THE GUILD SHAKESPEARE™

Hamlet

Troilus and Cressida

THE GUILD

HAMLET

TROILUS AND CRESSIDA

BY

WILLIAM SHAKESPEARE

EDITED BY

JOHN F. ANDREWS

Forewords by
Derek Jacobi and Celeste Holm

GuildAmerica Books™
Doubleday Book & Music Clubs, Inc.
Garden City, New York

Cover Painting: Hamlet.
Painting, frontispiece, endpapers, and book design by Barry Moser.
Text is in Baskerville, with display calligraphy by
Reassurance Wunder. Binding design by Barry Moser
and Hideo Ietaka.

Art Director: Diana Klemin, with Rhea Braunstein.
Project Editor: Mary Sherwin Jatlow.

The Guild Shakespeare™
GuildAmerica Books™
Trademark registration pending on behalf of Doubleday Book &
Music Clubs, Inc.

CONTENTS

FOREWORD
to
HAMLET
by Derek Jacobi

As an actor I thank God for William Shakespeare. An extraordinary, superhuman genius—I mean, where did he come from? And he wrote most of his plays while still a man in his 30s! Where did he get all that knowledge? Where did all that wisdom come from? If you go through all the plays, you find that he knew something about everything. He had a phrase or a sentence, a word for every conceivable human situation and emotion.

I think Shakespeare is for all ages. He is always relevant and exciting. He is loved and understood and respected and thrilled

---

DEREK JACOBI has acted in three professional productions of *Hamlet,* including one at the Old Vic and one that permitted him to perform the title role in Elsinore. In 1988 he made his directorial debut with the play in England. A veteran of the Royal Shakespeare Company, Mr. Jacobi has won the theatre's most coveted awards, and his television credits include such BBC series as *I, Claudius* and *The Shakespeare Plays* (for which he played both Hamlet and Richard II).

to no matter where you are in the world, no matter what age you are. He's survived four hundred years of reverence and idolatry. And during those four centuries he's also survived a great deal of iconoclasm. You can muck about with Shakespeare. You can do all sorts of things with and to him. It doesn't matter. He always survives.

He was a true man of the theatre, and he wrote wonderful parts. And I so hope he's looking down and approving of what we're doing with his plays when we try to be true to them. Whatever changes we make—textual transpositions, little felicities, whatever—we do so that the play and its characters will shine through. Our job is not to glorify any particular actor or director or designer, but to make the play as fresh and new-minted as we can.

I constantly remind myself that Shakespearean actors should approach their parts, in a sense, as they do contemporary roles. "Forget it's Shakespeare," I said to the actors I recently directed in *Hamlet,* and in a certain sense I meant it. When they come to Shakespeare, many actors tend to block off all those wonderful juices that naturally flow into modern parts. They cease to think, imagine, react, and feel as they would do normally. Their voices become different. Their bodies become different.

They must learn to make Shakespeare's language sound like the language they speak every day. They must live in the moment, create the words out of the air. They must forget that Shakespeare wrote them; get rid of the smell of ink; forget that anybody's ever said them before; pluck them out of the feeling and the situation and make them new.

I think that spontaneity comes from the immediacy of emotion. If actors regard these lines as speeches, famous speeches, then that is how they'll come out. Actors must not think that what they say and do is the result of what Shakespeare wrote. What actors say and do must be the result of what they're thinking and feeling, of what is happening in the play as the company has chosen to present it.

Of all of Shakespeare's plays, *Hamlet* probably holds the most interest for an actor. Because one of the things it's about is acting and pretending to be what you're not. It's a play that very much inhabits the world of the imagination: the world of what if, the world of finding out who you are, what you are, where you are in relation to other people and to the universe. This is true of most of Shakespeare, but *Hamlet* in particular comes very close to what acting itself is about, how actors react to a situation, and the whole craft of pretense, of being someone else.

Another reason *Hamlet* is so interesting for an actor is that a performance can never be definitive. There are as many *Hamlets* as there are actors to play Hamlet. Each one is different, because each production, to a great extent, turns on the personality of the actor who is playing Hamlet, and most actors have a Hamlet within them.

Hamlet is probably the clearest and most accessible of all of Shakespeare's plays, largely because it's such a wonderful story, with wonderful dramatic sweep rhythmically throughout the evening. Hamlet goes on a voyage of self-discovery. I don't believe he's ever truly mad. There are three occasions in the play, maybe four, when he drives himself to the edge of madness, but he never actually topples over that edge. He is in control of his own destiny for a great deal of the play.

This play has always been very important to me. Hamlet was the first major role I ever played as a schoolboy. That was when I was seventeen or eighteen. It really started my career as an actor, because my performance got a great deal of press and attention. I was very lucky in that respect. And so I had a very fond memory of the play long before I came to play it professionally in 1977. I played it again in 1979 at the Old Vic. Then I did it for television in 1980. And most recently, in 1988 I directed the very talented young actor, Kenneth Branagh, in a production for the Renaissance Theatre Company.

Over the years since I first began playing Hamlet, I have become more and more convinced that "To be or not to be" is to be treated not as a soliloquy, but as a dramatic speech to Ophelia. And my reasons are very much rooted in the text.

The way the Nunnery Scene is set makes it clear that Hamlet is not merely wandering round the castle with thoughts of death on his mind. Claudius has just told Ophelia that "We have closely sent for Hamlet hither." So Hamlet is on his way to a particular place at a certain time to fulfill an appointment.

The person he sees when he gets there is the person he least expected to see. For the last few weeks, every time he's met Ophelia she's run the other way; she's avoided him. If he saw her at the end of the corridor, she would turn the other way and off she'd go. Now he sees her and she doesn't run away. Of course, the last thing Polonius has said to her is "Walk you here. Read on this book." But most Ophelias have to not "walk you here" but go to the wings or hide behind a pillar, or do something to get out of Hamlet's way, whereas the whole point of the scene is for her to confront him.

If we presuppose that they have been lovers, that they are in love, then what better opportunity for him to be able to say "This is where my head is at the moment: I'm thinking about committing suicide." He speaks at her, through her, around her. He soliloquizes to her, if you like.

Well, what does Ophelia do while he's doing this? Does she just sit there? Yes indeed. What else can she do? She's in a very false situation, having been placed there by her father and the King. She knows they are listening behind the curtain. She doesn't want to be there. She knows she's a decoy. It's a completely false situation to her. Hamlet is the man she loves.

I played Hamlet this way with two Ophelias, and both said it helped them with their character. Because the irony is that the speech is about the very things that happen to Ophelia—madness and suicide. She goes mad, and commits suicide, virtually. Hamlet talks about both but experiences neither. In effect, though, hearing this speech plants the seed in Ophelia's mind.

The speech ends with "Soft you now, the fair Ophelia." This line is usually taken to mean "Oh look, there's Ophelia," but I take it to be one of those little titles he gives her, that we all give each other: the tedious Polonius, the villainous King. This is the way he sees her and he wants her to know it. Then he goes on to call her "Nymph." What he is saying is "Soft you now . . ." "I don't need you to say anything. Now you know where I am. Just remember me in your prayers. Now, off you go."

But of course, she's been placed there by her father and the King, so she's got to keep him there, however she can. "Oh, good my Lord," she blurts out, "how does your Honour for this many a day?" "How have you been lately?"

So the first thing she says is false, and immediately Hamlet knows that the whole situation is phony. We don't have to see the curtains moving to know that Hamlet senses Polonius' presence. From the beginning of the scene Hamlet has suspected that something is wrong, something is out of kilter. "She didn't run away like she usually does. She's had the most extraordinary reaction to what I've just said. Then she goes on to give back all these tokens of love and remembrance. Something is extremely wrong." And then when he confirms it by testing her, by asking her "Where's your father?" and she answers "At home, my Lord," in spite of the fact that everything in her being might be struggling to tell him the truth, their relationship, and their lives, can never be the same again.

From this point on, Hamlet realizes that there is no one in his world that he can trust. Everyone is acting, and survival will depend on choosing and playing one's own role as shrewdly as possible.

FOREWORD

by

Celeste Holm

The times in life we cherish most stay with us forever. Never can I forget the deep pleasure in the writings of Will Shakespeare that began when I was—what? six, I think—when I did a monologue of the balcony scene from *Romeo and Juliet* at our family camp in the Kittatinny Mountains, minus my front teeth. "The more I give, the more I have, for both are infinite"—a phrase I've always cherished and lived by. My father was very moved, and I was very proud.

CELESTE HOLM has played such diverse roles as Anna in *The King and I*, Anna in *Anna Christie*, Ado Annie in *Oklahoma!*, Judith in *Hay Fever*, and the title roles in *Mame* and *Candida*. Knighted by King Olav of Norway, jailed by the Mayor of New York, and appointed to the National Arts Council by the President of the United States, she is an ardent board member of the "Save the Theatres Committee" in New York City. She received the 1947 Academy Award for Best Supporting Actress in the film *Gentlemen's Agreement*. Her latest film was *Three Men and a Baby*, her latest play *The Road to Mecca*.

The following summer he and my grandfather found an ideal setting on the side of our hill, where they placed a cement stage with trees and shrubbery to provide wing space at each side. The background was one of mountains and the valley. One year we did a montage of several scenes, and my grandfather played Shakespeare—he had a beard anyway. I remember his magnificent lace ruff and the brass buckles on his shoes; and his voice, low and rhythmic as he presented the introduction to each scene from one of Shakespeare's plays, which he had written in iambic pentameter with great skill and charm.

That year I played Portia with a neighboring farmer's daughter, corralled into the role of Nerissa. But it was my mother's sleepwalking scene from "That Play!" which I remember with gut-wrenching clarity. She was so moving, so piteous, so mesmerizing in her anguish! My father and a cousin, playing the Doctor and a Gentlewoman, were rendered quite speechless, coming in late with the lines that should have followed. No Lady Macbeth I have ever seen could even touch her.

When I was about eleven, Fritz Leiber came to Chicago with his Shakespearean Company. We saw him in each production, *Hamlet, The Merchant of Venice,* and *King Lear.* Two weeks before we were to see the performance, my father would start reading aloud each of the plays. He spoke six languages without an accent in any of them and was fascinated with the subtleties of language. Whenever he came upon a word or phrase I could not understand, I would say so. What was Shakespeare trying to say in that scene? It took a long time! But my excitement grew in the anticipation of seeing what we had so lovingly and scrupulously examined—to see that our expectations were fulfilled. And oh my!

xiv

they were! Shakespeare's wisdom, his perception of people, his ability to make us identify the people with ourselves, all bespoke his infinite artistry. And I thought Fritz Leiber was wonderful! I believed him. He made all that elaborate language sound perfectly natural. And then he was quite different in every role, in shape and sound and look.

I remember sitting on a trunk backstage and looking up high into the dark flies and thinking, "This is where I will spend my life!"

My mother was a portrait painter, and *The Merchant of Venice* became a very special experience, because I saw change take place. The first time we saw the play Mr. Leiber played Shylock with an evil relish—with real villainy. My mother was not happy with this interpretation. She felt Shakespeare had written much more than that. By this time we had met the Leibers socially and my mother had arranged to do three portraits of him in his three major roles. I sat quietly when they discussed the role of Shylock. Surely this man was to be pitied as much as scorned. He had been ill treated, called upon only as a moneylender and not respected for that. His desire for vengeance was understandable, and his pathetic anguish at his daughter's desertion could be an agony for the audience. When he finally left the stage, the whole audience's heart could go out to him.

About two weeks later we came to see it again. And it was so! The "quality of mercy" was indeed felt by the audience in several directions. The play was infinitely richer. Was there an echo of this memory when I was given the opportunity to play in the film *Gentleman's Agreement,* which dealt with anti-Semitism?

And then my very first engagement in a major production

was touring the country in Leslie Howard's *Hamlet,* in which I understudied Ophelia. I had adored Leslie Howard on the screen, but now, to have the opportunity to appear on the same stage with him! Oh my!

Leslie Howard had opened in New York just three weeks after John Gielgud's triumphant *Hamlet,* which I much admired and in which Lillian Gish played Ophelia with red stockings. The critics were unkind—Leslie had not really been ready. But by the time he decided to take it on tour Leslie had grown tremendously in the part. We, the new members of the company, rehearsed under the stage manager's direction in the basement of a church on West 48th Street which had lots of pillars. It meant that much of the time we could not see each other, let alone the stage manager. We played ladies and gentlemen of the court, and we joined the company in Chicago. I never did see the show from the front.

We met Mr. Howard and company on Christmas Eve—the night before we opened at the Shubert Theater. We were lined up like servants on Boxing Day, and then the English contingent, Leslie, Mrs. Howard, Wilfred Walter (Claudius), Clifford Evans (Laertes), and Pamela Stanley (Ophelia) passed before us, formally shaking our hands. I was startled when Leslie suddenly leaned toward me and, gazing intently into my eyes, said, "Welcome to our company." I nearly swooned! Later I discovered he could only see when he was that close. How he and Clifford managed that duel in the last scene without killing each other or falling into the pit, I still cannot imagine.

The next night I entered Stuart Cheney's dark castle of Elsinore and was swept into the tragedy of the Danish Prince.

I asked Wilfred Walter how it was he could make his prayer so moving every night. He looked at me and said simply, "I've lived another day, haven't I?" He was a fine watercolorist and went out to paint wherever we were.

We played every major city between Chicago and Santa Barbara. It was a marvelous experience seeing America under such comfortable and exciting circumstances—our own sleeping cars, an observation car, and a diner was put on when needed. We played huge auditoriums; where the circus had played the week before, we could still smell the elephants. In the Grand Ole Opry in Nashville the dressing rooms were nil—all kinds of theaters, all filled with history. And we found ourselves in Shakespeare and Shakespeare in us, and we gave it to enraptured audiences every night! Once Pamela Stanley had a high fever, but I never got to play Ophelia.

Whenever I experience anything by Shakespeare, I am returned to that wonderful time when my father shared his enthusiasm so patiently with me. "Then" becomes "Now," which is what the arts are all about. They permit us to hold the "Now" a little longer; even to return to it again and again. Because of course "Now" is all we ever have.

Editor's Introduction to

HAMLET

and

TROILUS AND CRESSIDA

In an eloquent review of *Ulysses,* the most celebrated novel of the twentieth century, T.S. Eliot praised the brilliance with which James Joyce deployed classical myth and legend to mirror "the immense panorama of futility and anarchy which is contemporary history." What Eliot commended in his fellow writer was what he himself was endeavoring to accomplish in *The Waste Land,* our century's most famous poem. And something akin to what both authors had in mind was what Shakespeare appears to have been doing more than three centuries earlier when he produced *Hamlet* and *Troilus and Cressida.*

Of all the plays he wrote, these are the two that have most persistently been described as "modern." *Hamlet* features the most intellectually intriguing of Shakespeare's characters, a protagonist of dazzling wit and incomparable complexity whose irreducible "mystery" (III.ii.395) has made him the very emblem of man's problematic identity in the post-medieval world. The

xix

Prince of Denmark is a figure in whom entire nations have claimed to see their psyches registered, and his dilemmas have stimulated a body of commentary so vast that the literature generated by *Hamlet* is itself a subject of considerable significance. Meanwhile *Troilus and Cressida,* which crushes all the grandeur of antiquity into a squalid "Argument" about "a Whore and a Cuckold" (II.iii.82–83) and which seems to have been conceived as the most overtly provocative of Shakespeare's plays, has proven to be precisely that: a conundrum so riddling in its generic and thematic ambiguity that it has thus far defied even a consensus on how the work should be classified.

Both plays reflect the waning of an Elizabethan era whose glories were receding into gloom. As the sixteenth century gave way to the seventeenth, Shakespeare's contemporaries grew increasingly anxious over the position they felt placed in by a declining Queen who adamantly refused to forestall future chaos by naming her successor. A cosmos they had long thought stable and secure seemed threatened on every side by skepticism, pragmatism, and a Machiavellian "realism" that appeared to leave no room for traditional values. As they looked around them and saw the old order succumbing to what John Donne called the "new Philosophy," a way of thinking that cast "all in doubt," there were many who feared that they had been set adrift with neither moorings nor anchors. And they must have found their own uncertainties echoed in many of the characters, situations, and speeches of *Hamlet* and *Troilus and Cressida.*

Hamlet appears to have been written between late 1599 and early 1601; *Troilus and Cressida* appears to have been completed between late 1601 and early 1602. The two plays share a preoccupation with the lusts—the perversions of reason and will—that corrupt civic harmony and bring great kingdoms to ruin. They focus on appetite and disease as metaphors for the causes and consequences of fatal error. They dramatize the disillusionments that occur when men and women discover that "Words, Words, mere Words" offer no real defense against "the hot Passion of distemper'd Blood" (*Troilus and Cressida,* V.iii.109, II.ii.168). They allude to the great theological and philosophical debates of the Renaissance. And they share so many links in language, atmosphere, and subject matter that it is hard to resist the notion that there must have been some overlap between them as Shakespeare brought the two works to fruition. What little we know about the production and publication history of *Troilus and Cressida* would seem to make it the perfect candidate for what the Prince of Denmark describes as a play that "was never acted, or if it was, not above once"—a drama that "pleas'd not the Million" because it was "Caviary to the General" (*Hamlet,* II.ii.467–69). And the fiery speech that the Prince and the First Player recite about the Fall of Ilium in II.ii of *Hamlet* would almost seem to have been written as a backdrop for the events and non-events that constitute the "action" of Shakespeare's play about "the matter of Troy."

Troy was a city with symbolic ties to the London of Shakespeare's day. According to a tradition popularized by a twelfth-century chronicler known as Geoffrey of Monmouth, "Troynauvaunt" had been founded by a great-grandson of the same Aeneas who had established the original "new Troy" in Latium. This Trojan descendant had supposedly given his name, Brutus, to the island that became known as Britain, and in the process he had forged a kinship, both lineal and spiritual, that extended back from London through Rome (whose Republic had been instituted by another Brutus and defended by a third) to the plains of Phrygia. When an Elizabethan audience heard reference to the Fall of Troy, in other words, it was likely to connect that cataclysmic event both with the founding of London and with the cautionary moral that it was only through vigilance that a modern Troy could avoid the same fate that had overtaken its legendary forebears.

To a contemporary of Shakespeare's, then, "the matter of Troy" was closely related both to "the matter of Britain" and to "the matter of Rome." But Troy's significance was by no means limited to those associations. Like Rome, Troy was also an instance of what Saint Augustine had labeled "the City of Man." As such it frequently served as a metaphor not only for human civilization in general but for individual nations and individual human beings in particular. In a number of his plays, Shakespeare treats Troy as a figure for what Macbeth calls the "single State of Man." Troy's walls become symbols of the defense a soul must maintain against the siege of temptation, and for women those walls represent the virtue required to preserve chastity and honor. Troy's towers, her "wanton Tops," are emblems of pride, male lust, and a full panoply of ungoverned ambitions. And of course Troy's fall can be viewed as another version of the Biblical Fall of Man.

In many ways the battlements of Elsinore Castle function as a Danish counterpart to the walls of Troy, and it is thus very much to the point in *Hamlet* when the Prince of Denmark asks one of the visiting players to recite Aeneas' tale about "Priam's Slaughter."

Hamlet calls for this speech because he hopes to model his own vengeance after the mayhem the "hellish Pyrrhus" delivers in retaliation for his father's death at the hands of the Trojans. In Pyrrhus' cause the Prince sees an image of his own. Eventually, following a delay that recapitulates Pyrrhus' pause, the Prince succeeds in his aim to emulate his classical predecessor. As he does so, however, he himself dies and the kingdom of Denmark collapses around him.

The ironic consequence of Hamlet's Pyrrhic victory is that the crown he has been trying to wrest from the murderer of his father now falls to a Norwegian prince who has been skirting the borders of Elsinore in search of an opening that will enable him to avenge *his* father's death at the hands of the elder Hamlet. With no one left to rule Denmark from within, the expiring Hamlet correctly surmises that "th' Election lights / On Fortinbrasse."

Just what an Elizabethan audience would have made of Fortinbrasse's "Election," his conquest by default, is difficult to say. But it seems more than likely that many of the Globe's patrons would have read the play's conclusion as confirmation that a Troy-like Denmark had sown the seeds of its own destruction through vices analogous to those that had proven fatal to the original Ilium. Anyone who stopped to consider the implications of the Hamlet-Pyrrhus parallel, moreover, would probably have found it interesting that the Prince's role model is not a Trojan but a Greek. The effect of the playwright's allusion to the Fall of Troy is thus to align Hamlet with "Troy's" adversaries and portray him as the unwitting agent of another avenger who is left with nothing more to do than pick up the pieces and claim what remains of Denmark for Norway.

Like the Troy that Shakespeare depicts in *Troilus and Cressida*, the Elsinore the Prince seeks to set right in *Hamlet* is "rotten" at the core. For the Prince as for Thersites, the "Argument" is largely about "a Whore and a Cuckold." But of course in this case the cuckolder is also a murderer and a usurper; and that, for Hamlet, is the "necessary Question of the Play" (III.ii.49–50).

The protagonist appears to believe that there is only one real issue to be resolved before he proceeds with his "Course": he must "catch the Conscience of the King" (III.ii.633,641) and thereby determine whether the Ghost has spoken truthfully about how the elder Hamlet died. It may be that this is the only issue the playwright wanted his audience to consider, too, but it would seem more likely that Shakespeare expected the "judicious" (III.i.31) to ponder a pair of additional questions: (a) whether even a truth-telling Ghost should be regarded as "Honest" in a sense that would call for it to be taken at face value and obeyed, and (b) whether the Ghost's command should be weighed in the light of Biblical injunctions against private vengeance (most notably Romans 12:17–13:7).

The opening scenes of the play draw a significant contrast between the Prince's response to the Ghost and the reactions of more cautious observers such as Horatio and the Danish guard. And a number of Hamlet's speeches in the play, particularly the one he delivers as he observes Claudius at prayer in III.iii, would suggest that the Prince's approach to what he considers a sacred duty is difficult to reconcile with Christian precepts that are shown to be applicable elsewhere in the play. In the Prayer Scene, for example, Shakespeare arranges to have Hamlet look in on Claudius at a moment when the King's "Conscience" has been caught in a way that the Prince would not have wished for. At this juncture it is just possible that even so wicked a man as Claudius might repent. We are surely meant to be surprised at this development, and to ask ourselves what kind of "Consummation" is now most "devoutly to be wished" (III.i.60–61). Then, a moment later, we are probably meant to ask whether Hamlet's decision to delay his revenge until some time when the King's "Heels may kick at Heav'n" (III.iii.93) isn't one that raises questions about the Prince's own relationship with Heaven. In similar fashion we are probably expected to be brought up short when Hamlet tells Horatio in V.ii that he has arranged for Rosencrans and Guildenstern to be "put to sudden Death, / Not Shriving-time allow'd" and then says that "They are not near my Conscience."

The Prince's dealings with his former schoolmates offer a particularly instructive insight into the way *Hamlet* would appear to operate as a work of drama. On the one hand we have the Prince's view of Rosencrans and Guildenstern as "Adders fang'd" (III.iv.199), willing and presumably knowing tools of the King's treachery. On the other hand we have what might be said to be "the play's" more objective portrayal of them, as a pair of loyal public servants who come to Court at the request of the new King, who seek to help the Queen find out why her son is acting so strangely, and who then proceed to function in what they assume to be the best interests of a legitimate monarch. So far as we can determine, they know nothing of what Claudius has done in the past and they are never made privy to the King's plots against Hamlet.

Like Polonius, and indeed like virtually every other character in this world of deception and counter-deception, Hamlet attempts "by Indirections" to "find Directions out" (II.i.63). More often than not, for Hamlet as well as for others, those "Indirections" either result in or contribute tragically to "Purposes mistook / Fall'n on th' Inventors' Heads" (V.ii.396–97). To what extent the Prince himself is to be held accountable for the consequences of his misjudgments is a question the play leaves unresolved. A close examination of even his most eloquent soliloquies will disclose that Hamlet is frequently a man whose pride and passions get in the way of "That Capability and God-like Reason" that allows a person to discover the way "rightly to be Great" (IV.iv.35,50). But in the end he acts with a nobility that garners him what may well be the most touching benediction a tragic hero ever received: "Good night, sweet Prince, / And flights of Angels sing thee to thy Rest" (V.ii.371–72).

The pathos that marks the closing moments of *Hamlet* is generally absent from *Troilus and Cressida.* Drawing on a variety of sources, from Renaissance versions of Homer's *Iliad* and Vergil's *Aeneid* through such medieval treatments of the Trojan War as John Lydgate's *Sege of Troye* (circa 1412–20), William Caxton's *Recuyell of the Historyes of Troye* (1475), Geoffrey Chaucer's *Troilus and Criseyde* (1382–85), and Robert Henryson's *Testament of Cresseid* (1532), Shakespeare depicts most of the Greeks and Trojans as unheroic figures who bear little of the dignity associated with the honorifics tradition has bestowed on them.

"After sev'n years' Siege," as we learn in the Greek Council Scene near the beginning of the play (I.iii), Agamemnon and his fellow generals have nothing to show for their efforts to force the Trojans to surrender Helen. Menelaus, the Spartan King whose wife has been taken away from him by Paris to start this senseless war, remains a laughingstock to Greek and Trojan alike. Achilles, the champion of the Greeks, lies tented with his "masculine Whore" Patroclus. Meanwhile Aiax, second only to Achilles in might, grows "factious" and breeds dissension in an army that has degenerated into little more than a contending assembly of petty fiefdoms. As Ulysses makes clear in his splendid speech on "Degree," the Commander has lost his command, and "Hark, what Discord follows."

But if things are in disarray on the outside of Troy's walls, they are even worse on the inside. Hector, the champion of the Trojans, proclaims in the Trojan Council Scene (II.ii) that after many thousand dead it should now be clear that Helen "is not worth what she doth cost / The Keeping." The "Moral Laws / Of Nature and of Nations speak aloud," he says, "To have her back return'd." The "Divinations" of the prophetess Cassandra warn of retribution if the Trojans "persist / In doing Wrong." And only men with "Ears more deaf than Adders" would fail to heed such pleadings and enact "true Decision." So Hector affirms; but before he finishes speaking, he disregards everything he has just said and announces that he is more inclined to proceed on "Resolution" than to be rendered unmanly by what Hamlet would call "the pale Cast of Thought." Like his "spritely Brethren," Hector is more interested in doing what promotes "Honor and Renown" than in using his influence to guide Troy toward a settlement of the conflict that would save thousands of additional lives and preserve the city from ruin.

Hector's non sequitur is typical of what happens and fails to happen in this curious play. Over and over we see debates that lead to invalid or foolish conclusions, plots that turn out to be counterproductive, schemes that end either in comic frustration or in abject defeat. Small wonder, then, that in his 1982 television production of *Troilus and Cressida* Jonathan Miller hit upon *M*A*S*H* as the most appropriate twentieth-century analogue for Shakespeare's depiction of a war that represents the triumph of unreason, ennui, and debased nobility.

But of course *Troilus and Cressida* is about more than warfare. A love-plot is at the root of the conflict, and as long as Troy stands there would seem to be more than enough time for the leisure activities that Cressida associates with "Merry Greek" Helen. It may eventually turn out, as Helen jests, that "this Love will undo us all," but in the interim the "hot Blood" that is not being directed into battle may be devoted to Mars's more pleasurable pursuits with Venus.

In his choral comments on the action, the corrosive Thersites reduces every manifestation of love to lechery and the venereal diseases that follow. There can be no doubt that Thersites has a point, and the play's concluding bequest by an ostracized Pandarus makes it even more tellingly than do the railings of a deformed Court Fool. At the same time, however, a sensitive reading of the text will show that what draws Troilus and Cressida together for the first time is not limited to the base carnality we witness once events sweep Cressida over to the Grecian camp. The lovers clearly care for one another, and Cressida appears to speak her vows with just as much sincerity as Troilus. Later, as Cressida gives in to the degradation that is destined to define her name, Shakespeare allows us to witness an inner conflict and an awareness of consequences that earns her at least a degree of tragic pity. Like Troilus, she is a deeply flawed character, but there would seem to be at least some distinction between the charges leveled at her by Ulysses and Thersites and the qualities in her that make Troilus lament her fall from grace.

By and large, the final scenes of *Troilus and Cressida* are as dark in their portrayal of human depravity as anything in the modern Theatre of the Absurd. After fighting gloriously and chivalrously in a battle that offers us a glimpse of what Troy might have been, Hector gives in to a baser impulse and thereby makes himself vulnerable to an Achilles who has none of the magnanimity that Troy's champion displayed in an earlier encounter. Once this happens, the Greek champion reveals a streak of barbarity that proves to be the most shocking thing in a work that was evidently designed to assault its audience's sensibilities.

When the copyright for *Troilus and Cressida* was first registered in 1602, the play was described as a "History" that had been acted by Shakespeare's company at the Globe. That designation remained on the initial title-page for the Quarto that was printed in 1609. A different title-page was substituted before the print-run was completed, however, and in the "Epistle" that accompanied it the play was commended as a "Comedy" that had never been "stal'd with the Stage." A little more than a decade later, when the publishers of the First Folio began printing *Troilus and Cressida* for the volume that would be issued in 1623, their initial plan was to put the play in the section of the book reserved for "Tragedies." Owing to some problem that developed after work commenced, they abandoned their original intention, withheld the pages that had been printed, and eventually repositioned the play in a no-man's-land between the "Histories" and the "Tragedies."

In many ways the publishing history of the play has proven prophetic. Some of today's editors and commentators group *Troilus and Cressida* with the Comedies and some with the Tragedies. Others have pointed to its affinities with those histories that are now referred to as the Roman Plays. But most have found it more helpful to link the play with the "Comical Satires" that enjoyed a brief vogue during the period of thespian mudslinging known as the War of the Theatres. It may well be that Polonius would have been able to classify *Troilus and Cressida* under one of his ludicrously composite headings in II.ii of *Hamlet:* "Tragical-Comical-Historical-Pastoral" comes close to capturing the play's mixture of genres. But it probably makes best sense to cite the authority of Cressida's Servant in I.ii of *Troilus and Cressida* and affirm only that this is a work that "stands alone."

The control text for the Guild edition of *Troilus and Cressida* is the 1609 Quarto, which appears to have been printed either from an authorial manuscript or from a close transcript of one. The Folio text offers several passages not found in the Quarto, and those have been incorporated in this edition. The Folio also contains a number of variant readings that may or may not be authorial. In most cases the Quarto's readings have been retained here in preference to the Folio variants, but the notes provide information about a number of the Folio readings that have been adopted by other editors of the play.

The control text for the Guild edition of *Hamlet* is the 1604 Second Quarto. Here again the Quarto text has been supplemented on occasion with passages that appear only in the 1623 Folio. And in many cases where the Folio text is manifestly superior to the Quarto, the Folio's readings have been adopted in preference to those in the Quarto. Far more often than in most editions of *Hamlet,* however, the reader will find here the version of the text first printed in the Second Quarto, which may well have been set from Shakespeare's own manuscript of the play. Among other things, the Guild edition preserves the original names of such characters as Fortinbrasse (Fortinbras), Gertrard (Gertrude), Ostrick (Osric), and Rosencrans (Rosencrantz).

A corrupt version of *Hamlet* was published in 1603 in what is now known as the First Quarto. It appears to have been compiled from memory by one or more of the actors who had performed minor roles in the play, and it was probably consulted to some extent by the typesetters of the Second Quarto. None of its readings are adopted here in preference to readings in either of the more authoritative texts.

NAMES OF THE ACTORS

CLAUDIUS, King of Denmark
GERTRARD, Queen of Denmark and Mother to Hamlet
HAMLET, Prince of Denmark and Nephew to the King

POLONIUS, Lord Chamberlain
LAERTES, Son to Polonius
OPHELIA, Daughter to Polonius

HORATIO, Friend to Hamlet

ROSENCRANS
GUILDENSTERN
VOLTEMAND   Courtiers
CORNELIUS
OSTRICK (OSRICK)

MARCELLUS
BARNARDO   Officers of the Court

FRANCISCO, a Soldier

REYNALDO, Servant to Polonius

FORTINBRASSE, Prince of Norway
NORWEGIAN CAPTAIN
DOCTOR OF DIVINITY
PLAYERS

HAMLET

TWO CLOWNS, Gravediggers
ENGLISH AMBASSADORS

GHOST

LORDS, LADIES, OFFICERS, SOLDIERS, SAILORS,
  MESSENGERS, and ATTENDANTS

I.i   *The opening scene begins in the dark of midnight on the battlements of Elsinore Castle in Denmark. Barnardo is reporting for guard duty, relieving Francisco, whose watch is now scheduled to conclude.*

S.D.   **Barnardo**   *This spelling, a variant of* **Bernardo**, *occurs in both of the authoritative early texts, and reflects the way* **Bernardo** *would have been pronounced in Elizabethan England.*

1   **Nay answer me.**   *The emphatic* **me** *in this sentence suggests that there is an unusual tension in the air. Under normal circumstances the incoming guard would not be challenging another figure to identify himself, as Barnardo has just done; and under normal circumstances the guard awaiting relief would not feel the need to question the identity of a man appearing at the appointed "Hour" (line 3).*
      unfold   *disclose, reveal.*

2   **Long live the King.**   *Whether or not this is a watchword, it identifies Barnardo not as an enemy but as a friend to Denmark.*

3   **carefully**   *cautiously, nervously.*

4   **strook twelfe**   *struck twelve. These spellings are likely to reflect Shakespeare's pronunciation of these words.*

6   **Sick at Heart**   *We are given no reason for Francisco's sense of despondency, but the phrase provides another suggestion that all is not well.*
      quiet   *uneventful.*

4

Act One

Scene 1

Enter Barnardo and Francisco, two Sentinels.

BARNARDO Who's there?

FRANCISCO Nay answer me. Stand and unfold
Your self.

BARNARDO Long live the King.

FRANCISCO Barnardo.

BARNARDO He.

FRANCISCO You come most carefully upon your Hour.

BARNARDO 'Tis now strook twelfe: get thee to Bed,
Francisco.

FRANCISCO For this Relief, much thanks. 'Tis
bitter Cold,   5
And I am Sick at Heart.

BARNARDO Have you had quiet Guard?

7   Well   *that's good.*

9   Rivals   *partners. Like* competitors, *this word had a significance in Shakespeare's time that is the opposite of its present
meaning.*

11   ground   *land.*
Liegemen to   *loyal servants of.*
the Dane   *the King of Denmark.*

12   Give   *God give.*

15   A piece of him.   *This is probably Horatio's ironic way of
saying that his heart is not in this visit to the guard's post on
such a cold night; as we learn in line 22, he is here only
because Marcellus has "entreated him along" (urged him to
come).*

17   this Thing   *Horatio's phrasing conveys skepticism.*

21   Touching   *concerning.*
dreaded   *awesome, terrifying.*

23   watch   *both (a) observe, and (b) stay awake for.*

25   approve our Eyes   *verify that our eyes have not been deceived
by a seizure of "Fantasy" (here meaning delusion).*
speak to it   *Marcellus and Barnardo have been afraid to
confront the "Apparition." By implication, Horatio, being a
scholar (line 38), will know how to address it without endan-
gering either his life or his soul. In Shakespeare's time, Protes-
tants usually assumed that apparitions were likely to be demonic spirits. Catholics, who believed in Purgatory, were more
inclined to think that ghosts might be the spirits of departed
human beings; but Catholics too urged caution.*

6

FRANCISCO   Not a Mouse stirring.
BARNARDO   Well, good night.
    If you do meet Horatio and Marcellus,
    The Rivals of my Watch, bid them make haste.

Enter Horatio and Marcellus.

FRANCISCO   I think I hear them. —Stand ho: who is
    there?   10
HORATIO   Friends to this ground.
MARCELLUS   And Liegemen to the Dane.
FRANCISCO   Give you good night.
MARCELLUS   O farewell, honest Soldier;
    Who hath reliev'd you?
FRANCISCO   Barnardo hath my place:
    Give you good night.   *Exit.*
MARCELLUS   Holla, Barnardo!
BARNARDO   Say,
    What, is Horatio there?
HORATIO   A piece of him.   15
BARNARDO   Welcome, Horatio; welcome, good Marcellus.
HORATIO   What, has this Thing appear'd again
    tonight?
BARNARDO   I have seen nothing.
MARCELLUS   Horatio says 'tis but our Fantasy,
    And will not let Belief take hold of him   20
    Touching this dreaded Sight twice seen of us:
    Therefore I have entreated him along,
    With us to watch the Minutes of this Night,
    That if again the Apparition come
    He may approve our Eyes and speak to it.   25

7

27   **assail** *assault. Barnardo uses a military metaphor to suggest that Horatio's ears are walled behind a battlement.*

31   **Last Night of all** *this very last night. This short line is indented here to indicate that Barnardo commences his narrative only after a brief pause; during the three-beat interval, Barnardo, Marcellus, and Horatio have time to settle into their sitting positions.*

32   **Pole** *the pole (north) star.*

33   **his** *its. In Shakespeare's time "his" and "it" were the normal forms for the neuter possessive pronoun.*
        illume *light up.*

37   **Figure** *shape, appearance.*

40   **horrows** *The Folio prints* harrows, *the reading most editions accept here. The Second Quarto's word would seem more likely to be Shakespeare's; like* horrors *(the reading in the First Quarto), it means "horrifies."*

41   **It would be spoke to.** *Barnardo's line suggests that the Ghost is trying to establish communication; it was commonly believed that ghosts were not able to address living mortals until they were first spoken to.*

42   **usurp'st** *Horatio's verb suggests that he regards the Ghost's appearance as illegitimate, both because the spirit intrudes upon the night without warrant and because it borrows the apparel of the dead King.*

43   **fair** *handsome, impressive.*

HORATIO   Tush, tush, 'twill not appear.
BARNARDO   Sit down a while,
    And let us once again assail your Ears,
    That are so fortified against our Story,
    What we have two Nights seen.
HORATIO   Well, sit we down,
    And let us hear Barnardo speak of this.   30
BARNARDO   Last Night of all,
    When yond same Star that's Westward from the
        Pole
    Had made his Course t' illume that part of
        Heav'n
    Where now it burns, Marcellus and my self,
    The Bell then beating One—   35

                    Enter Ghost.

MARCELLUS   Peace, break thee off! Look where it
        comes again!
BARNARDO   In the same Figure like the King that's
        dead.
MARCELLUS   Thou art a Scholar: speak to it, Horatio.
BARNARDO   Looks 'a not like the King? Mark it,
        Horatio.
HORATIO   Most like: it horrows me with Fear and
        Wonder.   40
BARNARDO   It would be spoke to.
MARCELLUS   Speak to it, Horatio.
HORATIO   —What art thou that usurp'st this Time of
        Night,
    Together with that fair and warlike Form

9

44   buri'd Denmark   *the buried King of Denmark.*

45   sometimes   *both (a) on occasion, and (b) at one time.*
          By Heav'n   *Christians were told to "believe not every spirit,
          but try the spirits whether they are of God" (1 John 4:1).
          When Horatio says "I charge [command] thee speak" in the
          name of Heaven, then, he is following orthodox procedure.*

46   It is offended.   *Marcellus appears to believe that the Ghost is
          annoyed at Horatio's words, and particularly at his reference
          to Heaven.*

51–52   I might / Not this believe   *I would not be able to believe
          this.*

52   sensible   *both (a) through the senses, and (b) intelligent.*

53   true avouch   *reliable testimony.*

56   Norway   *King of Norway.*
          combated   *fought; accented on the first and third syllables.*

57   angry Parle   *fierce argument. This may refer to either (a) a
          heated verbal altercation, or (b) a hand-to-hand combat.*

58   smote . . . Pollax   *probably either (a) struck the ice with
          his studded poleaxe (a long-handled weapon), or (b) struck the
          sled-borne Polacks (Polish soldiers).*

60   jump   *exactly.*

62–64   In . . . State.   *Although I'm as yet unable to formulate a
          precise reason for my hunch, the general drift of my thinking is
          that this appearance portends something terrible.*

In which the Majesty of buri'd Denmark
Did sometimes march? By Heav'n I charge thee
   speak!   45

MARCELLUS   It is offended.
BARNARDO   See, it stalks away.
HORATIO   Stay, speak, speak, I charge thee, speak!
                                     Exit Ghost.

MARCELLUS   'Tis gone, and will not answer.
BARNARDO   How now, Horatio? You tremble and
   look pale.
Is not this something more than Fantasy?   50
What think you on't?
HORATIO   Before my God, I might
Not this believe without the sensible
And true avouch of mine own Eyes.
MARCELLUS   Is it
Not like the King?
HORATIO   As thou art to thy self.
Such was the very Armor he had on   55
When he th' ambitious Norway combated;
So frown'd he once when in an angry Parle
He smote the sleaded Pollax on the Ice.
'Tis strange.
MARCELLUS   Thus twice before, and jump at this
   Dead Hour,   60
With Martial Stalk hath he gone by our Watch.
HORATIO   In what partic'lar Thought to work I know
   not,
But in the gross and scope of mine Opinion
This bodes some strange Eruption to our State.

67   toils the Subject   *requires toil of the subjects.*

68   cost   *expense. The Folio prints* cast *(casting).*
Brazen   *both (a) brass, and (b) bold and aggressive.*

69   Mart   *trading.*

70   Impress   *impressment, forced labor.*
sore Task   *grievous burden, unceasing workload.*

72   toward   *in the offing, in the near future.*

77   Fortinbrasse   *The First Folio spelling (*Fortinbras*) reproduces a French word for "strong in arms." The earlier Quarto spelling, adopted here, suggests an additional link with "brass" (brazen mettle), reinforced by lines 68 and 91.*

78   prick'd on   *incited, motivated.*
emulate   *envious, rivalrous; here a two-syllable word.*

81   seal'd Compact   *official agreement; pronounced "com-páct."*

82   Well ratified . . . Heraldry   *properly subscribed to by the councils and heraldic officials of both countries.*

84   Which . . . seiz'd of   *which he stood to lose.*

85   Moi'ty competent   *equivalent portion (of land).*

86   gaged   *pledged, staked.*

88–89   as . . . Design   *as by the same mutual agreement and tenor of the articles designed for this purpose. Instead of* Comart *(bargain), many editors adopt the Folio's* Cov'nant *here. Most also amend* design *to* design'd, *a reading that first appears in the Second Folio.*

12

MARCELLUS   Good now sit down, and tell me, he that
        knows,   65
    Why this same strict and most observant Watch
    So nightly toils the Subject of the Land,
    And with such daily cost of Brazen Cannon
    And foreign Mart for Implements of War;
    Why such Impress of Shipwrights, whose sore Task   70
    Does not divide the Sunday from the Week;
    What might be toward that this sweaty Haste
    Doth make the Night joint Lab'rer with the Day?
    Who is't that can inform me?
HORATIO   That can I;
    At least the Whisper goes so. Our last King,   75
    Whose Image ev'n but now appear'd to us,
    Was, as you know, by Fortinbrasse of Norway,
    Thereto prick'd on by a most emulate Pride,
    Dar'd to the Combat; in which our valiant
        Hamlet
    (For so this side of our known World esteem'd
        him)   80
    Did slay this Fortinbrasse, who by a seal'd
        Compact
    Well ratified by Law and Heraldry
    Did forfeit, with his Life, all these his Lands
    Which he stood seiz'd of to the Conqueror;
    Against the which a Moi'ty competent   85
    Was gaged by our King, which had return
    To the Inheritance of Fortinbrasse
    Had he been Vanquisher, as by the same Comart
    And Carriage of the Article Design
    His fell to Hamlet. Now Sir, young Fortinbrasse,   90

13

91   unimproved Mettle   *probably both (a) unproven, raw vir-
      tue, not yet put to profitable use, and (b) untempered* metal *(a
      word that was yet to be fully distinguished from* mettle*), such
      as brass or steel that is still being treated to make it durable.*

93   Shark'd . . . Resolutes   *scavenged up an indiscriminate
      collection of desperadoes from the fringes of society.*

95   a Stomach   *both (a) an appetite (in keeping with the food
      metaphor), and (b) a touch of bravery (guts).*

101   Head   *both (a) source, and (b) reason, heading (as in a list of
      topics).*

102   Post-haste and Romage   *intense haste and bustling activity
      (rummage). The Quarto spelling anticipates "Rome" (line
      108).*

104   Well may it sort   *may it accord well (be a favorable sign).*
      portentous   *ominous, prophetic.*

107   Moth   *mote, tiny particle.*

108   palmy   *victorious, flourishing.*

113   Disasters   *literally, "malign stars" in the Heavens.*
      the Moist Star   *the Moon, which controls "Neptune's Em-
      pire" (the sea).*

116   Fear   *fearful, feared.*

117   still   *always.*
      the Fates   *the three Goddesses who determine human destiny.*

118   the Omen   *coming on the event foretold by the "Harbingers."*

120   Climatures   *climes, region.*

Of unimproved Mettle, hot and full,
Hath in the Skirts of Norway here and there
Shark'd up a List of lawless Resolutes
For Food and Diet to some Enterprise
That hath a Stomach in't, which is no other,   95
As it doth well appear unto our State,
But to recover of us by Strong Hand
And Terms Compulsatory those foresaid Lands
So by his Father lost; and this, I take it,
Is the main Motive of our Preparations,   100
The Source of this our Watch, and the chief Head
Of this Post-haste and Romage in the Land.
BARNARDO   I think it be no other but e'en so:
Well may it sort that this portentous Figure
Comes armed through our Watch so like the King   105
That was and is the Question of these Wars.
HORATIO   A Moth it is to trouble the Mind's Eye.
In the most high and palmy State of Rome
A little ere the mightiest Julius fell,
The Graves stood ten'ntless, and the Sheeted
    Dead   110
Did squeak and gibber in the Roman Streets
As Stars with trains of Fire and dews of Blood,
Disasters in the Sun; and the Moist Star
Upon whose Influence Neptune's Empire stands
Was sick almost to Doomsday with Eclipse.   115
And ev'n the like Precurse of Fear Events,
As Harbingers preceding still the Fates
And Prologue to the Omen coming on,
Have Heav'n and Earth together demonstrated
Unto our Climatures and Countrymen.   120

15

122   cross it   *literally, cross its path; confront it (perhaps with arms spread to form a cross-like figure).*
       blast   *wither.*
       Illusion   *apparition. Horatio is not suggesting that it is illusory.*

S.D.   his   *its.*

125–   If . . . Ease   *Horatio's "if" clause indicates that he is test-*
26   *ing to see whether the Ghost claims to be a departed human spirit who cannot rest until something he left undone has been attended to.*

129   happily   *both (a) by chance, and (b) fortunately.*

131   uphoarded   *hoarded and buried.*

132   Extorted   *wrested by force.*

135   Partizan   *partisan, a long-handled spear or pike.*

138   being so Majestical   *since it is so King-like.*

139   offer it the show   *threaten it with a display.*

140   invulnerable   *incapable of being harmed.*

141   vain   *useless, in vain.*
       malicious Mockery   *an empty threat of malice.*

144   Upon a fearful Summons   *upon receiving a frightening summons (either to trial or to execution).*

16

Re-enter Ghost.

But soft, behold, lo where it comes again!
I'll cross it though it blast me. —Stay,
  Illusion!   *It spreads his Arms.*
If thou hast any Sound or use of Voice,
Speak to me.
If there be any good thing to be done   125
That may to thee do Ease and Grace to me,
Speak to me.
If thou art privy to thy Country's Fate,
Which happily Foreknowing may avoid,
O speak.   130
Or if thou hast uphoarded in thy Life
Extorted Treasure in the Womb of Earth,
For which they say your Spir'ts oft walk in
  Death,   *The Cock crows.*
Speak of it, stay and speak. —Stop it,
  Marcellus!
MARCELLUS   Shall I strike it with my Partizan?   135
HORATIO   Do if it will not stand.
BARNARDO   'Tis here!
HORATIO   'Tis here!   *Exit Ghost.*
MARCELLUS   'Tis gone.
We do it wrong, being so Majestical,
To offer it the show of Violence:
For it is as the Air, invulnerable,   140
And our vain Blows malicious Mockery.
BARNARDO   It was about to speak when the Cock crew.
HORATIO   And then it started like a Guilty Thing
  Upon a fearful Summons. I have heard

147   Awake the God of Day   *bring on the dawn by waking up the Sun.*

149   Th' extravagant and erring Spirit   *the spirit that has strayed beyond its appointed bounds.*

151   made Probation   *offered proof, evidence.*

153   'gainst that Season comes   *in anticipation of the coming of that time.*

155   This Bird of Dawning   *the Cock.*

157   wholesome   *free both from contagion and from the powers of evil.*
       strike   *harm by pernicious influence. In this phrase Marcellus alludes to the belief, from astrology, that the stars and planets conditioned human behavior.*   .

158   No Fairy takes   *no fairy bewitches or captures. This line is a reminder that in Shakespeare's time fairies were often regarded as malevolent spirits; among other things, they were said to take human infants and leave "changelings" (bad children, or children possessed by evil fairy spirits) in their place.*
       charm   *enslave, bewitch.*

159   hallow'd   *holy, sanctified.*

161   in russet Mantle clad   *cloaked in a coarse, grayish-brown cloth.*

166   dumb   *speechless.*

170   convenient   *conveniently, readily.* Convenient *literally means "coming together."*

The Cock, that is the Trumpet to the Morn,   145
Doth with his lofty and shrill sounding Throat
Awake the God of Day; and at his Warning,
Whether in Sea or Fire, in Earth or Air,
Th' extravagant and erring Spirit hies
To his Confine; and of the Truth herein   150
This present Object made Probation.
MARCELLUS   It faded on the crowing of the Cock.
Some say that ever 'gainst that Season comes
Wherein our Savior's Birth is celebrated,
This Bird of Dawning singeth all Night long,   155
And then they say no Spir't dare stir abroad;
The Nights are wholesome, then no Planets
    strike,
No Fairy takes, nor Witch hath pow'r to charm,
So hallow'd and so gracious is that Time.
HORATIO   So have I heard, and do in part believe it;   160
But look, the Morn in russet Mantle clad
Walks o'er the Dew of yon high Eastward Hill.
Break we our Watch up, and by my Advice
Let us impart what we have seen tonight
Unto young Hamlet: for upon my Life,   165
This Spirit, dumb to us, will speak to him.
Do you consent we shall acquaint him with it
As needful in our Loves, fitting our Duty?
MARCELLUS   Let's do 't, I pray, and I this Morning
    know
Where we shall find him most convenient.   *Exeunt.*   170

I.ii   *The scene takes place at the Court in Elsinore Castle.*

S.D.   Claudius   *Apart from this opening stage direction and the initial speech assignment, Claudius is referred to solely as "King." Shakespeare probably drew the name from that of a Roman Emperor (A.D. 41–54) who married his niece Agrippina (mother of Nero) and was notorious for the vice and corruption of his reign.*

Gertradt   *a variant of* Gertrard, *as the Queen's name is normally spelled in the Second Quarto.* Gertrude *is the spelling in the First Folio text.*

cum Aliis   *with others.*

2   green   *fresh.*

5   Discretion   *prudence, judgment.*

8   sometime Sister   *former sister-in-law.*

9   Jointress   *inheritor. Claudius implies that the Queen has inherited the kingdom as a jointure (bequeathed estate), and that he has joined (grafted) himself to her and to the kingship by marriage. The root word* joint *epitomizes the other perversions of "marriage" described in lines 10–14; meanwhile it anticipates the images in I.ii.20 and I.v.179.*

10   as 'twere   *as it were, so to speak.*

11   auspicious   *happy, uplifted (contrast* dropping, *downcast).*

13   Dole   *grieving.*

14   barr'd   *excluded, acted without.*

18   weak Supposal   *low estimate.*

Scene 2

Flourish. Enter Claudius, King of Denmark, Gertradt
the Queen, and Council: as Polonius and his Son
Laertes, Hamlet, cum Aliis.

KING   Though yet of Hamlet our dear Brother's Death
      The Memory be green, and that it us befitted
      To bear our Hearts in Grief, and our whole
         Kingdom
      To be contracted in one Brow of Woe,
      Yet so far hath Discretion fought with Nature   5
      That we with wisest Sorrow think on him
      Together with Remembrance of our selves:
      Therefore our sometime Sister, now our Queen,
      Th' imperial Jointress to this warlike State,
      Have we, as 'twere with a defeated Joy,   10
      With an auspicious and a dropping Eye,
      With Mirth in Fun'ral, and with Dirge in
         Marriage,
      In Equal Scale weighing Delight and Dole,
      Taken to Wife. Nor have we herein barr'd
      Your better Wisdoms, which have freely gone   15
      With this Affair along. For all, our Thanks.
      Now follows that you know young Fortinbrasse,
      Holding a weak Supposal of our Worth,

20   **out of Frame**   *both (a) out of socket (like a disjointed limb), and (b) disordered.*

21   **Co-leagued**   *joined, linked.*
        Dream   *illusory hope.*

23   **Importing**   *both (a) concerning, and (b) importuning (pestering with demands for).*

24   **Bands**   *bonds, binding contracts.*

29   **impotent and Bed-rid**   *feeble and bed-ridden.*

31   **Gate**   *both (a) gait, proceeding, and (b) encroachment with a threat of entry.*
        Levies   *conscripted troops. So also with "Lists" and "Proportions" in line 32.*

33   **Subject**   *subjects.*

37   **To**   *to do.*
        Scope   *prescribed range.*

38   **delated**   *dilated, detailed at length.*
        Articles   *written provisions.*

39   **commend**   *speak for, be a witness to.*

41   **nothing**   *not at all.*

43   **Suit**   *request.*

44   **the Dane**   *the King (the embodiment of all Denmark).*

45   **lose your Voice**   *waste your breath, fail to obtain what you request.*

Or thinking by our late dear Brother's Death
Our State to be Disjoint and out of Frame,   20
Co-leagued with this Dream of his Advantage,
He hath not fail'd to pester us with Message
Importing the Surrender of those Lands
Lost by his Father with all Bands of Law
To our most valiant Broth'r; so much for him.   25
Now for our Self, and for this Time of Meeting,
Thus much the Bus'ness is: we have here writ
To Norway, Uncle of young Fortinbrasse,
Who, impotent and Bed-rid, scarcely hears
Of this his Nephew's Purpose, to suppress   30
His further Gate herein, in that the Levies,
The Lists, and full Proportions are all made
Out of his Subject. —And we here dispatch
You, good Cornelius, and you, Voltemand,
For Bearers of this Greeting to old Norway,   35
Giving to you no further pers'nal Power
To Bus'ness with the King, more than the Scope
Of these delated Articles allow.
                              He hands them a Document.
Farewell, and let your Haste commend your Duty.
CORNELIUS, VOLTEMAND   In that and all things will
     we show our Duty.   40
KING   We doubt it nothing: heartily farewell.
                         Exeunt Cornelius and Voltemand.
—And now, Laertes, what's the News with you?
You told us of some Suit: what is't, Laertes?
You cannot speak of Reason to the Dane
And lose your Voice: what would'st thou beg,
     Laertes,   45

47   native to   *born with, linked to as part of the same organism.*

48   instrumental to   *an instrument of. In lines 47–49 Claudius says that the Heart (Laertes' father) and the Mouth (Laertes in his role as a "Voice" making a request) are so powerful in the Body Politic of Denmark that they rule the Head (the King's mind and authority) and the Hand (the King's power to bestow favor).*

51   Fraunce   *France. Here and elsewhere, this edition adopts the -au- spellings in the Second Quarto, which may well have been set from Shakespeare's own manuscript of the play and is likely to reflect the pronunciations he preferred in particular contexts.*

56   bow   *submit. Combined with* bend *(incline) in line 55, this verb suggests that as Laertes curtsies to the King he also bends in the direction of France.*
         Leave   *permission (for Laertes to leave).*

65   A . . . Kind.   *What Hamlet means is that, as a result of his Uncle's marriage to his Mother, he is more "Kin" to the King than he wishes, since he is "less than Kind" (less than a real "Son" to this newly crowned "Father"). Hamlet does not want to be thought the "kind" of man the King is. Many editions mark this line as an aside; whether it is to be so treated is a matter of interpretation.*

67   Son   *Hamlet puns on* Sun *(the word to be found in the Folio), a traditional symbol of kingship.*

70   vailed   *both (a) lowered, and (b) veiled, as with the "Clouds" (black clothes) that hide the Sun (Son) in a "nighted Color."*

That shall not be my Offer, not thy Asking?
The Head is not more native to the Heart,
The Hand more instrumental to the Mouth,
Than is the Throne of Denmark to thy Father.
What would'st thou have, Laertes?

LAERTES   My dread Lord,   50
Your Leave and Favor to return to Fraunce,
From whence, though willingly I came to Denmark
To show my Duty in your Coronation,
Yet now I must confess, that Duty done,
My Thoughts and Wishes bend again tow'rd
    Fraunce,   55
And bow them to your gracious Leave and Pardon.

KING   Have you your Father's Leave? —What says
    Polonius?

POLONIUS   He hath, my Lord, wrung from me my slow
    Leave
By laborsome Petition, and at last
Upon his Will I seal'd my hard Consent.   60
I do beseech you give him leave to go.

KING   Take thy fair Hour, Laertes: Time be thine,
And thy best Graces spend it at thy Will.
—But now, my Cousin Hamlet, and my Son—

HAMLET   A little more than Kin, and less than Kind.   65

KING   How is it that the Clouds still hang on you?

HAMLET   Not so, my Lord: I am too much in the Son.

QUEEN   Good Hamlet, cast thy nighted Color off,
And let thine Eye look like a Friend on
    Denmark.
Do not for ever with thy vailed Lids   70

71 in the Dust *by looking to the ground. The Queen echoes Genesis 3:19 ("dust thou art, and unto dust thou shalt return").*

74 Common *a universally shared experience. But in view of what Hamlet says about his Mother later, it seems likely that he is punning on a sexual sense of "it is Common."*

75 so *both (a) thus, and (b) so intensely.*
  particular with thee *peculiar to you, or especially so to you.*

77 cold *Here the Second Quarto prints* coold. *Modern editions normally adopt the Folio's* good. *But Hamlet may well be using* cold *to remark upon the Queen's capacity for dispassionate philosophizing: what the Lord Chief Justice in* 2 Henry IV *commends as "cold Consid'rance" (V.ii.97).*

79 Suspiration *exhaling, sighing.*

81 Havior *behavior, expression.*

82 Chapes *Modern editions normally emend to* shapes *(for which the Second Quarto spelling may be either a variant or a pun); but* chapes *(plural for the metal plate protecting the end of a scabbard from the point of the blade "within," line 85) suits the context with equal precision.*

83 devote *Modern editions normally adopt the Folio's* denote *instead of the Quarto's* deuote; *but* devote *(consecrate, as with a monastic habit similar to Hamlet's "Suits of Woe") is by no means untenable here.*

85 passes *surpasses.*

92 obsequious *funereal (from* obsequies, *rites for the dead).*

Seek for thy noble Father in the Dust.
Thou know'st 'tis common all that lives must
   die,
Passing through Nature to Eternity.

HAMLET   Ay Madam, it is Common.

QUEEN   If it be,
Why seems it so particular with thee?   75

HAMLET   Seems, Madam? Nay it Is: I know not Seems.
'Tis not alone my Inky Cloak, cold Mother,
Nor customary Suits of solemn Black,
Nor windy Suspiration of forc'd Breath,
No, nor the fruitful River in the Eye,   .   80
Nor the dejected Havior of the Visage,
Together with all Forms, Moods, Chapes of
   Grief,
That can devote me truly. These indeed Seem,
For they are Actions that a Man might Play;
But I have that within which passes Show,   85
These but the Trappings and the Suits of Woe.

KING   'Tis sweet and commendable in your Nature,
   Hamlet,
To give these Mourning Duties to your Father;
But you must know your Father lost a Father,
That Father lost lost his, and the Survivor
   bound   90
In filial Obligation for some Term
To do obsequious Sorrow. But to persever
In obstinate Condolement is a Course
Of impious Stubbornness; 'tis unmanly Grief;
It shows a Will most incorrect to Heaven,   95
A Heart unfortified, or Mind impatient,

27

97   simple   *naive, infantile.*

99   vulgar   *common to all people.*

100   peevish   *obstinately childish.*

101   a Fault to Heaven   *an offense against God. Here and else-
       where the King rejects Hamlet's implication that his "Trap-
       pings" of grief are signs of filial and religious devotion. As
       Claudius depicts them, they are the very opposite: a rejection of
       Heaven's will, and thus an impious sin against God, Nature,
       Reason, and even the deceased himself.*

105   Corse   *corpse.*

107   unprevailing   *unavailing, ineffectual.*

109   the most immediate to our Throne   *the next in succession.*

113   Wittenberg   *This German university, founded in 1502 and
       made famous in 1517 as the setting where Martin Luther
       launched the Protestant Reformation, was the most popular
       institution of higher learning for Danes studying abroad in the
       later sixteenth century.*

114   retrogard   *a variant of* retrograde, *moving in a contrary
       direction. Unlike Laertes, whose request to return to Paris was
       granted immediately, Hamlet will not be encouraged in his suit
       to leave Denmark.*

118   lose her Prayers   *be denied her wishes. Compare line 45.*

123   Accord   *consent.*

125   jocund Health   *cheerful toast.*

An Understanding simple and unschool'd;
For what we know must be, and is as common
As any the most vulgar thing to Sense,
Why should we in our peevish Opposition   100
Take it to Heart? Fie, 'tis a Fault to Heaven,
A Fault against the Dead, a Fault to Nature,
To Reason most absurd, whose Common Theme
Is Death of Fathers, and who still hath cried
From the first Corse till he that died today   105
"This must be so." We pray you throw to Earth
This unprevailing Woe, and think of us
As of a Father: for let the World take note
You are the most immediate to our Throne,
And with no less Nobility of Love   110
Than that which dearest Father bears his Son
Do I impart tow'rd you. For your Intent
In going back to School in Wittenberg,
It is most retrograd to our Desire,
And we beseech you bend you to remain   115
Here in the Cheer and Comfort of our Eye,
Our chiefest Courtier, Cousin, and our Son.
QUEEN   Let not thy Mother lose her Prayers, Hamlet:
    I pray thee stay with us, go not to Wittenberg.
HAMLET   I shall in all my best obey you, Madam.   120
KING   Why 'tis a loving and a fair Reply:
    Be as our self in Denmark. —Madam, come;
    This gentle and unforc'd Accord of Hamlet
    Sits smiling to my Heart, in Grace whereof
    No jocund Health that Denmark drinks today   125
    But the great Cannon to the Clouds shall tell;

127   Rouse   *carouse; here a "Health" pledged by the King.*
           bruit again   *proclaim in reply (with a loud reverberation).*

129   salli'd   *a variant of* sullied, *blemished, defiled. The Folio prints* solid, *and Hamlet may be combining the two senses in an image of bloated flesh. Compare II.i.39.*

132   Cannon   *both (a) an aimed and firmly placed ("fix'd") weapon, and (b) an unbending divine law (*canon, *the spelling adopted by all modern editions).*
           Seal-Slaughter   *The Quarto's* seale *may be a misreading of* sealf *or* sealfe *or simply a variant of* self *(the word in the Folio text). But Shakespeare may have intended a play on* self *and* seal *(the insignia of a self, and particularly a monarch). If so, this line can refer to two options, both forbidden by "the Everlasting": suicide and regicide (Romans 12:17–13:7).*

133   wary   *(a) perilous, (b) cursed, and (c) weary (the Folio reading).*

137   merely   *completely.*
           come thus   *arrive at this point. Modern editions normally follow the Folio and print* come to this.

140   Hyperion to a Satyr   *the Sun God in comparison to a creature half human and half goat. Like goats, satyrs were proverbial for lechery.*

141   beteem   *permit.*

149   Niobe   *a heroine in Greek myth who wept so uncontrollably for her children (slain by Apollo and Diana) that she became a stone from which tears continued to flow. Ovid depicted her in Book VI of his* Metamorphoses.

And the King's Rouse the Heav'n shall bruit
   again,
Respeaking Earthly Thunder. Come away.
                Flourish. Exeunt all but Hamlet.
HAMLET   O that this too too salli'd Flesh would
   melt,
Thaw, and resolve it self into a Dew;   130
Or that the Everlasting had not fix'd
His Cannon 'gainst Seal-Slaughter. O God, God,
How wary, stale, flat, and unprofitable
Seem to me all the Uses of this World!
Fie on't, ah fie, 'tis an unweeded Garden   135
That grows to Seed: things rank and gross in
   Nature
Possess it merely. That it should come thus.
But two Months dead, nay not so much, not two;
So excellent a King, that was to this
Hyperion to a Satyr; so loving to my Mother   140
That he might not beteem the Winds of Heaven
Visit her Face too roughly. Heav'n and Earth,
Must I remember? Why she should hang on him
As if Increase of Appetite had grown
By what it fed on, and yet within a Month—   145
Let me not think on't! (Frailty, thy name is
   Woman)—
A little Month, or ere those Shoes were old
With which she follow'd my poor Father's Body
Like Niobe, all Tears, why she—
O God, a Beast that wants Discourse of Reason   150
Would have mourn'd longer! Marri'd with my Uncle,
My Father's Brother, but no more like my Father

153   Hercules   *a Greek hero proverbial for his strength. According to later traditions he became a God, and his virtues and labors were allegorized in such a way that he became a symbol of Christ in victory. He also appears to have been an emblem for the Globe playhouse and its actors.*

154   unrighteous   *both (a) unworthy, and (b) insincere.*

155   Had . . . Eyes   *had finished washing the red out of her irritated eyes.*

156   post   *hasten.*

157   incestious   *incestuous. In accordance with such Biblical passages as Leviticus 18:16 and 20:21, Hamlet regards as incestuous a union between a woman and her former husband's brother. His views would have had the support of both Catholics and Anglicans in Shakespeare's time. The matter was somewhat sensitive, because Queen Elizabeth was the daughter of Henry VIII, whose first wife, Catherine of Aragon, was the widow of Henry's brother Arthur.*

163   Sir—my good Friend   *Hamlet decides to drop the formality with which he had initially greeted Horatio and acknowledge him more warmly.*
        change   *exchange.*

164   what make you from   *what brings you from, what are you doing away from.*

166   Good ev'n, Sir.   *This greeting is probably addressed to Barnardo. The word* ev'n *indicates that it is now after noon.*

168   Truant   *irresponsible person. Horatio's self-description implies more than a disposition to play hooky from school.*

Than I to Hercules. Within a Month,
Ere yet the Salt of most unrighteous Tears
Had left the Flushing in her galled Eyes,   155
She marri'd. O most wicked Speed: to post
With such Dexter'ty to incestious Sheets!
It is not, nor it cannot come to, Good.
—But break, my Heart, for I must hold my
    Tongue.

Enter Horatio, Marcellus, and Barnardo.

HORATIO   Hail to your Lordship!
HAMLET   I am glad to see you well;   160
    Horatio, or I do forget my self.
HORATIO   The same, my Lord, and your poor Servant
    ever.
HAMLET   Sir—my good Friend: I'll change that Name
    with you!
    And what make you from Wittenberg, Horatio?
    —Marcellus.
MARCELLUS   My good Lord.   165
HAMLET   I'm very glad to see you. —Good ev'n,
    Sir.
    —But what in faith make you from Wittenberg?
HORATIO   A Truant Disposition, good my Lord.
HAMLET   I would not hear your Enemy say so,
    Nor shall you do my Ear that Violence   170
    To make it Truster of your own Report
    Against your Self: I know you are no Truant.
    But what is your Affair in Elsinore?

33

174   for to drink   *how to drink. The Folio's "to drink deep" has the same implications and is preferred by most modern editors.*

176   prethee   *pray thee. This spelling is the one to be found throughout the Second Quarto.*
       Student   *student; this spelling occurs frequently in Shakespeare's texts.*

178   hard upon   *quickly thereafter.*

179   Meats   *food, not limited to meat in the modern sense.*

180   coldly   *Hamlet means this literally; in lines 179–80 he is saying that the wedding was so soon after the funeral that the leftovers from the food served hot on the first occasion were served cold on the second. As in line 77, however,* coldly *also refers to an inappropriately dispassionate attitude.*

181   Would . . . Heav'n   *The sentiments Hamlet expresses here will be echoed later in the play. Compare III.iii.73–95 and V.ii.37–47.*

182   Or ever   *before.*

185   'a   *he.*

188   yesternight   *last night.*

191   Season your Admiration   *moderate your amazement.*

192   attent   *attentive; probably accented on the second syllable.*

197   dead Waste and Middle   *Horatio means midnight, the time when night is most still (dead), and when the spirits of the dead are most likely to walk. There is wordplay on* waist *(another kind of middle) and probably on* vast *(which is etymologically related to* waste*).*

34

We'll teach you for to drink ere you depart!

HORATIO   My Lord, I came to see your Father's
Funeral.   175

HAMLET   I prethee do not mock me, fellow Studient:
I think it was to my Mother's Wedding.

HORATIO   Indeed, my Lord, it follow'd hard upon.

HAMLET   Thrift, thrift, Horatio! The Funeral bak'd
Meats
Did coldly furnish forth the Marriage Tables.   180
Would I had met my dearest Foe in Heav'n
Or ever I had seen that Day, Horatio!
My Fath'r, me thinks I see my Father—

HORATIO   Where,
My Lord?

HAMLET   In my Mind's Eye, Horatio.

HORATIO   I saw him once: 'a was a goodly King.   185

HAMLET   'A was a Man, take him for all in all,
I shall not look upon his like again.

HORATIO   My Lord I think I saw him yesternight.

HAMLET   Saw, who?

HORATIO   My Lord, the King your Father.

HAMLET   The King my Father?   190

HORATIO   Season your Admiration for a while
With an attent Ear till I may deliver
Upon the Witness of these Gentlemen
This Marv'l to you.

HAMLET   For God's Love, let me hear!

HORATIO   Two Nights together had these Gentlemen,   195
Marcellus and Barnardo, on their Watch
In the dead Waste and Middle of the Night
Been thus encount'red: a Figure like your Father,

35

199   at Point   *precisely in every respect.*
            Cap-a-pe   *French for "head to foot."*

201   stately   *literally, "state-like," in the imperial manner of a monarch.*

202   surprised   *ambushed, overtaken by surprise.*

203   Truncheon   *a short, thick staff symbolizing military authority.*

205   dumb   *speechless.*

206   dreadful   *full of fear.*

211   like   *like each other than the Ghost is like your Father.*

215   it   *its. "His" and "it" were the normal forms for the neuter possessive pronoun.*

217   even then   *at that very moment.*

222   Indeed, Sirs   *This phrase can either refer back to what Horatio has just said (with Hamlet commending the sense of duty the three men have demonstrated) or intensify what follows (with Hamlet saying "This troubles me indeed").*

Arm'd at Point, exactly Cap-a-pe,
Appears before them, and with solemn March   200
Goes slow and stately by them; thrice he walk'd
By their oppress'd and Fear-surprised Eyes
Within his Truncheon's length, whil'st they, distill'd
Almost to Jelly with the act of Fear,
Stand dumb and speak not to him. This to me   205
In dreadful Secrecy impart they did,
And I with them the Third Night kept the Watch,
Where, as they had deliver'd, both in Time,
Form of the Thing, each Word made true and good,
The Apparition comes. I knew your Father: 210
These Hands are not more like.
HAMLET   But where was this?
MARCELLUS   My Lord, upon the Platform where we
    watch.
HAMLET   Did you not speak to it?
HORATIO   My Lord, I did,
But Answer made it none; yet once me thought
It lifted up it Head and did address   215
It self to Motion like as it would speak;
But even then the Morning Cock crew loud,
And at the Sound it shrunk in haste away
And vanish'd from our Sight.
HAMLET   'Tis very Strange.
HORATIO   As I do live, my honor'd Lord, 'tis true,   220
And we did think it writ down in our Duty
To let you know of it.
HAMLET   Indeed, Sirs, but
This troubles me. Hold you the Watch tonight?
ALL   We do, my Lord.

227   **Beaver**   *visor.*
    What . . . frowningly?   *It is not clear how this line is to be spoken. Among the possibilities are "What, look'd he frowningly?" and "What look'd he, frowningly?" In the second version* **What** *would mean "how."*

233   **tell a Hundreth**   *count to a hundred.*

234   **grisl'd**   *grizzled, mingled with gray.*

236   **Sable silver'd**   *black mixed with gray.*

238   **assume**   *take on. Hamlet seems perilously close to assuming that if the spirit assumes his "Father's Person" (appearance), it must be his father's spirit in fact. Horatio and the two watchmen have been much more cautious about drawing any conclusions about the Ghost.*

239   **gape**   *open its mouth widely. This verb is often used to describe an infant bird eagerly awaiting food.*

HAMLET   Arm'd, say you?
ALL   Arm'd, my Lord.
HAMLET   From Top to Toe?
ALL   My Lord, from Head to Foot.   225
HAMLET   Then saw you not his Face?
HORATIO   O yes, my Lord,
    He wore his Beaver up.
HAMLET   What look'd he frowningly?
HORATIO   A Count'nance more in Sorrow than in
    Anger.
HAMLET   Pale or Red?
HORATIO   Nay very Pale.
HAMLET   And fix'd
    His Eyes upon you?
HORATIO   Most constantly.
HAMLET   I would   230
    I had been there.
HORATIO   It would have much amaz'd you.
HAMLET   Very like; stay'd it long?
HORATIO   While one
    With mod'rate Haste might tell a Hundreth.
BOTH   Longer, longer.
HORATIO   Not when I saw 't.
HAMLET   His Beard was grisl'd, no?
HORATIO   It was as I have seen it in his Life,   235
    A Sable silver'd.
HAMLET   I will watch tonight:
    Perchance 'twill walk again.
HORATIO   I warr'nt it will.
HAMLET   If it assume my noble Father's Person,
    I'll speak to it though Hell it self should gape

242   ten'ble   *tenable, held tightly.*

243   whatsomever   *whatsoever.*

244   Give . . . Tongue   *note it but say nothing about it to any-
       one.*

245   requite   *reward.*

250   doubt   *fear, suspect.*

251   Fond   *Most editors print* Foul, *the word in the First Folio (as
       well as in the First Quarto). Here* Fond *would mean "fool-
       ish" or "mad" (referring to deeds an evildoer rashly expected
       to go undetected and unpunished).* Fond *was also a variant
       spelling for "found," and Hamlet could well be punning on
       that implication as a way of emphasizing the folly of the "Foul
       Play" (line 250) that is now to be found out.*

252   o'erwhelm   *literally, bury, cover over; suppress, overpower.*

I.iii   *This scene takes place in or near the chambers of Polonius.*

1   Necessaries   *necessities.*
       inbark'd   *embarked, loaded aboard ship.*

3   Convay   *conveyance, means of transport; accented on the first
       syllable.*
       in assistant   *in assisting them. Most editors adopt the Folio's*
       Convoy *here and emend* in *to* is.

40

And bid me hold my Peace. I pray you all,   240
If you have hitherto conceal'd this Sight,
Let it be ten'ble in your Silence still;
And whatsomever else shall hap tonight,
Give it an Understanding but no Tongue.
I will requite your Loves; so fare you well.   245
Upon the Platform 'twixt eleven and twelfe
I'll visit you.
ALL   Our Duty to your Honor.
HAMLET   Your Loves as mine to you: farewell.
                                        Exeunt all but Hamlet.
—My Father's Spir't in Arms: all is not well.
I doubt some Foul Play. Would the Night were
    come!   250
—Till then, sit still, my Soul. Fond Deeds will
    rise,
Though all the Earth o'erwhelm them to Men's
    Eyes.   *Exit.*

Scene 3

Enter Laertes and Ophelia, his Sister.

LAERTES   My Necessaries are inbark'd: farewell,
        And Sister, as the Winds give Benefit
        And Convay, in assistant do not sleep

5   For   *as for.*

6   Hold it a Fashion   *regard it as a passing fancy.*
a Toy in Blood   *an idle prompting of his youthful passions.*

7   primy Nature   *nature in the springtime.*

8   Forward   *over-eager (and thus likely to wither prematurely).*

9   Suppliance of a Minute   *something that supplies the needs of a brief moment and no more.*

10   so   *thus. Although the early texts do not so indicate, modern editors normally punctuate this speech as a question.*

11   cressant   *crescent; growing, increasing.*
alone   *solely.*

12   Thews and Bulks   *strength and stature.*
Temple waxes   *body grows. Laertes alludes to 1 Corinthians 6:19, "know yet not that your body is the temple of the Holy Ghost which is in you, which ye have of God, and ye are not your own?"*

14   Grows wide withal   *develops along with it. But* wide *also hints at "wide of the mark," out of control.*

15   Soil nor Cautel   *blemish nor deceitfulness.*

17   weigh'd   *considered, taken in the balance.*

21   Safety   *Here the Folio reads* sanctity. *If* Safety *is correct, the word is probably to be pronounced with three syllables.*

30   credent   *credulous, gullible.*
list   *listen to, heed.*

But let me hear from you.

OPHELIA   Do you doubt that?

LAERTES   For Hamlet, and the Trifling of his Favor,   5
    Hold it a Fashion, and a Toy in Blood,
    A Violet in the Youth of primy Nature,
    Forward, not Permanent, Sweet, not Lasting,
    The Perfume and Suppliance of a Minute,
    No more.

OPHELIA   No more but so.

LAERTES   Think it no more: 10
    For Nature cressant does not grow alone
    In Thews and Bulks, but as this Temple waxes
    The inward Service of the Mind and Soul
    Grows wide withal. Perhaps he loves you now,
    And now no Soil nor Cautel doth besmirch   15
    The Virtue of his Will; but you must fear,
    His Greatness weigh'd, his Will is not his own.
    For he himself is subject to his Birth.
    He may not, as Unvalued Persons do,
    Carve for himself: for on his Choice depends   20
    The Safety and Health of this whole State,
    And therefore must his Choice be circumscrib'd
    Unto the Voice and Yielding of that Body
    Whereof he is the Head. Then if he says he
      loves you,
    It fits your Wisdom so far to believe it   25
    As he in his partic'lar Act and Place
    May give his Saying deed, which is no further
    Than the Main Voice of Denmark goes withal.
    Then weigh what Loss your Honor may sustain
    If with too credent Ear you list his Songs,   30

32 Importunity *demanding persistence. The Latin root of this word refers to an urgent suit to gain admission to a* portus, *port or entrance.*

34 keep you in the Rear of your Affection *keep your "chaste Treasure" (virginity) away from the front lines of battle, so that neither your "Affection" (desires) nor Hamlet's may endanger its security.*

36 Chariest *literally, stingiest, most sparing; most modest.*
Prodigal *extravagant, spendthrift.*

37 Moon *The Moon was associated with Cynthia (Diana), Goddess of Chastity.*

38 scapes *escapes.*
calumnious Strokes *the blows of calumny (malicious scandal).*

39 Canker *cankerworm, a larva feeding on the buds ("Buttons") of flowers.*

42 Contagious . . . imminent *the danger of contagion from withering blasts of air (the cause of blight) is most urgent.*

47 ungracious Pastors *ministers (literally, shepherds) lacking in grace (spiritual discipline).*

48 Step *stairstep. Modern editors normally follow the Folio here and print* steep.

49 a puff'd and reckless Libertine *as a proud and heedlessly licentious man.*

50 Dalliance *wanton pleasure.*

51 reaks not his own Rede *heeds (recks) not his own advice.*
fear me not *don't worry about me.*

Or lose your Heart, or your chaste Treasure
  open
To his unmast'red Importunity.
Fear it, Ophelia; fear it, my dear Sister,
And keep you in the Rear of your Affection,
Out of the Shot and Danger of Desire.   35
The Chariest Maid is Prodigal enough
If she unmask her Beauty to the Moon.
Virtue it self scapes not calumnious Strokes.
The Canker galls the Infants of the Spring
Too oft before their Buttons be disclos'd.   40
And in the Morn and liquid Dew of Youth
Contagious Blastments are most imminent.
Be wary then: best Safety lies in Fear.
Youth to it self rebels, though none else near.
OPHELIA   I shall th' effect of this good Lesson
  keep   45
As Watchman to my Heart. But good my Brother,
Do not as some ungracious Pastors do,
Show me the Step and thorny Way to Heav'n
Whiles a puff'd and reckless Libertine
Himself the Primrose Path of Dalliance treads   50
And reaks not his own Rede.

Enter Polonius.

LAERTES   O fear me not.
I stay too long; but here my Father comes.
A double Blessing is a double Grace;
Occasion smiles upon a second Leave.

58   **Precepts** *proverbs, wise sentences (from Latin* sententiae*).*

59   character   *inscribe or engrave. As we have just seen from Laertes' advice to Ophelia, he has already "charactered" a large stock of prudent maxims.*

60   **unproportion'd**   *unsuitable, inordinate.*

61   **Familiar**   *friendly, informal, open.*
       Vulgar   *common, loose, indiscriminate.*

62   **and their Adoption tried**   *once they have been proven trust-worthy.*

63   **Grapple**   *grasp, embrace.*

64   **entertainment**   *hospitable reception.*

65   **unfledg'd Courage**   *ardent "hearts" too young to fly.*

69   **Censure**   *counsel, opinions, criticism.*
       reserve thy Judgment   *both (a) make up your own mind, and (b) keep your opinions to yourself.*

70   **Habit**   *apparel.*

71   **express'd in Fancy**   *displayed in ostentatious finery.*

74   **Gen'rous**   *highborn, noble (from Latin* generosus*). Here "class of men" is implied.*
       Chief in that   *most renowned for tasteful elegance.*

75   **Lender, Boy**   *Here the Folio reads* **Lender** be. *Polonius implies "be" in the Quarto version.*

77   **Husbandry**   *personal economy, thrifty management.*

46

POLONIUS   Yet here, Laertes? Aboard, aboard, for
      shame!   55
   The Wind sits in the Shoulder of your Sail,
   And you are stay'd for. There, my Blessing
      with thee,
   And these few Precepts in thy Memory
   Look thou character. Give thy Thoughts no
      Tongue,
   Nor any unproportion'd Thought his Act.   60
   Be thou Familiar, but by no means Vulgar.
   Those Friends thou hast, and their Adoption
      tried,
   Grapple them unto thy Soul with Hoops of Steel;
   But do not dull thy Palm with entertainment
   Of each new-hatch'd unfledg'd Courage. Beware   65
   Of entrance to a Quarr'l, but being in,
   Bear 't that the Opposed may beware of thee.
   Give ev'ry man thy Ear, but few thy Voice.
   Take each man's Censure, but reserve thy
      Judgment.
   Costly thy Habit as thy Purse can buy,   70
   But not express'd in Fancy; Rich, not Gaudy:
   For the Apparel oft proclaims the Man,
   And they in Fraunce of the best Rank and Station,
   Or of a most Select and Gen'rous, Chief in that.
   Neither a Borr'wer nor a Lender, Boy: 75
   For Loan oft loses both it Self and Friend,
   And Borr'wing dulls the Edge of Husbandry.
   This above all: to thine own Self be True,
   And it must follow as the Night the Day
   Thou canst not then be False to any Man.   · 80

47

81   season   *make palatable, preserve, and ripen.*

83   invests you   *clothes you (making you ready).*
         tend   *attend, wait on you.*

89   So   *if it.*
         touching   *concerning.*

90   Marry well bethought.   *Indeed, I'm glad you reminded me of that. Originally* marry *was an oath referring to the Virgin Mary.*

92   Private Time   *time alone. In Shakespeare's time maidens were often forbidden to spend unchaperoned time with young men. See lines 123–25.*

93   Audience   *willingness to hear.*

94   put   *pressed.*

97   behooves   *befits.*
         my Daughter   *the daughter of a respected counselor such as I.*
         Honor   *reputation.*

99   Tenders   *offers.*

101   green   *unripe, naive.*
         unsifted   *unproven. Polonius probably alludes to Luke 22:31, where Jesus says "Satan hath desired to have you, that he may sift you as wheat."*

102   per'lous   *perilous; here elided for metrical purposes. The word was probably pronounced "parlous" in Shakespeare's time.*

Farewell, my Blessing season this in thee.

LAERTES   Most humbly do I take my Leave, my Lord.

POLONIUS   The Time invests you: go, your Servants
tend.

LAERTES   —Farewell, Ophelia, and remember well
What I have said to you.

OPHELIA   'Tis in my Mem'ry lock'd   85
And you your self shall keep the Key of it.

LAERTES   Farewell.   *Exit.*

POLONIUS   What is't, Ophelia, he hath said to you?

OPHELIA   So please you, something touching the
Lord Hamlet.

POLONIUS   Marry well bethought.   90
'Tis told me he hath very oft of late
Giv'n Private Time to you, and you your self
Have of your Audience been most free and
bounteous.
If it be so (as so 'tis put on me,
And that in way of Caution), I must tell you   95
You do not understand your self so clearly
As it behooves my Daughter and your Honor.
What is between you? Give me up the Truth.

OPHELIA   He hath, my Lord, of late made many
Tenders
Of his Affection to me.

POLONIUS   Affection, puh!   100
You speak like a green Girl, unsifted in
Such per'lous Circumstance. Do you believe
His Tenders, as you call them?

OPHELIA   I do not know,
My Lord, what I should think.

106   **Sterling**   *legitimate currency.*

107   **Tender . . . dearly**   *hold (value) yourself at a higher rate.*

108   **Phrase**   *word.*
        roaming it thus   *leading it about in this roundabout fashion. This verb comes from the Folio printing; the Second Quarto reads* wrong, *and most editors emend to* wringing, wronging, *or* running.

109   **tender me a Fool**   *probably (a) give me a fool for a daughter, (b) give me a fool (baby) for a grandchild, and (c) make me a fool to the world.*

111   **go to**   *an expression of dismissal, like our "come on now!"*

112   **Count'nance**   *literally, face; assurance, warranty.*

114   **Springes**   *snares.*
        Woodcocks   *birds proverbial for their stupidity.*

117   **extinct**   *extinguished.*

121   **Intreatments**   *both (a) your treatment of him, your willingness to give him audience; and (b) your willingness to receive his entreaties to you [to surrender].*

122   **a Command to Parle**   *to call for negotiations.*

124   **larger Tider**   *longer tether.*

126   **Brokers**   *(a) lying panders, rather than (b) honest agents.*

127   **Die**   *probably both (a) dye (color), and (b) gambling die.*
        Investments show   *apparel (outward appearance) indicates.*

POLONIUS   Marry I will teach you.
     Think your self a Baby, that you have ta'en   105
     These Tenders for true Pay which are not Sterling.
     Tender your self more dearly, or (not to crack
     The Wind of the poor Phrase, roaming it thus)
     You'll tender me a Fool.
OPHELIA   My Lord, he hath
     Importun'd me with Love in honorable fashion—   110
POLONIUS   Ay, Fashion you may call 't; go to, go to!
OPHELIA   And hath given Count'nance to his Speech,
     My Lord, with almost all the holy Vows
     Of Heav'n.
POLONIUS   Ay, Springes to catch Woodcocks. I
     Do know, when the Blood burns, how prodigal   115
     The Soul lends the Tongue Vows. These Blazes,
          Daughter,
     Giving more Light than Heat, extinct in both
     Even in their Promise as it is a-making,
     You must not take for Fire. From this time
     Be something scanter of your Maiden Presence;   120
     Set your Intreatments at a higher Rate
     Than a Command to Parle. For Lord Hamlet,
     Believe so much in him: that he is Young,
     And with a larger Tider may he walk
     Than may be given you. In few, Ophelia,   125
     Do not believe his Vows, for they are Brokers,
     Not of that Die which their Investments show,
     But mere Implor'tors of unholy Suits
     Breathing like sanctified and pious Bonds

51

130   beguide   *Modern editors normally follow the Folio and print* beguile *(deceive, cheat). That is the sense called for here; but* beguide *may be a Shakespearean coinage to combine such senses as "misguide," "beguile," and "begild" (gild over). All of these would be fit with the seemingly "pious Bonds" (holy pledges or contracts) that Polonius accuses Hamlet of tendering to disguise the "unholy Suits" he implores (lines 128–29).*

132   moment   *moment's.*

134   charge   *command.*
         Come your ways.   *Come along now.*

I.iv   *This scene returns us to the battlements on which the play began.*

1   shroudly   *shrewdly, sharply.*

2   eager   *bitter.*

4   strook   *struck.*

5   Seas'n   *period of time.*

6   wont   *custom, habit.*

S.D.   Pieces goes off   *cannons are fired.*

7   takes his Rouse   *carouses.*

8   Wassel   *wassail, a word that derives from an Anglo-Saxon toast meaning "be hale [whole, healthy]."*
         up-spring Reels   *The up-spring was a wild dance, and reels were swirling, swaggering movements.*

9   Rennish   *Rhenish (Rhine) wine.*

The better to beguide. This is for all: 130
I would not, in plain Terms, from this Time
   forth
Have you so slander any moment Leisure
As to give Words or Talk with the Lord Hamlet.
Look to 't, I charge you. Come your ways.

OPHELIA   I shall obey, my Lord.   *Exeunt.* 135

Scene 4

Enter Hamlet, Horatio, and Marcellus.

HAMLET   The Air bites shroudly, it is very cold.

HORATIO   It is nipping, and an eager Air.

HAMLET   What Hour now?

HORATIO   I think it lacks of Twelve.

MARCELLUS   No, it is strook.

HORATIO   Indeed? I heard it not.
It then draws near the Seas'n wherein the Spirit 5
Held his wont to walk.

             A Flourish of Trumpets, and two Pieces goes off.
            What does this mean, my Lord?

HAMLET   The King doth wake tonight, and takes his
   Rouse,
Keeps Wassel and the swagg'ring up-spring Reels;
And as he drains his drafts of Rennish down

11 **The Triumph of his Pledge**   *his quaffing the entire cup after each toast.*

15 **More . . . Observance**   *that would be more honored by being broken than by being observed. In modern parlance the phrase is usually given a satirical twist.*

17 **traduc'd and tax'd**   *Both words mean vilified, censured.*

18 **clip**   *clepe, call.*

19 **Soil our Addition**   *befoul any titles or epithets they apply to us.*

21 **The Pith . . . Attribute**   *the core of our good reputation.*

22 **So . . . Men**   *similarly it happens with individual men.*

23 **for . . . them**   *because of some natural blemish in them.*

26 **Complexion**   *humour (an imbalance in one's disposition).*

27 **Pales**   *fences. This word is echoed in III.i.82.*

28–29 **some . . . Manners**   *some vice that spoils pleasing manners.*

31 **Being . . . Star**   *resulting from Nature (wearing her livery, uniform) or deriving from a malignant star (or planet) that sways one's fortune.*

34 **in . . . Corruption**   *in general opinion be judged corrupt.*

35–37 **the . . . Scandal**   *a drop of oil (symbolizing evil) clouds all their nobility of soul with a dubious character that scandalizes it, giving it a bad name.*

The Kettle-drum and Trumpet thus bray out   10
The Triumph of his Pledge.
HORATIO   Is it a Custom?
HAMLET   Ay marry, is't;
    But to my Mind, though I am Native here
    And to the Manner born, it is a Custom
    More honor'd in the Breach than the Observance.   15
    This heavy-headed Revel East and West
    Makes us traduc'd and tax'd of other Nations:
    They clip us Drunkards, and with Swinish Phrase
    Soil our Addition; and indeed it takes
    From our Achievements, though perform'd at
        Height,   20
    The Pith and Marrow of our Attribute.
    So oft it chaunces in Partic'lar Men
    That for some vicious Mole of Nature in them,
    As in their Birth, wherein they are not guilty
    (Since Nature cannot choose his Origin),   25
    By their o'er-growth of some Complexion
    Oft breaking down the Pales and Forts of
        Reason,
    Or by some Habit that too much o'er-leavens
    The Form of Plausive Manners, that these Men
    (Carrying, I say, the Stamp of one Defect,   30
    Being Nature's Livery or Fortune's Star,
    His Virtues else be they as pure as Grace,
    As infinite as Man may undergo)
    Shall in the Gen'ral Censure take Corruption
    From that Partic'lar Fault: the Dram of Eale   35
    Doth all the Noble Substance of a Doubt

55

41   charitable   *good, in keeping with* caritas *(Latin for "Christian love").*

42   Questionable   *The preceding phrases prepare us to interpret*
Questionable *here as "ambiguous"; but Hamlet appears to
mean "to be questioned" in a more positive sense. Rather than
"try the spirit" as Horatio has done in I.i.45, Hamlet simply
assumes that it is his Father's ghost and proceeds to query it on
that basis.*

46   canoniz'd   *sanctified; buried with the prescribed rites. In order
to preserve the meter in this line,* canoniz'd *either needs to be
syncopated to "can'niz'd" or accented on the second syllable.*
hearsed   *coffined; here pronounced as a two-syllable word.*

47   Cerements   *apparently a Shakespearean coinage that combines "cerecloth" (waxed burial cloth) and "ceremonies."*

51   Corse   *corpse.*
in complete Steel   *in full armor; here pronounced "cóm-
plete."*

52   the glimpses of the Moon   *This phrase reminds us that the
Ghost is from a realm the Moon does not reach with its beams.
It also suggests that the light of the Moon is pale and intermit-
tent on this ominous night.*

53   hideous   *terrifying.*
Fools of Nature   *mere mortals, subject to Nature's whims.*

56   What should we do?   *Hamlet's question reflects the belief
that Ghosts sometimes revisited the living in order to get them
to perform some unfinished task.*

58   Impartment   *communication.*

To his own Scandal.

Enter Ghost.

HORATIO   Look, my Lord, it comes.
HAMLET   Angels and Ministers of Grace, defend us!
    —Be thou a Spir't of Health or Goblin damn'd,
    Bring with thee Airs from Heav'n or Blasts
        from Hell,   40
    Be thy Intents wicked or charitable,
    Thou com'st in such a Questionable Shape
    That I will speak to thee: I'll call thee
        Hamlet,
    King, Father, Royal Dane. O answer me:
    Let me not burst in Ignorance, but tell   45
    Why thy canoniz'd Bones, hearsed in Death,
    Have burst their Cerements; why the Sepulcher
    Wherein we saw thee quietly interr'd
    Hath op'd his ponderous and marble Jaws
    To cast thee up again. What may this mean   50
    That thou, dead Corse, again in complete Steel
    Revisits thus the glimpses of the Moon,
    Making Night hideous, and we Fools of Nature
    So horridly to shake our Disposition
    With Thoughts beyond the reaches of our Souls?   55
    Say why is this? Wherefore? What should we do?
                                    The Ghost beckons.
HORATIO   It beckons you to go away with it
    As if it some Impartment did desire
    To you alone.
MARCELLUS   Look with what courteous Action

57

60   removed   *remote, isolated.*

62   then   *therefore.*

64   Fee   *value.*

65   what can it do to that   *Horatio provides the conventional Elizabethan answer to this question in the speech that follows.*

68   toward   *here a one-syllable word.*
      Flood   *sea.*

69   Somnet   *summit.*
      Cleef   *cliff. Horatio alludes to the notion that devils often lured troubled souls to promontories, where they could induce them to surrender to despair and commit suicide (a damnable act, as Hamlet has noted in I.ii.130–32). Shakespeare treats this subject again in IV.vi of* King Lear; *there Edgar tells Gloucester a "Fiend" has led him to the cliff from which the suicidal old man believes he has leaped.*

70   bettles   *beetles, overhangs. The word may derive from beetle-brows; or it may derive from a likeness between an overhanging precipice and a beam (beetle) used as a battering ram.*

74   Toys of Desperation   *desperate impulses (toward self-slaughter).*

76   Fadoms   *fathoms (lengths of six feet).*

81   Arture   *artery.*

82   Nemean Lion   *a mythical creature slain by Hercules as the first of his twelve labors.*
      Nerve   *sinew, muscle.*

It waves you to a more removed Ground: 60
But do not go with it.
HORATIO   No, by no means.
HAMLET   It will not speak, then I will follow it.
HORATIO   Do not, my Lord.
HAMLET   Why, what should be the Fear?
I do not set my Life at a Pin's Fee,
And for my Soul, what can it do to that,   65
Being a Thing Immortal as it self?
It waves me forth again, I'll follow it.
HORATIO   What if it tempt you toward the Flood, my
    Lord?
Or to the dreadful Somnet of the Cleef
That bettles o'er his Base into the Sea,   70
And there assume some other horr'ble Form
Which might deprive your Sovereignty of Reason
And draw you into Madness? Think of it:
The very Place puts Toys of Desperation,
Without more Motive, into ev'ry Brain   75
That looks so many Fadoms to the Sea
And hears it roar beneath.
HAMLET   It waves me still.
—Go on, I'll follow thee.
MARCELLUS   You shall not go, my Lord!
HAMLET   Hold off your Hands!
HORATIO   Be rul'd, you shall not go!
HAMLET   My Fate cries out   80
And makes each petty Arture in this Body
As hardy as the Nemean Lion's Nerve.
Still am I call'd: unhand me, Gentlemen!

84 lets *impedes.*

86 Imagination *irrational fantasies.*

88 Have after. *Proceed, and I'll follow.*

90 it *the issue, outcome (line 88).*

I.v *This scene continues immediately on the heels of I.iv. As Hamlet and the Ghost re-enter, we are to assume that they have arrived at the "removed Ground" referred to in I.iv.60.*

2 My Hour is almost come *The Ghost means that it is now approaching dawn.*

3 sulph'rous and tormenting Flames *This description of the Ghost's residence is compatible with pre-Shakespearean renderings of both Purgatory and Hell. But lines 10–12 suggest that the Ghost is referring to Purgatory. Since Elizabethans were no longer legally permitted to be Catholics (belonging to an Anglican Church that generally followed the reformers in denying the existence of Purgatory), it seems likely that many of them would have inferred that the Ghost is merely deceiving Hamlet by implying that he comes from somewhere other than Hell. It was a commonplace that the Devil was the Father of Lies and was capable of transforming himself "into an angel of light" to mislead the unwary (2 Corinthians 11:14). In the final analysis, the origin and nature of the Ghost in* Hamlet *remain profoundly ambiguous, like much else in this most enigmatic of Shakespearean tragedies. The issue of the Ghost's "honesty" re-emerges in III.ii.311.*

By Heav'n, I'll make a Ghost of him that lets
    me!
—I say away, go on, I'll follow thee.   85
                          Exeunt Ghost and Hamlet.
HORATIO   He waxes desp'rate with Imagination.
MARCELLUS   Let's follow: 'tis not fit thus to obey
    him.
HORATIO   Have after. To what Issue will this come?
MARCELLUS   Something is rotten in the State of
    Denmark.
HORATIO   Heav'n will direct it.
MARCELLUS   Nay let's follow him.   90
                                  Exeunt.

Scene 5

Enter Ghost and Hamlet.

HAMLET   Where wilt thou lead me? Speak: I'll go no
    further.
GHOST   Mark me.
HAMLET   I will.
GHOST   My Hour is almost come
    When I to sulph'rous and tormenting Flames
    Must render up my self.
HAMLET   Alas poor Ghost!
GHOST   Pity me not, but lend thy serious Hearing   5

12 But *except.*

15 harrow up *fill with horror. One of the early doctrines of the Church was that between the Crucifixion and the Resurrection, Jesus descended into the underworld for the "Harrowing of Hell." On this expedition, he gathered up the souls of the Old Testament patriarchs and other pre-Christian saints and released them to eternal rewards in Heaven. Though the Ghost uses the phrase* harrow up *in a very different sense here, the echo of Christ's harrowing would have probably given his words additional poignance to some members of Shakespeare's original audience.*

16 start *jump.*
    Spheres *eye-sockets, with an analogy to the concentric spheres in which the stars were thought to revolve around the globe.*

18 an end *on end.*

19 fearful Porpentine *frightened porcupine.*

20 eternal Blazon *catalogue of the horrors of eternity. The word* Blazon *was associated with heraldry (where it referred to the motto on a coat of arms), but it also referred to a loud proclamation. Here its first syllable keeps us mindful of the blazing flames of the underworld.*

21 List *listen and mark.*

24 Murther *murder.*

29 Meditation *thought. Here the choice of words picks up on* murther *by alliteration.*

To what I shall unfold.

HAMLET   Speak: I am bound
    To hear.

GHOST   So art thou to Revenge, when thou
    Shalt hear.

HAMLET   What?

GHOST   I am thy Father's Spirit,
    Doom'd for a certain Term to walk the Night
    And for the Day confin'd to fast in Fires   10
    Till the foul Crimes done in my Days of Nature
    Are burnt and purg'd away. But that I am forbid
    To tell the Secrets of my Prison-house,
    I could a Tale unfold whose lightest Word
    Would harrow up thy Soul, freeze thy young
        Blood,   15
    Make thy two Eyes like Stars start from their
        Spheres,
    Thy knotted and combined Locks to part,
    And each partic'lar Hair to stand an end
    Like Quills upon the fearful Porpentine;
    But this eternal Blazon must not be   20
    To Ears of Flesh and Blood. List, list, O list:
    If thou didst ever thy dear Father love—

HAMLET O God!

GHOST Revenge his foul and most unnat'ral Murther.

HAMLET Murther?   25

GHOST Murther most foul, as in the best it is;
    But this most foul, strange, and unnatural.

HAMLET Haste me to know 't, that I with Wings as
        swift
    As Meditation or the Thoughts of Love

30 Apt *ready, eager.*

31 fat Weed *a weed that has grown large and lethargic through overfeeding.*

32 Lethe Wharf *the bank of Lethe, the River of Forgetfulness in the classical Hades.*

34 given out *reported.*

35 Serpent *snake. Because this murder is elsewhere described as "primal" (III.iii.37), it is appropriate that it be introduced here with an image that associates it with the Fall of Man (Genesis 3).*

36 forged Process *counterfeited account.*

37 Rankly abus'd *egregiously deceived. But here* Rankly *carries associations with corruption and disease, and* abus'd *also means "misused."*

41 adult'rate *This adjective suggests that in addition to committing incest by marrying his brother's widow, Claudius also committed adultery with her before he killed the elder Hamlet. Since* adultery *was a word that could refer to licentiousness in general, however, there are other ways of interpreting this passage.*

45 Will *inclination.* Will *was also regularly used to refer to sexual desire and to the genitalia, and those implications are probably included in the Ghost's words.*

51 To *compared to.*

52 But . . . mov'd *but just as Virtue can never be seduced.*

55 sort *situate, place. Most editors adopt the Folio's* sate.

64

May sweep to my Revenge.

GHOST   I find thee Apt,
And Duller should'st thou be than the fat Weed
That roots it self in Ease on Lethe Wharf
Would'st thou not stir in this. Now Hamlet hear.
'Tis given out that, sleeping in my Orchard,
A Serpent stung me; so th' whole Ear of Denmark   35
Is by a forged Process of my Death
Rankly abus'd. But know, thou Noble Youth,
The Serpent that did sting thy Father's Life
Now wears his Crown.
HAMLET   O my prophetic Soul:
My Uncle?   40
GHOST   Ay, that incestuous, that adult'rate Beast,
With Witchcraft of his Wits, with trait'rous
     Gifts
(O wicked Wit, and Gifts that have the power
So to seduce!) won to his shameful Lust
The Will of my most seeming virtuous Queen.   45
O Hamlet, what a falling off was there!
From me, whose Love was of that Dignity
That it went Hand in Hand ev'n with the Vow
I made to her in Marriage; and to decline
Upon a Wretch whose Nat'ral Gifts were poor   50
To those of mine.
But Virtue, as it never will be mov'd,
Though Lewdness court it in a Shape of Heav'n,
So Lust, though to a radiant Angel link'd,
Will sort it self in a Celestial Bed   55
And prey on Garbage.
But soft, me thinks I scent the Morning Air:

65

60 Secure *free from cares. Elsewhere in Shakespeare this word refers to a condition of negligence resulting from overconfidence.*

61 Heb'na *hebona (ebony), a tree associated with blackness and possibly also with poison in Shakespeare's time. But Shakespeare may also have been thinking of another poison, henbane, and perhaps merging the names poetically.*

63 leperous *designed to produce scales on the body similar to those caused by leprosy.*

67 possess *Most editors adopt the Folio's* posset *here, a word meaning much the same thing as* curd *(coagulate) in the next line.*

68 eager *sour.*

70 Tetter *scab-like eruption.*

71 Lazar *leper.*

76 Unhousl'd *without having received the Eucharist (the Housel), the last communion.*
disappointed *unprepared, without having confessed and received forgiveness for my sins.*
unanel'd *literally, unanointed; deprived of extreme unction.*

77 Reck'ning *absolution (forgiveness of sins confessed).*
Account *judgment-day.*

82 Luxury *lust and other forms of sensual indulgence.*

85 ought *anything.*

88 Matin *morning.* Matin *is associated with morning prayers.*

66

Brief let me be. Sleeping within mine Orchard,
My Custom always of the Afternoon,
Upon my Secure Hour thy Uncle stole   60
With Juice of cursed Heb'na in a Vial,
And in the Porches of my Ears did pour
The leperous Distillment, whose Effect
Holds such an Enmity with Blood of Man
That swift as Quicksilver it courses through   65
The nat'ral Gates and Alleys of the Body,
And with a sudden Vigor it doth possess
And curd, like eager droppings into Milk,
The thin and wholesome Blood. So did it mine,
And a most instant Tetter bark'd about,   70
Most Lazar-like, with vile and loathsome Crust,
All my smooth Body.
Thus was I, sleeping, by a Brother's Hand
Of Life, of Crown, of Queen at once dispatch'd;
Cut off ev'n in the Blossoms of my Sin,   75
Unhousl'd, disappointed, unanel'd,
No Reck'ning made, but sent to my Account
With all my Imperfections on my Head.
O horrible, O horrible, most horrible!
If thou hast Nature in thee, bear it not: 80
Let not the Royal Blood of Denmark be
A Couch for Luxury and damned Incest.
But howsomever thou pursues this Act,
Taint not thy Mind, nor let thy Soul contrive
Against thy Mother ought: leave her to Heav'n,   85
And to those Thorns that in her Bosom lodge
To prick and sting her. Fare thee well at once:
The Glowworm shows the Matin to be near,

89   uneffectual Fire *a light that gives off no heat (compare I.iii.117) and is unable to hold its own in broad daylight.*

92   couple *add in; join.*

93   Sinows *sinews, muscles.*

96   this distracted Globe *this maddened head. But in its original performances this line would also have reminded the audience of the theatre in which the first Hamlet (Richard Burbage) was acting distraught.*

97   Table *tablet, notebook.*

98   fond *foolish, idle.*
       Records *accented on the second syllable here.*

99   Saws *wise sayings.*
       Forms *images.*
       Pressures *impressions.*

102   Book and Volume *Hamlet may be referring to different divisions of a larger work; he may be distinguishing between a book (the written text) and the volume (the bound cover) that contains it; or he may simply be using the terms with deliberately redundant duplication, as he and other speakers so often do in this play.*

103   Baser Matter *This term was often used to refer to the kinds of metal (often iron or lead) that alchemists sought to transform into gold.*

106   meet it is I set it down *it is appropriate for me to record.*

109   my Word *my watchword, my charge.*

And 'gins to pale his uneffectual Fire.
Adieu, adieu, adieu: remember me!   *Exit.*   90
HAMLET   —O all you Host of Heav'n! O Earth!
     What else?
And shall I couple Hell? —O fie! Hold, hold, my
     Heart!
And you, my Sinows, grow not instant Old,
But bear me swiftly up! —Remember thee?
Ay, thou poor Ghost, whiles Mem'ry holds a Seat   95
In this distracted Globe. Remember thee?
Yea, from the Table of my Memory
I'll wipe away all trivial fond Records,
All Saws of Books, all Forms, all Pressures past
That Youth and Observation copi'd there,   100
And thy Commandment all alone shall live
Within the Book and Volume of my Brain
Unmix'd with Baser Matter. Yes, by Heav'n!
—O most pernicious Woman!
—O Villain, Villain, smiling damned Villain!   105
—My Tables: meet it is I set it down
That one may smile, and smile, and be a
     Villain;
At least I'm sure it may be so in Denmark.
                                        He writes.
—So Uncle, there you are. —Now to my Word:
It is "Adieu, adieu, remember me."   110
I have sworn 't.
HORATIO AND MARCELLUS [*within*]   My Lord,
     my Lord!

          Enter Horatio and Marcellus.

69

112 **So be it!** *This "amen" is assigned to Marcellus in the Folio text.*

113 **Illo** *hello. In his next speech Hamlet plays on Horatio's greeting and implicitly compares it to a falconer's call to his hawk.*

114 **and come** *The Folio prints "bird, come."*

115 **wonderful** *to be wondered at.*

118 **think it,** *Many editors replace the Quarto's comma with a dash here; the Folio text employs a question mark. The usual interpretation is that Hamlet is on the verge of disclosing what he has just seen and then stops himself in mid-sentence.*

124 **Circumstance** *elaboration, ceremony.*

126 **Bus'ness and Desire** *Hamlet is probably alluding to the sexual senses of these two terms. In* **Romeo** and **Juliet,** *Romeo jokes that "my Business was great, and in such a Case as mine a Man may strain Courtesy" (II.iv.56–58). Here* **point** *reinforces the phallic innuendo.*
  point *both (a) direct, and (b) appoint.*

129 **I will go pray** *These words are often taken literally. But it seems more likely that Hamlet is simply saying that he will set off in a different direction. His primary purpose at this moment is not to communicate his intentions but to get rid of his companions as quickly as possible.*

MARCELLUS   Lord Hamlet!
HORATIO   Heav'ns secure him!
HAMLET   So be it!
HORATIO   Illo, ho, ho, my Lord!
HAMLET   Hillo, ho, ho:
     Boy, come, and come.
MARCELLUS   How is't, my Noble Lord?
HORATIO   What News, my Lord?
HAMLET   O wonderful!   115
HORATIO   Good my Lord, tell it.
HAMLET   No, you will reveal it.
HORATIO   Not I, my Lord, by Heav'n.
MARCELLUS   Nor I, my Lord.
HAMLET   How say you then, would Heart of Man once
     think it,
     But you'll be secret?
BOTH   Ay, by Heav'n.
HAMLET   There's nev'r a Villain dwelling in all
     Denmark   120
     But he's an arrant Knave.
HORATIO   There needs no Ghost,
     My Lord, come from the Grave to tell us this.
HAMLET   Why right, you are in the right.
     And so, without more Circumstance at all,
     I hold it fit that we shake Hands and part: 125
     You as your Bus'ness and Desire shall point
        you
     (For ev'ry man hath Bus'ness and Desire,
     Such as it is), and for my own poor part,
     I will go pray.

71

133   **by Saint Patrick**   *Saint Patrick (ca. 389–461), the patron saint of Ireland, was proverbial as the spiritual keeper of "Purgatory," an Irish cave visited by Pilgrims who wished to have their sins purged. He was also credited with ridding Ireland of all its serpents, and that association would relate to lines 38–39.*

134   **Touching this Vision here**   *with regard to this apparition we have seen.*

135   **Honest**   *good, genuine. Hamlet means that the Ghost is what it presents itself as being, not a demon counterfeiting the spirit of a deceased king. Later (II.ii. 634–39) it occurs to Hamlet to doubt what he has said here, but for now he seems to speak with complete assurance about the Ghost's reliability.*

136   **us**   *Hamlet and the Ghost.*

137   **O'ermaster**   *overcome, suppress.*

139   **poor**   *paltry.*

143   **Upon my Sword.**   *With its hilt the sword formed a cross. Hamlet demands that his companions place their right hands on it as they vow to keep secret what they have seen.*

145   **Truepenny**   *Hamlet's name for the Ghost is one that means "honest or trusty fellow."*

146   **Cellarage**   *the area below the stage. Like other Elizabethan amphitheatres, the Globe probably had a trapdoor to the cellarage; whether it was used in these scenes with the Ghost is uncertain.*

HORATIO   These are but wild and whirling Words,
    my Lord.   130
HAMLET   I'm sorry they offend you, heartily:
    Yes faith, heartily.
HORATIO   There's no Offense, my Lord.
HAMLET   Yes, by Saint Patrick, but there is,
    Horatio,
    And much Offense too! Touching this Vision
    here,
    It is an Honest Ghost, that let me tell you.   135
    For your desire to know what is between us,
    O'ermaster 't as you may. And now, good
    Friends,
    As you are Friends, Scholars, and Soldiers,
    Give me one poor Request.
HORATIO   What is't, my Lord? We will.
HAMLET   Never make known what you have seen
    tonight.   140
BOTH   My Lord, we will not.
HAMLET   Nay but swear 't.
HORATIO   In faith,
    My Lord, not I.
MARCELLUS   Nor I, my Lord, in faith.
HAMLET   Upon my Sword.
MARCELLUS   We've sworn, my Lord, already.
HAMLET   Indeed, upon my Sword, indeed.
GHOST *cries under the Stage*   Swear!
HAMLET   Ha, ha, Boy, say'st thou so? Art thou there,
    Truepenny?   145
    —Come on, you hear this Fellow in the Cellarage.
    Consent to swear.

149   **Hic et ubique?** *Latin for "here and everywhere." This phrase (and the capacity for omnipresence) was associated with both God and Satan.*

150   **Then . . . ground.** *Just why Hamlet wants to move to another site for the swearing is unclear. One possibility is that he wants to be directly over the Ghost; another is that he wants to be away from where the Ghost is.*

154   **old Mole** *Whether this nickname means anything other than that Hamlet is comparing the Ghost to a burrowing mammal is subject to debate. Some interpreters have suggested that the name would have associated the Ghost with the Devil.*

155   **Pioner** *miner; a soldier who dug trenches and tunnels to undermine enemy fortifications.*

156   **O Day . . . Strange!** *Horatio's reaction is surely meant to be shared by the audience. Hamlet's response (line 157) means "give it the welcome one is expected to give a stranger." Some commentators have interpreted this episode merely as Shakespeare's means of providing comic relief. Others, noting that the "Cellarage" (see line 146) was frequently associated with Hell in early English drama, have suggested that the episode is intended to serve a more serious purpose.*

159   **Philosophy** *In Shakespeare's time this word was associated with all the branches of natural science.*

161   **some'er** *so ever.*
        bear my self *conduct my self, appear in public.*

163   **To put . . . on** *to adopt the mannerisms of an idiot or a madman.* **Antic** *could refer to any kind of eccentric behavior.*

165   **encumb'red** *folded.*

74

HORATIO   Propose the Oath, my Lord.
HAMLET   Never to speak of this that you have seen.
    Swear by my Sword.
GHOST   Swear!
HAMLET   *Hic et ubique?*
    Then we'll shift our ground. Come hether,
        Gentl'men,   150
    And lay your Hands again upon my Sword.
    Swear by my Sword never to speak of this
    That you have heard.
GHOST   Swear by his Sword!
HAMLET   Well said, old Mole! Canst work i' th'
        Earth so fast?
    A worthy Pioner! —Once more remove, good
        Friends.   155
HORATIO   O Day and Night, but this is wondrous
        Strange!
HAMLET   And therefore as a Stranger give it Welcome.
    There are more things in Heav'n and Earth,
        Horatio,
    Than are dreamt of in your Philosophy. But
        come,
    Here as before, never, so help you Mercy   160
    (How strange or odd some'er I bear my self,
    As I perchance hereafter shall think meet
    To put an Antic Disposition on),
    That you at such times seeing me never shall
    With Arms encumb'red thus, or this Head-shake,   165
    Or by pronouncing of some doubtful Phrase,
    As "Well, well, we know," or "We could and if
        we would,"

75

168   list   *wished.*

170   ought   *anything.*

174   commend me   *offer myself.*

176   Friending   *friendliness.*

178   still   *continually, always.*

179   out of Joint   *This phrase can mean "out of socket" or "out of frame"; here its implication is that Denmark is in a state of utter disorder. The* joint *imagery echoes Claudius' opening speech, particularly I.ii.9, 20.*
        Spight   *spite, injury.*

181   Nay come, let's go together.   *Hamlet is reassuring his companions that it is all right for them to accompany him. In all likelihood he has separated himself from the group for a moment to speak lines 179–80 as a private reflection.*

Or "If we list to speak," or "There be and if
   they might,"
Or such ambiguous giving out, to note
That you know ought of me. This do swear,   170
So Grace and Mercy at your most need help you.

GHOST   Swear!   *They swear.*

HAMLET   Rest, rest, perturbed Spirit. —So
   Gentlemen,
With all my Love I do commend me to you;
And what so poor a man as Hamlet is   175
May do t' express his Love and Friending to you,
God willing, shall not lack. Let us go in
   together,
And still your Fingers on your Lips, I pray.
The Time is out of Joint. O cursed Spight
That ever I was born to set it Right!   180
Nay come, let's go together.   *Exeunt.*

II.i   *This scene takes place in Polonius' quarters. The Quarto stage direction, reproduced here, suggests that Shakespeare originally conceived the scene in such a way that Polonius' "Man" (Reynaldo) could be accompanied by another servant. The Folio reads "his man Reynaldo."*

3   marvel's   *marvelous[ly].*

7   Inquire me   *Here* me *has the force of "for me." It is an illustration of what grammarians call the "ethic dative," a form that Shakespeare uses to convey a colloquial familiarity or informality or to imitate the manner of the person being "presented."*

      Danskers   *Danish fellows.*

8   keep   *stay, lodge.*

10   By this . . . Question   *by these roundabout and yet subtly directed inquiries.*

11   more nearer   *closer to home.*

78

Act Two

Scene 1

Enter Old Polonius with his Man or Two.

POLONIUS   Give him this Money, and these Notes,
    Reynaldo.
REYNALDO   I will, my Lord.
POLONIUS   You shall do marvel's wisely, good
    Reynaldo,
Before you visit him, to make inquire
Of his Behavior.
REYNALDO   My Lord, I did intend it.   5
POLONIUS   Marry well said, very well said. Look
    you, Sir,
Inquire me first what Danskers are in Paris,
And how, and who; what means, and where they
    keep;
What company, at what expense; and finding
By this Encompassment and Drift of Question   10
That they do know my Son, come you more nearer

79

12   particular Demaunds   *individual, pointed questions.*

13   Take you . . . him   *adopt as your posture the perspective of someone who knows him from afar, as a distant acquaintance. Having just heard Hamlet speak of donning a persona (an "Antic Disposition") for his purposes, we now hear Polonius advise Reynaldo to do something similar for Polonius' as yet undisclosed purposes.*

19   put on him   *literally, clothe him in.*

20   Forgeries   *made-up tales.*
      rank   *corrupting, excessive.*

22   usual Slips   *common lapses or vices. The phrase "Of General Assault" (line 35) has the same implications.*

23   noted   *commonly observed and thus regularly associated with.*

24   Gaming   *Polonius probably means gambling.*

26   Drabbing   *resorting to prostitutes.*

28   as you may seas'n it in the Charge   *since you may flavor or temper it in the way you imply the accusation.*

30   Incontinency   *uncontrolled, habitual vice; libertinism.*

31   quently   *quaintly, artfully, with wit and urbanity. In this context, the word probably also has bawdy connotations.*

33   Flash . . . Mind   *sudden eruptions of a disposition comprised primarily of the noblest of the four elements, Fire.*

34   unreclaimed Blood   *as yet untamed passions.*

Than your particular Demaunds will touch it;
Take you as 'twere some distant Knowledge of him,
As thus, "I know his Father and his Friends,
And in part him." Do you mark this, Reynaldo?   15
REYNALDO   Ay, very well, my Lord.
POLONIUS   "And in part him, but" (you may say)
     "not well,
But if 't be he I mean, he's very Wild,
Addicted so and so"; and there put on him
What Forgeries you please. Marry not so rank   20
As may dishonor him, take heed of that;
But Sir, such wanton, wild, and usual Slips
As are Companions noted and most known
To Youth and Liberty.
REYNALDO   As Gaming, my Lord.
POLONIUS   Ay, or Drinking, Fencing, Swearing,   25
     Quarreling, Drabbing: you may go so far.
REYNALDO   My Lord, that would dishonor him.
POLONIUS   Faith no, as you may seas'n it in the
     Charge.
You must not put another Scandal on him,
That he is open to Incontinency: 30
That's not my Meaning. But breathe his Faults so
     quently
That they may seem the Taints of Liberty,
The Flash and Outbreak of a Fiery Mind,
A Savageness in unreclaimed Blood,
Of General Assault.
REYNALDO   But my good Lord—   35
POLONIUS   Wherefore should you do this?
REYNALDO   Ay my Lord,

38   a Fetch of Wit *a clever device. A* Fetch *was a trick or subterfuge; and* Wit *refers to any kind of cunning or intelligence. Here many editors follow the Folio, which substitutes* Warrant *for* Wit.

39   Sallies *probably both (a) sullies, blemishes, and (b) assaults. Compare I.ii.129.*

40   As . . . Working *as if he were something that has become a bit soiled from use (but is no worse for wear).*

42   prenom'nate Crimes *aforementioned vices.*

44   closes with you *concludes with you, confides to you.*
        in this Consequence *in the following way (as a result of what you have said to him).*

47   Of Man and Country *the name of the addressee and his country.*

49–51   What . . . leave? *Amusingly, when Polonius loses track of what he was saying, he also drifts away from regular verse into something more like prose.*

56   'a *he. The punctuation in this line is adapted from the Folio, which reads "There was he gaming, there o'retooke in's Rouse." The Quarto suggests a different interpretation: "There was a gaming there, or tooke in's rowse."*

59   Videlizet *namely; from Latin* videlicet.

61   Reach *apprehension.*

62   Windlesses *windlasses (hoists), roundabout means.*
        Assays of Bias *trials of the bias (curving course) on a bowl (a bowling ball with an off-center weight designed to prevent it from rolling in a straight line).*

I would know that.

POLONIUS   Marry Sir, here's my Drift,
And I believe it is a Fetch of Wit:
You laying these slight Sallies on my Son,
As 'twere a thing a little soil'd with Working,   40
Mark you, your Party in Converse, him you
    would sound,
Having ever seen in the prenom'nate Crimes
The Youth you breathe of Guilty, be assur'd
He closes with you in this Consequence:
"Good Sir," or so, or "Friend," or "Gentleman,"   45
According to the Phrase, or the Addition
Of Man and Country—

REYNALDO   Very good, my Lord—

POLONIUS   And then, Sir, does 'a this, 'a does—
What was I about to say?
By th' Mass, I was about to say something.   50
Where did I leave?

REYNALDO   At "closes in the Consequence."

POLONIUS   At "closes in the Consequence." Ay, marry,
He closes thus: "I know the Gentleman;
I saw him yesterday," or "th' other day,"
Or then, or then, with such or such, and "as
    you say,   55
There was 'a Gaming," "There o'ertook in's Rouse,"
"There falling out at Tennis," or perchance
"I saw him enter such a House of Sale"
(Videlizet, a Brothel), or so forth. See you now,
Your Bait of Falsehood take this Carp of Truth,   60
And thus do we of Wisdom and of Reach,
With Windlesses and with Assays of Bias,

63   By Indirections find Directions out   *by indirect means arrive at our desired destination.*

65   have   *understand.*

66   God buy ye   *God be with you (the ancestor of "goodbye").*

67–68 Observe . . . self.   *It is not clear whether Polonius is continuing his instructions and (a) telling Reynaldo to use direct means (his own observations) to find Laertes out, or (b) telling Reynaldo to follow and obey Laertes wherever his inclinations lead him. Both readings are compatible with the rest of the speech.*

69   And let him ply his Music.   *If Polonius means this metaphorically (let him play his own tune), it would appear to support the second reading of lines 67–68 as Polonius' primary intention. Music in the literal sense would probably have been one of the skills and pastimes of an accomplished courtier such as Laertes.*

73   Closet   *private chamber.*

74   his Doublet all unbrac'd   *his jacket all unlaced.*

75   his Stockins foul'd   *his stockings soiled and unkempt.*

76   down-gyved   *fallen down so that they resembled the gyves (fetters) around a prisoner's ankles.*

78   Purport   *implication. Since we hear only Ophelia's account of this episode, we are at a loss to determine its significance. Whether it reveals the "real" Hamlet, Hamlet in his "antic" mode, or some combination thereof is left ambiguous.*

By Indirections find Directions out.
So by my former Lecture and Advice
Shall you my Son. You have me, have you not?   65
REYNALDO My Lord, I have.
POLONIUS   God buy ye, fare ye well.
REYNALDO Good my Lord.
POLONIUS   Observe his Inclination
In your self.
REYNALDO   I shall, my Lord.
POLONIUS And let him ply his Music.
REYNALDO   Well, my Lord.

Enter Ophelia.

POLONIUS Farewell.   *Exit Reynaldo.*
                —How now, Ophelia? What's the matter?   70
OPHELIA O my Lord, my Lord, I have been so
Affrighted!
POLONIUS   With what, i' th' name of God?
OPHELIA My Lord, as I was sewing in my Closet,
Lord Hamlet, with his Doublet all unbrac'd,
No Hat upon his Head, his Stockins foul'd,   75
Ungart'red, and down-gyved to his Ankle,
Pale as his Shirt, his Knees knocking each
     other,
And with a Look so piteous in Purport
As if he had been loosed out of Hell
To speak of Horrors, he comes before me.   80
POLONIUS Mad for thy Love?
OPHELIA   My Lord, I do not know,
But truly I do fear it.

85

86   **Perusal** *careful examination.*

87   **draw it** *Ophelia probably means "draw a portrait of it." But another sense, "draw it out of me to him," may also be pertinent.*

88   **a little shaking of mine Arm** *while shaking my arm slightly.*

90   **profound** *from the depths of his being.*

91   **Bulk** *body.*

95   **Helps** *assistance.*

98   **Ecstasy** *seizure. Polonius uses a Greek word whose literal meaning is to be beside oneself, to be in a state that suspends the normal operations of reason and apprehension.*

99   **Whose . . . self** *whose nature is to take hold of a self with such violence as to undo it.*

100   **to desp'rate Undertakings** *to extremes of behavior. Here the word* desperate *suggests that Polonius believes Hamlet to be suicidal.*

102   **does** *probably understood as the verb for* Passions *(line 101); Elizabethan usage allowed for many constructions that would now be considered violations of subject-verb agreement.*

108   **coted** *observed; often spelled* quoted, *as at this point in the Folio.*

109   **wrack** *wreck, ruin.*
        beshrow my Jealousy *curse (beshrew) my suspiciousness.*

110   **it . . . Age** *it is as much a part of being old (my age).*

POLONIUS   What said he?

OPHELIA   He took me by the Wrist and held me hard,
Then goes he to the length of all his Arm
And with his other Hand thus o'er his Brow   85
He falls to such Perusal of my Face
As 'a would draw it; long stay'd he so;
At last, a little shaking of mine Arm,
And, thrice his Head thus waving up and down,
He rais'd a Sigh so piteous and profound   90
As it did seem to shatter all his Bulk
And end his Being; that done, he lets me go,
And, with his Head over his Shoulder turn'd,
He seem'd to find his Way without his Eyes,
For out a' Doors he went without their Helps,   95
And to the last bended their Light on me.

POLONIUS   Come, go with me, I will go seek the King:
This is the very Ecstasy of Love,
Whose violent Property fordoes it self
And leads the Will to desp'rate Undertakings   100
As oft as any Passions under Heaven
That does afflict our Natures. I am sorry.
What, have you giv'n him any hard Words of late?

OPHELIA   No, my good Lord, but as you did commaund
I did repel his Letters and denied   105
His Access to me.

POLONIUS   That hath made him mad.
I am sorry that with better Heed and Judgment
I had not coted him. I fear'd he did but trifle
And meant to wrack thee. But beshrow my Jealousy:
By Heav'n it is as proper to our Age   110

87

111   **To . . . Opinions** *to overshoot, to allow our anxieties to carry us too far.*

113   **Discretion** *prudence.*

114   **close** *secret.*

115   **More . . . Love** *more grief from our hiding it than displeasure over the love we show by speaking openly about Hamlet's love-malady.*

II.ii   *This scene takes place at Court. In the opening stage direction* cum Aliis *(from the Folio version) means "with others." In the two preceding scenes, we have heard first Hamlet and then Polonius talk about the use of indirect means to achieve ends that will not lend themselves to more direct approaches. Now we hear the King and Queen give similar instructions to two of Hamlet's former schoolmates, who have been summoned to see if they can be of assistance by helping to find out why the Queen's son is acting so strangely.*

2   **Moreover that** *in addition to the fact that.*

5   **Transformation** *Here the metrical context calls for the King to stretch the word out to its full five syllables.*

6   **Sith** *since, because. In line 12, the word may have the additional meaning of "since that time."*

9   **th' Understanding of himself** *his normal self, his proper use of his reasoning faculties.*

11   **of so young Days** *from an early age.*

12   **Havior** *behavior.*

To cast beyond our selves in our Opinions
As it is common for the Younger Sort
To lack Discretion. Come, go we to the King:
This must be known, which being kept close
    might move
More Grief to Hide than Hate to utter Love.   115
Come.   *Exeunt.*

Scene 2

*Flourish. Enter King and Queen, Rosencrans and
Guildenstern, cum Aliis.*

KING   Welcome, dear Rosencrans and Guildenstern.
Moreover that we much did long to see you,
The need we have to use you did provoke
Our hasty Sending. Something have you heard
Of Hamlet's Transformation; so call it,   5
Sith nor th' Exterior nor the Inward Man
Resembles that it was. What it should be
More than his Father's Death that thus hath
    put him
So much from th' Understanding of himself
I cannot dream of. I entreat you both   10
That, being of so young Days brought up with
    him,
And sith so neighbor'd to his Youth and Havior,

13   voutsafe your Rest   *vouchsafe (condescend) to stay.*

14   so   *in order.*

16   glean   *gather (like those who pick up leftover grain after the reapers have harvested a field). Claudius' advice ("draw him on to Pleasures") echoes what Polonius has said in the previous scene to Reynaldo (compare II.i.67–69); and gleaning is another form of indirection (II.i.63).*

17   ought   *anything.*

18   open'd   *Claudius means "disclosed." But the medical metaphor implied by "Remedy" also suggests the lancing of a boil or the opening of a patient's veins to rid his blood of infection.*

21   adheres   *clings.*

22   Gentry   *gentle behavior; the courtesy characteristic of gentlemen.*

24   the Supply and Profit of our Hope   *the fulfillment and reward of our hopes.*

26   Remembrance   *gratitude for services rendered.*

27   of   *over.*

28   dread   *fearful; to be held in awe and reverence.*

30   in the full Bent   *Guildenstern probably bows fulsomely as he speaks, thereby imitating a bow bent to the utmost to discharge an arrow. Compare I.ii.55–56.*

38   Practices   *endeavors. But the word often connoted deceits and tricks.*

That you voutsafe your Rest here in our Court
Some little time, so by your Companies
To draw him on to Pleasures, and to gather   15
So much as from Occasion you may glean,
Whether ought to us unknown afflicts him thus
That, open'd, lies within our Remedy.
QUEEN   Good Gentlemen, he hath much talk'd of you,
And sure I am two Men there is not living   20
To whom he more adheres. If it will please you
To show us so much Gentry and Good Will
As to expend your Time with us a while
For the Supply and Profit of our Hope,
Your Visitation shall receive such Thanks   25
As fits a King's Remembrance.
ROSENCRANS   Both your Ma'esties
Might by the Sovereign Pow'r you have of us
Put your dread Pleasures more into Commaund
Than to Entreaty.
GUILDENSTERN   But we both obey,
And here give up our selves in the full Bent   30
To lay our Service freely at your Feet
To be commaunded.
KING   Thanks, Rosencrans and gentle Guildenstern.
QUEEN   Thanks, Guildenstern and gentle Rosencrans.
And I beseech you instantly to visit   35
My too much changed Son. —Go some of you
And bring these Gentlemen where Hamlet is.
GUILDENSTERN   Heav'ns make our Presence and our
      Practices
Pleasant and helpful to him.
QUEEN   Ay, Amen.

91

40   Embassadors   *ambassadors, messengers.*

42   still   *both (a) yet, and (b) always.*

44   I . . . Soul   *my duty to you is just as important to me as the state of my soul in the eyes of God. Polonius alludes to the commonplace that the King was to be regarded as God's deputy on Earth (a doctrine derived from Romans 13:1–7).*

47   Policy   *This word often refers to statecraft, but here it probably means something closer to "sound judgment."*

52   Fruit   *dessert. Polonius refers to the "banquet," a course of fruits and wine that followed the main course of a feast.*

53   do Grace   *show proper courtesy.*

55   Head and Source   *both words mean "origin."*
        Distemper   *malady. The word literally means "lacking in temper" (balance or governance), and it derives from the view that a person's disposition was determined by how successfully the mind controlled the four humours that constituted a human body.*

56   doubt   *suspect, fear.*
        the Main   *the problem that has been troubling him all along.*

57   hasty   *Most editors adopt the Folio's* o'er*hasty here. But there is reason to doubt that that was Shakespeare's intention: at this point it is not clear that the Queen regards the marriage as* over*hasty. The Folio reading would appear to improve the meter; but if* our *is treated as a two-syllabic word, the meter in the Quarto is perfectly regular.*

Exeunt Rosencrans and Guildenstern.
Enter Polonius.

POLONIUS   Th' Embassadors from Norway, my good
   Lord,   40
   Are joyfully return'd.
KING   Thou still hast been the Father of Good News.
POLONIUS   Have I, my Lord? I assure my good Liege
   I hold my Duty as I hold my Soul,
   Both to my God and to my Gracious King;   45
   And I do think, or else this Brain of mine
   Hunts not the Trail of Policy so sure
   As it hath us'd to do, that I have found
   The very Cause of Hamlet's Lunacy.
KING   O speak of that, that do I long to hear.   50
POLONIUS   Give first admittance to th' Embassadors;
   My News shall be the Fruit to that great Feast.
KING   Thy self do Grace to them, and bring them in.
                             Exit Polonius.
   —He tells me, my dear Gertrard, he hath found
   The Head and Source of all your Son's
   Distemper.   55
QUEEN   I doubt it is no other but the Main:
   His Father's Death and our hasty Marriage.

Enter Polonius and the Embassadors.

KING   Well, we shall sift him. —Welcome, my good
   Friends.
   Say, Voltemand, what from our Brother Norway?

61   Upon our first   *as soon as we had delivered our message.*

62   Levies   *pressing men into military service.*

65   griev'd   *aggrieved, offended.*

67   falsely borne in hand   *dishonestly manipulated.*
      Arrests   *restraining orders, summons to appear before the King.*

69   in fine   *finally, in the end.*

71   Assay   *trial, threat.*

75   as   *as noted.*

76   shone   *exhibited, displayed, shown.*

77   to give quiet Pass   *to permit peaceful passage.*

80   likes   *pleases.*

81   at our more consider'd Time   *when we have time to consider it more thoroughly.*

82   Answer   *reply.*

84   at night we'll Feast together   *No doubt one of Shakespeare's purposes in including this detail is to show Claudius' ability to be gracious in hospitality; another is to remind us once again of how much the King indulges in food and drink.*

94

VOLTEMAND   Most fair return of Greetings and
    Desires.   60
    Upon our first, he sent out to suppress
    His Nephew's Levies, which to him appear'd
    To be a Preparation 'gainst the Polack,
    But, better look'd into, he truly found
    It was against your Highness; whereat griev'd   65
    That so his Sickness, Age, and Impotence
    Was falsely borne in hand, sends out Arrests
    On Fortinbrasse, which he in brief obeys,
    Receives Rebuke from Norway, and in fine
    Makes Vow before his Uncle never more   70
    To give th' Assay of Arms against your Majesty:
    Whereon old Norway, overcome with Joy,
    Gives him threescore thousand Crowns in annual
      Fee
    And his Commission to employ those Soldiers
    So levi'd (as before) against the Polack,   75
    With an Entreaty herein further shone
              He hands the King a Document.
    That it might please you to give quiet Pass
    Through your Dominions for this Enterprise
    On such Regards of Safety and Allowance
    As therein are set down.
KING   It likes us well,   80
    And at our more consider'd Time we'll read,
    Answer, and think upon this Business.
    Mean time we thank you for your well took
      Labor.
    Go to your Rest: at night we'll Feast together.
    Most welcome home.   *Exeunt Embassadors.*

95

86   expostulate   *expound upon.*

90   Brev'ty   *The meter calls for a witty abbreviation of* brevity.

91   And Tediousness . . . Flourishes   *Appropriately a line
        about tediousness (a boringly lengthy exposition) is two sylla-
        bles longer than the pentameter norm, even when* Tedious-
        ness *is rendered as a three-syllable word. The superfluous
        syllables illustrate the "outward Flourishes" they denote.*

94   is't   *Here* it *refers to "true Madness."*

95   Art   *a display of rhetorical devices to convey one's wit.*

97   'tis Pity   *it is a pity.*

98   Figure   *figure of speech. Polonius probably refers to his use of
        what rhetoricians called* antimetabole, *the repetition of
        words or phrases in reverse order (in a chiasmic or crossing
        pattern named after the Greek letter* chi, X*). But he may also
        be referring to other schematic "figures" such as* ploce *(the
        repetition of a word with others in between),* epizeuxis *(the
        immediate repetition of a word), and* anadiplosis *(the repeti-
        tion of a word at the end of one unit and the beginning of the
        next). In the lines that follow, after promising that he will
        "use no Art," Polonius parades such schemes as* traductio
        *(the repetition of a word in varying grammatical forms, as
        with "Defect"/"Defective," and "remains,"/"remainder")
        and* antithesis *(the use of repetition or parallel structure to
        draw attention to contrasting elements, as with the phrases
        ending in "Effect" and "Defect" in lines 101–2).*

105   Perpend   *weigh, consider.*

96

POLONIUS   This Bus'ness is well ended.   85
  My Liege and Madam, to expostulate
  What Majesty should be, what Duty is,
  Why Day is Day, Night Night, and Time is Time,
  Were nothing but to waste Night, Day, and Time:
  Therefore, since Brev'ty is the Soul of Wit   90
  And Tediousness the Limbs and outward
      Flourishes,
  I will be brief. Your Noble Son is Mad.
  Mad call I it, for to define true Madness
  What is't but to be nothing else but Mad.
  But let that go.
QUEEN   More Matter with less Art.   95
POLONIUS   Madam, I swear I use no Art at all.
  That he's Mad 'tis True, 'tis True 'tis Pity,
  And Pity 'tis 'tis True: a foolish Figure,
  But farewell it, for I will use no Art.
  Mad let us graunt him then, and now remains   100
  That we find out the Cause of this Effect,
  Or rather say, the Cause of this Defect,
  For this Effect Defective comes by Cause:
  Thus it remains, and the Remainder thus
  Perpend.   105
  I have a Daughter (have while she is mine)
  Who in her Duty and Obedience, mark,
  Hath giv'n me this. Now gather and surmise:
                              He reads the Letter.
    "To the Celestial and my Soul's Idol, the
      most beautified Ophelia—"   110
  That's an ill Phrase, a vile Phrase;
  "beautified" is a vile Phrase. But you shall

97

117   stay   *wait, be patient.*
       faithful   *as good as my word.*

120   Doubt   *suspect. Elsewhere in this passage* doubt *is used in the normal modern sense.*

122   ill at these Numbers   *inept at these verses.*

123   reckon   *count. Hamlet plays on the more usual sense of "Numbers."*
       Groans   *love pangs. Hamlet uses the word in a more bawdy sense in III.ii.273.*

127   whilst this Machine is to him   *while this body belongs to him. Here* machine *is used in the Renaissance sense of a complex mechanism. Like the behavior described in II.i.73–96, Hamlet's letter is subject to interpretation. Is it a sincere love-note, or is it a ruse (in keeping with the Prince's "Antic Disposition," I.v.163) to convey the impression that Hamlet is mad from love-sickness?*

130   more about   *Most editors adopt the Folio's* more above *here; but it is difficult to derive any better sense from that phrasing. In this line Polonius appears to mean "and still more about his entreaties."*

131   fell out   *occurred, came to her.*

136   fain   *gladly, eagerly.*

141   play'd the Desk or Table-book   *Polonius' metaphor means "encouraged their wooing by cooperating as readily as if I were a desk or writing-tablet to aid and abet their communications."*

hear:
    "thus in her excellent white Bosom, these
      etc." 115
QUEEN   Came this from Hamlet to her?
POLONIUS   Good Madam, stay awhile: I will be
    faithful.
      "Doubt thou the Stars are Fire,
      Doubt that the Sun doth move,
      Doubt Truth to be a Liar, 120
      But never doubt I love.
    O dear Ophelia, I am ill at these Numbers.
    I have not Art to reckon my Groans, but
    that I love thee best, O most Best, believe
    it. Adieu. 125
        Thine evermore, most dear Lady,
            whilst this Machine is to him,
                    Hamlet."
    This in Obedience hath my Daughter shown me,
    And more about hath his Solicitings 130
    As they fell out by Time, by Means, and Place,
    All given to mine Ear.
KING   But how hath she receiv'd his Love?
POLONIUS   What do you think of me?
KING   As of a Man faithful and honorable. 135
POLONIUS   I would fain prove so. But what might
    you think,
    When I had seen this hot Love on the wing,
    (As I perceiv'd it, I must tell you that,
    Before my Daughter told me), what might you,
    Or my dear Majesty your Queen here, think 140
    If I had play'd the Desk or Table-book,

142   Or giv'n . . . dumb   *or turned my heart into an instrument that failed to report what it perceived. Most editors substitute the Folio's* winking *(blindfolding or eye-shutting) for* working; *but the word in the Second Quarto would seem more compatible with* Heart *(a word that could refer to the eye's perceptions, but usually implied all the senses).*

143   Idle Sight   *either (a) dysfunctional eyes, or (b) neglectful eyes that chose not to register what they saw (and were thus irresponsible).*

145   bespeak   *speak to.*

146   out of thy Star   *beyond your sphere (based on the belief that each star or planet occupied its own crystalline sphere as it revolved around the earth).*

147   Prescripts   *orders, prescribings.*

148   from her Resort   *from where she is usually to be found, and where he could partake of her company. Most editors adopt the Folio's* his resort.

149   Tokens   *gifts, favors, expressions of affection.*

151   repell'd   *Here the elision derives from the Quarto text. If in fact* repelled *is to be treated as a two-styllable word,* short *is probably to be lengthened to two syllables.*
       a short Tale to make   *to make a long story short.*

152   a Fast   *Forlorn lovers were proverbially inaccessible.*

153   a Watch   *a habitual sleeplessness.*
       a Weakness   *a weakened, vulnerable condition.*

154   Lightness   *mental distraction, a lack of rational "gravity."*

164   the Center   *the center of the earth, proverbially inaccessible.*

Or giv'n my Heart a working mute and dumb,
Or look'd upon this Love with Idle Sight?
What might you think? No, I went round to
   work,
And my young Mistress thus I did bespeak: 145
"Lord Hamlet is a Prince out of thy Star;
This must not be." And then I Prescripts gave
   her
That she should lock her self from her Resort,
Admit no Messengers, receive no Tokens;
Which done, she took the Fruits of my Advice,   150
And he, repell'd, a short Tale to make,
Fell into a Sadness, then into a Fast,
Thence to a Watch, thence into a Weakness,
Thence to Lightness, and by this Declension
Into the Madness wherein now he raves   155
And we all mourn for.
KING   —Do you think this?
QUEEN   —It may be very like.
POLONIUS   Hath there been such a time, I'd fain
   know that,
That I have positively said " 'Tis so"
When it prov'd otherwise?
KING   Not that I know.   160
POLONIUS   Take this from this if this be otherwise.
If Circumstances lead me, I will find
Where Truth is hid, though it were hid indeed
Within the Center.
KING   How may we try it further?
POLONIUS   You know sometimes he walks four Hours
   together   165

167   loose   *release (from the tether, the restraints, that Polonius has imposed on her). This verb frequently refers to a man's setting a woman at liberty (to be accosted by male wooers).*

168   Arras   *a large tapestry, named after a town (Artois) in France.*

170   thereon   *because of that (his love for Ophelia).*

171   Assistant for a State   *counsel to the throne.*

172   Carters   *drivers of farm carts.*

175   board   *approach (a nautical term that usually referred to one ship's pulling alongside another).*
presently   *immediately.*
give me leave   *pardon me (for interrupting you).*

178   Fishmonger   *fish merchant. But because* fish *is frequently a word with sexual implications in Shakespeare's plays, it seems likely that Hamlet is also hinting at a less respectable profession. In view of what Polonius has said in line 167, the innuendo is apt.*

180   Honest   *virtuous, with a play on "chaste" as well.*

186   a good kissing Carrion   *a good corpse to kiss. In the context of his reference to breeding maggots (fly larvae), Hamlet's image suggests that he is now depicting the Sun as a lover who sates his lust on putrefying flesh. The image may be meant to recall I.v.54–56 and I.ii.140, Hamlet's earlier reference to Hyperion (the Sun God), and thus to suggest that in Claudius' rotten Denmark the Sun (a traditional symbol for the King) is even more loathsome than a Satyr.*

Here in the Lobby.

QUEEN   So he does indeed.

POLONIUS   At such a time I'll loose my Daughter to
    him.
    Be you and I behind an Arras then,
    Mark the Encounter; if he love her not,
    And be not from his Reason fall'n thereon,   170
    Let me be no Assistant for a State
    But keep a Farm and Carters.

KING   We will try it.

Enter Hamlet, reading on a Book.

QUEEN   But look where sadly the poor Wretch comes
    reading.

POLONIUS   Away, I do beseech you, both away:
    I'll board him presently.   *Exeunt King and Queen.*
                        —O give me leave,   175
    How dooes my good Lord Hamlet?

HAMLET   Well, God 'a mercy.

POLONIUS   Do you know me, my Lord?

HAMLET   Excellent well: you are a Fishmonger.

POLONIUS   Not I, my Lord.

HAMLET   Then I would you were so Honest a Man.   180

POLONIUS   Honest, my Lord?

HAMLET   Ay Sir, to be Honest as this World goes is
    to be One Man pick'd out of Ten Thousand.

POLONIUS   That's very true, my Lord.

HAMLET   For if the Sun breed Maggots in a dead Dog,   185
    being a good kissing Carrion— Have you a
    Daughter?

103

189   Let . . . Sun. *In light of the previous image, Hamlet's implication is "don't let her become a piece of breeding carrion."*

194   'A *he.*

199   Matter *Polonius means "subject matter." In the next line Hamlet mis-takes him to mean "quarrel."*

204   purging *discharging.*

205   Amber *a brownish-yellow resin, similar to the gum (sap) from a plumtree.*

207   Hams *rear thighs and hips.*

208   potently *a synonym for "powerfully."*
        Honesty *virtue, decent behavior. Hamlet is saying "I do not regard it as honesty [good manners] to be so brutally honest."*

210   old *Hamlet probably means "as old" (that is, as young); that appears to be how Polonius takes his words. But since Hamlet is in his "Antic Disposition" (I.v.163), it is not necessary to assume that his remarks conform to normal logic. He may be pretending to describe himself as "old" here and pretending to believe that Polonius is young.*

211   go backward *walk backward (probably with the implication "go backwards in time").*

213   out of the Air *inside (with the implication that outside air is unhealthy, particularly for invalids).*

217   Pregnant *full of meaning.*
        a Happiness *a chance (lucky) aptness.*

POLONIUS   I have, my Lord.

HAMLET   Let her not walk i' th' Sun. Conception is
a Blessing, but as your Daughter may conceive,   190
Friend, look to 't.

POLONIUS   —How say you by that? Still harping on
my Daughter. Yet he knew me not at first: 'a
said I was a Fishmonger. 'A is far gone; and
truly in my Youth I suff'red much Extremity   195
for Love, very near this. I'll speak to him
again. —What do you read, my Lord?

HAMLET   Words, words, words.

POLONIUS   What is the Matter, my Lord?

HAMLET   Between who?   200

POLONIUS   I mean the Matter that you read, my Lord?

HAMLET   Slander, Sir: for the Satirical Rogue says
here that Old Men have Gray Beards, that their
Faces are Wrinkled, their Eyes purging thick
Amber and Plumtree Gum, and that they have a   205
plentiful lack of Wit, together with most weak
Hams; all which, Sir, though I most powerfully
and potently believe, yet I hold it not Honesty
to have it thus set down. For your self, Sir,
shall grow old as I am, if like a Crab you   210
could go backward.

POLONIUS   —Though this be Madness, yet there is
Method in 't. —Will you walk out of the Air,
my Lord?

HAMLET   Into my Grave.   215

POLONIUS   Indeed, that's out of the Air. —How
Pregnant sometimes his Replies are, a Happiness
that often Madness hits on, which Reason and

219   Sanctity   *virtue, holiness of life. Here the Folio reads* sanity.

224   withal   *with.*

233   doost   *Here and elsewhere, this edition preserves verb forms that may provide a clue to Shakespeare's pronunciation.*

236   indifferent   *ordinary. Normally in Shakespeare* indifferent *means "not different," without pejorative connotations.*

238   Happy . . . Over-happy   *blessed in that we are not too well endowed by Fortune. It was a commonplace of Christian theology that a person's happiness should not be judged by his fortune (his worldly possessions, position, or favor). Indeed, according to Boethius'* Consolation of Philosophy *(a classic treatise on Fortune written while the author awaited execution in the year 524), Fortune was most kind to a person when she seemed most unkind; then a person was forced to recognize that worldly happiness could never be relied upon, that the only lasting fulfillment derived from one's favor and union with God. Queen Elizabeth herself had translated Boethius' treatise from Latin to English, and Shakespeare's audience probably included many who knew it well.*

239   Button   *crown of a cap.*

243   middle   *Hamlet plays on at least two senses: (a) midpoint (frequently associated with the Aristotelian mean between two extremes, the idea that a virtue could be defined as the avoidance of vices at either end of an ethical spectrum), and (b) midst (mingling with and encompassed by). Guildenstern adds a bawdy sense in line 244.*

Sanctity could not so prosperously be delivered
of. I will leave him and suddenly contrive the   220
means of Meeting between him and my Daughter.
—My Lord, I will take my Leave of you.

HAMLET   You cannot take from me any thing that I
will not more willingly part withal: except my
Life, except my Life, except my Life.   225

Enter Guildenstern and Rosencrans.

POLONIUS   Fare you well, my Lord.
HAMLET   —These tedious old Fools!
POLONIUS   —You go to seek the Lord Hamlet: there
    he is.
ROSENCRANS   God save you, Sir.   *Exit Polonius.*   230
GUILDENSTERN   My honor'd Lord.
ROSENCRANS   My most dear Lord.
HAMLET   My excellent good Friends. —How doost
    thou, Guildenstern? —Ah Rosencrans. —Good Lads,
    how do you both?   235
ROSENCRANS   As the indifferent Children of the
    Earth.
GUILDENSTERN   Happy in that we are not Over-happy:
    on Fortune's Cap we are not the very Button.
HAMLET   Nor the Soles of her Shoe.   240
ROSENCRANS   Neither, my Lord.
HAMLET   Then you live about her Waist, or in the
    middle of her Favors.
GUILDENSTERN   Faith, her Privates we.
HAMLET   In the Secret Parts of Fortune: O most   245
    true, she is a Strumpet. What News?

107

247   but   *but that.*

249   Then is Doomsday near. *Hamlet is probably alluding to the peaceful millennium to precede the Last Judgment (the thousand years during which Satan is to be bound, "that he should deceive the nations no more," Revelation 20). Only then, Hamlet implies, will the world have "grown Honest."*

252   Prison *Hamlet's image may be another allusion to "the bottomless pit" into which Satan will be cast and "bound," according to Revelation 20:1–3. Compare line 266.*

262   but *unless, except when.*

264   Ambition *Rosencrans is probably fishing to find out if Hamlet's being passed over for the monarchy is what troubles him.*

270   Substance *desired condition or position.*

271   Shadow *image (not limited to what Shakespeare sometimes refers to as a "shade," though Hamlet focuses on that meaning in lines 276–78).*

274   Light *both (a) insubstantial, and (b) frivolous.*

276–   Then . . . Shadows. *Hamlet takes Rosencrans' image of*
78   *"Ambition" as a "Shadow's Shadow" and implies that "Monarchs" (overgrown or "out-stretch'd" shadows) are but the shades cast by beggars. His point is that beggars, who have no ambition and who are normally thought to be nothing more than "shadows" (insignificant human beings) are actually more substantial than monarchs (who personify ambition). Hamlet reduces all ambition (worldly pride and aspiration) to the nothing that the word "vanity" literally denotes.*

ROSENCRANS   None, my Lord, but the World's grown
    Honest.
HAMLET   Then is Doomsday near. But your News is
    not true. Let me question more in particular.   250
    What have you, my good Friends, deserv'd at the
    hands of Fortune that she sends you to Prison
    hither?
GUILDENSTERN   Prison, my Lord?
HAMLET   Denmark's a Prison.   255
ROSENCRANS   Then is the World one.
HAMLET   A goodly one, in which there are many
    Confines, Wards, and Dungeons, Denmark being
    one o' th' worst.
ROSENCRANS   We think not so, my Lord.   260
HAMLET   Why then 'tis none to you: for there is
    Nothing either Good or Bad but Thinking makes
    it so. To me it is a Prison.
ROSENCRANS   Why then your Ambition makes it one:
    'tis too Narrow for your Mind.   265
HAMLET   O God, I could be bounded in a Nutshell
    and count my self a King of Infinite Space,
    were it not that I have Bad Dreams.
GUILDENSTERN   Which Dreams indeed are Ambition:
    for the very Substance of the Ambitious is   270
    merely the Shadow of a Dream.
HAMLET   A Dream it self is but a Shadow.
ROSENCRANS   Truly, and I hold Ambition of so Airy
    and Light a Quality that it is but a Shadow's
    Shadow.   275
HAMLET   Then are our Beggars Bodies; and our
    Monarchs and out-stretch'd Heroes the Beggars'

278   Fay   *faith.*

281   No such matter.   *That's out of the question. Hamlet says that*
       he refuses to regard his old friends as "Servants" (line 282)
       who "wait upon" him (attend to his needs).

283–   dreadfully attended   *both (a) poorly served, and (b) accom-*
84   *panied by feelings of dread and melancholy (line 268).*

284   Beaten Way   *well trodden path.*

285   what make you at   *what brings you to.*

290   too dear a Halfpenny   *too expensive at a halfpenny. In other*
       words, I can't even afford a halfpenny's worth of thanks to you
       (and besides that, you'll be thanked by the person who sent for
       you).

292   free   *both (a) of your own free will, and (b) free of any obliga-*
       tion that may derive from your pleasing someone else.

295   but to th' Purpose   *either (a) so long as it is to the point, or*
       (b) except for something that would be to the point. The
       implication of the phrase depends upon whether Hamlet is to
       be thought of as (a) exhorting his former schoolmates to tell
       him the truth, or (b) telling them that he knows that anything
       they say will be a lie.

297   Modesties   *self-control, dignity. Hamlet is probably referring*
       to the skill with which actors adhere to their roles: the "color"
       (disguise) they have donned for their parts.

304–5 by . . . withal   *by any higher claim a dearer friend may*
       invoke.

Shadows. Shall we to th' Court? For by my Fay
I cannot reason.

BOTH   We'll wait upon you.   280

HAMLET   No such matter. I will not sort you with
the rest of my Servants: for to speak to you
like an Honest Man, I am most dreadfully
attended. But in the Beaten Way of Friendship,
what make you at Elsinore?   285

ROSENCRANS   To visit you, my Lord, no other
Occasion.

HAMLET   Beggar that I am, I am even poor in Thanks,
but I thank you; and sure, dear Friends, my
Thanks are too dear a Halfpenny. Were you not   290
sent for? Is it your own Inclining? Is it a
free Visitation? Come, come, deal justly with
me; come, come, nay speak.

GUILDENSTERN   What should we say, my Lord?

HAMLET   Any thing but to th' Purpose. You were sent   295
for, and there is a kind of Confession in your
Looks which your Modesties have not Craft
enough to color. I know the good King and
Queen have sent for you.

ROSENCRANS   To what end, my Lord?   300

HAMLET   That you must teach me. But let me conjure
you, by the Rights of our Fellowship, by the
Consonancy of our Youth, by the Obligation of
our ever-preserved Love, and by what more dear
a better Proposer can charge you withal, be   305
even and direct with me whether you were sent
for or no.

ROSENCRANS   —What say you?

310   hold not off   *do not hold back from me.*

313   prevent your Discovery   *forestall your having to discover it.*

313–   your . . . Feather   *your secret mission for the King and*
14   *Queen be accomplished to your full credit, without so much as*
          the loss of a feather.

316   forgone . . . Exercises   *given up my normal athletic pur-*
          suits.

319   Promontory   *jutting ("o'erhanging") piece of rock.*

320   brave   *splendid.*

321   Firmament   *the Heavens. As the original Hamlet spoke these*
          lines, he probably gestured not only to the sky but to the
          "Canopy" or "Roof" above the Globe stage.

322   fretted with Golden Fire   *adorned with the Sun and stars.*
          Shakespeare is probably alluding to the decorations on the
          underside of the canopy.

324   Congregation of Vapors   *cluster of illuminated gases (such*
          as the ignis fatuus, *the will-o'-the-wisp).*
          Piece of Work   *artistic creation. Compare III.ii.54.*

326   Express   *probably both (a) precise, and (b) expressive.*

329   Paragon   *touchstone, highest exemplar.*

338   Lenten Entertainment   *the spare hospitality provided dur-*
          ing Lent.

339   coted   *either (a) noted, or (b) overtook, encountered.*

HAMLET   Nay then I have an Eye of you: if you love
    me, hold not off.   310
GUILDENSTERN   My Lord, we were sent for.
HAMLET   I will tell you why. So shall my
    Anticipation prevent your Discovery, and your
    Secrecy to the King and Queen moult no Feather.
    I have of late, but wherefore I know not, lost   315
    all my Mirth, forgone all Custom of Exercises;
    and indeed it goes so heavily with my
    Disposition that this goodly Frame the Earth
    seems to me a sterile Promontory; this most
    excellent Canopy the Air, look you, this brave   320
    o'erhanging Firmament, this majestical Roof
    fretted with Golden Fire, why it appeareth
    nothing to me but a foul and pestilent
    Congregation of Vapors. What a Piece of Work
    is a Man, how Noble in Reason, how Infinite in   325
    Faculties, in Form and Moving, how Express and
    Admirable in Action, how like an Angel in
    Apprehension, how like a God: the Beauty of
    the World, the Paragon of Animals. And yet to
    me, what is this Quintessence of Dust? Man   330
    delights not me, nor Women neither, though by
    your Smiling you seem to say so.
ROSENCRANS   My Lord, there was no such Stuff in my
    Thoughts.
HAMLET   Why did ye laugh then, when I said "Man   335
    delights not me"?
ROSENCRANS   To think, my Lord, if you delight not
    in Man, what Lenten Entertainment the Players
    shall receive from you. We coted them on the

113

343   Tribute on   *reward from.*

344   Foil   *light fencing sword.*

345   Target   *small shield (targe).*

345–   the Humourous Man   *the man subject to humours (obses-*
46   *sions or caprices), here probably choler (wrath).*

348   tickle a' th' Sere   *easily fired off [easily provoked to laugh],*
      like a gun whose sere (catch) is easily triggered.

351   wont   *accustomed. So also with* wonted *in line 362.*

353   travail   *both (a) travel, and (b) suffer hardship.*

356   their Inhibition   *their inability to perform at home. Hamlet*
      alludes to the fact that because of "the late Innovation" (the
      rise of children's companies), the adult acting companies have
      lost prestige ("Estimation," line 358) and "profit."

359   so followed   *thus regarded [still].*

363   Aery   *nest.*

364   Eyases   *baby hawks. Hamlet refers to the schoolboy actors.*

364–   cry . . . Question   *scream contentiously at the tops of their*
65   *voices.*

366–   and . . . Stages   *and they have so terrorized the public play-*
67   *houses.*

368–   many . . . Goose-quills   *many rapier-bearing gallants are*
69   *afraid of ridicule from the pens of the poets writing satirical*
      plays for the boys' companies to perform.

way, and hether are they coming to offer you   340
    Service.
HAMLET   He that plays the King shall be welcome:
    His Majesty shall have Tribute on me. The
    adventurous Knight shall use his Foil and
    Target; the Lover shall not sigh Gratis; the   345
    Humourous Man shall end his Part in Peace;
    the Clown shall make those laugh whose Lungs
    are tickle a' th' Sere; and the Lady shall say
    her Mind freely, or the Blank Verse shall halt
    for 't. What Players are they?   350
ROSENCRANS   Even those you were wont to take
    such Delight in: the Tragedians of the City.
HAMLET   How chances it they travail? Their
    Residence, both in Reputation and Profit, was
    better both ways.   355
ROSENCRANS   I think their Inhibition comes by
    means of the late Innovation.
HAMLET   Do they hold the same Estimation they did
    when I was in the City? Are they so followed?
ROSENCRANS   No indeed, are they not.   360
HAMLET   How comes it? Do they grow Rusty?
ROSENCRANS   Nay, their Endeavor keeps in the wonted
    Pace. But there is, Sir, an Aery of Children,
    little Eyases, that cry out on the Top of
    Question, and are most tyrannically clapp'd   365
    for 't. These are now the Fashion, and so
    be-rattled the Common Stages (so they call
    them) that many wearing Rapiers are afraid of
    Goose-quills and dare scarce come thither.
HAMLET   What, are they Children? Who maintains   370

371   escotted   *supported. The word comes from* scot, *payment.*

372   Quality   *profession (acting).*
no longer than they can sing   *The actors in the London boys' companies were choristers associated with such institutions as St. Paul's Cathedral and the Chapel Royal.*

377   their own Succession   *the "Common Players" (professional actors) they will become once they grow up.*

378   to do   *ado.*

380   tarre   *incite, encourage.*

381   bid for Argument   *paid for themes (plays).*

382   in the Question   *over the matter at issue.*

387–88   Hercules and his Load too   *Hercules relieved Atlas of his load (the world) while Atlas went in search of the apples of the Hesperides. The motto of Shakespeare's own playhouse probably depicted Hercules bearing the Globe. Now that the boys "carry it away" (line 386), Hercules and Globe alike, the common players have no choice but to perform elsewhere.*

389   It . . . strange   *Hamlet says that the "late Innovation" in the theatres has its parallel in the new King's usurpation of another kind of globe (the orb that was a symbol of royalty).*

393   Picture in Little   *portrait in miniature.*

400   Extent   *extension of welcome. Hamlet is complying with the "Garb" (outward form) that pertains to "Fashion and Ceremony" (a "show" of etiquette) as he takes the hands of his schoolmates to bid them a formal welcome.*

'em? How are they escotted? Will they pursue
the Quality no longer than they can sing? Will
they not say afterwards, if they should grow
themselves to Common Players (as it is most
like if their Means are no better), their   375
Writers do them wrong to make them exclaim
against their own Succession?

ROSENCRANS   Faith there has been much to do on
both Sides; and the Nation holds it no Sin to
tarre them to Controversy. There was for a   380
while no Money bid for Argument unless the Poet
and the Player went to Cuffs in the Question.

HAMLET   Is't possible?

GUILDENSTERN   O there has been much throwing
about of Brains.   385

HAMLET   Do the Boys carry it away?

ROSENCRANS   Ay that they do, my Lord: Hercules
and his Load too.

HAMLET   It is not very strange, for my Uncle is
King of Denmark, and those that would make   390
Mouths at him while my Father lived give
twenty, forty, fifty, a hundred Ducats apiece
for his Picture in Little; 'Sblood, there is
something in this more than Natural, if
Philosophy could find it out.   *A Flourish.*   395

GUILDENSTERN   There are the Players.

HAMLET   Gentlemen, you are welcome to Elsinoure.
Your Hands, come then: th' Appurtenance of
Welcome is Fashion and Ceremony. Let me
comply with you in this Garb, lest my Extent to   400
the Players, which I tell you must show fairly

117

406   I . . . Northwest   *I am mad only when the wind is blowing from the north northwest.*

407   a Hawk from a Handsaw   *Hamlet is probably punning on two kinds of implements (a plasterer's tool and a cutting blade) and two kinds of birds; a* Handsaw *(hernshaw or heron) is a bird preyed upon by hawks. Hamlet's point is that, despite his intermittently "Antic Disposition," he is able to make such discriminations as the difference between a harmless bird and a bird of prey.*

411   Swaddling Clouts   *the cloths used to wrap an infant.*

412   Happily   *haply, perhaps.*

415   —You say right, Sir   *With this sentence Hamlet shifts from confidential dialogue with Rosencrans and Guildenstern to the appearance of ordinary discourse with one of them.*

419   Roscius   *the most celebrated of Roman actors.*

421   Buzz, buzz.   *probably a phrase of contemptuous dismissal, indicating that Polonius' report contains no new information.*

423   on his Ass   *Hamlet may be quoting from a contemporary poem or ballad.*

428   Scene Individable   *It is not clear whether this refers to a play that cannot be sorted into constituent elements (such as "Pastoral"), a play that is unclassifiable, or a play that is not divided into separate scenes or settings. "Poem Unlimited" could be anything from a synonym to an opposite of "Scene Individable."*

118

outwards, should more appear like Entertainment
than yours. You are welcome; but my Uncle-
Father and Aunt-Mother are deceived.

GUILDENSTERN   In what, my dear Lord?   405

HAMLET   I am but Mad North Northwest; when the
Wind is Southerly, I know a Hawk from a Handsaw.

Enter Polonius.

POLONIUS   Well be with you, Gentlemen.

HAMLET   —Hark you, Guildenstern, and you too (at
each Ear a Hearer): that great Baby you see   410
there is not yet out of his Swaddling Clouts.

ROSENCRANS   Happily he is the second time come to
them, for they say an Old Man is twice a Child.

HAMLET   I will prophesy he comes to tell me of the
Players: mark it. —You say right, Sir, a Monday   415
morning, 'twas then indeed.

POLONIUS   My Lord, I have News to tell you.

HAMLET   "My Lord, I have News to tell you:
When Roscius was an Actor in Rome—"

POLONIUS   The Actors are come hether, my Lord.   420

HAMLET   Buzz, buzz.

POLONIUS   Upon my Honor—

HAMLET   "Then came each Actor on his Ass."

POLONIUS   The best Actors in the World, either for
Tragedy, Comedy, History, Pastoral, Pastoral-   425
Comical, Historical-Pastoral, Tragical-
Historical, Tragical-Comical-Historical-
Pastoral, Scene Individable, or Poem Unlimited.
Seneca cannot be too heavy, nor Plautus too

119

430   for . . . Liberty *for the "rules" (the laws of probability) governing Senecan tragedy and the freedom from such restraints in Plautine comedy.*

431   These . . . Men. *These are the best players.*

432   Jeptha *Hamlet alludes to Jephthah (Judges 11), an Israelite judge who vowed that if the Lord would grant him a victory over the Ammonites he would sacrifice whatever emerged from his house to greet him on his return from battle. That turned out to be his only child, a maiden daughter, and after she had been given two months to bewail her virginity in the mountains, the grieving Jepthah offered her up to God.*

441   passing *surpassingly.*

442   Nay . . . not. *Hamlet says that a man's being a Jephthah does not prove him to be a father who loves his daughter.*

445   As by lot, God wot *Like the other quotations here, this one is from a ballad about Jephthah and his daughter. Its implication is that God's will was done "by lot" (by random chance) as a result of Jephthah's rash vow.*

449   Row *stanza.*
        pious Chanson *religious song.*

449–   will show you more *will tell you more about the moral of this*
50   *story.*

450   my Abridgment *the players, who (a) abridge (cut off) Hamlet's story, and (b) promise to abridge (shorten) the time.*

453   Valanc'd *fringed. Hamlet then plays on* beard *(confront).*

light for the Law of Writ and the Liberty.   430
These are the only Men.

HAMLET   O Jeptha, Judge of Israel, what a Treasure
hadst thou?

POLONIUS   What a Treasure had he, my Lord?

HAMLET   Why   435
      "One fair Daughter and no more,
         The which he loved passing well."

POLONIUS   —Still on my Daughter!

HAMLET   Am I not i' th' Right, old Jeptha?

POLONIUS   If you call me Jeptha, my Lord, I have a   440
Daughter that I love passing well.

HAMLET   Nay that follows not.

POLONIUS   What follows then, my Lord?

HAMLET   Why
      "As by lot, God wot,"   445
and then you know
      "It came to pass,
         As most like it was."
The first Row of the pious Chanson will show
you more, for look where my Abridgment comes.   450

Enter the Players.

—You are welcome, Maisters, welcome all. I am
glad to see thee well, welcome good Friends.
—O old Friend, why thy Face is Valanc'd since
I saw thee last! Com'st thou to beard me in
Denmark? —What, my young Lady and Mistress: 455
by'r Lady, your Ladyship is nearer to Heaven
than when I saw you last by the altitude of a

121

458 Chopine *a high-soled woman's shoe. Hamlet is addressing one of the company's boy actors and alluding to female roles he has seen him play.*

459 uncurrent Gold *a gold coin that will no longer be accepted as currency because it has been "cracked" or clipped enough to penetrate the "Ring" surrounding the Sovereign's engraved head. Hamlet puns on the "ring" of a boy's high-pitched voice; he may also be noting that if a female's "ring" (virginity) has been "cracked," she can no longer pass as a maiden.*

460 Maisters *masters (from the Latin* magister*).*

461 friendly *undiscriminating. Modern editions normally adopt the Folio's* French, *a word with similar import.*

463 Quality *expertise.*

469 'twas Caviary to the General *it was like offering a delicacy (caviar) to the undiscriminating general populace.*

471 cried in the Top of mine *proclaimed with even more vehemence and authority than my judgment could claim.*

473 Modesty *decorum, restraint.*
   Cunning *probably both (a) skill, and (b) cleverness.*

474 Sallets *salads; spicy morsels, such as shallots and other herbs.*

477 Affection *excess, affectation.*

478– more . . . Fine *more disciplined and straightforward than*
79 *overrefined.*

484 Hyrcanian Beast *a tiger from Hyrcania in the Caucasus.*

Chopine. Pray God your Voice, like a piece of
uncurrent Gold, be not crack'd within the Ring.
—Maisters, you are all welcome. We'll e'en   460
to 't like friendly Falc'ners: fly at any
thing we see. We'll have a Speech straight:
come give us a Taste of your Quality; come, a
passionate Speech.

PLAYER   What Speech, my good Lord?   465

HAMLET   I heard thee speak me a Speech once, but it
was never acted, or if it was, not above once;
for the Play I remember pleas'd not the Million,
'twas Caviary to the General; but it was, as I
received it, and others, whose Judgments in   470
such Matters cried in the Top of mine, an
excellent Play, well digested in the Scenes,
set down with as much Modesty as Cunning. I
remember one said there were no Sallets in the
Lines to make the Matter savory, nor no Matter   475
in the Phrase that might indict the Author of
Affection, but call'd it an Honest Method,
as Wholesome as Sweet, and by very much more
Handsome than Fine. One Speech in 't I chiefly
loved: 'twas Aeneas' Talk to Dido, and there   480
about of it especially when he speaks of
Priam's Slaughter. If it live in your Memory,
begin at this Line: let me see, let me see.
"The rugged Pyrrhus like th' Hyrcanian Beast—"
'Tis not so: it begins with   485

                    "Pyrrhus,
     The rugged Pyrrhus, he whose Sable Arms,

489   couched   *crouched, ready to spring.*
      th' omynous Horse   *the ominous Trojan Horse. Shakespeare draws this and many other details from Book II, "Aeneas' Talk to Dido" (line 480) in Vergil's* Aeneid. *There Pyrrhus avenges the death of his father, Achilles, by leading the assault that destroys Troy.*

492   total Gules   *totally blood-red. In keeping with the vocabulary of "Heraldry" (line 491), Pyrrhus is described as if his body were a coat of arms, originally smeared all black ("Sable Arms," line 487) and now "trick'd" (adorned) in blood.*

494   parching   *burning. Once they got their wooden horse inside the walls, the Greeks emerged and set Troy on fire.*

495   tyr'nnous   *Here and elsewhere, Shakespeare uses* tyrannous *to mean "cruel and merciless."*

497   o'er-sized   *coated as with sizing (glaze).*
      coagulate Gore   *congealed blood; here pronounced "co-ág-lut."*

498   Carbuncles   *fiery red jewels, thought to glow in the dark.*

502   Discretion   *judgment, discipline.*

504   antic   *both (a) antique, old-fashioned, and (b) foolish. Priam, the elderly King of Troy, is here depicted as lacking either the strength or the weapon to withstand the onslaught of the "fell" (fierce) invaders.*

506   Repugnant to Commaund   *resisting the will of its master.*
      Unequal match'd   *matched with a defenseless old man.*

509   senseless Ilium   *the insensible (inanimate) citadel of Troy.*

Black as his Purpose, did the Night
   resemble,
When he lay couched in th' omynous Horse,
Hath now this dread and black Complexion
   smear'd   490
With Heraldry more dismal Head to Foot:
Now is he total Gules, horridly trick'd
With Blood of Fathers, Mothers, Daughters,
   Sons,
Bak'd and impasted with the parching Streets,
That lend a tyr'nnous and a damned Light   495
To their Lord's Murther. Roasted in Wrath
   and Fire,
And thus o'er-sized with coagulate Gore,
With Eyes like Carbuncles, the hellish
   Pyrrhus
Old Grandsire Priam seeks."
So proceed you.   500
POLONIUS   'Fore God, my Lord, well spoken: with
   good Accent and good Discretion!
PLAYER   "Anon he finds him;
Striking too short at Greeks, his antic
   Sword,
Rebellious to his Arm, lies where it falls,   505
Repugnant to Commaund. Unequal match'd,
Pyrrhus at Priam drives, in Rage strikes wide;
But with the Whiff and Wind of his fell
   Sword
Th' unnerved Father falls. Then senseless
   Ilium,

511   Stoops to his Base   *collapses to its foundations.*

513   milky   *milk-white. In* Macbeth, *I.v, milk is associated with "Human Kindness." This implication also occurs in line 552.*

516   a Neutral to his Will and Matter   *one caught midway between his intent and his execution of it.*

518   against   *in anticipation of; just before.*

519   the Rack   *the mass of clouds broken up by the wind.*

520   Orb   *globe (Earth).*

521   anon   *shortly.*

524   Cyclops' Hammers   *The Cyclopes (one-eyed giants) were the smiths in Vulcan's shop who made armor for Mars, the God of War.*

525   forg'd for Proof eterne   *made so durable as to be eternally proof against penetration.*

526   Remorse   *pity.*

529   Synod   *assembly, council.*

530   Follies   *a variant spelling for* felloes *or* fellies, *the exterior rims on wooden wheels. But Shakespeare probably also intends a reference to the "follies" (infidelities and deceits) that "strumpet Fortune" (line 528) bequeaths to those who trust in her. Modern editors normally emend to* fellies *(a reading first introduced in the Fourth Folio, 1685).*

531   Nave   *hub.*

Seeming to feel this Blow, with flaming Top   510
Stoops to his Base, and with a hideous Crash
Takes pris'ner Pyrrhus' Ear: for lo his Sword,
Which was declining on the milky Head
Of rev'rent Priam, seem'd i' th' Air to
    stick.
So as a painted Tyrant Pyrrhus stood   515
And, like a Neutral to his Will and Matter,
Did nothing.
But as we often see, against some Storm,
A Silence in the Heavens, the Rack stand
    still,
The bold Winds speechless, and the Orb below   520
As hush as Death, anon the dreadful Thunder
Doth rend the Region: so after Pyrrhus'
    Pause
A roused Vengeance sets him new a-work,
And never did the Cyclops' Hammers fall
On Mars's Armor forg'd for Proof eterne   525
With less Remorse than Pyrrhus' bleeding
    Sword
Now falls on Priam.
Out, out, thou strumpet Fortune, all you
    Gods
In gen'ral Synod take away her Power!
Break all the Spokes and Follies from her
    Wheel   530
And bowl the round Nave down the Hill of
    Heav'n
As low as to the Fiend's!"

535   Jig   *a song and dance routine following the play proper.*

535–   Tale of Bawdry   *bawdy story.*
36

537   mobled   *muffled (with face covered). Hamlet's reaction in the next line suggests that he regards the word as obscure and affected; that does not bother Polonius, whose taste is more to the "Fine" (overwrought) than to the "Handsome" (line 479).*

541   Bisson Rheum   *blinding discharge (tears).*
       Clout   *cloth.*

542   Diadem   *either a small crown or an ornamental headband.*

543   o'er-teemed   *exhausted from childbearing (52 children).*

545   Who this had seen   *whoever had seen this (rephrasing line 537).*

546   'Gainst . . . pronounc'd   *would have uttered treasonous pronouncements against the sway of Fortune.*

552   milch   *milky. The poet's point is that even the stars of Heaven would have been moved to compassion if they had seen Priam's widow in her lamentations.*

553   Passion   *compassion. In accordance with Epicurean philosophy, the Olympian Gods are here depicted as remote and uninvolved in human affairs.*

554   where   *both (a) whether, and (b) where.*

558   bestow'd   *lodged and cared for.*

POLONIUS   This is too long.

HAMLET   It shall to the Barber's with your Beard.
  —Prethee say on: he's for a Jig, or a Tale of   535
  Bawdry, or he sleeps. Say on, come to Hecuba.

PLAYER   "But who, ah Woe, had seen the mobled
    Queen—"

HAMLET   "The mobled Queen"?

POLONIUS   That's good: "mobled Queen" is good!

PLAYER   "Run barefoot up and down, threat'ning
    the Flames   540
  With Bisson Rheum, a Clout upon that Head
  Where late the Diadem stood, and for a Robe
  About her lank and all o'er-teemed Loins
  A Blanket in th' Alarm of Fear caught up;
  Who this had seen, with Tongue in Venom
    steep'd,   545
  'Gainst Fortune's State would Treason have
    pronounc'd.
  But if the Gods themselves did see her then,
  When she saw Pyrrhus make malicious Sport
  In mincing with his Sword her Husband's Limbs,
  The instant burst of Clamor that she made,   550
  Unless things Mortal move them not at all,
  Would have made milch the burning Eyes of
    Heaven
  And Passion in the Gods."

POLONIUS   Look where he has not turn'd his Color
  and has Tears in's Eyes: prethee no more.   555

HAMLET   'Tis well: I'll have thee speak out the
  rest of this soon. —Good my Lord, will you
  see the Players well bestow'd? Do you hear,

560   **Abstract** *both (a) brief, and (b) artful (extracting and preserving the essence of "the Time").*

565   **God's Bodkin** *God's little body; an oath alluding to the Crucifixion, and thus one that is appropriate to a speech in which Hamlet reminds Polonius that "all have sinned and come short of the glory of God" (Romans 3:23) and "scape" condemnation only through the "Whipping" (Matthew 26:27) and sacrifice of Christ in their stead.*

566   **after his Desert** *in accordance with what he deserves.*
        scape *escape.*

567   **Whipping** *The punishment Hamlet chooses is apt; players who traveled and performed without a license (usually secured through the patronage of a Lord) were subject to flogging, the penalty the law provided for those convicted of being vagabonds.*

568–   **the less . . . Bounty** *Hamlet's phrasing echoes that of the*
69   *Apostle Paul in such passages as Romans 5:20 ("where sin abounded, grace did much more abound") and Ephesians 2:8 ("by grace are ye saved through faith; and that not of yourselves: it is the gift of God"). Both passages were central to the Lutheran theology promulgated at Wittenberg in 1517.*

571   **hear a Play** *In Shakespeare's time, discriminating audiences spoke of "hearing" (attending to the "Matter") rather than "seeing" (being amused by the spectacle of) a play.*

576   **ha't** *have it.*

581   **look you** *see that you.*

586   **God buy** *goodbye.*

let them be well used, for they are the
Abstract and Brief Chronicles of the Time: 560
after your Death you were better have a bad
Epitaph than their Ill Report while you live.
POLONIUS   My Lord, I will use them according to
   their Desert.
HAMLET   God's Bodkin, Man, much better! Use   565
   every Man after his Desert, and who shall scape
   Whipping? Use them after your own Honor and
   Dignity: the less they deserve, the more Merit
   is in your Bounty. Take them in.
POLONIUS   —Come, Sirs.   570
HAMLET   —Follow him, Friends: we'll hear a Play
   tomorrow.
               Exit Polonius with all but the First Player.
   —Dost thou hear me, old Friend: can you play
   "The Murther of Gonzago"?
PLAYER   Ay, my Lord.   575
HAMLET   We'll ha't tomorrow night. You could for
   need study a Speech of some dozen Lines or
   sixteen Lines, which I would set down, and
   insert in't, could you not?
PLAYER   Ay, my Lord.   580
HAMLET   Very well, follow that Lord. And look you
   mock him not.   *Exit First Player.*
   —My good Friends, I'll leave you till Night.
   You are welcome to Elsinoure.
ROSENCRANS   Good my Lord.   585
HAMLET   Ay so, God buy to you.
               Exeunt Rosencrans and Guildenstern.
                      —Now I am alone.

588   monstrous   *a violation of nature's norms. Things that were monstrous were frequently regarded as portents, omens of disaster (from Latin* monere, *to warn).*

589   a Dream of Passion   *a fictitious set of emotions.*

590   Conceit   *here, a concept generated and elaborated by imagination.*

591   all the Visage wan'd   *his face waned to a completely wan (bloodless) complexion. Hamlet is probably combining* waned *and* wanned *here.*

592   Distraction . . . Aspect   *a distraught (semi-mad) condition manifested in his expression.*

593–   his . . . Conceit   *all his bodily functions finding external*
94   *appearances in keeping with his ruling idea.*

595   Hecuba   *Priam's wife and Troy's Queen.*

598   the Cue   *the prompting, reason. Here the Folio reading seems clearly superior to the Second Quarto's "that."*

600   cleave the Gen'ral Ear   *split the ears of the general populace.*

601   appall the Free   *astonish the innocent (those free of guilt), by telling them the tale Hamlet has heard from the Ghost.*

602   Confound   *bewilder.*

604   muddy-mettl'd   *equipped with a dull spirit, no better than a metal rendered inferior by its admixture of baser matter.* peak   *mope, look peaked.*

605   unpregnant of   *not filled to the bursting point with.*

O what a Rogue and peasant Slave am I!
Is it not monstrous that this Player here,
But in a Fiction, in a Dream of Passion,
Could force his Soul so to his own Conceit   590
That from her working all the Visage wan'd,
Tears in his Eyes, Distraction in's Aspect,
A broken Voice, and his whole Function suiting
With Forms to his Conceit; and all for nothing,
For Hecuba!   595
What's Hecuba to him, or he to her,
That he should weep for her? What would he do
Had he the Motive and the Cue for Passion
That I have? He would drown the Stage with
   Tears
And cleave the Gen'ral Ear with Horrid Speech,   600
Make Mad the Guilty and appall the Free,
Confound the Ign'rant, and amaze indeed
The very Faculties of Eyes and Ears. Yet I,
A dull and muddy-mettl'd Rascal, peak
Like John-a-Dreams, unpregnant of my Cause,   605
And can say Nothing; no, not for a King
Upon whose Property and most dear Life
A damn'd Defeat was made. Am I a Coward?
Who calls me Villain, breaks my Pate across,
Plucks off my Beard and blows it in my Face,   610
Tweaks me by th' Nose, gives me the Lie i'
   th' Throat
As deep as to the Lungs? Who does me this?
Hah, 'Swounds, I should take it: for it cannot be
But I am Pigeon-liver'd and lack Gall
To make Oppression bitter, or ere this   615

617 **Offal** *entrails. The word literally means "off-fall," waste.*

620 **a Deer Murthered** *If this reading from the Second Quarto is correct (the Folio reads "the Deere murthered"), it probably combines two senses: (a) a murdered deer (the hart, a stag deer, was sometimes treated as a symbol of royalty, as Hamlet does in III.ii.297), and (b) a dear one murdered. Modern editions normally follow the First and Third Quartos here and print "a dear father murdered." Neither of these texts has the authority of the Second Quarto and the First Folio. In line 621, the word* Heart *is spelled* hart *in the Quarto. Other words reinforcing* deer *in this soliloquy include "Rascal" (line 604) and "dear" (line 607). One early meaning of* rascal *is "a young, lean, or inferior deer."*

624 **Stallion** *a male drab (prostitute). Most modern editions adopt the Folio's* Scullion *(a kitchen wench).*

625 **About** *either (a) turn around, or (b) get on with it.*

627 **Cunning** *art, skill.*

628 **presently** *immediately.*

629 **Malefactions** *evil-doings.*

634 **tent** *probe.*
   blench *flinch, wince.*

639 **such Spirits** *the souls of persons weakened by melancholy.*

640 **Abuses** *both (a) deceives, and (b) misuses.*

641 **relative** *relating to verification.*

I should 'a fatted all the region Kites
With this Slave's Offal! Bloody, bawdy Villain!
Remorseless, treach'rous, lech'rous, kindless Villain.
Why what an Ass am I? This is most brave,
That I, the Son of a Deer Murthered,   620
Prompted to my Revenge by Heav'n and Hell,
Must like a Whore unpack my Heart with Words
And fall a-Cursing like a very Drab,
A Stallion. Fie upon 't, foh!
About, my Brains! Hum, I have heard   625
That Guilty Creatures sitting at a Play
Have by the very Cunning of the Scene
Been strook so to the Soul that presently
They have proclaim'd their Malefactions:
For Murther, though it have no Tongue, will
    speak   630
With most mirac'lous Organ. I'll have these
    Players
Play something like the Murther of my Father
Before mine Uncle. I'll observe his Looks;
I'll tent him to the Quick. If 'a do blench,
I know my Course. The Spir't that I have seen   635
May be a Devil, and the Dev'l hath Pow'r
T' assume a pleasing Shape; yea, and perhaps
Out of my Weakness and my Melancholy
(As he is very potent with such Spirits)
Abuses me to damn me. I'll have Grounds   640
More relative than this: the Play's the thing
Wherein I'll catch the Conscience of the King.

Exit.

III.i   *This scene takes place in Elsinore Castle.*

1   Conference   *conversation. Here the Folio prints* circumstance.

2   puts on this Confusion   *adopts such a confused, disruptive mode of behavior. The King's verb, "puts on," implies a suspicion that Hamlet is only feigning.*

5   dooes   *does. The spelling of this word in the Second Quarto is probably an indication of how it was often spoken in Shakespeare's time.*

    Distracted   *mentally and emotionally disturbed; distraught. We would probably use a word like "neurosis" to describe what the Elizabethans called "distraction."*

7   forward to be sounded   *willing to have us test him with "soundings." The metaphor refers to the lowering of lines to plumb for the depth of a body of water.*

8   Crafty Madness   *Guildenstern too assumes that Hamlet's "Madness" is a cunning defensive technique rather than genuine insanity.*

Act Three

Scene 1

Enter King, Queen, Polonius, Ophelia, Rosencrans,
Guildenstern, Lords.

KING An' can you by no Drift of Conference
    Get from him why he puts on this Confusion,
    Grating so harshly all his Days of Quiet
    With turbulent and dang'rous Lunacy?
ROSENCRANS He dooes confess he feels himself
    Distracted,   5
    But from what Cause 'a will by no means speak.
GUILDENSTERN Nor do we find him forward to be
    sounded,
    But with a Crafty Madness keeps aloof
    When we would bring him on to some Confession
    Of his true State.
QUEEN   Did he receive you well?   10
ROSENCRANS Most like a Gentleman.

11–12   forcing / Of his Disposition   *What Guildenstern probably means is that, though Hamlet was formally courteous, he also allowed his friends to see that it required some effort on his part to be so.*

12   Niggard of Question   *not disposed to ask questions or initiate conversations.*

13   of our Demaunds   *in response to our inquiries.*

14   assay him to any Pastime   *attempt to interest him in any pastime.*

16   o'er-raught   *overtook.*

22   the Matter   *the material to be performed.*

24   Edge   *spur, incitement.*

26   two   *This is the reading of the Second Quarto; many editors follow the Folio and print* too. *If the Quarto reading is correct, it would appear that the King refers to himself and Polonius, the two who will remain once Ophelia has been "loosed" to Hamlet. It is also possible, however, that the King simply overlooks Ophelia when calculating the number who really matter from his point of view. After all, Ophelia is only a lowly maiden.*

28   as 'twere   *as if it were.*

29   Affront   *meet, encounter.*

30   bestow   *stow, hide away.*

31   frankly   *freely and directly.*

138

GUILDENSTERN   But with much forcing
    Of his Disposition.
ROSENCRANS   Niggard of Question,
    But of our Demaunds most free in his
    Reply.
QUEEN   Did you assay him to any Pastime?
ROSENCRANS   Madam, it so fell out that certain
        Players   15
    We o'er-raught on the way; of these we told him,
    And there did seem in him a kind of Joy
    To hear of 't. They are here about the Court,
    And, as I think, they have already Order
    This Night to play before him.
POLONIUS   'Tis most true;   20
    And he beseech'd me to entreat your Majesties
    To hear and see the Matter.
KING   With all my Heart,
    And it doth much content me t' hear him so
        inclin'd.
    Good Gentlemen, give him a further Edge,
    And drive his Purpose into these Delights.   25
ROSENCRANS   We shall, my Lord.
                    Exeunt Rosencrans and Guildenstern.
KING   Sweet Gertrard, leave us two,
    For we have closely sent for Hamlet hether,
    That he, as 'twere by Accident, may here
    Affront Ophelia. Her Father and my self,
    We'll so bestow our selves that, seeing unseen,   30
    We may of their Encounter frankly judge,
    And gather by him, as he is behav'd,
    If 't be th' Affliction of his Love or no

139

36   happy   *fortunate.*

37   Wildness   *ungovernable behavior.*

38   Wonted   *accustomed, normal.*

40   gracious, so please you   *in a gracious (pious) manner, if you please. Most editors assume that Polonius addresses this phrase and "We will bestow ourselves" to the King. But nowhere else in Shakespeare is "Gracious" used alone as a title.*

41   this Book   *probably either a devotional manual or a Bible, in view of what Polonius says in lines 42–46 and what Hamlet says in lines 86–87.*

42   Exercise   *activity (here referring to a religious meditation).*
color   *account for, appear to conform to.*

43   Lowliness   *pious humility. Modern editions normally adopt the Folio's* loneliness *here. But what Ophelia is being asked to "Show" (display) is "Devotion's Visage" (line 44).*
too blame   *too much to blame, too blameworthy.*

44   prov'd   *demonstrated by experience.*

48   plast'ring Art   *cosmetics.*

49   to   *either (a) in the eye of, or (b) compared to.*

50   painted Word   *words that cover over ugly thoughts and deeds.*

52   withdraw, my Lord   *Polonius' phrasing in the Quarto suggests that he and Claudius are standing far enough apart that they retire to separate hiding places. The Folio reads "let's withdraw my Lord."*

That thus he suffers for.

QUEEN   I shall obey you.
    —And for your part, Ophelia, I do wish   35
    That your good Beauties be the happy Cause
    Of Hamlet's Wildness. So shall I hope your
        Virtues
    Will bring him to his Wonted Way again,
    To both your Honors.

OPHELIA   Mad'm, I wish it may.

POLONIUS   Ophelia, walk you here, gracious, so
        please you: 40
    We will bestow our selves. Read on this Book,
    That Show of such an Exercise may color
    Your Lowliness. We are oft too blame in this:
    'Tis too much prov'd that with Devotion's
        Visage
    And pious Action we do sugar o'er   45
    The Devil himself.

KING   —O 'tis too true:
    How smart a Lash that Speech doth give my
        Conscience!
    The Harlot's Cheek, beauti'd with plast'ring
        Art,
    Is not more ugly to the thing that helps it
    Than is my Deed to my most painted Word.   50
    O heavy Burthen!

Enter Hamlet.

POLONIUS   I hear him coming: withdraw, my Lord.
                            Polonius and the King retire.

141

54   **suffer**   *endure patiently, without resistance.*

57   **by opposing**   *It is not clear whether Hamlet is here referring to direct self-slaughter or to a Quixotic attack against overwhelming odds that will result in certain death. In either event, the outcome will be a release from his "Sea of Troubles."*

60   **a Consummation**   *both (a) a conclusion, and (b) a consuming (annihilation).*

62   **Rub**   *resistance, impediment. The term derives from the game of bowls, and it refers to anything that throws a bowl off course.*

64   **shuffl'd . . . Coil**   *sloughed off this skin (as does a snake when molting). Coil suggests not only (a) the body, but (b) all the turmoils of human life, and (c) a rope or chain coiled around a struggling prisoner.*

65   **Respect**   *consideration; matter to take into account.*

66   **That . . . Life**   *that makes suffering so long-lived.*

68   **Contumely**   *scorn, insulting haughtiness.*

70   **Spurns**   *kicks.*

72   **Quietus**   *settlement of an account (with a play on quietude). Hamlet's words can apply either to suicide or to regicide (killing the King). He hesitates because he realizes that either action could result in his damnation.*

73   **a bare Bodkin**   *a simple, unsheathed dagger.*
       Fardels   *burdens, bundles.*

76   **Bourn**   *boundary, borders.*

HAMLET To be or to be, that is the Question:
Whether 'tis Nobler in the Mind to suffer
The Slings and Arrows of outrageous Fortune   55
Or to take Arms against a Sea of Troubles
And by opposing end them. To die, to sleep
No more, and by a Sleep to say we end
The Heartache and the thousand nat'ral Shocks
That Flesh is heir to: 'tis a Consummation   60
Devoutly to be wish'd. To die to sleep,
To sleep, perchance to dream: ay there's the
   Rub,
For in that Sleep of Death what Dreams may
   come
When we have shuffl'd off this Mortal Coil
Must give us Pause. There's the Respect   65
That makes Calamity of so long Life:
For who would bear the Whips and Scorns of
   Time,
Th' Oppressor's Wrong, the Proud Man's
   Contumely,
The Pangs of Despis'd Love, the Law's Delay,
The Insolence of Office, and the Spurns   70
That patient Merit of th' Unworthy takes,
When he himself might his Quietus make
With a bare Bodkin? Who would Fardels bear,
To grunt and sweat under a Weary Life,
But that the Dread of Something after Death,   75
The Undiscover'd Country from whose Bourn
No Traveler returns, puzzles the Will
And makes us rather bear those Ills we have
Than fly to others that we know not of.

80   Conscience   *both (a) consciousness, and (b) the moral sense.*

81   Native Hew of Resolution   *Hamlet puns on* hew *(a swinging stroke with an ax or blade to chop down or slaughter) and* hue *(color, complexion, vigor), to describe both the natural expression and the in-born disposition (sanguine, blood-red) of courage and resolve.*

82   sickl'd . . . Thought   *Here the Second Quarto's* sickled *combines two basic meanings: (a) sickened, and (b) cut down with a sickle (a curved blade). These cohere with two meanings for* Cast *to yield a complex of related implications: (a) replaced with a pale, sickly cast (complexion), and (b) cut down and left to languish under the cast-off stalks of what has now become a faded overlay of "Thought." The Folio's* sicklied *yields only the first set of meanings.*

84   Regard   *consideration; compare* Respect *in line 65.*
      their Currents turn awry   *divert their flow into a channel that leads away from "Action" (the fulfillment of "Will," line 77) into puzzled paralysis. After contemplating his dilemma from the perspective of either a Pyrrhus or an "antique Roman" (V.ii.353), Hamlet has allowed Christian "Regard" to stay his hand. Now he upbraids himself for cowardice.*

85–86 Soft . . . Ophelia.   *This sentence is here treated as something Hamlet says to himself upon first noticing Ophelia. For a different reading, see Derek Jacobi's eloquent foreword.*

86   Orizons   *orisons, prayers; probably pronounced "o-rý-zons."*

98   Unkind   *This is the play's first suggestion that Hamlet has been unkind to Ophelia; it signals to Hamlet that Ophelia is not to be trusted.*

Thus Conscience dooes make Cowards of us all, 80
And thus the Native Hew of Resolution
Is sickl'd o'er with the Pale Cast of Thought,
And Enterprises of great Pitch and Moment
With this Regard their Currents turn awry
And lose the name of Action. Soft you now, 85
The fair Ophelia. —Nymph, in thy Orizons
Be all my Sins rememb'red.

OPHELIA   Good my Lord,
How dooes your Honor for this many a Day?

HAMLET   I humbly thank you, well.

OPHELIA   My Lord, I have Remembrances of yours 90
That I have longed long to redeliver:
I pray you now receive them.

HAMLET   No, not I: I never gave you ought.

OPHELIA   My honor'd Lord, you know right well you
did,
And with them Words of so sweet Breath compos'd 95
As made these things more rich. Their Perfume
lost,
Take these again: for to the Noble Mind
Rich Gifts wax poor when Givers prove Unkind.
There my Lord.

HAMLET   Ha, ha, are you Honest? 100

OPHELIA   My Lord?

HAMLET   Are you Fair?

OPHELIA   What means your Lordship?

HAMLET   That if you be Honest and Fair, your Honesty
should admit no Discourse to your Beauty. 105

OPHELIA   Could Beauty, my Lord, have better
Commerce than with Honesty?

145

112   the Time gives it Proof   *In lines 104–5 and 108–11 Hamlet has implied that Ophelia's "Honesty" (chastity) is failing to shield her "Beauty" from the kind of "Discourse" that can corrupt a maiden. What Hamlet probably means is that Ophelia's "Honesty" in another sense (her truthfulness) has been compromised. From the comments he made to Polonius in II.ii, it seems likely that Hamlet had already begun to suspect that Ophelia's "Fishmonger" father was inserting himself into his daughter's affairs. When he says "the Time gives it Proof," then, Hamlet probably means that Ophelia's devious behavior now confirms those earlier suspicions. Ophelia's "Honesty" has been transformed into a kind of "Bawd" who "looses" her Beauty to Hamlet in a way that serves not love but the will of her conniving father and his crafty King. What was once a "Paradox" (a statement to be treated skeptically) is now proven true.*

115–
17   Virtue . . . it   *we cannot graft virtue into our original stock so thoroughly as to remove all traces of the original plant. Hamlet echoes the same doctrines as in II.ii.565–69.*

119   Nunn'ry   *convent.* Nunn'ry *could also mean brothel.*

120–
21   indifferent Honest   *as virtuous as (no different from) the next person.*

124   beck   *call, command.*

133   play the Fool   *be the fool he is.*

136–
37   this Plague for thy Dowry   *this curse as your wedding settlement.*

138   Calumny   *scandal.*

HAMLET   Ay truly, for the Power of Beauty will
          sooner transform Honesty from what it is to a
          Bawd than the Force of Honesty can translate   110
          Beauty into his Likeness. This was sometime a
          Paradox, but now the Time gives it Proof. I
          did love you once.
OPHELIA   Indeed my Lord, you made me believe so.
HAMLET   You should not have believ'd me, for Virtue   115
          cannot so inoculate our old Stock but we shall
          relish of it. I loved you not.
OPHELIA   I was the more deceived.
HAMLET   Get thee to a Nunn'ry: why would'st thou be
          a Breeder of Sinners? I am my self indifferent   120
          Honest, but yet I could accuse me of such
          things that it were better my Mother had not
          borne me: I am very Proud, Revengeful,
          Ambitious, with more Offenses at my beck than
          I have Thoughts to put them in, Imagination to   125
          give them Shape, or Time to act them in. What
          should such Fellows as I do crawling between
          Earth and Heaven? We are arrant Knaves: believe
          none of us. Go thy ways to a Nunn'ry. Where's
          your Father?   130
OPHELIA   At home, my Lord.
HAMLET   Let the Doors be shut upon him, that he
          may play the Fool no where but in's own House.
          Farewell.
OPHELIA   —O help him, you sweet Heavens!   135
HAMLET   If thou doost marry, I'll give thee this
          Plague for thy Dowry: be thou as Chaste as Ice,
          as Pure as Snow, thou shalt not escape Calumny.

140   Fool   *Here Hamlet means a man who has been fooled
       (deceived) by an unfaithful wife.*

141   Monsters   *horned cuckolds (deceived husbands).*

145   Paintings   *use of cosmetics.*

147   jig and amble   *dance in a suggestive way.*
       lisp   *speak with seductive affectations.*

148   nickname God's Creatures   *give wanton names to your
       lovers and their bodily parts. Compare IV.vii.164–67.*

148–   make your Wantonness your Ignorance   *when you get
49   caught acting wanton, [you] pretend that you didn't know
       what you were doing.*

149–   I'll no more on't   *I'll have no more of it. Hamlet cannot bear
50   to be reminded of or to reenact what his Father suffered.*

151   moe   *more.*

156   Th' Expectation . . . State   *the heir apparent and favorite
       of the state. The Folio prints* expectancy.

157   Glass of Fashion   *mirror (exemplar) of dress and appearance.*

159   Deject   *both (a) cast down, and (b) rejected.*

161   what   *Most editors adopt* that *from the Folio.*

162   out of Time   *with no order or rhythm. The Folio prints* out
       of tune, *an idea conveyed by* Harsh.

163   blown Youth   *youth in full bloom.*

164   Blasted with Ecstasy   *blighted with madness; beside itself.*

148

Get thee to a Nunn'ry, farewell. Or if thou
wilt needs marry, marry a Fool: for Wise-men   140
know well enough what Monsters you make of
them. To a Nunn'ry go, and quickly too.
Farewell.

OPHELIA   —Heavenly Powers restore him!

HAMLET   I have heard of your Paintings well enough.   145
God hath given you one Face and you make your
selves another; you jig and amble; and you lisp
and nickname God's Creatures, and make your
Wantonness your Ignorance. Go to, I'll no more
on't: it hath made me Mad. I say we will have   150
no moe Marriage. Those that are married
already, all but one shall live, the rest
shall keep as they are. To a Nunn'ry go.   *Exit.*

OPHELIA   O what a Noble Mind is here o'erthrown!
The Courtier's, Soldier's, Scholar's Eye,
    Tongue, Sword,   155
Th' Expectation and Rose of the fair State,
The Glass of Fashion and the Mould of Form,
Th' Observ'd of all Observers, quite quite
    down;
And I of Ladies most Deject and Wretched,
That suck'd the Honey of his Music'd Vows!   160
Now see what Noble and most Sov'reign Reason,
Like sweet Bells jangl'd out of Time and Harsh,
That unmatch'd Form and Stature of blown Youth—
Blasted with Ecstasy. O woe is me,
T' have seen what I have seen, see what I see!   165

Enter King and Polonius.

167   Form   *formal order, the self-control of deliberate discourse.*

169   sits on brood   *sits brooding, like a mother bird incubating eggs until they are ready to hatch and yield a brood of off-spring.*

170   doubt   *fear.*
        Disclose   *disclosure [of what the egg contains]. Brutus uses a similar image to justify his decision to intercept another source of Danger "in the Shell" before it can hatch* (Julius Caesar, *II.i.33–34*).

172–   I have . . . down   *This announcement would seem to con-*
73   *firm that the King and Polonius have watched Hamlet and Ophelia from different hiding places. We should also note that the King and Polonius engage in private conversation, ignoring the distraught Ophelia.*

174   neglected Tribute   *overdue payment.*

175   Haply   *both (a) perhaps, and (b) happily (it is to be hoped).*

176   variable Objects   *new sights (to distract his attention).*

177   something settl'd   *unidentified but firmly fixed.*

179   From Fashion of himself   *away from his normal behavior.*

182   How now   *how are you?*

186   entreat   *urge.*

187   show his Grief   *reveal what troubles him.*
        round   *open, direct.*

189   find him not   *fail to discover what is really on his mind.*

KING   Love: his Affections do not that way tend,
       Nor what he spake, though it lack'd Form a
           little,
       Was not like Madness. There's something in his
           Soul
       O'er which his Melancholy sits on brood,
       And I do doubt the Hatch and the Disclose   170
       Will be some Danger; which for to prevent
       I have in quick Determination
       Thus set it down: he shall with speed to
           England
       For the Demaund of our neglected Tribute.
       Haply the Seas, and Countries different,   175
       With variable Objects, shall expel
       This something settl'd Matter in his Heart,
       Whereon his Brains still beating puts him thus
       From Fashion of himself. What think you on't?
POLONIUS   It shall do well. But yet do I believe   180
       The Or'gin and Commencement of his Grief
       Sprung from neglected Love. —How now,
           Ophelia?
       You need not tell us what Lord Hamlet said:
       We heard it all. —My Lord, do as you please,
       But if you hold it fit, after the Play   185
       Let his Queen-Mother all alone entreat him
       To show his Grief; let her be round with him,
       And I'll be plac'd (so please you) in the Ear
       Of all their Conf'rence. If she find him not,
       To England send him; or confine him where   190
       Your Wisdom best shall think.

III.ii *This scene takes place in the Castle. As it opens, Hamlet is advising the Players on how to perform their parts.*

2 trippingly *skippingly, with lightness, ease, and rapidity.*

3 mouth it *speak it with labored, exaggerated delivery.*

4 as live *as lief; as soon, as willingly.*

6 use all gently *moderate your gestures, in the manner of a gentleman.*

8 acquire and beget *obtain (through training) and deliver (in performance).*

9 Temperance *restraint, self-control.*

10 robustious *blustering, excessively histrionic.*

11 Periwig-pated *wig-covered (and thus looking pretentious).* Totters *tatters, scraps.*

12 spleet *split.*

13 Groundlings *members of the audience who paid only a penny to enter and who stood in the yard surrounding the stage.*

13–14 capable of *able to appreciate.*

14 inexplicable Dumb-shows *inscrutable pantomimes. Hamlet's point seems to be that what the dumb-shows signify is of no consequence for the groundlings.*

16 Termagant *like Herod, a ranting tyrant in medieval mystery plays; he was a Saracen deity, traditionally presented as a counterpart to Mohammed.*

KING   It shall be so:
    Madness in Great Ones must not unwatch'd go.

Exeunt.

Scene 2

Enter Hamlet and three of the Players.

HAMLET   Speak the Speech, I pray you, as I
    pronounc'd it to you, trippingly on the Tongue;
    but if you mouth it as many of our Players do,
    I had as live the Town-crier spoke my Lines.
    Nor do not saw the Air too much with your   5
    Hand thus, but use all gently: for in the very
    Torrent, Tempest, and, as I may say, Whirlwind
    of your Passion, you must acquire and beget a
    Temperance that may give it Smoothness. O it
    offends me to the Soul to hear a robustious   10
    Periwig-pated Fellow tear a Passion to Totters,
    to very Rags, to spleet the Ears of the
    Groundlings, who for the most part are capable
    of nothing but inexplicable Dumb-shows and
    Noise. I would have such a Fellow whipp'd for   15
    o'er-doing Termagant: it out-Herods Herod, pray
    you avoid it.
PLAYER   I warrant your Honor.
HAMLET   Be not too Tame neither, but let your own

20   Discretion   *judgment.*

22   Observance   *concern, point of caution.*

23   Modesty of Nature   *norms and manners of ordinary human behavior.*

24   from   *a departure from.*
      End   *rationale; what Aristotle referred to as a "final cause."*

26   as 'twere   *so to speak.*

28   Age and Body of the Time   *historical setting and physical realities of the period (as represented both in the play and in the audience).*

28–29 his Form and Pressure   *its defining shape and impression (as in a seal).*

29–30 come Tardy off   *underdone (performed with hesitancy or inadequacy).*

30   Unskillful   *unknowing, undiscriminating.*

31   the Judicious   *those with sophisticated taste and judgment.*

32   Censure   *judgment (either approving or disapproving).*
      Allowance   *reckoning, consideration.*

39–40 Nature's Journeymen   *Nature's day-laborers (rather than Nature or God).*

41   abhominably   *the normal Shakespearean spelling of* abominably. *The word was thought to derive from* ab homine *(Latin for "away from humanity," un-human).*

42   indifferently   *well enough, tolerably.*

49   necessary Question   *crucial issue.*

Discretion be your Tutor: suit the Action to 20
the Word, the Word to the Action, with this
special Observance, that you o'er-step not the
Modesty of Nature. For anything so o'er-done
is from the Purpose of Playing, whose End,
both at the first and now, was and is, to hold 25
as 'twere the Mirror up to Nature, to show
Virtue her Feature, Scorn her own Image, and
the very Age and Body of the Time his Form and
Pressure. Now this Over-done, or come Tardy
off, though it makes the Unskillful laugh, 30
cannot but make the Judicious grieve, the
Censure of which One must in your Allowance
o'er-weigh a whole Theater of Others. O there
be Players that I have seen play, and heard
others praise, and that highly, not to speak 35
it profanely, that neither having th' Accent
of Christians, nor the Gait of Christian,
Pagan, nor Man, have so strutted and bellowed
that I have thought some of Nature's Journeymen had made Men, and not made them well, 40
they imitated Humanity so abhominably.
PLAYER   I hope we have reform'd that indifferently
with us.
HAMLET   O reform it altogether. And let those
that play your Clowns speak no more than is 45
set down for them: for there be of them that
will themselves laugh to set on some quantity
of barren Spectators to laugh too, though
in the mean time some necessary Question of
the Play be then to be considered. That's 50

155

51   pitiful Ambition   *lamentable arrogance (here the overween-
      ing audacity of a mere player who believes himself superior
      both to the play and to the intentions, the "purpose," of the
      playwright).*

52   uses it   *does it.*

55   presently   *immediately.*

S.D. Exeunt they two.   *This stage direction, from the Second
      Quarto, indicates the departure of Rosencrans and Guilden-
      stern.*

59   What how   *What ho. Hamlet is bidding Horatio to come. In
      the early texts that appear to derive from Shakespeare's own
      manuscripts, the "how" spelling for "ho" or "hoa" is quite
      common.*

61   just   *probably both (a) honest, and (b) judicious.*

62   As . . . withal   *as I have ever encountered in my dealings
      with people.*

63   flatter   *curry favor by telling pleasing lies.*

65   Revenue   *wealth, income; here accented on the second syllable.*

68–69 crook . . . Fawning   *curtsy where profit may derive from
      obsequious bowing and scraping. Here* crook *means "bend";*
      pregnant Hinges *refers to "ready knee-joints," eager to
      discharge their devotion to "absurd Pomp," fools in positions
      of power.*

70   dear   *precious.*
      Mistress of her Choice   *in a position to decide for herself.*

71   And could . . . Election   *and could make a selection from
      the men she had to choose from.*

156

Villainous, and shows a most pitiful Ambition
in the Fool that uses it. Go make you ready.

Exeunt Players.

Enter Polonius, Guildenstern, and Rosencrans.

—How now, my Lord, will the King hear this
piece of Work?
POLONIUS   And the Queen too, and that presently.   55
HAMLET   Bid the Players make haste. —Will you two
help to hasten them?
ROSENCRANS   Ay my Lord.   *Exeunt they two.*
HAMLET   —What how, Horatio!

Enter Horatio.

HORATIO   Here, sweet Lord, at your Service.   60
HAMLET   Horatio, thou art e'en as just a Man
As e'er my Conversation cop'd withal.
HORATIO   O my dear Lord—
HAMLET   Nay do not think I flatter:
For what Advancement may I hope from thee
That no Revenue hast but thy good Spirits   65
To feed and clothe thee? Why should the Poor
be flatter'd?
No, let the candi'd Tongue lick absurd Pomp,
And crook the pregnant Hinges of the Knee
Where Thrift may follow Fawning. Doost thou
hear:
Since my dear Soul was Mistress of her Choice,   70
And could of Men distinguish her Election,

74 Buffets *blows (as from a boxer).*

76 Blood *emotions, passions.*
co-meddled *mingled. In lines 70–81 Hamlet defines Horatio as a man of exemplary objectivity and self-control.*

78 Stop *fingering for a particular note on a recorder or other musical instrument.*

83 Circumstance *pertinent details.*

86 Comment *noting; consideration, observation.*

87 occulted *hidden, secret.*

88 unkennel *come out of hiding (like a rabbit or fox being driven out of its hole or lair in a hunt).*

90 foul *filthy, besmudged, wicked.*

91 Vulcan's Stithy *the forge of Vulcan, blacksmith of the Gods.*
heedful Note *attentive scrutiny.*

93 after *afterwards.*

94 Censure of his Seeming *This phrase can mean something as neutral as "assessment of his behavior"; but in fact Hamlet appears to have made up his mind already that the King will only be "Seeming" (feigning) if he appears unaffected by the play. The "Purpose" of Hamlet's "Playing" (line 24) will be to obtain grounds for "Censure" (condemnation) of a murderer. He assumes that his stagecraft will disclose the King's statecraft.*

95 steal ought *steal anything; manage to get away with any guilty behavior that a good detective should catch (line 96).*

S' hath seal'd thee for her self; for thou
   hast been
As one in Suff'ring all that suffers nothing,
A Man that Fortune's Buffets and Rewards
Hast ta'en with equal Thanks; and blest are
   those   75
Whose Blood and Judgment are so well co-meddled
That they are not a Pipe for Fortune's Finger
To sound what Stop she please. Give me that
   Man
That is not Passion's Slave, and I will wear him
In my Heart's Core, ay in my Heart of Heart   80
As I do thee. Something too much of this.
There is a Play tonight before the King;
One Scene of it comes near the Circumstance
Which I have told thee of my Father's Death.
I prethee when thou seest that Act a-foot,   85
Ev'n with the very Comment of thy Soul
Observe my Uncle. If his occulted Guilt
Do not it self unkennel in one Speech,
It is a damned Ghost that we have seen,
And my Imaginations are as foul   90
As Vulcan's Stithy. Give him heedful Note,
For I mine Eyes will rivet to his Face,
And after we will both our Judgments join
In Censure of his Seeming.
HORATIO   Well, my Lord,
If he steal ought the whilst this Play is
   playing   95
And scape detecting, I will pay the Theft.

97–98   **be idle**   *resume my antic disposition.*

100–1   **of the Chameleon's Dish**   *fed like a chameleon (thought to be able to draw sustenance from the air).*

101   **Promise-cramm'd**   *Hamlet implies that the promises he has received are so much thin air (heir). He is probably alluding to the King's assurance that Hamlet is the heir apparent to the throne (I.ii.109)—rather than the rightful King even now.*

102   **Capons**   *castrated male chickens, which were fattened up before they were slaughtered and served.*

103–4   **I have . . . mine.**   *I refuse to acknowledge that any of these words have anything to do with me.*

110–11   **I . . . me.**   *The same actor who first spoke these lines as Polonius had probably performed Julius Caesar a few months before* Hamlet *joined* Julius Caesar *in the Globe repertory. Meanwhile the same actor who played Brutus (Richard Burbage) would surely have been playing Hamlet. An Elizabethan audience would thus have enjoyed multiple ironies in an exchange that proves both retrospective and prophetic.*

112   **Brute Part**   *both (a) a brutish, brutal act, and (b) the part of Brutus. Shakespeare probably intends an additional reference to the ancestral Brutus, who feigned an antic disposition (idiocy) of his own in order to outwit and in time defeat the tyrannical Tarquins and found the Roman Republic in 509 B.C. Hamlet may also be alluding to* Brutus *as a name meaning dull and brutish.*

117–18   **Mettle more attractive**   *Hamlet compares Ophelia to a magnetic metal.*

Enter Trumpets and Kettle-drums, King, Queen,
Polonius, Ophelia, Rosencrans, Guildenstern,
and other Lords Attendant, then his Guard
carrying Torches. Danish March. Sound
a Flourish.

HAMLET   They are coming to the Play. I must be
  idle. Get you a place.
KING   How fares our Cousin Hamlet?
HAMLET   Excellent i' faith, of the Chameleon's   100
  Dish: I eat the Air, Promise-cramm'd. You
  cannot feed Capons so.
KING   I have nothing with this Aunswer, Hamlet:
  these Words are not mine.
HAMLET   No, nor mine now, my Lord. —You play'd   105
  once in the University, you say?
POLONIUS   That did I, my Lord, and was accounted
  a good Actor.
HAMLET   What did you enact?
POLONIUS   I did enact Julius Caesar: I was kill'd   110
  i' th' Capitol. Brutus kill'd me.
HAMLET   It was a Brute Part of him to kill so
  Capital a Calf there. —Be the Players ready?
ROSENCRANS   Ay my Lord, they stay upon your
  Patience.   115
QUEEN   Come hether, my dear Hamlet; sit by me.
HAMLET   No, good Mother: here's Mettle more
  attractive.
POLONIUS   —O ho, do you mark that?
HAMLET   Lady, shall I lie in your Lap?   120
OPHELIA   No, my Lord.

161

122   Country Matters   *Hamlet puns on the sound of the first syllable to imply that Ophelia thought him to be referring to "Wom-
en's matters"* (Julius Caesar, *I.i.27*), *female genitalia.*

127   Nothing.   *another common name for "Women's matters,"
based on the Elizabethan jest that a female either has "no
thing" or has one that resembles the figure for nothing (0). In
the next line Hamlet may be playing on* I *and* eye *as figures
for the male and female genitalia.*

128   merry   *mischievously (here erotically) playful.*

131   Jig-maker   *either (a) a composer, or (b) a performer of jigs, the
comic song-and-dance routines that followed a play.*

134   within's two Hours   *within these [last] two hours.*

136–   Nay . . . Sables.   *In that case, let's cast my black mourning
37   apparel to the Devil [traditionally depicted as wearing black],
because I'll now outfit myself in luxurious sable furs [also
dark, but not associated with mourning].*

141   build Churches   *have his name memorialized in the chapels
he has endowed.*

142   not thinking on   *not being thought about (remembered).*
with the Hobby-horse   *along with the Hobby-horse character in the May-games that took place in the country before the
Puritans put a stop to them.*

143   Epitaph   *tombstone memorial. The words Hamlet goes on to
quote are from a ballad mourning the demise of May-game
entertainments.*

146–   makes Show of Protestation   *puts on a display of her devo-
47   tion.*

HAMLET   Do you think I meant Country Matters?

OPHELIA   I think Nothing, my Lord.

HAMLET   That's a fair Thought, to lie between Maids'
Legs.   125

OPHELIA   What is, my Lord?

HAMLET   Nothing.

OPHELIA   You are merry, my Lord.

HAMLET   Who, I?

OPHELIA   Ay, my Lord.   130

HAMLET   O God, your only Jig-maker, what should
a Man do but be merry? For look you how
cheerfully my Mother looks, and my Father
died within's two Hours.

OPHELIA   Nay, 'tis twice two Months, my Lord.   135

HAMLET   So long? Nay then let the Devil wear Black,
for I'll have a Suit of Sables. O Heavens, die
two Months ago, and not forgotten yet: then
there's Hope a Great Man's Memory may out-live
his Life half a Year! But by'r Lady, 'a must   140
build Churches then, or else shall 'a suffer
not thinking on with the Hobby-horse, whose
Epitaph is "For O, for O, for O, the Hobby-
horse is forgot."

The Trumpet sounds. Dumb-show follows.

Enter a King and Queen, the Queen embracing   145
him and he her. She kneels and makes Show of
Protestation unto him. He takes her up and
declines his Head upon her Neck. He lies him
down upon a Bank of Flowers; she, seeing him

163

154   passionate Action   *uncontrolled lamentation.*

155   condole   *mourn, commiserate.*

158   harsh   *The Folio substitutes* loath and unwilling *for this word.*

160   munching Mallico   *mouthing malice (referring to the exaggerated "munching" gestures of the dumb-show actors as they mime speech and enact a deed of malice).* Mallico *probably derives from* malhecho *(Spanish for malefaction, evil deed). Modern editors normally substitute the Folio's* Miching *(usually interpreted to mean "sneaking") for* munching, *the adjective to be found in the Second Quarto text of the play.*

162   Belike   *likely, probably.*
       imports the Argument   *implies the theme (story).*

165   keep   *The Folio reads* keep Counsel *(maintain a secret); that spells out Hamlet's implication.*

167   Show   *display. As Ophelia's reply makes clear, Hamlet refers to a show of flesh, and probably to an overt display of sexual behavior.*

170   Naught   *naughty.*
       mark   *pay attention to. Ophelia's point is that rather than listen to Hamlet's bawdy innuendo, she will focus on the play.*

173   stooping to your Clemency   *bowing to beg your mercy.*

175   the Posy of a Ring   *a motto (usually in verse) engraved inside a ring.* Ring *was another word that frequently referred to a woman's virginity, and Hamlet plays on that sense of "the Posy of a Ring" in line 177. See the note to line 127.*

>asleep, leaves him. Anon comes in an other Man,   150
>takes off his Crown, kisses it, pours Poison
>in the Sleeper's Ears, and leaves him. The
>Queen returns, finds the King dead, and makes
>passionate Action. The Pois'ner with some
>three or four comes in again, seems to condole   155
>with her. The dead Body is carried away. The
>Pois'ner woos the Queen with Gifts; she seems
>harsh awhile, but in the end accepts love.

OPHELIA   What means this, my Lord?
HAMLET   Marry this munching Mallico, it means   160
  Mischief.
OPHELIA   Belike this Show imports the Argument
  of the Play.
HAMLET   We shall know by this Fellow.

Enter Prologue.

The Players cannot keep: they'll tell all.   165
OPHELIA   Will 'a tell us what this Show meant?
HAMLET   Ay, or any Show that you will show him.
  Be not you asham'd to show, he'll not shame
  you to tell you what it means.
OPHELIA   You are Naught, you are Naught! I'll mark   170
  the Play.
PROLOGUE   "For us and for our Tragedy,
        Here stooping to your Clemency,
        We beg your Hearing patiently."
HAMLET   Is this a Prologue, or the Posy of a Ring?   175
OPHELIA   'Tis brief, my Lord.

178   Phoebus' Cart   *the chariot of the Sun God.*

179   Neptune's salt Wash   *the ocean, of which Neptune was the God in Roman mythology.*
Tellus' orbed Ground   *the Earth, of which Tellus was the Roman Goddess.*

180   borrow'd Sheen   *reflected brightness.*

182   Hymen   *the Greek God of Marriage.*

183   Bands   *both (a) wedding bands (rings), and (b) the bonds of matrimony.*

185   doone   *done; here spelled to rhyme with* Moon.

188   distrust you   *fear for your health.*

189   Discomfort   *worry, trouble.*

191   hold Quantity   *weigh equally on the balance scales.*

192   Eith'r . . . Extremity   *either holding no quantity (neither weighing anything) or both holding maximum quantity (weighing as much as possible). The Player Queen's image depicts Fear and Love as two quantities being weighed on a set of balance scales. Her point is that, whether light or heavy, they are of equal weight.*

193   Proof   *experience (which has proven it).*

194   is siz'd   *is in size.*

198   op'rant   *vital, living.*
leave   *begin ceasing.*

200   haply   *both (a) perhaps, and (b) happily.*

HAMLET   As Woman's Love.

Enter the Player King and Queen.

PLAYER KING   "Full thirty times hath Phoebus' Cart
      gone round
   Neptune's salt Wash and Tellus' orbed Ground,
   And thirty dozen Moons with borrow'd Sheen   180
   About the World have times twelve thirties been
   Since Love our Hearts and Hymen did our Hands
   Unite co-mutual in most sacred Bands."
PLAYER QUEEN   "So many Journeys may the Sun
      and Moon
   Make us again count o'er ere Love be doone.   185
   But Woe is me, you are so Sick of late,
   So far from Cheer and from your former State,
   That I distrust you; yet though I distrust,
   Discomfort you, my Lord, it nothing must.
   For Women fear too much, ev'n as they love,   190
   And Women's Fear and Love hold Quantity:
   Eith'r None (in neither Ought) or in Extremity.
   Now what my Love is, Proof hath made you know,
   And as my Love is siz'd, my Fear is so:
   Where Love is great, the littlest Doubts are Fear; 195
   Where little Fear grows great, great Love
      grows there."
PLAYER KING   "Faith I must leave thee, Love, and
      shortly too:
   My op'rant Pow'rs their Functions leave to do,
   And thou shalt live in this fair World behind,
   Honor'd, belov'd; and haply one as kind   200

167

204   None . . . first   *either (a) let none wed a second husband but those who killed their first, or (b) no women wed second husbands but those who killed their first husbands.*

205   Wormwood   *Hamlet refers to an herb whose extract was a bitter-tasting oil. The Nurse says that she applied it to her dug to wean the infant Juliet* (Romeo and Juliet, *I.iii.26, 30*). *Hamlet probably means either (a) "That's so much wormwood!" or (b) "That's the bitter truth!"*

206–7   The Instances . . . Thrift   *the considerations that motivate second marriage are base calculations of profit.*

211   determine   *resolve to bring to pass.*

213   Validity   *strength, health, staying power.*

215   Mellow   *ripe. What the Player King says in lines 212–15 is that Purpose holds firm for about as long as it takes a fruit to ripen and fall to the ground of its own accord.*

218   propose   *propose to do, state as our purpose.*

220–21   The Violence . . . destroy   *Because of the violent passions (irrational impulses) they entail, both Grief and Joy sow the seeds of destruction for any "Enactures" (avowed purposes) they prompt in the very moment when such vows are sworn: because as soon as the passion that gave rise to the vow subsides, the vow subsides with it.*

223   on slender Accident   *on the basis of insupportable chance circumstances.*

224   aye   *ever.*

226   prove   *put to the test.*

For Husband shalt thou—"
PLAYER QUEEN   "O confound the rest:
    Such Love must needs be Treason in my Breast.
    In Second Husband let me be accurst:
    None wed the second but who kill'd the first."
HAMLET   That's Wormwood!   205
PLAYER QUEEN   "The Instances that second Marriage
        move
    Are base Respects of Thrift, but none of Love;
    A second time I kill my Husband dead
    When second Husband kisses me in Bed."
PLAYER KING   "I do believe you think what now you
        speak;   210
    But what we do determine, oft we break.
    Purpose is but the Slave to Memory,
    Of violent Birth, but poor Validity,
    Which now, the Fruit Unripe, sticks on the
        Tree,
    But fall unshaken when they Mellow be.   215
    Most necessary 'tis that we forget
    To pay our selves what to our selves is Debt;
    What to our selves in Passion we propose,
    The Passion ending, doth the Purpose lose.
    The Violence of either, Grief or Joy,   220
    Their own Enactures with themselves destroy.
    Where Joy most revels, Grief doth most lament:
    Grief joys, Joy grieves, on slender Accident.
    This World is not for aye, nor 'tis not strange
    That ev'n our Loves should with our Fortunes
        change.   225
    For 'tis a Question left us yet to prove,

169

229   The Poor . . . Enemies.   *The unworthy man, once he is up in fortune, discovers that his former enemies are now eager to be friends.*

230   hetherto   *hitherto, up to now.*
       doth Love on Fortune tend   *does Love prove to be sub-servient to Fortune.*

231   not needs   *needs none.*

232   Want   *need, poverty.*
       try   *put to test, call upon for help.*

233   Directly . . . Enemy   *immediately turns him into, or proves him to be, an enemy (by applying the "season" of "Want," need, to him and finding him wanting).*

234   orderly   *in an orderly fashion.*

235   Wills and Fates   *desires (motives) and fortunes.*

236   Devices still   *plans always.*

237   their Ends   *what will happen to them under the pressure of time and changing circumstances.*

240   Nor   *neither.*

243   Anchor's . . . Scope   *let my freedom and comfort be limited to that of a religious hermit's fare in his solitude.*

244   Each Opposite   *every obstacle or reversal.*
       blanks   *turns white (by removing blood from the complexion).*

250   fain I would beguile   *gladly would I cheat (by escaping it through sleep.)*

Wheth'r Love lead Fortune or else Fortune Love.
The Great Man down, you mark his Fav'rite
    flies;
The Poor, advaunc'd, makes Friends of Enemies.
And hetherto doth Love on Fortune tend: 230
For who not needs shall never lack a Friend;
And who in Want a Hollow Friend doth try
Directly seasons him his Enemy.
But orderly to end where I begun,
Our Wills and Fates do so contrary run   235
That our Devices still are overthrown.
Our Thoughts are ours, their Ends none of our
    own:
So think thou wilt no Second Husband wed,
But die thy Thoughts when thy First Lord is
    dead."
PLAYER QUEEN   "Nor Earth to me give Food, nor
    Heaven Light;   240
Sport and Repose lock from me Day and Night;
To Desperation turn my Trust and Hope;
And Anchor's Cheer in Prison be my Scope.
Each Opposite that blanks the Face of Joy
Meet what I would have well, and it destroy;   245
Both here and hence pursue me lasting Strife,
If, once a Widow, ev'r I be a Wife."
HAMLET   If she should break it now!
PLAYER KING   " 'Tis deeply sworn, Sweet, leave me
    here a while:
My Spir'ts grow Dull, and fain I would beguile   250
The tedious Day with Sleep."
QUEEN   "Sleep rock thy Brain

171

256   the Argument   *a thematic summary of the action to be dramatized.*

257   Offense   *offending (seditious or blasphemous) material.*

258   in jest   *in sport. Hamlet means "it's only a play," not real life.*

261   tropically   *figuratively. The word derives from the Greek word* trope *(literally, turn or twist), and it refers to any use of language that is other than strictly straightforward.* Tropically *is itself a trope (play or spin) on* trap, *here a device to "catch the Conscience of the King" (II.ii.642).*

264   knavish   *Hamlet probably means "depicting knavery."*

266   Free Souls   *souls free of guilt, with free consciences.*

266–   Let the Galled Jade winch   *let the chafed jade (a worn-out*
67   *horse) wince.*

267   Withers   *the ridges between a horse's shoulder blades.*
        unwrung   *not rubbed sore.*

270–   I could . . . dallying.   *Hamlet compares himself to the*
71   *Chorus who "interprets" (provides running commentary) for a puppet show. Here* dallying *refers to both (a) playful dangling, and (b) erotic foreplay.*

272   keen   *Ophelia probably means (a) sharp-witted, but in line 273 Hamlet takes her to mean (b) sexually aroused (compare the play on "point" in I.v.126).*

275   Still better and worse.   *yet wittier and naughtier.*

276   mistake   *Hamlet means "mis-take" (deceive, abuse), with a reference to the phrase "for better, for worse" in the marriage ceremony.*

And never come Mischance between us Twain."

Exeunt.

HAMLET   Madam, how like you this Play?

QUEEN   The Lady doth protest too much, me thinks.

HAMLET   O but she'll keep her Word. 255

KING   Have you heard the Argument? Is there no
Offense in't?

HAMLET   No, no, they do but jest, poison in jest:
no Offense i' th' World.

KING   What do you call the Play? 260

HAMLET   "The Mousetrap." Marry, tropically: this
Play is the Image of a Murther doone in Vienna.
Gonzago is the Duke's name, his Wife Baptista.
You shall see anon. 'Tis a knavish Piece of
Work, but what of that? Your Majesty, and we 265
that have Free Souls, it touches us not. Let
the Galled Jade winch; our Withers are unwrung.

Enter Lucianus.

This is one Lucianus, Nephew to the King.

OPHELIA   You are as good as a Chorus, my Lord.

HAMLET   I could interpret between you and your 270
Love if I could see the Puppets dallying.

OPHELIA   You are keen, my Lord, you are keen!

HAMLET   It would cost you a Groaning to take off
mine Edge.

OPHELIA   Still better and worse. 275

HAMLET   So you mistake your Husbands. —Begin,
Murtherer, leave thy damnable Faces and begin.
Come, the croaking Raven doth bellow for

173

279   **Revenge** *By introducing the theme of revenge, Hamlet manages a neat variation on both Claudius' crime and the crime depicted in "The Murther of Gonzago" (there too the villain is motivated by lust and ambition rather than by revenge). Meanwhile, by presenting the "Nephew to the King" (line 268) as the murderer, Hamlet sends the King a signal that another King's nephew is brooding over another regicide.*

281   **Consid'rate Season** *the time well considered (chosen prudently). The Folio prints* **Confederate** *(cooperative).*
      else no Creature seeing *otherwise no one else around to see.*

282   **rank** *foul, evil.*
      of *out of, from.*

283   **Hecate's Ban** *the curse (probably with a play on* **bane**, *poison) of the Goddess associated with magical arts. Puck invokes "Triple Hecate" (Cynthia, Diana, and Persephone) in the Epilogue to* **A** Midsummer Night's Dream.
      blasted *blighted, withered.*
      invected *both (a) cursed (from* **invective**, *denunciation), and (b) imported, introduced. The Folio prints* **infected.**

292   **False Fire** *a shot with a blank [empty] shell. This line occurs only in the First Folio.*

299   **watch** *both (a) stay awake, and (b) observe.*

302   **turn Turk with me** *betray me. The Mohammedan Turks were viewed as untrustworthy infidels.*

304   **Fellowship . . . Players** *part ownership in an acting troupe. Hamlet alludes to the plumes ("Feathers") and rosette-adorned shoes worn by the players.*

Revenge.

LUCIANUS "Thoughts black, Hands apt, Drugs fit,
 and Time agreeing: 280
 Consid'rate Season, else no Creature seeing.
 —Thou Mixture rank, of Midnight Weeds
  collected,
 With Hecate's Ban thrice blasted, thrice
  invected,
 Thy nat'ral Magic and dire Property,
 On wholesome Life usurps immediately." 285
      He pours the Poison in his Ears.

HAMLET 'A poisons him i' th' Garden for 's Estate.
 His name's Gonzago. The Story is extant, and
 written in very choice Italian. You shall see
 anon how the Murtherer gets the Love of
 Gonzago's Wife. 290

OPHELIA The King rises.

HAMLET What, frighted with False Fire?

QUEEN How fares my Lord?

POLONIUS Give o'er the Play.

KING Give me some Light. Away! 295

POLONIUS Lights, lights, lights!
      Exeunt all but Hamlet and Horatio.

HAMLET Why let the strooken Deer go weep,
  The Hart ungalled play,
 For some must watch while some must sleep.
  Thus runs the World away. 300
 Would not this, Sir, and a Forest of Feathers,
 if the rest of my Fortunes turn Turk with me,
 with provincial Roses on my raz'd Shoes, get
 me a Fellowship in a Cry of Players?

175

306   Damon   *a poetic shepherd's name here chosen, perhaps, to recall an era before the fall of the "Realm."*

307-8   This . . . himself   *This clause is usually interpreted to mean "this kingdom was stripped away [literally dis-mantled, its mantle stolen] from Jove himself [Hamlet's father]." Another possibility is that* of *means "from" or "by," in which case Hamlet is saying that "Jove himself" (the present King) is the usurping dismantler. In either case, Hamlet now has the "Grounds / More relative" he was seeking.*

309   Pajock   *a pun on (a) peacock, and (b) patchock (base savage).*

310   rim'd   *The word* Ass *would have provided the expected rhyme in line 309; Hamlet's substitution allows him to convey both that notion and the stronger one he imports with* Pajock.

311   I'll . . . Word   *Hamlet believes that the King's reaction has confirmed the truth of the Ghost's testimony. Whether this "trial" has also proven the Ghost to be the spirit of Hamlet's father, however, is another question. In I.iii of* Macbeth Banquo *notes that "oftentimes to win us to our Harm, / The Instruments of Darkness tell us Truths." It is conceivable that an "honest" (truth-telling) ghost may not be "an Honest Ghost" (I.v.135), a benign spirit.*

316   Recorders   *wind instruments with eight air holes.*

318   perdy   *by God (from the French* pardieu*).*

320   voutsafe   *vouchsafe, grant.*

326   distemper'd   *disturbed with a passion (in this case "Choler," anger) beyond tempering or controlling by reason.*

HORATIO Half a Share.

HAMLET   A whole one, I.   305
    For thou doost know, O Damon dear,
      This Realm dismantl'd was
    Of Jove himself, and now reigns here
      A very very Pajock.

HORATIO You might have rim'd.   310

HAMLET O good Horatio, I'll take the Ghost's Word
    for a thousand Pound! Did'st perceive?

HORATIO Very well, my Lord.

HAMLET Upon the Talk of the Poisoning.

HORATIO I did very well note him.   315

HAMLET —Ah ha, come, some Music! Come, the
    Recorders:
      —For if the King like not the Comedy,
      Why then belike he likes it not perdy.
    —Come, some Music!

Enter Rosencrans and Guildenstern.

GUILDENSTERN Good my Lord, voutsafe me a Word   320
    with you.

HAMLET Sir, a whole History.

GUILDENSTERN The King, Sir—

HAMLET Ay Sir, what of him?

GUILDENSTERN Is in his Retirement marvelous   325
    distemp'red.

HAMLET With Drink, Sir?

GUILDENSTERN No, my Lord, with Choler.

HAMLET Your Wisdom should show it self more
    richer to signify this to the Doctor: for for me to   330

331   Purgation   *cure (a treatment to remove disease by bleeding).*
*Hamlet implies that if he purged the King, he would make him
angrier by wrathfully plunging a sword into him.*

333– put . . . Frame   *control what you are saying.*
34

334– stare . . . Affair   *do not act like a wide-eyed madman when
35   I come to you on the King's affairs. Modern editors normally
adopt the Folio's* start, *but* stare *conveys the crazed look that
Guildenstern seems to be associating with Hamlet's "wild and
whirling Words" (I.v.130).*

339   welcome   *Hamlet extends the courtesy due an ambassador.*

342   wholesome Aunswer   *proper (polite) response. In lines
347–48 Hamlet plays on another sense of* wholesome
(healthy, a word that means "whole").

348   diseas'd   *both (a) unhealthy, and (b) ill at ease.*

353   Admiration   *astonishment.*

354   wonderful   *to be wondered at, marveled over.*

358   Closet   *private chamber.*

359– We . . . Mother.   *I would obey her even if she were my
60   Mother ten times over. Alluding to the commandment that
children are to "honor" their mothers (Exodus 20:12), Hamlet implies that he will obey the Queen despite the fact that she
is his Mother, rather than because of it.*

360   Trade   *commerce. This word, combined with Hamlet's use of
the royal plural ("us"), implies that he regards his old schoolmates as nothing more than the King's mercenaries.*

put him to his Purgation would perhaps plunge
him into more Choler.

GUILDENSTERN   Good my Lord, put your Discourse
into some Frame, and stare not so wildly from
my Affair.   335

HAMLET   I am tame, Sir: pronounce.

GUILDENSTERN   The Queen your Mother in most
great Affliction of Spirit hath sent me to you.

HAMLET   You are welcome.

GUILDENSTERN   Nay good my Lord, this Courtesy   340
is not of the right Breed. If it shall please you
to make me a wholesome Aunswer, I will do your
Mother's Commaundment; if not, your Pardon and
my Return shall be the end of my Business.

HAMLET   Sir, I cannot.   345

ROSENCRANS   What, my Lord?

HAMLET   Make you a wholesome Answer: my Wit's
diseas'd. But Sir, such Answer as I can make,
you shall commaund, or rather, as you say, my
Mother. Therefore no more, but to the Matter: 350
my Mother, you say—

ROSENCRANS   Then thus she says: your Behavior
hath strook her into Amazement and Admiration.

HAMLET   O wonderful Son, that can so 'stonish a
Mother! But is there no Sequel at the Heels   355
of this Mother's Admiration? Impart.

ROSENCRANS   She desires to speak with you in her
Closet ere you go to Bed.

HAMLET   We shall obey, were she ten times our
Mother. Have you any further Trade with us?   360

ROSENCRANS   My Lord, you once did love me.

362 **Pickers and Stealers** *hands. Hamlet alludes to the Cate-*
  chism, which exhorts against "picking and stealing."

364 **Distemper** *disturbance.*

364– **You do surely . . . Friend.** *Rosencrans probably means*
66 *that Hamlet fails to avail himself of a source of comfort if he*
  denies himself the chance to unburden himself to a friend. But
  his words could also be interpreted as a threat that Hamlet
  risks incarceration if he does not become more forthcoming.

367 **Advancement** *promotion to my rightful position.*

371 **While the Grass grows** *The proverb concludes with the*
  words "the Steed starves."

372– **O the Recorders** *Hamlet addresses this line to one of the*
73 *players. He has called for them in lines 316 and 319; either*
  they have taken this long to respond, or they have held back
  while Hamlet conversed with Rosencrans and Guildenstern.

373– **To withdraw with you** *to speak privately. As he speaks,*
74 *Hamlet probably draws Guildenstern aside.*

374– **to recover the Wind of me** *to get downwind from me.*
75 *Hamlet compares Guildenstern to a hunter stalking prey.*

375 **Toil** *snare, net.*

376– **if my Duty . . . Unmannerly** *if in my show of duty I*
77 *appear to be too forward, it is only because my love is so great*
  that it sometimes offends as a result of excessive diligence.

384 **Touch** *technique, skill.*

386 **Ventages** *vents, stops.*

HAMLET   And do still, by these Pickers and Stealers.

ROSENCRANS   Good my Lord, what is your Cause of
    Distemper? You do surely bar the Door upon
    your own Liberty if you deny your Griefs to   365
    your Friend.

HAMLET   Sir, I lack Advancement.

ROSENCRANS   How can that be, when you have the
    Voice of the King himself for your Succession
    in Denmark?   370

                Enter the Players with Recorders.

HAMLET   Ay Sir, but "While the Grass grows . . . ."
    The Proverb is something musty. —O the
    Recorders: let me see one. —To withdraw with
    you, why do you go about to recover the Wind
    of me, as if you would drive me into a Toil?   375

GUILDENSTERN   O my Lord, if my Duty be too Bold,
    my Love is too Unmannerly.

HAMLET   I do not well understand that: will you
    play upon this Pipe?

GUILDENSTERN   My Lord, I cannot.   380

HAMLET   I pray you.

GUILDENSTERN   Believe me, I cannot.

HAMLET   I do beseech you.

GUILDENSTERN   I know no Touch of it, my Lord.

HAMLET   It is as easy as Lying. Govern these   385
    Ventages with your Fingers and Thumb;
    give it Breath with your Mouth, and it will
    discourse most eloquent Music. Look you,
    these are the Stops.

391   Utt'rance of Harmony   *harmonious sound. To* utter *is to
        speak out.*

395   the Heart of my Mystery   *my essence, the core of my being.*

396   Compass   *range.*

398   Organ   *instrument (the recorder).*

401–2   fret me   *Hamlet plays on two senses: (a) finger me, as one does
        when playing a stringed instrument with "frets" (bars of wood
        or wire to guide the positioning of the fingers), and (b) irritate
        or vex me. There may also be a third implication: (c) make
        frets (ridges and furrows) in my brows by the way you treat me.*

405   presently   *right away.*

411   It is back'd   *it has a back.*

414   by and by   *shortly.*

415   fool me   *toy with me.*
        top of my Bent   *to the limit of my ability to bear it patiently.*

GUILDENSTERN   But these cannot I commaund to   390
     any Utt'rance of Harmony: I have not the Skill.
HAMLET   Why look you now, how unwoorthy a thing
     you make of me: you would play upon me, you
     would seem to know my Stops, you would pluck
     out the Heart of my Mystery, you would sound   395
     me from my Lowest Note to the Top of my
     Compass; and there is much Music, excellent
     Voice, in this little Organ, yet cannot you
     make it speak. 'Sblood, do you think I am
     easier to be play'd on than a Pipe? Call me   400
     what Instrument you will, though you can fret
     me, you cannot play upon me.

Enter Polonius.

     —God bless you, Sir.
POLONIUS   My Lord, the Queen would speak with
     you, and presently.   405
HAMLET   Do you see yonder Cloud that's almost in
     shape of a Camel?
POLONIUS   By th' Mass and 'tis, like a Camel
     indeed.
HAMLET   Me thinks it is like a Weasel.   410
POLONIUS   It is back'd like a Weasel.
HAMLET   Or like a Whale.
POLONIUS   Very like a Whale.
HAMLET   Then I will come to my Mother by and by.
     They fool me to the top of my Bent. I will   415
     come by and by.
POLONIUS   I will say so.   *Exit.*

419   Witching Time   *when the forces of evil are most potent.*

422   bitter Day   *Hamlet may be referring to Judgment Day. It seems more likely, however, that his immediate subject is daylight, which is now bitter for him because of the situation in which he finds himself.*

423   Soft   *hush. Hamlet summons himself to attention.*

424   thy Nature   *your share of human nature. Hamlet is exhorting himself not to be so caustic with his mother that he forgets that he is her son.*

425   Nero   *Nero executed his mother Agrippina after she poisoned her husband, the Emperor Claudius.*

428   Hypocrites   *liars, deceivers (to each other). Hamlet may be aware that in Greek the word for actor is* hypocrite; *if so, what he is saying is that his Tongue and his Soul should play different roles and try thereby to keep each other separate, the Tongue being cruel, the Soul kind.*

429–   How . . . consent   *however she may be rebuked in my*
30   *words, to give them the seals of my approval without allowing my soul to become a party to the deeds the harsh judgments would seem to call for.*

III.iii   *This scene takes place in the King's chambers of the Castle.*

1   I like him not   *I am not pleased with his behavior.*

2   range   *have free rein.*

3   Commission   *official authorization of responsibilities.*
     dispatch   *prepare in an expeditious fashion.*

5   The terms of our Estate   *my position as King.*

HAMLET "By and by" is easily said. —Leave me,
    Friends.   *Exeunt all but Hamlet.*
  —'Tis now the very Witching Time of Night,
  When Churchyards yawn, and Hell it self
    breathes out   420
  Contagion to this World. Now could I drink hot
    Blood
  And do such Bus'ness as the bitter Day
  Would quake to look on. Soft, now to my Mother.
  —O Heart, lose not thy Nature; let not ever
  The Soul of Nero enter this firm Bosom;   425
  Let me be Cruel, not Unnatural.
  I will speak Daggers to her, but use none;
  My Tongue and Soul in this be Hypocrites,
  How in my Words somever she be shent,
  To give them Seals, never my Soul consent.   *Exit.*   430

Scene 3

Enter King, Rosencrans, and Guildenstern.

KING   I like him not, nor stands it safe with us
  To let his Madness range. Therefore prepare
    you:
  I your Commission will forthwith dispatch,
  And he to England shall along with you.
  The terms of our Estate may not endure   5

7 his Brows *Shakespeare frequently treats threatening brows (here symbolic of a brooding mind) as symbols of imminent danger.*
 provide *make ready.*

8 holy and religious Fear *Guildenstern alludes to the commonplace that the monarch is God's deputy on Earth, and that the good of the commonwealth is dependent on his health and security. This doctrine derives ultimately from Romans 13:1–7.*

11 peculiar *individual.*

13 Noyance *annoyance, mortal danger.*

15 Cesse *cessation, cease.*

16 Gulf *whirlpool.*

17 massy *massive.*

18 Somnet *summit.*

20 mortis'd *notched.*

21 Annexment *appendage.*

22 Attends *accompanies.*
 boist'rous Ruin *tumultuous downfall.*

23 sigh *suffer pain.*

24 Viage *voyage.*

25 Fetters *shackles, to impede the leg movements of a prisoner.*
 Fear *source of danger.*

Hazard so near us as doth hourly grow
Out of his Brows.

GUILDENSTERN   We will our selves provide.
Most holy and religious Fear it is
To keep those many many Bodies safe
That live and feed upon your Majesty.   10

ROSENCRANS   The single and peculiar Life is bound
With all the Strength and Armor of the Mind
To keep it self from Noyance, but much more
That Spir't upon whose Weal depends and rests
The Lives of many. The Cesse of Majesty   15
Dies not alone, but like a Gulf doth draw
What's near it with it. Or it is a massy Wheel
Fix'd on the Somnet of the highest Mount,
To whose huge Spokes ten thousand lesser
     things
Are mortis'd and adjoin'd; which when it falls   20
Each small Annexment, petty Consequence,
Attends the boist'rous Ruin. Never alone
Did the King sigh, but with a gen'ral Groan.

KING   Arm you, I pray you, to this speedy Viage:
For we will Fetters put about this Fear,   25
Which now goes too free-footed.

ROSENCRANS   We will haste us.
                    Exeunt Rosencrans and Guildenstern.

                    Enter Polonius.

POLONIUS   My Lord, he's going to his Mother's
     Closet.
Behind the Arras I'll convey my self

29   the Process   *the proceedings, what transpires.*
         I'll . . . home.   *I guarantee she'll take him to task.*

33   of Vantage   *from a more objective point of view (an advantageous perspective that is not "partial," line 32).*

37   primal eldest Curse   *the curse associated with the original murder, Cain's slaughter of Abel (Genesis 4).*

39   as sharp as Will   *as powerful as all that the human will can summon.*

41   to . . . bound   *committed to two equally pressing tasks.*

42   I stand in Pause   *Claudius' condition recalls that of Pyrrhus in II.ii.509–17). The "Mousetrap" has caught "the Conscience of the King" (II.ii.641), and now the issue is in doubt: will he or won't he repent?*

43   both neglect   *fail to do either.*

46   wash . . . Snow   *Claudius' words recall several Biblical passages, among them Isaiah 1:18 ("Come now, and let us reason together, saith the Lord: though your sins be as scarlet, they shall be as white as snow") and Matthew 27:24 ("When Pilate saw that he could prevail nothing, but that rather a tumult was made, he took water, and washed his hands before the multitude, saying, I am innocent of the blood of this just person").*

49–50   To . . . down   *Claudius echoes the Lord's Prayer: "And forgive us our debts, as we forgive our debtors. And lead us not into temptation, but deliver us from evil" (Matthew 6:12–13).*

54   Effects   *gains, possessions.*

To hear the Process. I'll warr'nt she'll tax
   him home.
And as you said, and wisely was it said,   30
'Tis meet that some more Audience than a
   Mother,
Since Nature makes them partial, should
   o'erhear
The Speech of Vantage. Fare you well, my Liege;
I'll call upon you ere you go to Bed
And tell you what I know.

KING   Thanks, dear my Lord.   35

Exit Polonius.

—O my Offense is rank: it smells to Heav'n.
It hath the primal eldest Curse upon 't,
A Brother's Murther. Pray can I not,
Though Inclination be as sharp as Will:
My stronger Guilt defeats my strong Intent,   40
And, like a Man to double Bus'ness bound,
I stand in Pause where I shall first begin
And both neglect. What if this cursed Hand
Were thicker than it self with Brother's Blood:
Is there not Rain enough in the sweet Heav'ns   45
To wash it white as Snow? Whereto serves Mercy
But to confront the Visage of Offense?
And what's in Prayer but this two-fold Force,
To be forestalled ere we come to fall,
Or pardon being down? Then I'll look up.   50
My Fault is past, but O what form of Prayer
Can serve my Turn? Forgive me my foul Murther?
That cannot be, since I am still possess'd
Of those Effects for which I did the Murther:

189

56 **retain th' Offense** *Unless he surrenders what his sin has gained him, Claudius must retain the guilt itself.*

57 **Currents** *courses (with wordplay on* currencies*).*

58 **gilded Hand** *both (a) gold-covered (because of the wealth and hypocrisy of the offender), and (b) gold-bearing (to bribe Justice).*
   shove by Justice *push Justice aside. This reading is from the Folio; the Second Quarto reads "showe by iustice."*

59–60 **the . . . Law** *the ill-gotten gains themselves are used to bribe the Law to look the other way. Claudius' own situation is an illustration of this principle; the Queen he has won through his crime has brought him a throne and the support of a Council that has "freely gone / With this Affair along" (I.ii.15–16).*

61 **There is no Shuffling** *there no sleight of hand is allowed.*

61–62 **there . . . Nature** *there (before God) the case (legal "Action") is presented in its true character, with no trickery.*

64 **rests** *remains (with wordplay on resting a case).*

65 **can** *can do.*

68 **limed** *trapped, as in a sticky snare of birdlime.*

69 **make Assay** *make an attempt.*

75 **scann'd** *examined more carefully.*

79 **Hire and Sal'ry** *Here the Folio reading seems superior to the Quarto's* base and silly.

81 **broad blown** *in full flower ("flush," filled, with vigor).*

My Crown, mine own Ambition, and my Queen.   55
May one be pardon'd and retain th' Offense?
In the corrupted Currents of this World,
Offense's gilded Hand may shove by Justice,
And oft 'tis seen the Wicked Prize it self
Buys out the Law. But 'tis not so Above: 60
There is no Shuffling; there the Action lies
In his true Nature, and we our selves compell'd,
Ev'n to the Teeth and Forehead of our Faults,
To give in Evidence. What then? What rests?
Try what Repentance can. What can it not?   65
Yet what can it when one cannot repent?
O wretched State, O Bosom black as Death!
O limed Soul, that, struggling to be Free,
Art more Engag'd! —Help, Angels, make Assay!
—Bow, stubborn Knees. —And Heart with
   Strings of Steel,   70
Be soft as Sinews of the new-born Babe.
All may be well.

Enter Hamlet.

HAMLET   Now might I do it pat, now 'a is a-praying;
And now I'll do 't, and so 'a goes to Heaven,
And so am I reveng'd. That would be scann'd: 75
A Villain kills my Father, and for that
I his sole Son do this same Villain send
To Heaven.
Why, this is Hire and Sal'ry, not Revenge.
'A took my Father grossly, full of Bread,   80
With all his Crimes broad blown, as flush as May,

82   Audit   *reckoning, account (when he comes to the Last Judgment).*

83   But . . . Thought   *but given the perspective we have, based on what we know and can infer.*

85   in the Purging of his Soul   *while he is purifying his soul of its guilt. Hamlet is now referring to Claudius.*

86   fit . . . Passage   *in proper spiritual condition for his departure to the next world (by contrast with his victim, who was caught unawares, out of season, bearing his sins on his soul unconfessed and unabsolved). As we learn in lines 97–98, Claudius only appears to be in a state of grace.*

88   know . . . Hent   *wait till you can seize on a more horrible occasion.* Hent *combines a verb meaning "seize" and a noun meaning "time" or "opportunity."*

89   Rage   *This noun could refer to any surrender to passion, including lust; here, however, it seems most likely to mean an angry frenzy.*

90   incestious   *incestuous.*

92   Relish   *trace. But in view of the other culinary metaphors in the speech ("full of Bread," "season'd"), the word probably means "taste" as well. Compare III.i.115–17.*

95   stays   *awaits me.*

96   Physic   *medication. Hamlet refers to Claudius' praying.*

III.iv   *This scene takes place in the Queen's Closet (private chamber).*

1   lay home to him   *rebuke him as only a mother can do.*

And how his Audit stands who knows save Heaven?
But in our Circumstance and Course of Thought,
'Tis Heavy with him: and am I then reveng'd
To take him in the Purging of his Soul,   85
When he is fit and season'd for his Passage?
No.
—Up, Sword, and know thou a more horrid Hent:
When he is Drunk, Asleep, or in his Rage,
Or in th' incestious Pleasure of his Bed,   90
At Game a-swearing, or about some Act
That has no Relish of Salvation in't,
Then trip him, that his Heels may kick at
   Heav'n,
And that his Soul may be as damn'd and black
As Hell, whereto it goes. —My Mother stays.   95
—This Physic but prolongs thy sickly Days.   *Exit.*
KING   My Words fly up, my Thoughts remain below;
   Words without Thoughts never to Heaven go.   *Exit.*

Scene 4

Enter Gertrard and Polonius.

POLONIUS 'A will come straight. Look you lay home
   to him:
   Tell him his Pranks have been too broad to bear
   with,

3   your Grace   *both (a) an honorific for the Queen, and (b) a reference to her gracious (loving) intercessions for her wayward son.*

4   Heat   *Polonius alludes to the smoldering wrath of the King.*
         silence me   *both (a) cease speaking, and (b) seclude myself silently. Polonius' phrasing will prove ironically prophetic.*

5   round   *forthright.*
         wait you   *serve you, do as you bid me to do. Most editors adopt the Folio's* warrant you.
         fear me not   *don't worry.*

10   Idle   *both (a) willfully irrelevant (evading the issue), and (b) irreverent, insolent.*

13   forgot me   *forgotten who I am (and your relationship to me).*
         Rood   *Cross.*

14   your . . . Wife   *Hamlet's point is that the Queen is guilty of incest.*

16   I'll . . . speak   *I'll turn you over to those who can command more respect from you.*

18   Glass   *mirror.*

21   how   *The word means "ho" the first two times it is used in this line.*
         a Rat   *Hamlet alludes not only to the loathsomeness and sneakiness of this creature, but also to its tendency to make sounds that eventually attract attention and thereby get it killed.*

And that your Grace hath screen'd and stood
  between
Much Heat and him. I'll silence me ev'n here.
Pray you be round.
QUEEN   I'll wait you, fear me not.   5
Withdraw, I hear him coming.

Enter Hamlet.

HAMLET   Now Mother, what's the matter?
QUEEN   Hamlet, thou hast thy Father much offended.
HAMLET   Mother, you have my Father much offended.
QUEEN   Come, come, you answer with an Idle Tongue.   10
HAMLET   Go, go, you question with a Wicked Tongue.
QUEEN   Why how now, Hamlet?
HAMLET   What's the matter now?
QUEEN   Have you forgot me?
HAMLET   No, by th' Rood, not so:
You are the Queen, your Husband's Brother's
  Wife,
And, would it were not so, you are my Mother.   15
QUEEN   Nay, then I'll set those to you that can
  speak.
HAMLET   Come, come, and sit you down. You shall
  not budge;
You go not till I set you up a Glass
Where you may see the Inmost Part of you.
QUEEN   What wilt thou do? Wilt thou murther me?   20
Help, how!
POLONIUS   What how, help!
HAMLET   How now, a Rat?

22   for a Ducat   *probably either (a) I'll wager a ducat (a gold coin), or (b) for the price of a ducat.*

30   I . . . Better   *What Hamlet means is "I mistook you for the King."*

31   Thou . . . Danger.   *you discover that to be too much of a busybody is somewhat dangerous.*

32   Leave   *give over, quit. Hamlet speaks to Gertrard.*

34   Penetrable Stuff   *material that is not too hard to be wrung or pierced.*

35   damned Custom   *damnable habit (the vicious practices it has become accustomed to).*
       braz'd it   *plated it with brass or turned it to solid brass.*

36   Proof . . . Sense   *completely shielded against normal human feelings and common sense.*

39   blurs   *obscures.*

40   Calls Virtue Hypocrite   *turns Virtue into a hypocrite (by pretending to be virtuous).*

42   Blister   *Hamlet refers to the blister branded on the foreheads of whores to subject them to public shame.*

43   Dicer's Oaths   *the promises of habitual gamblers, proverbially unreliable. Compare I.iii.125–30.*

Hamlet draws his Sword and stabs through the Arras.
Dead for a Ducat, dead!
POLONIUS   O I am slain!
QUEEN   —O me, what hast thou done?
HAMLET   Nay I know not:
    Is it the King?
QUEEN   O what a rash and bloody Deed is this!   25
HAMLET   A bloody Deed: almost as bad, good Mother,
    As kill a King and marry with his Brother.
QUEEN   As kill a King?
HAMLET   Ay Lady, 'twas my Word.
            Hamlet opens the Arras and discovers Polonius.
    —Thou wretched, rash, intruding Fool, farewell!
    I took thee for thy Better: take thy Fortune.   30
    Thou find'st to be too Busy is some Danger.
    —Leave wringing of your Hands; peace, sit you
        down,
    And let me wring your Heart. For so I shall
    If it be made of Penetrable Stuff:
    If damned Custom have not braz'd it so   35
    That it be Proof and Bulwark against Sense.
QUEEN   What have I done that thou dar'st wag thy
        Tongue
    In Noise so rude against me?
HAMLET   Such an Act
    That blurs the Grace and Blush of Modesty,
    Calls Virtue Hypocrite, takes off the Rose   40
    From the fair Forehead of an inn'cent Love,
    And sets a Blister there; makes Marriage Vows
    As false as Dicer's Oaths; O such a Deed

197

44 Contraction *contract-making, the swearing of solemn oaths.*

45–46 sweet . . . Words *turns the beauty and order of religious observances into a uncontrolled jumble of profane ecstasies.*

47 this Solidity and compound Mass *the heart described in lines 33–36.*

48 as . . . Doom *in anticipation of Judgment Day.*

50 That roars . . . Index. *Here* Index *probably refers to a prefatory summary of the contents of a book. If this line belongs to Hamlet (the Folio assigns it to the Queen), it is probably meant to illustrate the "Rhapsody of Words" he describes in line 46. His point would seem to be either (a) that Heaven's present "Visage" is only an index of the "Doom" to follow, or (b) that a description of the Queen's "Act" is like a thundering table of contents, fortelling the fearful judgment to be detailed in the volume itself.*

52 counterfeit Presentment *artificial rendering. Hamlet is probably holding up two portraits side by side.*

56 Station *bearing.*

57 a Heave *an up-swelling of the earth to "kiss" the alighting Mercury. Most editors adopt the Folio's* Heaven-kissing Hill *in this line.*

62 mildew'd Ear *blighted ("blasting") ear of grain.*

65 batten on this Moor *gorge on this marshland (with a pun on Blackamoor).*

67 Heyday *prime vigor (literally, "high day").*

As from the Body of Contraction plucks
The very Soul, and sweet Religion makes   45
A Rhapsody of Words. Heav'n's Face dooes glow
O'er this Solidity and compound Mass
With heated Visage, as against the Doom,
Is Thought-sick at the Act—
QUEEN   Ay me, what Act?
HAMLET   That roars so loud, and thunders in the
     Index.   50
Look here upon this Picture, and on this:
The counterfeit Presentment of two Brothers.
See what a Grace was seated on this Brow:
Hyperion's Curls, the Front of Jove himself,
An Eye like Mars, to threaten and command,   55
A Station like the Herald Mercury
New lighted on a Heave, a kissing Hill;
A Combination and a Form indeed
Where ev'ry God did seem to set his Seal
To give the World assurance of a Man.   60
This was your Husband. Look you now what
     follows:
Here is your Husband, like a mildew'd Ear,
Blasting his wholesome Brother. Have you Eyes?
Could you on this fair Mountain leave to feed
And batten on this Moor? Ha, have you Eyes?   65
You cannot call it Love, for at your Age
The Heyday in the Blood is Tame; it's Humble,
And waits upon the Judgment; and what Judgment
Would step from this to this? Sense sure you
     have,

70   Sense   *In this passage the word means (a) the senses by which
       one perceives, (b) common sense, and (c) sensual appetite.*

71   apoplex'd   *paralyzed, rendered inoperable.*

72   Ecstasy   *a seizure in which one is beside oneself or enslaved
       (thrall'd) to another.*

74   Difference   *departure from normal behavior.*

75   cozen'd   *deceived, cheated.*
       Hoodman Blind   *blindman's buff.*

77   sans   *without (from the French).*

78–79 Or . . . mope   *or even a sickly portion of one properly func-
       tioning sense would have prevented such a dazed state.*

81   mutine   *lead a mutiny (rebellion).*
       in a Matron's Bones   *in the body of a respectable married
       woman.*

84   compulsive Ardure   *irresistible ardor (desire).*

86   Reason panders Will   *Reason (supposedly predominant in
       frosty-haired elders) serves as the go-between for, rather than
       the defense against, lust-driven Will.*

88   grieved   *both (a) grievous, and (b) lamentable. The Folio
       reads* grained.

89   Tinct   *color, taint.*

90   enseamed   *seamy, greasy. Compare I.v.49–55.*

95   Kyth   *kith, kin (kind of man). The Folio prints* tithe.

Else could you not have Motion; but sure that
  Sense   70
Is apoplex'd. For Madness would not err,
Nor Sense to Ecstasy was ne'er so thrall'd,
But it reserv'd some quantity of Choice
To serve in such a Difference. What Devil was 't
That thus hath cozen'd you at Hoodman Blind?   75
Eyes without Feeling, Feeling without Sight,
Ears without Hands or Eyes, Smelling sans all,
Or but a sickly Part of one true Sense,
Could not so mope. O Shame, where is thy Blush?
                  —Rebellious Hell,   80
If thou canst mutine in a Matron's Bones,
To flaming Youth let Virtue be as Wax
And melt in her own Fire! Proclaim no Shame
When the compulsive Ardure gives the Charge,
Since Frost it self as actively doth burn,   85
And Reason panders Will.
QUEEN   O Hamlet, speak no more:
Thou turn'st my very Eyes into my Soul,
And there I see such black and grieved Spots
As will leave there their Tinct.
HAMLET   Nay but to live
In the rank Sweat of an enseamed Bed   90
Stew'd in Corruption, honeying and making love
Over the nasty Sty!
QUEEN   O speak to me no more:
These Words like Daggers enter in my Ears.
No more, sweet Hamlet.
HAMLET   A Murth'rer and a Villain,
A Slave that is not twenti'th part the Kyth   95

96 precedent *both (a) previous, and (b) of a higher order of precedence. Here pronounced "pre-cée-dent."*
    a Vice of Kings *a vice-ridden parody of a true king (like the buffoonish Vice character in late-medieval morality plays).*

97 A Cutpurse . . . Rule *a pickpocket [who has stolen] both the empire (Denmark and its tributaries) and its throne.*

98 Diadem *crown.*

100 Of Shreds and Patches *Hamlet is probably thinking once more of the Vice figure and his clown-like particolored costume. His point is that by comparison with the paragon of divinity he supplanted (the epitome of human perfection), Claudius is a beggarly thief rather than a man of King-like stature.*

102 Heav'nly Guards *angels.*

106 important *urgent (as in "importunate").*

108 whet *sharpen, as one does with a "blunted" (dull) knife.*

109 Amazement *a maze-like bewilderment.*

111 Conceit *imagination (or, more literally, imaginary conceptions).*

114 bend your Eye on Vacancy *focus your eye on nothingness.*

115 incorp'ral *bodiless.*

116 your Spirits *The Queen refers to the fluids that were thought to permeate the blood and animate the brain.*

117 in th' Alarm *when the alarm (call to arms for battle) is sounded.*

Of your precedent Lord; a Vice of Kings,
A Cutpurse of the Empire and the Rule,
That from a Shelf the precious Diadem stole
And put it in his Pocket—

QUEEN   No more!

HAMLET   A King
Of Shreds and Patches—   100

Enter Ghost.

—Save me, and hover o'er me with your Wings,
You Heav'nly Guards! —What would your Gracious
    Figure?

QUEEN   —Alas, he's Mad!

HAMLET   —Do you not come your tardy Son to chide,
That, laps'd in Time and Passion, lets go by   105
Th' important Acting of your dread Command?
O say.

GHOST   Do not forget: this Visitation
Is but to whet thy almost blunted Purpose.
But look, Amazement on thy Mother sits:
O step between her and her fighting Soul.   110
Conceit in weakest Bodies strongest works:
Speak to her, Hamlet.

HAMLET   —How is it with you, Lady?

QUEEN   Alas, how is't with you,
That you do bend your Eye on Vacancy,
And with th' incorp'ral Air do hold Discourse?   115
Foorth at your Eyes your Spirits wildly peep,
And, as the sleeping Soldiers in th' Alarm,

118   like Life in Excrements   *as if there were life in outgrowths of the body such as hair and nails.*

119   an   *on.*

120   Distemper   *imbalanced disposition. The Queen assumes that Hamlet is experiencing a fit of madness.*

121   Patience   *self-control, to temper (regulate) the heat of passion.*

123   His Form and Cause conjoin'd   *considering the combined power of his form and the cause that brings him here.*

124   capable   *capable of response. In Luke 19:40 Jesus says "I tell you that, if these should hold their peace, the stones would immediately cry out."*

126   My stern Effects   *my fierce impulses.*

127   Will want true Color   *will lack the resolve that bloodthirsty passion would give them.*
       Tears perchance for Blood   *shedding tears, perhaps, instead of blood.*

132   Habit   *habitual apparel.*

135–   This . . . in.   *This conjuring up of imaginary bodies is some-*
36   *thing madness is very skillful in prompting.*

137   temp'rately   *moderately, not agitated with excitement.*

140   reword   *recount. Hamlet's point is that, if tested, he would be able to describe what he has seen in a coherent fashion that would prove that it was not the "Coinage" (hallucination) of a disturbed brain.*

Your bedded Hair, like Life in Excrements,
Start up and stand an end. O gentle Son,
Upon the Heat and Flame of thy Distemper   120
Sprinkle cool Patience. Whereon do you look?
HAMLET   On him, on him. Look you how Pale he
    glares:
His Form and Cause conjoin'd, preaching to
    Stones
Would make them capable! —Do not look upon me
Lest with this piteous Action you convert   125
My stern Effects: then what I have to do
Will want true Color, Tears perchance for
    Blood.
QUEEN   To whom do you speak this?
HAMLET   Do you see Nothing there?
QUEEN   Nothing at all, yet all that is I see.
HAMLET   Nor did you Nothing hear?
QUEEN   No, Nothing but our Selves.   130
HAMLET   Why look you there: look how it steals away,
My Father in his Habit as he liv'd!
Look where he goes ev'n now out at the Portal!
                                        Exit Ghost.
QUEEN   This is the very Coinage of your Brain:
This bodiless Creation Ecstasy   135
Is very cunning in.
HAMLET   Ecstasy?
My Pulse as yours doth temp'rately keep Time,
And makes as healthful Music. It is not Madness
That I have utt'red: bring me to the Test,
And I the Matter will reword, which Madness   140

140–
41   which Madness / Would gambol from *which madness*
       would make impossible, gamboling (leaping) away from the
       topic in an incoherent manner.

142   Lay not . . . Soul *do not deceive your soul by soothing it*
       with an ointment that merely masks its disease in a deceptively
       flattering way without treating it.

144   skin and film *cover over with a thin film of skin.*
       Ulc'rous *ulcerous, cancerous.*

145   mining *undermining.*

148   Compost *organic fertilizer.*

149   ranker *more prolific.*

150   Fatness *bloatedness. Compare I.v.31–33.*
       Pursy *pursed up, flabby, diseased.*

152   curb *bow, curtsy.*
       leave *permission.*

153   cleft *split.*

155   leave *remain, probably with wordplay on* live *(the word to be*
       found in the Folio and in most modern editions).

157   Assume *act as if you have, as one assumes (puts on) a gar-*
       ment. Compare I.ii.238, II.ii.635–37.

159   Of Habits Dev'l *who acts like a Devil in devouring our*
       "Sense" (awareness) of the bad things we do habitually.
       Habits *are garments; compare I.iii.70.*

166   [shame] *The Quarto text appears to be missing a word;*
       shame *is used elsewhere in similar contexts and is thus sup-*
       plied here. Compare 1 Henry IV, *III.i.54–58.*

Would gambol from. Mother, for love of Grace,
Lay not that flatt'ring Unction to your Soul,
That not your Trespass but my Madness speaks:
It will but skin and film the Ulc'rous Place
Whiles rank Corruption, mining all within,   145
Infects unseen. Confess your self to Heav'n,
Repent what's past, avoid what is to come,
And do not spread the Compost on the Weeds
To make them ranker. Forgive me this my Virtue,
For in the Fatness of these Pursy Times   150
Virtue it self of Vice must pardon beg,
Yea curb and woo for leave to do him good.
QUEEN   O Hamlet, thou hast cleft my Heart in twain.
HAMLET   O throw away the Worser Part of it,
And leave the Purer with the other half.   155
Good night, but go not to my Uncle's Bed.
Assume a Virtue if you have it not:
That monster Custom, who all Sense doth eat,
Of Habits Dev'l, is Angel yet in this,
That to the Use of Actions fair and good   160
He likewise gives a Frock or Livery
That aptly is put on. Refrain tonight,
And that shall lend a kind of Easiness
To the next Abstinence, the next more easy.
For Use almost can change the Stamp of Nature,   165
And either [shame] the Devil or throw him out
With wondrous Potency. Once more good night,
And when you are desirous to be blest,
I'll Blessing beg of you. For this same Lord
I do repent; but Heav'n hath pleas'd it so   170
To punish me with this, and this with me,

207

172   their Scourge and Minister   *their [Heaven's] agent.*
        Scourge *was often used to refer to an agent of Heaven who*
        was himself evil, and who was cast off to damnation after
        punishing other evildoers. But Hamlet appears to be using the
        term as a synonym for Minister *(a worthy instrument of*
        Divine justice). Strictly speaking, the same person could not be
        both a Scourge and a Minister; but Hamlet does not tend to
        think in rigorous theological terms. In II.ii.620, for example,
        he says he is "Prompted to my Revenge by Heav'n and Hell."
        As it turns out, the consequences of his inadvertent slaying do
        "punish" Hamlet as well as Polonius (line 171).

173   answer well   *Hamlet probably means "give a good answer*
        for"; but he could also mean "answer [pay for] thoroughly."

176   behind   *still to come.*

178–   Not . . . Craft.   *Hamlet tells his Mother neither to submit to*
85   *the King's lust, nor to let him know that Hamlet is sane.*

181   reechy   *reeky, filthy.*

183   rovel   *ravel, unwind.*

187   Paddock   *frog.*
        Gib   *tomcat.*

189–   No . . . down.   *No, despite the claims of "Sense" (desire)*
93   *and "Secrecy" (a wife's obligation to share her secrets with her*
        husband, especially when he is the King), if you open the
        basket and let the birds (my secret) out, the conclusion of your
        story will be like that of the ape who fell off the roof and broke
        his neck by creeping into a basket in a foolish effort to imitate
        the birds that flew out of it.

That I must be their Scourge and Minister.
I will bestow him and will answer well
The Death I gave him. So again good night.
I must be cruel only to be kind: 175
This Bad begins, and Worse remains behind.
One Word more, good Lady.
QUEEN   What shall I do?
HAMLET   Not this, by no means that I bid you do:
Let the bloat King tempt you again to Bed,
Pinch wanton on your Cheek, call you his Mouse, 180
And let him for a pair of reechy Kisses,
Or paddling in your Neck with his damn'd
    Fingers,
Make you to rovel all this Matter out,
That I essentially am not in Madness
But Mad in Craft. 'Twere good you let him
    know, 185
For who that's but a Queen, fair, sober, wise,
Would from a Paddock, from a Bat, a Gib,
Such dear Concernings hide? Who would do so?
No, in despite of Sense and Secrecy,
Unpeg the Basket on the House's Top, 190
Let the Birds fly, and, like the famous Ape,
To try Conclusions, in the Basket creep
And break your own Neck down.
QUEEN   Be thou assur'd,
If Words be made of Breath, and Breath of Life,
I have no Life to breathe what thou hast said 195
To me.
HAMLET   I must to England, you know that.
QUEEN   Alack, I had forgot: 'tis so concluded on.

198   seal'd   *written and certified with the King's official seal in wax.*

199   Adders fang'd   *poisonous snakes.*

200   Mandate   *commission, the King's commands.*

201   marshal   *conduct. One of the duties of the Marshal at formal occasions was to see that participants were properly bestowed (seated).*

        to Knavery   *Hamlet probably means "to some kind of knavish plot against me." But he may also mean the knavish plot he will devise to counter them. He assumes that Rosencrans and Guildenstern are themselves privy to the King's "Mandate." The play provides no clear evidence that they are.*

        Let it work   *let their plans go forward.*

202   Enginer   *engineer (agent) of the plot.*

203   Hoist with his own Petar   *blown up by his own explosive. A Petar or petard was a kind of bomb.*

        an't shall go hard   *and it will be difficult.*

204   delve   *dig.*

        Mines   *tunnels (used to undermine fortifications, among other things by the planting of bombs).*

206   in one Line   *straight on, in head-to-head confrontation.*

209   good night indeed   *Hamlet means that he is now ready to say goodnight in earnest.*

210   Still   *Hamlet alludes to the idea that Counselors were expected to be solemn and attentive.*

        Secret   *confidential (able to keep secrets).*

        Grave   *sober, wise. One of Hamlet's implications is that the only place where Polonius could be truly grave is in the grave.*

HAMLET   There's Letters seal'd, and my two
     Schoolfellows,
     Whom I will trust as I will Adders fang'd,
     They bear the Mandate; they must sweep my Way   200
     And marshal me to Knavery. Let it work,
     For 'tis the Sport to have the Enginer
     Hoist with his own Petar; an't shall go hard
     But I will delve one Yard below their Mines
     And blow them at the Moon. O 'tis most sweet   205
     When in one Line two Crafts directly meet.
     This Man shall set me packing:
     I'll lug the Guts into the neighbor Room.
     Mother, good night indeed. This Counselor
     Is now most Still, most Secret, and most Grave,   210
     Who was in Life a most foolish prating Knave.
     —Come Sir, to draw toward an End with you.
     —Good night, Mother.
                    Exit Hamlet tugging in Polonius.

IV.i   *This scene takes place immediately after the just-concluded Closet Scene. Whether the Queen simply remains on stage at the end of the preceding scene, or exits and re-enters as the Second Quarto entrance direction would seem to imply, is an open question.*

1   profound Heaves   *deep heaving motions.*

7   Mad   *The Queen's first words about the preceding interview indicate that she has indeed shifted her loyalty to Hamlet.*

8   lawless Fit   *uncontrolled seizure.*

11   brainish Apprehension   *misjudgment, based on a figment of his imagination. The Queen implies that Hamlet thought Polonius really was a rat.*

Act Four

Scene 1

Enter the King and Queen, with Rosencrans and Guildenstern.

KING   There's Matter in these Sighs; these profound
    Heaves
    You must translate; 'tis fit we understand them.
    Where is your Son?
QUEEN   —Bestow this place on us a little while.
                    Exeunt all but the King and Queen.
    —Ah mine own Lord, what have I seen tonight!   5
KING   What, Gertrard, how dooes Hamlet?
QUEEN   Mad as the Sea and Wind when both contend
    Which is the mightier! In his lawless Fit,
    Behind the Arras hearing something stir,
    Whips out his Rapier, cries "A Rat, a Rat!"   10
    And in this brainish Apprehension kills
    The unseen good Old Man.

16   answer'd   *explained, responded to.*

17   Providence   *"providing," management of the royal household.*

18   short   *on a short leash.*
      out of haunt   *sequestered from society.*

20   fit   *suitable, appropriate.*

22   divulging   *being disclosed. Hamlet has used a similar disease image in III.iv.144–46.*

23   Pith   *vital core.*

25   Ore   *either (a) a piece of pure metal (usually referring to gold), or (b) a vein of a particular metal in a mine.*

26   Mineral   *either (a) a piece of unrefined extract from a mine (ore in the more usual modern sense), or (b) a mine itself.*

27   pure   *both (a) unmixed with baser metals (in this case any touches of sanity), and (b) pure in heart, innocent.*
      'A weeps for what is done.   *Again, the Queen appears to be attempting to "screen" Hamlet (III.iv.3).*

29   The Sun . . . touch   *as soon as morning comes.*

32   count'nance and excuse   *tolerate and explain satisfactorily.*

33   go . . . Aid   *go assemble some others to help you.*

35   dregg'd   *dragged.*

36   speak fair   *speak gently (not reprovingly or threateningly).*

KING   O heavy Deed!
    It had been so with us had we been there.
    His Liberty is full of Threats to all:
    To you your self, to us, to ev'ry one.   15
    Alas, how shall this bloody Deed be answer'd?
    It will be laid to us, whose Providence
    Should have kept short, restrain'd, and out of
        haunt
    This mad Young Man; but so much was our Love
    We would not understand what was most fit,   20
    But like the Owner of a foul Disease,
    To keep it from divulging, let it feed
    Ev'n on the Pith of Life. Where is he gone?
QUEEN   To draw apart the Body he hath kill'd,
    O'er whom his very Madness, like some Ore   25
    Among a Mineral of Metals Base,
    Shows it self pure. 'A weeps for what is done.
KING   O Gertrard, come away:
    The Sun no sooner shall the Mountains touch
    But we will ship him hence, and this vile Deed   30
    We must with all our Majesty and Skill
    Both count'nance and excuse. —Ho Guildenstern!

            Enter Rosencrans and Guildenstern.

    —Friends both, go join you with some further Aid:
    Hamlet in Madness hath Polonius slain,
    And from his Mother's Closet hath he dregg'd him.   35
    Go seek him out: speak fair, and bring the Body
    Into the Chapel. I pray you haste in this.
                    Exeunt Rosencrans and Guildenstern.

41   Whose Whisper *rumors of which ("what's untimely doone"). Modern editors tend to assume that a phrase is missing from the preceding line. Perhaps, but it seems equally likely that Shakespeare deliberately inserted a short (metrically "untimely") line at this point to signal a brief pause after "doone" for dramatic emphasis. The word* doone *provides a near rhyme for* do *in line 39 (a word it balances rhetorically).*
        o'er the World's Diameter *Claudius depicts the world as flat, and he means "from one extreme to the other."*

42   Blank *target; literally, a white spot in the target one aims at when firing at blank (level) range, as opposed to the arched trajectory required for shooting at longer ranges.*

44   Woundless Air *unwoundable air. Claudius hopes that the "Whisper" (the news of Polonius' death) will find a target other than the King.*

IV.ii   *This scene shifts to another part of the Castle, probably one near the "neighbor Room" (III.iv.208) adjacent to the Queen's Closet.*

6   Compound it *mix it. Modern editors normally follow the Folio here and print* Compounded. *But since Hamlet hasn't buried the corpse, it seems quite possible that he answers Rosencrans' question with a command for Rosencrans to take care of the burial. Hamlet remains "antic" in his behavior, and we should not expect any of his replies to adhere to conventional logic. An alternative possibility here is that* Compound *means "compounded."*

6–7   Dust whereto 'tis Kin *Hamlet alludes to Genesis 3:19, "dust thou art, and unto dust shalt thou return."*

—Come Gertrard, we'll call up our wisest
  Friends,
And let them know both what we mean to do
And what's untimely doone,   40
Whose Whisper o'er the World's Diameter,
As level as the Cannon to his Blank
Transports his poison'd Shot, may miss our Name
And hit the Woundless Air. O come away:
My Soul is full of Discord and Dismay.   *Exeunt.*   45

Scene 2

Enter Hamlet.

HAMLET Safely stow'd.
GENTLEMEN *within* Hamlet, Lord Hamlet!
HAMLET But soft, what Noise? Who calls on Hamlet?

Enter Rosencrans and Guildenstern.

  O here they come.
ROSENCRANS What have you doone, my Lord,
  with the dead Body?   5
HAMLET Compound it with the Dust whereto 'tis
  Kin.

10   keep your Counsel *act in accordance with your counsel (advice or judgment), with wordplay on the more usual "keep your secrets."*

11   demaunded of a Spunge *ordered around by a sponge.*

12   Replication *reply. But Hamlet is probably playing on other senses of* replication, *among them (a) fold or bend (to squeeze), and (b) echo or reverberate (as in a musical tone repeated an octave higher or lower). Murellus uses the word to mean "echo" in I.i.52 of* Julius Caesar.

16   Countenaunce *favor.*

20   glean'd *picked up, as with leftovers from a harvested field. The King has used this verb in II.ii.16.*

24   sleeps *is to no avail (because it doesn't awaken the hearing).*

28–29 The Body . . . Body *Hamlet alludes to the doctrine of "the King's two bodies," the idea that a monarch has both a normal, mortal body and a mystical, spiritual body as the epitome of his realm. As usual, Hamlet's meanings are equivocal and multiple. One implication is that the body of Claudius is now attached to the Kingship, but that the true King (either the elder Hamlet or the younger Hamlet) is not identical with the Body (Claudius) who is now pretending to be King. In that sense, this "King" is "a thing of Nothing" (lines 30, 32), a Body that is not the thing it is taken to be. The obscene innuendo in "Nothing" anticipates Hamlet's calling Claudius "Mother" in IV.iii.49. (See the note to III.ii.127.)*

31–32 Hide . . . after. *a hunting call appropriate for the "Fox" (Claudius) whom Hamlet is warning to hide.*

ROSENCRANS   Tell us where 'tis, that we may take
    it thence
And bear it to the Chapel.
HAMLET   Do not believe it.
ROSENCRANS   Believe what?
HAMLET   That I can keep your Counsel and not mine   10
    own. Besides, to be demaunded of a Spunge, what
    Replication should be made by the Son of a
    King?
ROSENCRANS   Take you me for a Spunge, my Lord?
HAMLET   Ay Sir, that soaks up the King's   15
    Countenaunce, his Rewards, his Authorities. But
    such Officers do the King best Service in the
    end: he keeps them like an Apple in the Corner
    of his Jaw, first mouth'd to be last swallow'd.
    When he needs what you have glean'd, it is but   20
    squeezing you, and, Spunge, you shall be dry
    again.
ROSENCRANS   I understand you not, my Lord.
HAMLET   I am glad of it: a Knavish Speech sleeps
    in a Foolish Ear.   25
ROSENCRANS   My Lord, you must tell us where the
    Body is, and go with us to the King.
HAMLET   The Body is with the King, but the King
    is not with the Body. The King is a thing—
GUILDENSTERN   A Thing, my Lord?   30
HAMLET   Of Nothing. Bring me to him. Hide, Fox,
    and all after.   *Exeunt.*

IV.iii   *This scene takes place immediately after IV.ii in another room of the Castle. The "two or three" with whom Claudius enters are probably the "wisest Friends" he has referred to in IV.i.38.*

3   put . . . him   *prosecute him to the full extent of the law.*

4   distracted   *not rational, easily diverted from an objective appraisal. But Claudius may be concerned about the masses' becoming "distracted" in a more severe sense (frenzied) once they hear about and become agitated over the death of Polonius.*

5   like   *form their preferences.*

6   th' Offender's Scourge   *the punishment given the criminal.*
     weigh'd   *taken into consideration.*

7   To bear all smooth and even   *to keep things peaceful and calm.*

9   Delib'rate Pause   *the result of a dispassionate weighing of all the alternatives. The King is saying that a reaction that must be "sudden" must seem to be "deliberate" (unhurried, reflective). In fact the King's plans for Hamlet have been devised with some deliberation: Claudius told Polonius of his scheme to send Hamlet to England immediately after the two of them eavesdropped on the conversation between Hamlet and Ophelia (III.i.168–74).*
     desp'rate grown   *at the critical stage (where the patient is desperate, at the point where life is in the balance).*

10   By desperate Appliance   *by the application of desperate measures (measures equal to the severity of the crisis).*

Scene 3

Enter the King, and two or three.

KING   I have sent to seek him, and to find the
    Body.
    How dang'rous is it that this Man goes loose,
    Yet must not we put the strong Law on him:
    He's lov'd of the distracted Multitude,
    Who like not in their Judgment but their Eyes;   5
    And where 'tis so, th' Offender's Scourge is
      weigh'd,
    But never the Offense. To bear all smooth and
      even,
    This sudden sending him away must seem
    Delib'rate Pause. Diseases desp'rate grown
    By desperate Appliance are reliev'd   10
    Or not at all.

Enter Rosencrans and all the Rest.

          —How now, what hath befall'n?
ROSENCRANS   Where the dead Body is bestow'd, my
    Lord,
    We cannot get from him.
KING   But where is he?

14 Without   *just outside the chamber.*
   guarded   *under guard.*
   to know your Pleasure   *to learn what you have decided to do
       with him.*

15 How   *ho.*

19 Convocation   *solemn assembly.*
   politic Worms   *worms who are occupied with affairs of state.*

20 Your . . . Diet.   *Hamlet plays on two senses of* Diet: *(a)
   food, and (b) a council or convocation. He alludes in particular to the Diet of Worms (a famous council in the German city
   of Worms); here the Holy Roman Emperor presided over an
   assembly at which Martin Luther was condemned for heresy in
   1521. Hamlet adopts the colloquial* your *throughout this
   dialogue; it is a familiar, informal way of saying "the," and
   here it reinforces the satirical reductiveness of everything
   Hamlet utters about matters that are normally treated with
   formal reverence and stately reserve.*

21 fat   *feed to make fat.*

23 Variable Service   *different dishes or servings.*

31 go a Progress   *Hamlet alludes to the pompous ceremonies
   whereby royal personages were welcomed when they went on
   progresses, official state journeys; he suggests that a King's
   final progress may be somewhat less dignified than the ones he
   grew accustomed to in life.*

35 Other Place   *Hell.*

36 nose   *smell.*

ROSENCRANS Without, my Lord, guarded to know
      your Pleasure.
KING Bring him before us.
ROSENCRANS   —How, bring in the Lord!   15

      Enter Hamlet and Guildenstern.

KING Now, Hamlet, where's Polonius?
HAMLET   At Supper.
KING At Supper, where?
HAMLET Not where he eats, but where 'a is eaten.
      A certain Convocation of politic Worms are e'en
      at him. Your Worm is your only Emperor for Diet.   20
      We fat all Creatures else to fat us, and we fat
      our selves for Maggots. Your Fat King and your
      Lean Beggar is but Variable Service: two Dishes
      to one Table, that's the End.
KING Alas, alas.   25
HAMLET A Man may fish with the Worm that hath eat
      of a King, and eat of the Fish that fed of that
      Worm.
KING What doost thou mean by this?
HAMLET Nothing but to show you how a King may   30
      go a Progress through the Guts of a Beggar.
KING Where is Polonius?
HAMLET In Heav'n. Send thether to see; if your
      Messenger find him not there, seek him i' th'
      Other Place your self. But if indeed you find   35
      him not within this Month, you shall nose him
      as you go up the Stairs into the Lobby.
KING —Go seek him there.

223

41   **tender**   *treat with careful regard.*
        as   *both (a) at the same time as, and (b) just as much as.*

43   **With fiery Quickness**   *This phrase, which may or may not be authorial, occurs only in the Folio printing of the play.*

44   **Bark**   *boat.*
        at help   *in a favorable disposition.*

45   **Th' Associates tend**   *those who will go with you are at your service.*

48   **Cherub**   *presiding angel.*

48–49 **But . . . England.**   *This sentence may be addressed to "Th' Associates," as is almost certainly true of line 52.*

52   **Man and Wife is one Flesh**   *Hamlet alludes to the marriage ceremony and to such Biblical passages as Genesis 2:24 and Matthew 19:5–6. Here the reference is a reminder that the "one Flesh" created by this incestuous marriage is a grotesque parody of "holy matrimony."*
        so my Mother   *therefore it follows that you are my Mother. Hamlet implies that it is as appropriate to call Claudius his Mother as it is to call him his Father or his King. Here and in line 49* **Mother** *becomes charged with innuendo that anticipates one of the most pervasive expletives of the 1960s.*

54   **at foot**   *at his heels (keeping a close eye on him).*
        tempt   *incite, spur.*

60   **Cicatrice**   *scar. Claudius implies that Danish forces have recently disciplined "England" (here referring primarily to the English King).*

HAMLET   —'A will stay till you come.

Exeunt Attendants.

KING   —Hamlet, this Deed, for thine especial
    Safety   40
    (Which we do tender as we dearly grieve
    For that which thou hast done), must send thee
        hence
    With fiery Quickness. Therefore prepare thy self.
    The Bark is ready, and the Wind at help;
    Th' Associates tend, and ev'ry thing is bent   45
    For England.
HAMLET   For England.
KING   Ay Hamlet.
HAMLET   Good.
KING   So is it if thou knew'st our Purposes.
HAMLET   I see a Cherub that sees them. But come,
    for England. Farewell, dear Mother.
KING   Thy loving Father, Hamlet.   50
HAMLET   My Mother. Father and Mother is Man and
    Wife; Man and Wife is one Flesh; so my Mother.
    —Come, for England.   *Exit.*
KING   —Follow him at foot: tempt him with Speed
        aboard.
    Delay it not: I'll have him hence tonight.   55
    Away: for ev'ry thing is seal'd and done
    That else leans on th' Affair. Pray you make
        haste.   *Exeunt all but the King.*
    —And England, if my Love thou hold'st at ought
    (As my great Pow'r thereof may give thee Sense,
    Since yet thy Cicatrice looks raw and red   60
    After the Danish Sword), and thy free Awe

62   coldly set   *aloofly disregard.*

63   Our Sov'reign Process   *the command ("Mandate," III.iv.200) that I, as the King of England's sovereign, am dispatching.*
       which imports at full   *spells out with complete clarity.*

64   congruing to that Effect   *in accordance with that objective.*

66   the Hectic   *a severe, unbroken fever.*

68   How e'er my Haps   *however my fortunes.*
       were ne'er begun   *This phrase means "will ne'er begin," the reading in the Second Quarto. Here the Folio reading is adopted because it conforms to Shakespeare's usual pattern of concluding a scene-ending soliloquy with a rhymed couplet (compare I.iii, I.v, II.i, II.ii, III.ii, and III.iii).*

IV.iv   *This scene takes place on the way to the harbor, just prior to the departure for England.*

2   License   *authorization (earlier referred to in II.ii.77–80).*

3   Craves . . . March   *requests an official Danish escort for the conduct of a march across Danish territory for which permission has already been requested and granted.*

4   the Rendezvous   *Fortinbrasse probably means "where to find him." But he may mean "where to meet us."*

5   would . . . us   *either (a) would like to speak directly to me, or (b) has any business to conduct with us.*

6   in his Eye   *to his face, in his presence.*

8   Pow'rs   *military forces.*

Pays Homage to us, thou may'st not coldly set
Our Sov'reign Process, which imports at full,
By Letters congruing to that Effect,
The present Death of Hamlet. Do it, England,   65
For like the Hectic in my Blood he rages,
And thou must cure me. Till I know 'tis done,
How e'er my Haps, my Joys were ne'er begun.   *Exit.*

Scene 4

Enter Fortinbrasse with his Army over the Stage.

FORTINBRASSE   Go, Captain, from me greet the
     Danish King;
Tell him that by his License Fortinbrasse
Craves the Conveyance of a promis'd March
Over his Kingdom. You know the Rendezvous.
If that his Majesty would ought with us,   5
We shall express our Duty in his Eye,
And let him know so.
CAPTAIN   I will do 't, my Lord.
FORTINBRASSE   Go softly on.
                    Exeunt all but the Captain.

Enter Hamlet, Rosencrans, and Guildenstern.

HAMLET   Good Sir, whose Pow'rs are these?

12   Main   *primary territory.*

14   Addition   *exaggeration.*

16   Profit   *value, advantage.*

17   farm   *lease.*

19   ranker Rate   *higher return.*
      in Fee   *outright.*

21   garrison'd   *fortified with armed soldiers.*

23   Will not debate   *will not be sufficient to contest.*

24   Impostume   *abcess, festering sore. Hamlet uses yet another
      image from the vocabulary of disease.*

25   inward breaks   *erupts within the body. Compare Hamlet's
      similar reference to an "Ulc'rous Place" in III.iv.144–46.*

27   God buy you   *God be with you.*

28   before   *ahead of me.*

29   How . . . me   *How everything that happens and everyone I
      encounter bears witness against me. Hamlet is employing a
      metaphor from legal terminology.*

31   Market   *profitable use.*

33   large Discourse   *ample powers of reasoning.*

34   Looking before and after   *with an eye to both the past and
      the future. The ambiguous syntax permits this phrase to modify
      both* He *(God) and* Discourse.

CAPTAIN   They are of Norway, Sir.
HAMLET   How purpos'd, Sir, I pray you?
CAPTAIN   Against some part of Poland.
HAMLET   Who commaunds them, Sir?   10
CAPTAIN   The Nephew to old Norway: Fortinbrasse.
HAMLET   Goes it against the Main of Poland, Sir,
    Or for some Frontier?
CAPTAIN   Truly to speak, and with no Addition,
    We go to gain a little Patch of Ground   15
    That hath in it no Profit but the Name.
    To pay five Ducats, five, I would not farm it;
    Nor will it yield to Norway or the Pole
    A ranker Rate should it be sold in Fee.
HAMLET   Why then the Polack never will defend it.   20
CAPTAIN   Yes, it is already garrison'd.
HAMLET   Two thousand Souls, and twenty thousand
    Ducats
    Will not debate the Question of this Straw:
    This is th' Impostume of much Wealth and Peace,
    That inward breaks, and shows no Cause without   25
    Why the Man dies. I humbly thank you, Sir.
CAPTAIN   God buy you, Sir.   *Exit.*
ROSENCRANS   Will 't please you go, my Lord?
HAMLET   I'll be with you straight: go a little
        before.   *Exeunt all but Hamlet.*
    —How all Occasions do inform against me
    And spur my dull Revenge! What is a Man   30
    If his chief Good and Market of his Time
    Be but to Sleep and Feed? A Beast, no more.
    Sure He that made us with such large Discourse,
    Looking before and after, gave us not

36   fust *grow musty.*

37   Bestial Oblivion *beastlike forgetfulness.*
craven Scruple *slavish, cowardly doubt.*

38   Of . . . Event *of dwelling excessively on the outcome.*

39   quarter'd *both (a) broken into fourths (as with the shield on a coat of arms), and (b) cornered like a prey.*

43   gross *both (a) obvious, and (b) dirty, foul.*

44   Mass and Charge *massive numbers and expenditure.*

47   Makes . . . Event *defies the unknown risks he undertakes.*

51   great Argument *a significant cause or reason for the combat.*

53   at the Stake *both (a) staked, as in a wager, and (b) tied to the stake, like a bear attacked by baying dogs in a baiting arena.*

55   Blood *passion. A number of Hamlet's phrases suggest analogies with manly "Excitements" of a different kind.*

58   a Fantasy . . . Fame *an illusory "Argument" and a trifling cause prompted by a desire for "Fame." Fortinbrasse is here presented as the kind of Soldier the melancholy Jaques describes as "Seeking the Bubble Reputation / Ev'n in the Cannon's Mouth" (*As You Like It, *II.vii.152–53).*

60   Cause *case (*causa *in Latin); another legal metaphor.*

61   Continent *container. Hamlet's point in lines 59–62 is that the plot being fought over is too small to hold the massive numbers who will "debate" it.*

That Capability and God-like Reason   35
To fust in us unus'd. Now wheth'r it be
Bestial Oblivion or some craven Scruple
Of thinking too precisely on th' Event
(A Thought which, quarter'd, hath but one part
    Wisdom
And ever three parts Coward), I do not know   40
Why yet I live to say "This thing's to do":
Sith I have Cause, and Will, and Strength, and
    Means
To do 't. Examples gross as Earth exhort me:
Witness this Army of such Mass and Charge,
Led by a delicate and tender Prince,   45
Whose Spirit, with divine Ambition puff'd,
Makes Mouths at th' invisible Event,
Exposing what is Mortal and Unsure
To all that Fortune, Death, and Danger dare,
Ev'n for an Eggshell. Rightly to be Great   50
Is not to stir without great Argument,
But greatly to find Quarrel in a Straw
When Honor's at the Stake. How stand I then
That have a Father kill'd, a Mother stain'd,
Excitements of my Reason and my Blood,   55
And let all Sleep, while to my Shame I see
The imm'nent Death of twenty thousand Men
That for a Fantasy and Trick of Fame
Go to their Graves like Beds, fight for a Plot
Whereon the Numbers cannot try the Cause,   60
Which is not Tomb enough and Continent
To hide the Slain? O from this Time forth
My Thoughts be Bloody or be Nothing worth.   *Exit.*

IV.v   *This scene returns us to the Castle, where the Queen has just received word that Ophelia wishes to talk with her.*

1   Importunate   *impatiently demanding; an echo of I.iii.32.*

2   Distract   *deranged.*
    Mood   *agitated emotional and mental state. Normally this word refers to a seizure of passion, usually anger.*

6   Spurns enviously   *kicks maliciously.*
    Straws   *trifling things. This word, picking up on Hamlet's two uses of it in the previous scene (IV.iv.23, 52), hints at a relationship between Hamlet's situation and that of Ophelia.*
    in Doubt   *that have doubtful meaning at best.*

8   unshaped Use of it   *incoherent way of speaking.*

9   to Collection   *to attempts to put the fragments together into something that makes sense.*
    yawn   *gape, listen in open-mouthed concentration. Most editors follow the Folio and print* aim, *conjecture.*

10   botch the Words . . . Thoughts   *patch the words together in a way that conforms to their own notions of what she is trying to say.*

11   yield them   *yield up words (produce words to accompany them). In this line* Which *refers to* Words *(line 10).*

13   sure   *secure, certain.*
    unhappily   *unaptly, incoherently.*

14   strew   *spread. This verb, which echoes* straw, *will recur in V.i.261.*

Scene 5

Enter Horatio, the Queen, and a Gentleman.

QUEEN   I will not speak with her.

GENTLEMAN   She is Importunate,
Indeed Distract: her Mood will needs be pitied.

QUEEN   What would she have?

GENTLEMAN   She speaks much of her Father, says she
hears
There's Tricks i' th' World, and hems, and beats
her Heart,   5
Spurns enviously at Straws, speaks things in
Doubt
That carry but half Sense. Her Speech is Nothing,
Yet the unshaped Use of it doth move
The Hearers to Collection: they yawn at it,
And botch the Words up fit to their own
Thoughts,   10
Which, as her Winks and Nods and Gestures yield
them,
Indeed would make one think there might be
Thought,
Though nothing sure, yet much unhappily.

HORATIO   'Twere good she were spoken with, for she
may strew

15   **ill-breeding Minds**   *minds inclined to thoughts that might endanger the security of the throne. Horatio is advising the Queen to allow Ophelia to be admitted.*

18   **Toy**   *trifle.*
       Amiss   *misfortune.*

19   **artless Jealousy**   *uncontrollable anxiety.*

20   **spills**   *both (a) undoes, destroys, and (b) pours out, reveals.*

S.D.   **Enter Ophelia.**   *The First Quarto, which undoubtedly preserves some authentic staging detail despite its generally unreliable rendering of the text of the play, indicates that Ophelia enters "playing on a Lute," singing, and with her "hair down" (a conventional sign of madness). The songs she sings in this scene are probably snatches from ballads that would have been familiar to the original audience.*

22   **How now**   *both (a) how are you, and (b) what may I do for you.*

25   **Cockle Hat**   *a hat with a cockle shell on it. Such hats were worn by pilgrims who had visited the shrine of Saint James of Compostela in Spain.*

26   **Shoone**   *an archaic (poetic) plural for* shoe.

27   **imports**   *signifies.*

32   **Stone**   *gravestone. The placement of the marker at the feet, rather than the head, of the deceased anticipates other irregularities to be dwelled on later in the ballad, and then later in the play.*

38   **Larded**   *bestrewn, covered over.*

Dangerous Conjectures in ill-breeding Minds.   15
QUEEN   Let her come in.   *Exit Gentleman.*
    —To my Sick Soul, as Sin's true Nature is,
    Each Toy seems Prologue to some great Amiss;
    So full of artless Jealousy is Guilt,
    It spills it self in fearing to be spilt.   20

Enter Ophelia.

OPHELIA   Where is the beauteous Majesty of Denmark?
QUEEN   How now, Ophelia?
OPHELIA *sings*
            " 'How should I your True-love know
                From another one?'
              'By his Cockle Hat and Staff   25
                And his Sandal Shoone.' "
QUEEN   Alas, sweet Lady, what imports this Song?
OPHELIA   Say you? Nay pray you mark:
            "He is dead and gone, Lady,
                He is dead and gone;   30
                At his Head a Grass-green Turf,
                At his Heels a Stone."
    O ho!
QUEEN   Nay but Ophelia—
OPHELIA   Pray you mark: 35
            "White his Shroud as the Mountain Snow."

Enter King.

QUEEN   Alas, look here, my Lord!
OPHELIA   "Larded all with sweet Flowers,

235

39–40 Which . . . Showers *Ophelia's song implies that the "True-love" who has died has not been properly mourned. Spoken in the Queen's presence, these words are a reminder of the insufficiency of her devotion to the elder Hamlet. But they have a more direct bearing on another recent burial whose circumstances are hinted at in lines 87–88.*

42 good-dild *a garbled version of "God yield" (bless).*

42–43 They say . . . Daughter. *Ophelia is probably quoting some version of a folk-tale in which a baker's daughter, having been stingy when asked for bread by Christ, was transformed into an owl. Baker's daughters appear to have been held in low esteem generally, and in many ballads and tales they are depicted as lascivious.*

46 Conceit upon her Father. *The King means that Ophelia's words reflect her grief for her father.*

50 betime *early.*

55 dupp'd *opened.*

61 Gis *an abbreviation of "Jesus."*
Saint Charity *divine love.*

64 Cock *both (a) a corruption of* God, *and (b) a reference to the male member.*
too blame *too much to blame.*

65 tumbled me *took my maidenhead.*

Which, beweept to the Ground, did not go
  With True-love Showers."   40

KING How do you, pretty Lady?

OPHELIA Well, good-dild you. They say the Owl was
a Baker's Daughter. Lord, we know what we are,
but know not what we may be. God be at your
Table.   45

KING Conceit upon her Father.

OPHELIA Pray let's have no Words of this; but when
they ask you what it means, say you this.

    "Tomorrow is Saint Valentine's Day,
      All in the Morning betime,   50
    And I a Maid at your Window
      To be your Valentine.

      Then up he rose,
      And donn'd his Clothes,
    And dupp'd the Chamber Door;   55
      Let in the Maid
      That out a Maid
      Never departed more."

KING Pretty Ophelia—

OPHELIA Indeed without an Oath I'll make an End on't.   60

    "By Gis and by Saint Charity,
      Alack and fie for Shame,
    Young Men will do't if they come to't,
      By Cock they are too blame."

    Quoth she: 'Before you tumbled me,   65
      You promis'd me to wed.' "

He answers:

69   And *if.*

73   lay . . . Ground   *place him without proper ceremony in the earth, rather than accord him the dignity of a stone vault.*

79–80   O this . . . behold!   *The King's momentary lapse into prose is an indication of his own disturbed condition; he has temporarily lost his secure command of the discourse habitual to him. In the speech that follows, moreover, there are several lines (among them 86–87) that contain enough metrical irregularities to make them seem like eruptions of prose beneath an otherwise smooth overlay of verse.*

82   single Spies   *as individual scouts to gather intelligence for the army preparing an attack.*

84   Author   *instigator, responsible party.*

85   muddied   *stirred up, agitated.*

87   greenly   *foolishly (like a naive child).*

88   In Hugger-mugger   *with haste, secrecy, and little ceremony.*

90   Pictures   *only images of human beings.*

93   keeps himself in Clouds   *hides himself away in a suspicious obscurity.*

94   wants . . . Ear   *is not lacking for gossips and malcontents to incite him to rebellion.* Buzzers *is an echoic word to imitate the sound of those who whisper; it also suggests buzzing insects (pests) and buzzards as they infect Laertes' ear.*

95   pest'lent   *both (a) contagious, and (b) pest-borne.*

      "So would I 'a done, by yonder Sun,
        And thou hadst not come to my Bed."

KING How long hath she been thus? 70

OPHELIA I hope all will be well; we must be
    patient. But I cannot choose but weep to think
    they would lay him i' th' cold Ground. My
    Brother shall know of it, and so I thank you
    for your good Counsel. —Come, my Coach. 75
    —God night, Ladies, God night. Sweet Ladies,
    God night, God night. *Exit.*

KING Follow her close: give her good Watch, I pray
    you. *Exit Horatio.*
    O this is the Poison of deep Grief: it springs
    all from her Father's Death, and now behold! 80
    O Gertrard, Gertrard,
    When Sorrows come, they come not single Spies
    But in Battalions. First her Father slain;
    Next your Son gone, and he most violent Author
    Of his own just Remove; the People muddied, 85
    Thick, and unwholesome in Thoughts and Whispers
    For good Polonius' Death; and we have done
      but greenly
    In Hugger-mugger to inter him; Poor Ophelia,
    Divided from her Self and her fair Judgment,
    Without the which we're Pictures or mere Beasts; 90
    Last, and as much containing as all these,
    Her Brother is in secret come from Fraunce,
    Feeds on this Wonder, keeps himself in Clouds,
    And wants not Buzzers to infect his Ear
    With pest'lent Speeches of his Father's Death, 95
    Wherein Necessity, of Matter beggar'd,

96–98   Wherein . . . Ear   *with which [Polonius' death] those who have no real "Matter" (substantive basis) for their discontent, and need to find a justification for it, will not hesitate to blame "our Person" (Claudius) in one ear after another.*

99   a Murd'ring-piece   *a type of cannon that discharged a scattering of shots and could thus hit many men with one firing.*

100   superfluous Death   *enough blows to kill me many times over.*

101   Swissers   *Swiss guards, mercenaries from Switzerland.*

103   over-peering of his List   *looking over its boundary (overflowing its shore).*

104   Flats   *flat land, beaches.*
      impitious   *both (a) pitiless, and (b) impetuous.*

105   in a riotous Head   *at the head of an uncontrollable force.*

106   O'erbears   *overwhelms.*

107   as   *as if.*

108   Antiquity forgot   *all age and tradition forgotten or disregarded.*

109   The Ratifiers . . . Word   *the basis and support for every pledge and compact in civilized society.*

113   cheerfully   *excitedly (like baying dogs "crying" after their prey).*

114   Counter   *To run counter was to pursue the scent in the wrong direction.*

Will nothing stick our Person to arraign
In Ear and Ear. O my dear Gertrard, this,
Like to a Murd'ring-piece, in many places
Gives me superfluous Death.   *A Noise within.*   100
KING   Attend, where is my Swissers? Let them guard
   the Door.

Enter a Messenger.

—What is the Matter?
MESSENGER   Save your self, my Lord.
  The Ocean over-peering of his List
Eats not the Flats with more impitious Haste
Than young Laertes in a riotous Head   105
O'erbears your Officers. The Rabble call him
   Lord,
And (as the World were now but to begin,
Antiquity forgot, Custom not known,
The Ratifiers and Props of ev'ry Word),
They cry "Choose we, Laertes shall be King!"   110
Caps, Hands, and Tongues applaud it to the
   Clouds:
"Laertes shall be King! Laertes King!"
                          A Noise within.
QUEEN   How cheerfully on the False Trail they cry!

Enter Laertes with Others.

—O this is Counter, you false Danish Dogs!
KING   The Doors are broke!
LAERTES   Where is the King?   115

241

117   give me Leave   *permit me [to speak with the King alone].*

121–   brands . . . Mother   *places the brand of a whore even here*
23   *[probably accompanied by a gesture to the center of Laertes'*
       forehead] between the chaste, unblemished brows of my virtu-
       ous mother. Hamlet has used a similar image in III.iv.42.

124   looks so Giant-like   *manifests itself in such an audacious*
       fashion. The King alludes to the rebellion of the ancient Gi-
       ants of the Earth, who piled Mount Pelion atop Mount Ossa
       in an attempt to storm Heaven and overthrow the Olympian
       Gods. Shakespeare would have known the story from Ovid's
       Metamorphoses *(Book I) and* Fasti *(Book V).*

125   fear our Person   *be afraid for me.*

126–   There's . . . Will.   *A King, being God's deputy on Earth, is*
28   *so thoroughly surrounded with Divine power that Treason can*
       do no more than lift its head without having its will sup-
       pressed. In view of what "Treason" has done to Claudius'
       predecessor, the King's words are undercut by an irony that is
       lost on Laertes but not on the audience.

132   juggl'd with   *subjected to tricks and sleight of hand.*

133   To Hell, Allegiance   *What Laertes says here and in the*
       following lines is that he is prepared to forswear his Christian
       faith (and particularly the injunction that subjects leave ven-
       geance to God and obey their rulers, Romans 12, 13) and risk
       damnation in order to avenge his father's death.

135   To this Point I stand   *to this pledge I commit myself, and I*
       will not be moved.

    —Sirs, stand you all without.

ALL   No, let's come in.

LAERTES   I pray you give me Leave.

ALL   We will, we will.

LAERTES   I thank you: keep the Door.

                       Exeunt Laertes' Followers.

                      —O thou vile King,

    Give me my Father!

QUEEN   Calmly, good Laertes!

LAERTES   That Drop of Blood that's calm proclaims

    me Bastard,   120

    Cries Cuckold to my Father, brands the Harlot

    Ev'n here between the chaste unsmirched Brow

    Of my true Mother.

KING   What is the Cause, Laertes,

    That thy Rebellion looks so Giant-like?

    —Let him go, Gertrard. Do not fear our Person: 125

    There's such Divinity doth hedge a King

    That Treason can but peep to what it would,

    Acts little of his Will. —Tell me, Laertes,

    Why thou art thus incens'd. —Let him go,

      Gertrard.

    —Speak, Man.

LAERTES   Where is my Father?

KING   Dead.   130

QUEEN   But not by him.

KING   Let him demaund his Fill.

LAERTES   How came he Dead? I'll not be juggl'd with.

    —To Hell, Allegiance; Vows, to the blackest Devil;

    Conscience and Grace, to the profoundest Pit!

    I dare Damnation! —To this Point I stand,   135

136   That . . . Negligence *that I will henceforth refuse to concern myself with either Heaven or Hell, "Let come what comes" (line 137).*

138   throughly *thoroughly.*

140   husband *manage; conserve and employ.*

144   Soopstake *swoopstake, a variant of* sweepstake, *a word that describes a winner's sweeping away all the stakes (money wagered) in a betting game. Laertes is ready to sweep not only what he is entitled to but everything else as well.*

148   Life-rend'ring Pelican *Laertes alludes to the bestiary fable about the mother Pelican who, in order to preserve her starving offspring, feeds them the blood of her own breast. An emblem of self-sacrifice, the Pelican was a popular medieval symbol for a ruler's devotion to the well-being of his commonwealth.*

149   Repast *feed. Shakespeare's wording in this passage reminds us that the Pelican's sacrifice is an emblem of the Pastor (shepherd) who opened his arms wide on the Cross and laid down "his life for his friends" (John 15:13).*

152   sensibly *feelingly (with all my senses).*

153   level *even, clear. The King may be thinking of himself as a target (with his pure heart as the "blank" or center) at which Laertes' Judgment may "level" (take aim). His implication is that because he is innocent, he can withstand the most penetrating scrutiny.*
       'pear *appear.*

That both the Worlds I give to Negligence,
Let come what comes: only I'll be reveng'd
Most throughly for my Father.
KING   Who shall stay you?
LAERTES   My Will, not all the World's;
And for my Means, I'll husband them so well,   140
They shall go far with little.
KING   Good Laertes,
If you desire to know the Certainty
Of your dear Fath'r, is't writ in your Revenge
That, Soopstake, you will draw both Friend and
    Foe,
Winner and Loser?
LAERTES   None but his Enemies.   145
KING   Will you know them then?
LAERTES   To his good Friends thus wide I'll ope my
    Arms,
And like the kind, Life-rend'ring Pelican,
Repast them with my Blood.
KING   Why now you speak
Like a good Child and a true Gentleman!   150
That I am Guiltless of your Father's Death,
And am most sensibly in Grief for it,
It shall as level to your Judgment 'pear
As Day does to your Eye.
A Noise within: Let her come in!
LAERTES   How now? What Noise is that?   155

Enter Ophelia.

157   **Sense and Virtue**   *sensation and operative power.*

158–   **paid . . . Beam**   *Laertes promises to pile enough "Weight"*
59   *of revenge on "our Scale" (his family's) to tip the balance*
         beam in his favor. It will not be enough to get "even"; Laertes
         insists on more than compensatory damages.

163–   **Nature . . . loves.**   *Nature (and human nature in particu-*
65   *lar) is shown to be most "fine" (pure, refined) when it*
         manifests itself through Love; and where it is present in its
         noblest form (as in Ophelia's love for her father), it sends some
         precious part or sign ("Instance") of itself (in this case, Ophe-
         lia's "Wits" or sanity) to the object of its devotion (the "Poor
         Man's Life").

170   **persuade Revenge**   *urge me by arguments to commit revenge.*

172   **A-down**   *Like the nonsense words in line 168, this refrain*
         would normally function simply as melodic filler; in this con-
         text, however, it reminds us that like Ophelia's father, Ophe-
         lia's wits are now "quite quite down" (III.i.158). She is "of
         Ladies most Deject and Wretched," and her own "Noble and
         most Sov'reign Reason, / Like sweet Bells jangl'd out of Time
         and Harsh," is "Blasted with Ecstasy" (III.i.159–64).

173   **Wheel**   *refrain (but with an echo of the Wheel of Fortune, also*
         "down").

182   **Fennel**   *an herb associated with (a) flattery, and (b) weddings.*
         Columbines   *flowers associated with (a) ingratitude, and (b)*
         infidelity.

183   **Rue**   *an herb associated with sorrow and repentance.*

—O Heat, dry up my Brains. Tears sev'n times
   salt
Burn out the Sense and Virtue of mine Eye!
—By Heav'n, thy Madness shall be paid with
   Weight
Till our Scale turn the Beam! O Rose of May,
Dear Maid, kind Sister, sweet Ophelia! 160
—O Heav'ns, is't possible a Young Maid's Wits
Should be as mortal as a Poor Man's Life?
Nature is fine in Love, and where 'tis fine
It sends some precious Instance of it self
After the thing it loves. 165
OPHELIA   "They bore him Bare-fac'd on the Bier,
          And in his Grave rain'd many a Tear."
            Hey non nonny, nonny hey nonny."
Fare you well, my Dove.
LAERTES   Hadst thou thy Wits, and didst persuade
   Revenge, 170
It could not move thus.
OPHELIA   You must sing "A-down a-down," and you
   call him "A-down-a." O how the Wheel becomes
   it! It is the false Steward that stole his Maister's
   Daughter. 175
LAERTES   This Nothing's more than Matter.
OPHELIA   There's Rosemary: that's for Remembrance.
   Pray you, Love, remember. And there is Pansies:
   that's for Thoughts.
LAERTES   A Document in Madness: Thoughts and 180
   Remembrance fitted.
OPHELIA   There's Fennel for you, and Columbines;
   there's Rue for you, and here's some for me.

184   Herb of Grace   *another name for Rue. The Gardener uses this same phrase in III.iv.104 of* Richard II.

185   with a Difference   *Ophelia's words derive from heraldry; a difference (such as the Daisy she now presents along with the Rue) was a variation in a coat of arms to allow individual members of a family to be distinguished by their heraldic insignia.*

189   bonny sweet Robin   *The song Ophelia quotes here is likely to have been a bawdy one (similar to the Valentine song she sang in IV.v.49–69), with Robin referring to both a lover and a male organ. But, as Laertes points out in the next speech, Ophelia's pitiful innocence in madness can turn "Hell it self" to "Favor and to Prettiness."*

198   Flaxen   *white.*
       Pole   *poll (head), with a possible play on the same kind of "pole" that "Robin" signifies.*

201   'a   *have.*

202   buy   *be with.*

204   commune with   *share in; accented on the first syllable.*

208   collat'ral Hand   *collateral, indirect involvement (that is, through an agent or associate).*

209   us touch'd   *me touched with guilt [of the crimes you wish to avenge].*

We may call it Herb of Grace a' Sundays; you
may wear your Rue with a Difference. There's a   185
Daisy. I would give you some Violets, but they
wither'd all when my Father died. They say 'a
made a Good End.
    "For bonny sweet Robin is all my Joy."
LAERTES   Thoughts and Afflictions, Passion, Hell
    it self,   190
  She turns to Favor and to Prettiness.

OPHELIA   "And will 'a not come again,
      And will 'a not come again?
        No, no, he is dead;
        Go to thy Death-bed;   195
      He never will come again.

      His Beard was as white as Snow;
      All Flaxen was his Pole.
        He is gone, he is gone,
        And we cast away Moan.   200
      God 'a mercy on his Soul."

  And of all Christians' Souls, God buy you.   *Exit.*
LAERTES   —Do you see this, O God?
KING   Laertes, I must commune with your Grief,
  Or you deny me Right. Go but apart,   205
  Make choice of whom your wisest Friends you
    will,
  And they shall hear and judge 'twixt you and
    me;
  If by direct or by collat'ral Hand
  They find us touch'd, we will our Kingdom give,
  Our Crown, our Life, and all that we call Ours   210

211   in Satisfaction   *to satisfy your honor and its demand that you have justice.*

214   due Content   *proper rest (as a result of its achieving satisfaction). In IV.vii.59 the King uses the word* Peace *to refer to the same state of contentment.*

215   Obscure Funeral   *secret burial service. The word* obscure *literally means "covered over"; what Laertes is implying is that the manner of his father's hasty disposal was shady.*

216   Hatchment   *a memorial tablet above the tomb bearing the deceased's coat of arms.*

217   Ostentation   *public ceremony.*

219   That   *so that.*

220   the great Axe   *the axe of the executioner. Claudius assumes that the order he has sent to England will shortly provide for the fulfillment of this pledge; he expects to hear soon that Hamlet has been beheaded.*

IV.vi   *This scene is probably to be thought of as occurring somewhere in the Castle.*

1   What   *what kind of messengers.*

To you in Satisfaction. But if not,
Be you content to lend your Patience to us,
And we shall jointly labor with your Soul
To give it due Content.

LAERTES   Let this be so.
His Means of Death, his Obscure Funeral   215
(No Trophy, Sword, nor Hatchment o'er his Bones,
No Noble Rite, nor Formal Ostentation)
Cry to be heard, as 'twere from Heav'n to Earth,
That I must call 't in Question.

KING   So you shall,
And where th' Offense is, let the great Axe fall.   220
I pray you go with me.   *Exeunt.*

Scene 6

Enter Horatio and Others.

HORATIO   What are they that would speak with me?
GENTLEMAN   Sea-faring Men, Sir: they say they have
   Letters for you.
HORATIO   Let them come in.
   I do not know from what part of the World   5
   I should be greeted, if not from Lord Hamlet.

Enter Sailors.

251

10   Embassador   *The "ambassador" the Sailor refers to is Hamlet.*

14   Means   *way of transporting his letters.*

16   were two Days old at Sea   *had been at sea for two days.*

17   Appointment   *appearance and equipment.*

18-19   put on a compelled Valor   *fought bravely out of necessity.*

19   boorded   *boarded.*

22-23   but they knew what they did   *but they did it in the knowledge that it would be to their advantage to do so.*

25-26   as thou wouldst fly Death   *as you would use if you were fleeing death.*

27   make thee Dumb   *stun you to speechlessness.*

27-28   too light . . . the Matter   *Hamlet compares his words to bullets that are too tiny for the bore (width) of the cannon from which they are to be shot. Here* the Matter *refers to the subject that occasions the words.*

33   give you way   *guide you (to someone who will bear your letters to the King).*

SAILOR   God bless you, Sir.

HORATIO   Let him bless thee too.

SAILOR   'A shall, Sir, and 't please him. There's a
    Letter for you, Sir: it came from th' Embassador   10
    that was bound for England, if your name be
    Horatio, as I am let to know it is.

HORATIO [*reads*]   "Horatio, when thou shalt have
    over-look'd this, give these Fellows some Means
    to the King: they have Letters for him. Ere we   15
    were two Days old at Sea, a Pirate of very
    warlike Appointment gave us Chase; finding our
    selves too slow of sail, we put on a compelled
    Valor, and in the Grapple I boorded them on the
    instant they got clear of our Ship, so I alone   20
    became their Prisoner. They have dealt with me
    like Thieves of Mercy, but they knew what they
    did: I am to do a Turn for them. Let the King
    have the Letters I have sent, and repair thou
    to me with as much speed as thou wouldst fly   25
    Death. I have Words to speak in thine Ear will
    make thee Dumb, yet are they much too light
    for the Bore of the Matter. These good Fellows
    will bring thee where I am. Rosencrans and
    Guildenstern hold their Course for England: 30
    of them I have much to tell thee. Farewell.
            So that thou knowest thine, Hamlet."

HORATIO   Come, I will give you way for these your
        Letters,
    And do 't the speedier that you may direct me
    To him from whom you brought them.   *Exeunt.*   35

253

IV.vii   *This scene takes us to another room in the Castle, where the King is concluding a meeting with Laertes.*

1   my Acquittance seal   *give its seal to (formal recognition of) my innocence (acquittal).*

3   Sith   *since.*

6   proceeded   *This reading derives from the First Folio; the Second Quarto prints* proceed.
     Feats   *deeds.*

7   Capital   *punishable by death (literally decapitation, cutting off the* capus, *head, of the offender).*

9   mainly   *both (a) powerfully, and (b) especially.*

10   unsinowed   *unsinewed, lacking in strength.*

11   th'   *they.*

14   conjunctive to   *joined to. This is one of many images of jointure in the play. Claudius is saying that he is as totally devoted to his wife as she is to her son. The King's phrasing is yet another reminder that his illegitimate union with Gertrard constitutes his principal claim to legitimacy as Denmark's monarch. See the note to I.ii.9.*

15   as the Star . . . Sphere   *Claudius alludes to the Ptolemaic conception of the universe, whereby each of the heavenly bodies revolved around the Earth fixed in a crystalline sphere.*

17   Count   *both (a) recounting (telling of what happened), and (b) accounting (trial and execution of the murderer).*

Scene 7

Enter the King and Laertes.

KING   Now must your Conscience my Acquittance seal,
And you must put me in your Heart for Friend,
Sith you have heard, and with a knowing Ear,
That he which hath your Noble Father slain
Pursu'd my Life.

LAERTES   It well appears. But tell me   5
Why you proceeded not against these Feats
So Crim'nal and so Capital in nature,
As by your Safety, Wisdom, all things else
You mainly were stirr'd up.

KING   O for two special Reasons,
Which may to you, perhaps, seem much
   unsinowed,   10
And yet to me th' are strong. The Queen his
   Mother
Lives almost by his Looks; and for my self,
(My Virtue or my Plague, be 't either which),
She's so conjunctive to my Life and Soul
That as the Star moves not but in his Sphere,   15
I could not but by her. The other Motive,
Why to a Public Count I might not go,

18   Gen'ral Gender   *common people. Here* Gender *means "kind."*

20   the Spring . . . Stone   *There were a number of springs in Elizabethan England that were reputed to petrify wood.*

21   Gyves   *shackles, here used as symbols of Hamlet's criminality.* Graces   *virtues, signs of favor.*

22   Too slightly timb'red   *made of too light a shaft.* loud   *strong and noisy. The loud wind is an apt metaphor for the currents of popular feeling as Claudius depicts them.*

23   reverted   *blown back.*

26   into Desp'rate Terms   *into a desperate (hopeless) condition.*

27   if Praises may go back again   *Laertes' phrase can be interpreted in two ways: (a) if praises may return to an earlier condition (what Ophelia was before she went mad), and (b) if I may be forgiven for seeming to praise myself in praising one so near to me. Both ideas echo the King's image of the reverted arrows (lines 21–23).*

28   Stood . . . Age   *could stand on the top of the highest mountain for all the ages and challenge all comers.*

33   Pastime   *a matter of idle interest.* You . . . more.   *The King expects an ambassador to come soon with word of Hamlet's execution in England. Ironically, a messenger enters almost as he speaks, but with news of a very different nature.*

Is the great Love the Gen'ral Gender bear him,
Who, dipping all his Faults in their Affection,
Would, like the Spring that turneth Wood to
    Stone,   20
Convert his Gyves to Graces, so that my Arrows,
Too slightly timb'red for so loud a Wind,
Would have reverted to my Bow again,
And not where I had aim'd them.
LAERTES   And so have I a Noble Father lost,   25
A Sister driven into Desp'rate Terms,
Whose Worth, if Praises may go back again,
Stood Challenger on Mount of all the Age
For her Perfections. But my Revenge will come.
KING   Break not your Sleeps for that. You must
    not think   30
That we are made of Stuff so Flat and Dull
That we can let our Beard be shook with Danger
And think it Pastime. You shortly shall hear
    more.
I lov'd your Father, and we love our Self,
And that I hope will teach you to imagine—   35

Enter a Messenger with Letters.

—How now? What News?
MESSENGER   Letters, my Lord, from Hamlet.
This to your Majesty, this to the Queen.
KING   From Hamlet? Who brought them?
MESSENGER   Sailors, my Lord, they say; I saw them
    not.
They were given me by Claudio: he receiv'd them   40

44 Naked *unattended, alone. But in fact there is a "naked" (unceremonious, unadorned) quality to Hamlet's whole letter. "High and Mighty" sounds jauntily familiar, if not downright disrespectful, and it implies that the King is to be regarded as an overweening usurper rather than revered as a monarch deserving of his exalted position. In this edition the letter is rendered as it appears in the Second Quarto. The less "naked" version in the Folio (adopted by most modern editions) adds the phrase* and more strange *before* Return. *It also affixes the name* Hamlet *to the end of the message.*

46 thereunto *for it. Because of the ambiguity of Hamlet's syntax, "first asking you Pardon" can relate to either (a) Hamlet's recounting (telling) of his story, or (b) his "Return."*

49 Abuse *deception, trick, lie.*

50 Char'cter *handwriting.*

52 devise me *explain it to me.*

56 didst *Modern editions normally adopt the Folio's* diest *here. The implications are much the same: in charging and challenging Hamlet, Horatio would in effect be telling him that he must die at the hands of an avenger.*

59 to a Peace *to be reconciled with my enemy.*

61 checking at his Voyage *reproving, rejecting the idea of his voyage, like a hawk that checks at (attacks) any prey it sees.*

62–63 I will . . . Device *I will manipulate him into undertaking an exploit the idea for which has just matured in my thinking (though the seeds for it were present before this moment).*

    Of him that brought them.

KING   —Laertes, you shall hear them.

    —Leave us.   *Exit Messenger.*

    [*Reads*] "High and Mighty, you shall know I

    am set Naked on your Kingdom. Tomorrow shall

    I beg leave to see your Kingly Eyes, when I   45

    shall, first asking you Pardon, thereunto

    recount the Occasion of my sudden Return."

    What should this mean? Are all the rest come back,

    Or is it some Abuse and no such thing?

LAERTES   Know you the Hand?

KING   'Tis Hamlet's Char'cter. "Naked,"   50

    And in a Postscript here he says "Alone."

    Can you devise me?

LAERTES   I'm lost in it, my Lord, but let him come:

    It warms the very Sickness in my Heart

    That I shall live and tell him to his Teeth   55

    "Thus didst thou."

KING   If it be so, Laertes

    (As how should it be so, how otherwise?),

    Will you be rul'd by me?

LAERTES   Ay my Lord,

    So you will not o'errule me to a Peace.

KING   To thine own Peace. If he be now returned   60

    As checking at his Voyage, and that he means

    No more to undertake it, I will work him

    To an Exploit now ripe in my Device,

    Under the which he shall not choose but fall;

    And for his Death no Wind of Blame shall

      breathe,   65

66   uncharge the Practice   *exonerate the activity. Here* un-
      charge *means the opposite of* charge *(accuse).* Practice *can
      refer to the execution of any kind of plan; but here it carries the
      connotation of a trick or stratagem.*

68   The rather   *and all the more so.*

69   Organ   *agent, instrument.*

70   Travail   *travel. The Elizabethan spelling reminds us that
      travel in the Renaissance involved considerable effort.*

72   Parts   *abilities, accomplishments.*

75   unworthiest Siege   *least importance. Here* Siege *is used in
      the earlier sense of "seat" (throne) or "rank."*

76   Riband   *ribbon, decorative flourish.*

79   Sables   *dark fur coats. Compare III.ii.136–37.*
      Weeds   *apparel.*

80   Importing . . . Graveness   *signifying maturity and dig-
      nity.*
      since   *ago.*

83   can well   *are highly skilled. Here* can *combines knowledge and
      capability.*

86–87 Incorps'd . . . With   *combined into a single composite
      body.*

87   topp'd   *excelled.*

88   in Forgery . . . Tricks   *in an attempt to forge an adequate
      description with all the flourishes that rhetoric supplies.*

But ev'n his Mother shall uncharge the Practice
And call it Accident.
LAERTES   My Lord, I will be rul'd,
The rather if you could devise it so
That I might be the Organ.
KING   It falls right.
You have been talk'd of since your Travail much,   70
And that in Hamlet's Hearing, for a Quality
Wherein they say you shine. Your Sum of Parts
Did not together pluck such Envy from him
As did that One, and that in my Regard
Of the unworthiest Siege.
LAERTES   What Part is that, my Lord?   75
KING   A very Riband in the Cap of Youth,
Yet needful too, for Youth no less becomes
The Light and Careless Liv'ry that it wears
Than settl'd Age his Sables and his Weeds
Importing Health and Graveness. Two Months
    since   80
Here was a Gentleman of Normandy.
I've seen my self, and serv'd against, the
    French,
And they can well on Horseback, but this
    Gallant
Had Witchcraft in't: he grew unto his Seat,
And to such Wondrous Doing brought his Horse   85
As he had been Incorps'd and Demi-natur'd
With the brave Beast. So far he topp'd, me
    thought,
That I in Forgery of Shapes and Tricks
Come short of what he did.

261

---

90   Lamord   *This name may be intended to suggest both* le mords *(old French for the jaw bit by which a rider controls a horse) and* La Mort *(French for "death"). Some editors follow the Folio and print* Lamound *(which would suggest* le monde *and describe an ideal man of the world).*

91   Brooch   *ornament, here one to be worn in the hat of a courtier.*

92   He . . . of you   *he confessed his inferiority to you.*

93   Masterly Report   *report of your mastery.*

94   Art and Exercise in your Defense   *technique and execution in the courtly arts of self-defense.*

97   Scrimures   *scrimers, fencers (from* escrimeurs *in French).*

98   Motion, Guard, nor Eye   *offensive maneuvers, defensive skills, nor precision in thrusting.*

105   the Painting of a Sorrow   *a mere imitation of true sorrow.*

109   in Passages of Proof   *through proven experience (evidence that has accumulated over the passage of time).*

110   qualifies   *moderates and thus lessens. This passage echoes a theme of "The Mousetrap," especially III.ii.210–39.*

112   Week   *wick.*
        Snuff   *either (a) a device for snuffing out a flame, or (b) the cutting off of the end of a wick.*
        abate   *diminish or extinguish.*

113   at a like Goodness still   *at the same intensity forever.*

LAERTES   A Norman was 't?
KING   A Norm'n.
LAERTES   Upon my Life, Lamord.
KING   The very same.   90
LAERTES   I know him well: he is the Brooch indeed
    And Gem of all the Nation.
KING   He made Confession of you,
    And gave you such a Masterly Report
    For Art and Exercise in your Defense,
    And for your Rapier most especial,   95
    That he cried out 'twould be a Sight indeed
    If one could match you. The Scrimures of their
        Nation
    He swore had neither Motion, Guard, nor Eye
    If you oppos'd them. Sir, this Report of his
    Did Hamlet so envenom with his Envy   · 100
    That he could nothing do but wish and beg
    Your sudden coming o'er to play with you.
    Now out of this—
LAERTES   What out of this, my Lord?
KING   Laertes, was your Father dear to you?
    Or are you like the Painting of a Sorrow,   105
    A Face without a Heart?
LAERTES   Why ask you this?
KING   Not that I think you do not love your Father,
    But that I know Love is begun by Time,
    And that I see in Passages of Proof
    Time qualifies the Spark and Fire of it.   110
    There lives within the very Flame of Love
    A kind of Week, or Snuff that will abate it,
    And nothing is at a like Goodness still:

114   Plurisy   *surfeit, superfluity ("Too Much"). The King is think-
       ing of* pleurisy *(an inflammation of the pleura, the thin
       membrane enveloping the lungs); its discharges were thought
       to result from the excessive consumption of fluids.*

117   Abatements   *legal impediments, quashing forbidden practices.*
       Delays   *This word recalls "the Law's Delay" (III.i.69); and
       Claudius' speech as a whole echoes several of Hamlet's solilo-
       quies. Like his nephew, the King is aware that "the Native
       Hew of Resolution" (III.i.81) may itself be hewn down by
       any of a variety of "Accidents."*

119–   Spendthrift's Sigh . . . easing   *Every sigh was thought to
20   cause the loss of a drop of blood.*

124   should Murther sanctuarize   *should provide asylum for a
       murderer (an ironic reminder of Hamlet's words in the Prayer
       Scene, III.iii.73–96).*

125   have no Bounds   *acknowledge no limits on its scope.*

126   Will you do this   *if you will do this.*

130   in fine   *in the end.*

131   Remiss   *neglectful, lacking in prudence.*

133   Foils   *fencing swords.*

135   unbated   *its end not blunted with a button to cover the tip.*
       a Pass of Practice   *a thrust in a practice match for sport.*

138   an Unction . . . Mountebank   *an ointment from an itin-
       erant drug salesman.*

For Goodness, growing to a Plurisy,
Dies in his own Too Much. That we would do   115
We should do when we would: for this "Would"
    changes,
And hath Abatements and Delays as many
As there are Tongues, are Hands, are Accidents.
And then this "Should" is like a Spendthrift's
    Sigh,
That hurts by easing. But to the Quick of th'
    Ulcer,   120
Hamlet comes back: what would you undertake
To show your self in Deed your Father's Son
More than in Words?
LAERTES   To cut his Throat i' th' Church!
KING   No place indeed should Murther sanctuarize:
    Revenge should have no Bounds. But good Laertes,   125
    Will you do this, keep close within your Chamber.
    Hamlet return'd shall know you are come home;
    We'll put on those shall praise your Excellence,
    And set a double Varnish on the Fame
    The Frenchman gave you, bring you in fine
        together,   130
    And wager o'er your Heads. He, being Remiss,
    Most Generous, and Free from all Contriving,
    Will not peruse the Foils, so that with ease,
    Or with a little Shuffling, you may choose
    A Sword unbated, and in a Pass of Practice   135
    Requite him for your Father.
LAERTES   I will do 't,
    And for that Purpose I'll anoint my Sword.
    I bought an Unction of a Mountebank

139   Mortal   *deadly.*

140   Cataplasm   *poultice; a soft, moist plaster applied to a wound or sore.*

141   Simples   *herbal extracts for use as drugs.*
      Virtue   *power (to cure).*

143   withal   *therewith.*

144   Contagion   *poison.*
      gall   *chafe, scratch.*

146   Convenience   *expedient; literally, a coming together of "Time and Means."*

147   fit us to our Shape   *suit us to our roles (as avengers).*

148–   And . . . assay'd   *and should our intention be disclosed as a*
49   *result of our inept performance [of this "play" we are scheming to produce], it would be better for us if we hadn't attempted it in the first place.*

150   Back or Second   *backup plan.*

151   blast in Proof   *fail (literally, blight) in execution.*

152   Cunnings   *abilities, skills.*

154   As make   *as you should contrive to make.*
      Bouts   *individual rounds of fencing.*

155   prefarr'd   *preferred, offered.*

156   A Chalice for the nonce   *a goblet for the occasion (literally, "the once"). Chalice often carries religious connotations.*

So Mortal that, but dip a Knife in it,
Where it draws Blood, no Cataplasm so rare,   140
Collected from all Simples that have Virtue
Under the Moon, can save the thing from Death
That is but scratch'd withal. I'll touch my
    Point
With this Contagion, that if I gall him slightly,
It may be Death.
KING   Let's further think on this.   145
Weigh what Convenience both of Time and Means
May fit us to our Shape if this should fail;
And, that our Drift look through our bad
    Performance,
'Twere better not assay'd; therefore this
    Project
Should have a Back or Second that might hold   150
If this did blast in Proof. Soft, let me see:
We'll make a solemn Wager on your Cunnings.
I ha't: when in your Motion you are hot and dry,
As make your Bouts more violent to that end,
And that he calls for drink, I'll have prefarr'd
    him   155
A Chalice for the nonce, whereon but Sipping
If he by chance escape your venom'd Stuck,
Our Purpose may hold there. But stay, what
    Noise?

Enter the Queen.

QUEEN   One Woe doth tread upon another's Heel,

162 askaunt *aslant over. The Folio prints* aslant.

163 his hoary *its whitish.*

164 fantastic *intricately wrought, the product of fantasy.*

165 Long Purples *probably a kind of wild orchid with an extended phallus-like purple spike (hence the "grosser Name).*

167 cull-cold *chaste (cold to "culling," embracing).*

168 pendant *hanging.*
Crownet Weeds *weeds formed into crowns (with a play on weeds,"apparel").*

169 envious *malicious.*

170 Trophies *the precious garlands she had woven from flowers.*

171 weeping Brook *The Queen poetically absolves the water from blame.*

173 Lauds *hymns of praise.*

174 incap'ble . . . Distress *unable to recognize her own danger.*

175– Native . . . Element *born in and accustomed to that envi-*
76 *ronment. Compare Hamlet's phrasing in I.iv.13–14.*

178 melodious Lay *Here the liquids ("l"-sounds) in the Queen's description evoke the element in which Ophelia sang her last "Lay" (song).*

183 our Trick *an involuntary manifestation of weakness in keeping with the "Custom" of human nature: to cry despite the "Shame" a man feels when acting "The Woman" (line 185).*

So fast they follow. —Your Sister's drown'd,
     Laertes.   160
LAERTES   Drown'd? O where?
QUEEN   There is a Willow grows askaunt the Brook
     That shows his hoary Leaves in th' glassy Stream;
     Therewith fantastic Garlands did she make
     Of Crowflow'rs, Nettles, Daisies, and Long
          Purples,   165
     That lib'ral Shepherds give a grosser Name,
     But our cull-cold Maids do Deadmen's Fingers
          call them.
     There on the pendant Boughs, her Crownet Weeds
     Clamb'ring to hang, an envious Sliver broke,
     When down her weedy Trophies and her self   170
     Fell in the weeping Brook. Her Clothes spread
          wide
     And Mermaid-like awhile they bore her up,
     Which time she chaunted Snatches of old Lauds
     As one incap'ble of her own Distress,
     Or like a Creature Native and Endu'd   175
     Unto that Element; but long it could not be
     Till that her Garments, heavy with their Drink,
     Pull'd the poor Wretch from her melodious Lay
     To muddy Death.
LAERTES   Alas, then she is drown'd!
QUEEN   Drown'd, drown'd.   180
LAERTES   —Too much of Water hast thou, poor
          Ophelia,
     And therefore I forbid my Tears. But yet
     It is our Trick, Nature her Custom holds:
     Let Shame say what it will, when these are gone,

185   will be out   *will come out.*

186   fain   *gladly, fervently.*

187   Folly   *Laertes refers to his "foolish" lack of manly self-control. He exits because he can no longer suppress his tears. Hamlet appears to use* Foolery *with the same implications (womanish) in V.ii.226.*

The Woman will be out. —Adieu, my Lord,   185
I have a Speech o' Fire that fain would blaze
But that this Folly drowns it.   *Exit.*
KING   —Let's follow, Gertrard.
How much I had to do to calm his Rage:
Now fear I this will give it Start again,
Therefore let's follow.   *Exeunt.*   190

V.i   *This scene takes place in a graveyard. The two "Clowns" re-*
      ferred to in the opening stage direction are a pair of rustics—
      one the chief gravedigger, the other apparently his assistant.
      They enter carrying spades and mattocks, and it soon becomes
      evident that they are here to prepare for the burial of Ophelia.

2   Salvation   *release. If the clown is a genuine bumpkin, he prob-*
      ably means to say "damnation." At issue is whether Ophelia
      committed suicide; if it had been determined that she did, she
      would be regarded as one who was guilty of mortal sin (as
      Hamlet notes in I.ii.131–32 and III.i.53–86) and would
      thus not be entitled to Christian burial rites.

4   Crowner   *coroner, the official who ruled on the cause of death*
      for anyone whose demise was not clearly by normal means.
      sate on her   *sat on her (conducted a formal inquest into her*
      death).

7   in her own Defense   *while attempting to save her life.*

8   found so   *so determined by the Coroner's inquest.*

9   Se offendendo   *offending against herself.*

11   wittingly   *knowingly. An "Act" requires the conscious will of*
      its agent.

13   Argal   *a rustic pronunciation of* Ergo, *Latin for "therefore."*
      Shakespeare is probably having an extra measure of fun with a
      pun on the name of an Elizabethan scholar, John Argall, who
      wrote learned treatises on logic.

14   Goodman Delver   *a title more or less equivalent to "Neigh-*
      bor Digger."

Act Five

Scene 1

Enter two Clowns.

CLOWN Is she to be buried in Christian Burial,
when she willfully seeks her own Salvation?
OTHER I tell thee she is, therefore make her
Grave straight: the Crowner hath sate on her,
and finds it Christian Burial.   5
CLOWN How can that be, unless she drown'd her
self in her own Defense?
OTHER Why 'tis found so.
CLOWN It must be *Se offendendo,* it cannot be else:
for here lies the Point. If I drown my self   10
wittingly, it argues an Act, and an Act hath
three Branches: it is to Act, to Do, to Perform.
Argal, she drown'd her self wittingly.
OTHER Nay, but hear you, Goodman Delver—
CLOWN Give me Leave. Here lies the Water, good.   15

273

17–18 will he nill he   *will he or will he not.*

18   he goes   *he that goes (he who is accountable for his act). What the Clown fails to note is that* nill he *would not apply to an act for which the victim was responsible.*

23   Quest   *inquest.*

24   ha'   *have.*
an't   *of it.*

28   have Count'naunce   *be indulged (have their deeds countenanced or overlooked).*

30   even Christen   *ordinary fellow Christians.*

35   bore Arms   *was entitled to bear a coat of arms as a gentleman (a distinction conferred by the College of Heralds in Shakespeare's England).*

41   to the Purpose   *with an answer that directly and truthfully addresses the question. Hamlet has used this expression earlier in his first conversation with Rosencrans and Guildenstern (II.ii.295).*
confess thy self   *The Clown alludes to a proverb, "Confess thy self and be hanged."*

45   Frame   *structure.*

46   Tenants   *occupants (hanged criminals).* Tenant *literally means "holder," and it can also refer to that which "hangs from" something.*

Here stands the Man, good. If the Man go to
this Water and drown himself, it is, will he
nill he, he goes; mark you that. But if the
Water come to him, and drown him, he drowns
not himself. Argal, he that is not guilty of   20
his own Death shortens not his own Life.

OTHER   But is this Law?

CLOWN   Ay marry is't, Crowner's Quest Law.

OTHER   Will you ha' the Truth an't? If this had
not been a Gentlewoman, she should have been   25
buried out a' Christian Burial.

CLOWN   Why there thou say'st; and the more Pity
that Great Folk should have Count'naunce in
this World to drown or hang themselves more
than their even Christen. Come, my Spade.   30
There is no auncient Gentlemen but Gard'ners,
Ditchers, and Grave-makers: they hold up
Adam's Profession.

OTHER   Was he a Gentleman?

CLOWN   'A was the first that ever bore Arms.   35

OTHER   Why he had none.

CLOWN   What, art a Heathen? How dost thou
understand the Scripture? The Scripture says
Adam digg'd: could he dig without Arms? I'll
put another Question to thee. If thou answerest   40
me not to the Purpose, confess thy self—

OTHER   Go to.

CLOWN   What is he that builds stronger than either
the Mason, the Shipwright, or the Carpenter?

OTHER   The Gallows-maker, for that Frame outlives a   45
thousand Tenants.

48   does well   *answers the question well. But in the next sentence the Clown gives a different twist to the expression, with* it *now referring not to the assistant's answer but to the Gallows made by the Gallows-maker.*

49   It does Well   *it does its job well.*

50   doost Ill   *commits a sin.*

55   unyoke   *be freed from further labor (like an ox), and (b) be cut down from the gallows.*

56   Marry   *truly. This expression probably originated as an oath referring to the Virgin Mary. Like* Mass *(referring to the Eucharist), it was a very mild oath by Shakespeare's time.*

60   your Ass   *an ass. The Clown uses the familiar article.*
      mend   *improve.*

63   stoup   *tankard.*

65–68 In Youth . . . meet.   *The song that the Clown begins here and continues later is a garbled version of "The Aged Lover Renounceth Love," a poem by Thomas Lord Vaux that had been printed in a popular anthology,* Tottel's Miscellany, *in 1557. Many of the* O *and* ah *words appear to be the Clown's grunts as he digs.*

67   To . . . Behove   *to shorten the time for my benefit.*

69   no Feeling of his Business   *no sensitivity to the kind of work he does.*

71–72 Custom . . . Easiness.   *Long habit has made it something he does with complete ease (without thinking deeply about it).*

CLOWN   I like thy Wit well, in good faith; the
        Gallows-maker does well. But how does it well?
        It does Well to those that do Ill. Now thou
        doost Ill to say the Gallows is built stronger   50
        than the Church: argal, the Gallows may do Well
        to thee. To 't again, come.
OTHER   Who builds stronger than a Mason, a Ship-
        wright, or a Carpenter?
CLOWN   Ay, tell me that and unyoke.   55
OTHER   Marry now I can tell.
CLOWN   To 't.
OTHER   Mass, I cannot tell.

                Enter Hamlet and Horatio afar off.

CLOWN   Cudgel thy Brains no more about it: for
        your Ass will not mend his Pace with Beating.   60
        And when you are ask'd this Question next, say
        "A Gravemaker: the Houses he makes lasts till
        Doomsday." Go get thee in, and fetch me a stoup
        of Liquor.   *Exit Other Clown.*
          "In Youth when I did love, did love,   *Song.*   65
             Me thought it was very sweet
           To contract, O, the Time for, ah, my
               Behove,
             O me thought there a was nothing, ah,
                 meet."
HAMLET Has this Fellow no Feeling of his Business?
        'A sings in Grave-making!   70
HORATIO Custom hath made it in him a Property of
        Easiness.

73–74   the Hand . . . Sense   *the hand that has been little employed is more sensitive (dainty), because it is not yet calloused.*

76   claw'd   *gripped.*

77   intil the Land   *into the land. Here the phrase suggests "into the grave."*

80   jowls it to the Ground   *dashes its jowls to the ground. The Clown is digging up old bones to make room for the fresh corpse.*

81   Cain's Jawbone   *This reference to the first murder (Genesis 4) reminds us of a more recent fratricide and of the murderer's own awareness of "the primal eldest Curse" (III.iii.37).*

82   the Pate of a Politician   *the head of a crafty intriguer (not limited to one involved in politics in the modern sense).*

83   o'er-reaches   *Hamlet enjoys the irony that one who sought to undo others with his plots is now being bumped by a bumpkin.*

83–84   one that would circumvent God   *one so overweening in his arrogance that he sought to get around (outwit) God himself.*

93   Chop-less   *without "chops" (jaws).*
Massene   *probably a variant of* mazzard, *head, and* mazer, *bowl or cup. The Folio prints* mazard.

94–95   and we . . . 't   *if we had the skill to perceive it.*

96   Loggets   *a game in which pieces of wood were tossed at a stake.*

103   Quiddities   *subtle arguments, fine legal distinctions.*

HAMLET   'Tis e'en so: the Hand of little Employment
hath the Daintier Sense.
CLOWN   "But Age with his stealing Steps   *Song.*   75
            Hath claw'd me in his Clutch
            And hath shipp'd me intil the Land
            As if I had never been such."
HAMLET   That Skull had a Tongue in it, and could
sing once. How the Knave jowls it to the Ground,   80
as if 'twere Cain's Jawbone, that did the first
Murder. This might be the Pate of a Politician
which this Ass now o'er-reaches: one that would
circumvent God. Might it not?
HORATIO   It might, my Lord.   85
HAMLET   Or of a Courtier, which could say "Good
Morrow, sweet Lord; how doost thou, sweet Lord?"
This might be My Lord Such-a-One, that prais'd
My Lord Such-a-One's Horse when 'a went to beg
it, might it not?   90
HORATIO   Ay my Lord.
HAMLET   Why e'en so, and now My Lady Worm's
Chop-less, and knock'd about the Massene with a
Sexton's Spade. Here's fine Revolution, and we
had the Trick to see 't. Did these Bones cost   95
no more the Breeding but to play at Loggets
with 'em? Mine ache to think on 't.
CLOWN   "A Pickaxe and a Spade, a Spade,   *Song.*
            For and a Shrouding Sheet,
            O a Pit of Clay for to be made   100
            For such a Guest is meet."
HAMLET   There's another. Why may not that be the
Skull of a Lawyer? Where be his Quiddities now,

104-5 his Quillities . . . Tricks *Hamlet notes that none of the Lawyer's tricks will be of any use to him in the court of last resort presided over by the Gravedigger. Like quiddities, "Quillities" are quibbles over minutiae. "Tenures" are titles to real estate.*

106 Sconce *head, but with a pun on a type of fine.*

107-8 his Action of Battery *the Clown's liability for a suit (action) for his action of battery (battering the Lawyer's skull).*

109–11 Buyer of Land . . . Recoveries *Lawyers were notorious for using their expertise to amass great holdings. "Statutes" and "Recognizances" were bonds in which debts had been secured with land and property. "Fines" and "Recoveries" were procedures for transferring land and property. "Vouchers" were devices to guarantee (vouch for) an owner's title.*

111–13 Is this . . . Dirt? *Is this the end of his fines, and the final return from his recoveries, to have his fine head full of fine-grained dirt?* Dirt *anticipates V.ii.87–89.*

113–18 Will . . . ha? *"Indentures" were duplicate copies of a deed, inscribed on a single sheet of parchment which was then cut in an indented (toothlike) line so that the buyer's and seller's halves could later be matched, if necessary, to prove their authenticity. The Lawyer's final estate (the "Box" he is buried in) is too small to hold even the pieces of parchment (the "Conveyances") that record the "Dirt" he went to so much effort to acquire. So much for the "Assurance" (security) to be found in "Sheep-skins."*

134 the Quick *the living (with wordplay on quick-witted, cheeky).*

his Quillities, his Cases, his Tenures, and his
Tricks? Why dooes he suffer this mad Knave now   105
to knock him about the Sconce with a dirty
Shovel and will not tell him of his Action of
Battery? Hum, this Fellow might be in's Time
a great Buyer of Land, with his Statutes, his
Recognizances, his Fines, his double Vouchers,   110
his Recoveries. Is this the Fine of his Fines,
and the Recovery of his Recoveries, to have his
fine Pate full of fine Dirt? Will his Vouchers
vouch him no more of his Purchases, and double
ones too, than the Length and Breadth of a Pair   115
of Indentures? The very Conveyances of his Lands
will scarcely lie in this Box, and must th'
Inheritor himself have no more, ha?

HORATIO   Not a iot more, my Lord.

HAMLET   Is not a Parchment made of Sheep-skins?   120

HORATIO   Ay my Lord, and of Calve-skins too.

HAMLET   They are Sheep and Calves which seek out
Assurance in that. I will speak to this Fellow.
—Whose Grave's this, Sirrah?

CLOWN   Mine Sir: 125
          "O a Pit of Clay for to be made
           For such a Guest is meet."

HAMLET   I think it be thine indeed: for thou liest
in't.

CLOWN   You lie out on't, Sir, and therefore 'tis   130
not yours. For my part, I do not lie in't, yet
it is mine.

HAMLET   Thou doost lie in't, to be in't and say it
is thine. 'Tis for the Dead, not for the Quick:

136   Quick Lie   *The Clown probably means a lie that spurts back and forth with the rapidity of quicksilver (mercury). In lines 128–35, he and Hamlet have used* lie *to mean (a) tell a lie, (b) stand, and (c) lie down, thereby demonstrating that* lie *is not a word to lie still. Since* Quick Lie *was a term for the kind of woman with whom one could have a quick sexual encounter (whence the name Mistress Quickly, a pun on "Quick-lie," in* 1 *and* 2 Henry IV*), the Clown is probably implying that the word* Lie *is itself a wanton.*

145   Absolute   *uncompromising in his insistence on absolute precision.*

146   by the Card   *perhaps an allusion to the "Shipman's Card" (*Macbeth, I.iii*), a chart used by sailors to navigate the seas.*
       Equivocation   *ambiguity; literally, speaking one word with two or more equally possible meanings. Hamlet is a master of equivocation himself, and in the world of this play equivocation is a way of life and death.*

147–   this three . . . it   *during the last three years I have noticed.*
48

148   Picked   *picky, finicky in its use of language.*

150   galls his Kibe   *chafes his chilblain (inflamed sore on the heel).*

163   seen   *noticed.*

therefore thou liest.   135

CLOWN   'Tis a Quick Lie, Sir: 'twill away again
from me to you.

HAMLET   What Man doost thou dig it for?

CLOWN   For no Man, Sir.

HAMLET   What Woman then?   140

CLOWN   For none neither.

HAMLET   Who is to be buried in't?

CLOWN   One that was a Woman, Sir; but rest her
Soul, she's dead.

HAMLET   —How Absolute the Knave is! We must speak   145
by the Card, or Equivocation will undo us. By
the Lord, Horatio, this three years I have took
note of it, the Age is grown so Picked that the
Toe of the Peasant comes so near the Heel of
the Courtier he galls his Kibe. —How long hast   150
thou been Grave-maker?

CLOWN   Of the Days of th' Year I came to 't that Day
that our last King Hamlet overcame Fortinbrasse.

HAMLET   How long is that since?

CLOWN   Cannot you tell that? Every Fool can tell   155
that! It was that very Day that young Hamlet
was born: he that is Mad and sent into England.

HAMLET   Ay marry, why was he sent into England?

CLOWN   Why because 'a was Mad. 'A shall recover
his Wits there; or if 'a do not, 'tis no great   160
Matter there.

HAMLET   Why?

CLOWN   'Twill not be seen in him there: there the
Men are as Mad as he.

HAMLET   How came he Mad?   165

283

167 How strangely? *Strangely in what way or sense?*

169 Upon what Ground? *For what reason or cause?*

175 pocky Corses *pock-marked corpses. The Clown is probably referring to victims of the pox (syphilis).*

177 A Tanner *a craftsman who tans hides to make leather. The Clown goes on to point out that by his use of tannin (a substance from the barks of oak trees) to tan the hides of animals, a tanner tans (and thereby waterproofs) his own skin as well.*

182 sore *severe.*

183 whoreson *bastard, a mild expletive that was often used with jocular familiarity.*

184 lyen *lain.*

190 a flagon of Renish *a pitcher of Rhine wine.*

193 This? *As Hamlet speaks this line, he probably takes the skull from the Gravedigger's hand. In the next line the Clown shifts from* This *(line 191) to* that *in reference to Yorick's head. The Folio adds the clause "Let me see," at the beginning of line 195; that would appear to be an interpolation rendered unnecessary by the fact that the skull has already changed hands, so in this as in most modern editions Hamlet's speech begins with "Alas, poor Yorick," as in the Second Quarto.*

CLOWN   Very strangely, they say.

HAMLET   How strangely?

CLOWN   Faith, e'en with losing his Wits.

HAMLET   Upon what Ground?

CLOWN   Why here in Denmark: I have been Sexton   170
here, Man and Boy, thirty years.

HAMLET   How long will a Man lie i' th' Earth ere
he rot?

CLOWN   Faith, if 'a be not Rotten before 'a die,
as we have many pocky Corses that will scarce   175
hold the laying in, 'a will last you some eight
year or nine year. A Tanner will last you nine
year.

HAMLET   Why he more than another?

CLOWN   Why Sir, his Hide is so tann'd with his   180
Trade that 'a will keep out Water a great while;
and your Water is a sore Decayer of your
whoreson dead Body. Here's a Skull now hath
lyen you i' th' Earth two and twenty years.

HAMLET   Whose was it?   185

CLOWN   A whoreson Mad Fellow's it was. Whose do
you think it was?

HAMLET   Nay I know not.

CLOWN   A Pestilence on him for a Mad Rogue, 'a
pour'd a flagon of Renish on my Head once.   190
This same Skull, Sir, was Sir Yorick's Skull,
the King's Jester.

HAMLET   This?

CLOWN   E'en that.

HAMLET   Alas, poor Yorick! —I knew him, Horatio: 195
a Fellow of infinite Jest, of most excellent

285

197   Fancy   *invention (imagination, wit).*

198   abhorred   *abhorrent (literally, to be shuddered away from).*

199   my Gorge rises   *my gullet threatens to regurgitate.*

201   Gibes   *sarcastic jests.*
       Gambols   *skipping movements.*

203   wont   *accustomed.*

204   Grinning   *Hamlet refers to the exposed teeth of the skull.*
       Chop-fall'n   *fallen down in the jaws; literally, down in the
       mouth.*

206   paint   *apply cosmetics.*
       Favor   *Hamlet is probably combining such senses as (a) facial
       appearance, (b) beauty, and (c) love-token.*

210   Alexander   *Alexander the Great (356–323 B.C.), the Greek
       general who amassed more territory than anyone prior to him;
       he sat down and wept when he realized that there were no more
       lands for him to conquer.*

213   pah   *an expression of disgust.*

218   Bunghole   *the spout hole in a cask for beer or wine. The word
       could also refer to the anus, and that may be a secondary
       implication.*

219   curiously   *ingeniously, precisely.*

221   iot   *jot; from the Greek word* iota, *the name of the letter corre-
       sponding to our* i.

222   Modesty   *rational and measured deliberation.*

Fancy. He hath bore me on his Back a thousand
times, and now how abhorred in my Imagination
it is: my Gorge rises at it. Here hung those
Lips that I have kiss'd I know not how oft. 200
—Where be your Gibes now? Your Gambols, your
Songs, your flashes of Merriment, that were
wont to set the Table on a Roar? Not one now
to mock your own Grinning? Quite Chop-fall'n!
Now get you to my Lady's Table, and tell her, 205
let her paint an Inch thick, to this Favor she
must come. Make her laugh at that. —Prethee,
Horatio, tell me one thing.

HORATIO   What's that, my Lord?

HAMLET   Doost thou think Alexander look'd a' this 210
Fashion i' th' Earth?

HORATIO   E'en so.

HAMLET   And smelt so, pah?

HORATIO   E'en so, my Lord.

HAMLET   To what base Uses we may return, 215
Horatio! Why, may not Imagination trace the
Noble Dust of Alexander till 'a find it stopping a
Bunghole?

HORATIO   'Twere to consider too curiously to
consider so. 220

HAMLET   No faith, not a iot. But to follow him
thether with Modesty enough, and Likelihood to
lead it, as thus: Alexander died, Alexander was
buried, Alexander returneth to Dust, the Dust
is Earth, of Earth we make Loam; and why of 225
that Loam whereto he was converted might they
not stop a Beer-barrel?

228   Imperious Caesar   *Here* Imperious *means both (a) imperial (possessing the power and attributes of an emperor), and (b) haughty. Hamlet is probably referring to Julius Caesar (100–44 B.C.), but he may also be thinking of Octavius Caesar (63 B.C.–A.D. 14), who assumed the title Caesar Augustus after he became Emperor in 27 B.C. After Augustus every Roman emperor was known as Caesar, and the name became synonymous with* monarch. *Hamlet may well be meditating on that as he plots to undo an "Imperious Caesar" who keeps "the World in Awe" in his own time.*

231   t' expel the Water's Flaw   *to keep out the rain. Here* Flaw *is probably either a variant of* flow *(so spelled to rhyme with* Awe*) or a word referring to a shaft of ice. Most editors adopt the Folio's* Winter's flaw, *referring either to a shaft of ice or to a squall of gusty wind.*

234   maim'd Rites   *curtailed ceremony.*

236   Fordo it   *destroy its.*
of some Estate   *of some high station.*

237   Couch we   *let us conceal ourselves.*

241   DOCTOR   *Doctor of Divinity, Priest.*
Obsequies   *funeral ceremonies.*

243   great . . . Order   *an order from the King supersedes the proper "Order" (liturgical practice) of the Church.*

245   For   *instead of.*

246   Peebles   *pebbles.*

247   Virgin Crants   *garlands strewn on an unblemished maiden.*

Imperious Caesar, dead and turn'd to Clay,
Might stop a Hole to keep the Wind away.
O that that Earth which kept the World in Awe   230
Should patch a Wall t' expel the Water's Flaw.

Enter the King, the Queen, Laertes,
and the Corse.

But soft, but soft a while, here comes the King,
The Queen, the Courtiers. Who is this they
   follow?
And with such maimed Rites? This doth betoken
The Corse they follow did with desp'rate Hand   235
Fordo it own Life. 'Twas of some Estate.
Couch we a while and mark.
LAERTES   What Ceremony else?
HAMLET   This is Laertes, a very Noble Youth: mark.
LAERTES   What Ceremony else?   240
DOCTOR   Her Obsequies have been as far enlarg'd
   As we have Warranty. Her Death was doubtful,
   And but that great Commaund o'er-sways the
      Order,
   She should in Ground Unsanctified been lodg'd
   Till the Last Trumpet. For charitable Prayers,   245
   Flints and Peebles should be thrown on her;
   Yet here she is allow'd her Virgin Crants,
   Her Maiden Strewments, and the bringing home
   Of Bell and Burial.
LAERTES   Must there no more be done?
DOCTOR   No more be done.   250
   We should profane the Service of the Dead

252   sage Requiem   *a solemn Mass for the peaceful repose of the deceased.*

253   Peace-parted Souls   *souls that departed at peace with God. Suicides were regarded as souls who died in despair, with no trust in God's grace.*

257   howling   *a state proverbially associated with the damned.* the fair Ophelia   *This is Hamlet's first realization that Ophelia is dead. His words echo III.i.86.*

258   Sweets to the Sweet   *sweet flowers to the sweet soul.*

260   thought   *expected. The Queen's sentiments in lines 259–61 not only endear her to the audience; they also remind us that Ophelia was the victim of tragically misguided interference by both her brother and her father.*

261   treble   *triple.*

263   most ingenious Sense   *sanity. Laertes uses* ingenious *in the Latin sense referring to intellectual vitality.*

266   Quick   *living.*

268   Pelion   *the mountain the primordial Giants piled on Mount Ossa in their challenge to the Olympian Gods. Claudius has associated an earlier outburst from Laertes with "Giant-like" rebellion in IV.v.124.*

271   Conjures   *casts under its spell.*

272   Wonder-wounded   *struck with amazement, from "wand'ring" (orbiting) to arrested "Wonder" at such a display of hubris (overweening pride).*

To sing sage Requiem and such Rest to her
As to Peace-parted Souls.
LAERTES   Lay her i' th' Earth,
And from her fair and unpolluted Flesh
May Violets spring. I tell thee, churlish
  Priest,   255
A min'st'ring Angel shall my Sister be
When thou li'st howling!
HAMLET   What, the fair Ophelia!
QUEEN   Sweets to the Sweet, farewell.
                        She strews Flowers on Ophelia's Corpse.
  —I hop'd thou should'st have been my Hamlet's
    Wife;
I thought thy Bride-bed to have deck'd, sweet
    Maid,   260
And not t' have strew'd thy Grave.
LAERTES   O treble Woe
Fall ten times double on that cursed Head
Whose wicked Deed thy most ingenious Sense
Depriv'd thee of! —Hold off the Earth a while
Till I have caught her once more in mine Arms.   265
                        He leaps in the Grave.
Now pile your Dust upon the Quick and Dead
Till of this Flat a Mountain you have made
T' o'ertop old Pelion, or the skyish Head
Of blue Olympus!
HAMLET [*Stepping forward*] What is he whose Grief
Bears such an Emphasis, whose Phrase of Sorrow   270
Conjures the wand'ring Stars and makes them
    stand
Like Wonder-wounded Hearers? This is I,

273   **Hamlet the Dane** *Hamlet's phrasing echoes earlier uses of "the Dane" by Claudius, and implies that Hamlet is not only asserting his superiority to Laertes but staking his claim to the Crown itself.*

276   **splen'tive Rash** *Hamlet uses the adjective* splenitive *to refer to the kind of passion that was thought to derive from the spleen, the seat of the impulsive emotions. The Folio adds an* and *before* Rash *to yield a metrically regular line, and modern editors normally follow suit. It may be, however, that Shakespeare deliberately inserted a short line here in keeping with the short-tempered rashness Hamlet describes.*

282   **wag** *move up and down (traditionally regarded as the last sign of life).*

287   **forbear** *restrain. By this point, both young men are probably being held to keep them from attacking each other physically.*

288   **S'wounds** *God's wounds, an oath referring to the Crucifixion.*

289   **Woo't** *wilt thou.*

290   **Esill** *vinegar. Hamlet may be alluding to the bitter gall given to Jesus on the Cross (Matthew 27:34).*

293   **quick** *alive.*

294   **prate** *speak idly and boastfully.*

296   **Singing . . . Zone** *pushing its head so high that it will be singed by the heat of the Sun.*

297   **Ossa** *another reference to the Giants' rebellion (see the note to line 268).*

Hamlet the Dane!
>   *He leaps into the Grave and Laertes seizes him.*
LAERTES   The Devil take thy Soul!
HAMLET   Thou pray'st not well.
I prethee take thy Fingers from my Throat,   275
For, though I am not splen'tive Rash,
Yet have I in me something Dangerous,
Which let thy Wisdom fear. Hold off thy Hand!
KING   Pluck them asunder!
QUEEN   Hamlet, Hamlet!
ALL   Gentl'men!
HORATIO   Good my Lord, be quiet!   280
HAMLET   Why, I will fight with him upon this Theme
Until my Eyelids will no longer wag!
QUEEN   O my Son, what Theme?
HAMLET   I lov'd Ophelia. Forty thousand Brothers
Could not with all their Quantity of Love   285
Make up my Sum. —What wilt thou do for her?
KING   O he is Mad, Laertes!
QUEEN   For love of God, forbear him!
HAMLET   S'wounds, show me what thou't do:
Woo't weep? Woo't fight? Woo't fast? Woo't tear
      thy Self?
Woo't drink up Essil, eat a Crocodile?   290
I'll do 't. Doost come here to whine?
To out-face me with leaping in her Grave?
Be buri'd quick with her, and so will I.
And if thou prate of Mountains, let them throw
Millions of Acres on us, till our Ground,   295
Singing his Pate against the Burning Zone,
Make Ossa like a Wart! Nay and thou'lt mouth,

298   mere   *pure.*

300   **Anon**   *in a short while.*
        Patient   *passive, contented.*

301   **golden Cuplets**   *the golden-downed couplets (offspring) of the Dove, a traditional symbol of peace, love, deliverance, and Divine grace (see Genesis 8:8–12 and Matthew 3:16).*
        disclosed   *hatched. The dove normally lays two eggs at a time.*

302   **drooping**   *with eyelids lowered, spent. The Queen's words imply that Hamlet will also feel remorse for his outburst.*

306   **The Cat will mew**   *the cat is bound to meow (despite the efforts of even the most powerful man on earth).*
        and Dog will have his Day   *and the dog, too, will act in accordance with his nature. What Hamlet means by this parting line is unclear. He may be saying that he and Laertes have just gone at each other like a dog and a cat; he may be trying to excuse his own passion; or he may be warning Laertes that "his Day" (Hamlet's) will come (to finish what he was prevented from doing on this occasion).*

307   wait upon him   *tend to him.*

309   **We'll . . . Push.**   *The King is speaking privately to Laertes, and he is telling him "we'll strike while the iron is hot."*

312   thereby   *as a result. The King implies to the Queen that he will place a memorial over Ophelia's grave to ensure a period of harmony ("An Hour of Quiet"); meanwhile he is probably implying to Laertes that true "Quiet" will result from a more fitting "Monument" to Ophelia, namely the death of Hamlet.*

I'll rant as well as thou.

QUEEN   This is mere Madness,
And thus a while the Fit will work on him;
Anon as Patient as the female Dove   300
When that her golden Cuplets are disclosed,
His Silence will sit drooping.

HAMLET   —Hear you, Sir,
What is the Reason that you use me thus?
I lov'd you ever, but it is no Matter:
Let Hercules himself do what he may,   305
The Cat will mew, and Dog will have his Day.   *Exit.*

KING   —I pray thee, good Horatio, wait upon him.
                                        Exit Horatio.

—Strengthen your Patience in our last night's
   Speech;
We'll put the Matter to the present Push.
—Good Gertrard, set some Watch over your Son.   310
This Grave shall have a living Monument:
An Hour of Quiet thereby shall we see;
Till then in Patience our Proceeding be.   *Exeunt.*

V.ii   *This scene returns us to the Castle, where Hamlet is telling Horatio what happened aboard the ship to England.*

1   now shall you see the other   *now shall I tell you about the other matter (the "Words" Hamlet promised Horatio in the letter delivered in IV.vi).*

6   Mutines in the Bilbo   *mutineers shackled to the bilbo, the long iron bar with which Renaissance ships were equipped to discourage insurrections. The Folio prints* bilboes.
      rashly   *irrationally, instinctively, intuitively.*

8   Indiscretion   *impulsive behavior; "rashness."*

9   deep Plots   *deeply meditated, deliberate plans.*
      pall   *falter, grow weary and prove useless.*

10–11   There's . . . will   *Hamlet's metaphor suggests a number of related ways in which Providence "shapes our Ends": (a) it gives our lives a well-carved shape, despite our own tendency to "hew" (chop) them in a rough, shapeless manner; (b) it takes our "Ends" (intentions) and gives them a shape we can only approach in a rough-hewn fashion; and (c) it takes the "Ends" of our lives (both literally, and in the sense pertaining to God's purpose for them) and gives them a shape (fits them into a design) that we can at best approximate with our rough-hewn plans and actions.* Rough-hew *echoes Hamlet's earlier reference to "the Native Hew of Resolution" (III.i.81).*

13   scarf'd   *wrapped.*

15   in fine   *in the end, eventually.*

17   unfold   *open up. Most editors adopt the Folio's* unseal *here.*

Scene 2

Enter Hamlet and Horatio.

HAMLET   So much for this, Sir; now shall you see the
    other.
    You do remember all the Circumstance.
HORATIO   Remember it, my Lord!
HAMLET   Sir, in my Heart there was a kind of
    Fighting
    That would not let me sleep; me thought I lay   5
    Worse than the Mutines in the Bilbo, rashly,
    And prais'd be Rashness for it. Let us know
    Our Indiscretion sometime serves us well
    When our deep Plots do pall; and that should
    learn us
    There's a Divinity that shapes our Ends   10
    Rough-hew them how we will.
HORATIO   That is most certain.
HAMLET   Up from my Cabin,
    My Sea-gown scarf'd about me in the Dark,
    Grop'd I to find them; had my Desire,
    Finger'd their Packet, and in fine withdrew   15
    To mine own Room again, making so bold,
    My Fears forgetting Manners, to unfold
    Their graund Commission; where I found, Horatio

20 **Larded** *garnished.*

21 **Importing** *pertaining to.*

22 **With . . . Life** *with more bugbears than I've ever heard in all my life.*

23 **Supervise** *overlooking, perusal [of the document].*
 no Leisure bated *with no time deducted (abated) for leisure.*

24 **stay** *wait for.*

29 **benetted round** *caught in a net.*

 Villains *Most editors emend to* villainies. *But Hamlet seems to be thinking primarily of the enemies arrayed against him at this moment: the two agents he assumes to be privy to the King's intentions, Rosencrans and Guildenstern.*

30 **Or** *before; an alternative spelling of* ere.

32 **fair** *in a neat hand, similar to the calligraphy of a professional scribe.*

33 **Statists** *"statesmen," men in high office.*

34 **A Baseness** *a demeaning skill.*

36 **Yeman's Service** *the benefit accruing to a reliable craftsman (yeoman).*

40 **As** *so that.*

42 **a Comma . . . Amities** *a link to tie them together in friendship.*

43 **Ases of great Charge** *as clauses of great weight and importance.*

(Ah Royal Knavery!), an exact Command,
Larded with many sev'ral sorts of Reasons,   20
Importing Denmark's Health and England's too,
With ho such Bugs and Goblins in my Life,
That on the Supervise, no Leisure bated,
No, not to stay the Grinding of the Axe,
My Head should be strook off.

HORATIO   Is't possible?   25

HAMLET   Here's the Commission: read it at more
     Leisure.
But wilt thou hear now how I did proceed?

HORATIO   I beseech you.

HAMLET   Being thus benetted round with Villains
     (Or I could make a Prologue to my Brains,   30
     They had begun the Play), I sat me down,
     Devis'd a new Commission, wrote it fair.
     I once did hold it, as our Statists do,
     A Baseness to write Fair, and labor'd much
     How to forget that Learning. But Sir now   35
     It did me Yeman's Service. Wilt thou know
     Th' Effect of what I wrote?

HORATIO   Ay, good my Lord.

HAMLET   An earnest Conjuration from the King,
     As England was his faithful Tributary,
     As Love between them like the Palm might
        flourish,   40
     As Peace should still her wheaten Garland wear
     And stand a Comma 'tween their Amities,
     And many such like *As*es of great Charge,
     That on the View and Knowing of these Contents,
     Without Debatement further more or less,   45

47   Not Shriving-time allow'd   *without allowing enough time for them to confess their sins and prepare their souls for death. The haste Hamlet calls for parallels that of the commission calling for his own execution (line 24). We must remember that at the time Hamlet wrote this death order he was assuming that he would arrive in England with his former schoolmates; he would thus have wanted them silenced before they could say anything that would jeopardize the Prince's own life. Even so, however, the harshness of Hamlet's sentence (going beyond that of even so evil a character as Claudius in its explicit call for what the Prince assumes will be the damnation of his victims) is surely designed by the playwright to give the audience pause.*

48   ordinant   *ordering matters.*

52   Subscrib'd it   *signed it (literally, "wrote under" it).*

53   Changeling   *Hamlet compares the exchanged document to a mischievous imp substituted by fairies for a stolen child.*

59   Insinuation   *winding into affairs of state; obsequious flattery.*

61   Pass . . . Points   *thrust of the fierce, enraged sword-tips.*

65   Popp'd . . . Hopes   *inserted himself between the throne and my expectations.*

66   Thrown . . . Life   *cast out his hook for my own life.*

67   Cous'nage   *a pun on (a) cozenage (trickery), and (b) cousin-like behavior. Any relative, including an uncle or a nephew, could be called a cousin.*

68   quit him   *both (a) requite (repay) him, and (b) kill him.*

He should those Bearers put to sudden Death,
Not Shriving-time allow'd.

HORATIO   How was this seal'd?

HAMLET   Why ev'n in that was Heaven ordinant:
I had my Father's Signet in my Purse,
Which was the Model of that Danish Seal;   50
Folded the Writ up in the Form of th' other,
Subscrib'd it, gave 't the Impression, plac'd
     it safely,
The Changeling never known. Now the next Day
Was our Sea-fight, and what to this was sequent
Thou know'st already.   55

HORATIO   So Guildenstern and Rosencrans go to 't.

HAMLET   Why Man, they did make love to this
     Employment:
They are not near my Conscience. Their
     Defeat
Dooes by their own Insinuation grow.
'Tis Dang'rous when the Baser Nature comes   60
Between the Pass and fell incensed Points
Of Mighty Opposites.

HORATIO   Why what a King is this!

HAMLET   Dooes it not, think thee, stand me now upon,
He that hath kill'd my King and whor'd my
     Mother,
Popp'd in between th' Election and my Hopes,   65
Thrown out his Angle for my proper Life,
And with such Cous'nage, is't not perfect
     Conscience
To quit him with this Arm? And is't not to be
     damn'd

69   **Canker**   *here either (a) a cancer or (b) a cankerworm.*

73   **the Int'rim's mine**   *I'll succeed within the brief interval I have to work with.*

74   **no more than to say "one"**   *lasts no longer than it takes a person either to say the word "one" or to count to "one."*

76   **I forgot my self**   *I lost control of my true nature.*

77–78   **by the Image . . . his**   *for if I look at my own situation, I now recognize that the one he faces is identical with it. Like the Latin word* causa, cause *can mean both "cause" and "case."*

78   **I'll count his Favors**   *I'll weigh (take into full account) his virtues and the kindnesses he has done me. Modern editions normally emend* count *to* court.

79   **the Brav'ry of his Grief**   *the bravado with which Laertes proclaimed his "Grief" (grievances) against "the cursed Head" (V.i. 262) responsible for his griefs (sorrows).*

80   **a Tow'ring Passion**   *Hamlet uses* Tow'ring *with nice precision here. To avoid having Laertes "out-face" him (V.i. 292), he engaged his opponent in a match to see whose rage could be more "Giant-like."*

86–87   **his Crib . . . Mess**   *his trough will have a place in the King's dining hall. Hamlet's point is that obsequious flatterers, however base, are more than welcome in a degenerate court that depends on such abominable creatures for its survival.*

87   **Chough**   *either a crow or a jackdaw (a smaller bird that could be taught to speak).*

To let this Canker of our Nature come
In further Evil? 70
HORATIO   It must be shortly known to him from
    England
What is the Issue of the Bus'ness there.
HAMLET   It will be short, the Int'rim's mine;
And a Man's Life's no more than to say "one."
But I am very sorry, good Horatio, 75
That to Laertes I forgot my self:
For by the Image of my Cause I see
The Portraiture of his. I'll count his Favors;
But sure the Brav'ry of his Grief did put me
Into a Tow'ring Passion.
HORATIO   Peace, who comes here? 80

Enter a Courtier.

COURTIER   Your Lordship is right welcome back to
    Denmark.
HAMLET   I humbly thank you, Sir.
   —Doost know this Water-fly?
LAERTES   No, my good Lord.
HAMLET   Thy State is the more gracious: for 'tis a
Vice to know him. He hath much Land and fertile. 85
Let a Beast be Lord of Beasts, and his Crib
shall stand at the King's Mess. 'Tis a Chough;
but, as I say, spacious in the Possession of
Dirt.
COURTIER   Sweet Lord, if your Lordship were at 90
Leisure, I should impart a thing to you from

303

94   **Bonnet**   *hat. The Courtier has removed his bonnet out of deference, and Hamlet is telling him to put it back on. In line 206 we learn that the Courtier's name is Ostrick (probably a play on Ostrich), and it seems likely that his headdress in the original staging was designed to make him resemble a bird stupid enough to believe itself invisible if its head were buried.*

100   **Sully**   *Possibly either a misreading for or a variant of* sultry *(the Folio reads* soultry, *which Ostrick appears to understand, line 102). But Hamlet may be coining an adjective that combines* sultry *(humid) and* sullied *(soiled, dirty).*

107   **remember**   *be reminded. Prompted, perhaps, by "great Wager on your Head," Hamlet tells Ostrick once more to cover his head.*

111   **Differences**   *distinctions.*
       soft Society   *refined, delicate manners.*

112   **Showing**   *appearance.*
       sellingly   *as if to market him.*

113   **Card or Calendar of Gentry**   *chart or inventory of gentlemanly attributes.*

114   **Continent**   *container.*

116–   **Sir . . . more.**   *Hamlet parodies Ostrick's ridiculously pre-*
25   *tentious vocabulary. Here* Definement *means "definition,"* Perdition *means "loss,"* dazzy *means "dizzy,"* Raw *means "unripe,"* Verity of Extolment *means "truth of praise,"* Article *means "substance,"* Infusion *means "quality," and* Dearth *means "preciousness."*

his Majesty.

HAMLET   I will receive it, Sir, with all Diligence
of Spirit. Your Bonnet to his right Use: 'tis
for the Head.   95

COURTIER   I thank your Lordship, it is very Hot.

HAMLET   No, believe me, 'tis very Cold: the Wind
is Northerly.

COURTIER   It is indifferent Cold, my Lord, indeed.

HAMLET   But yet me thinks it is very Sully and Hot,   100
or my Complexion—

COURTIER   Exceedingly, my Lord, it is very Soultery,
as 'twere, I cannot tell how. But my Lord his
Majesty bade me signify to you that 'a has laid
a great Wager on your Head: Sir, this is the   105
Matter—

HAMLET   I beseech you remember.

COURTIER   Nay good my Lord, for my Ease, in good
faith, Sir. Here is newly come to Court Laertes,
believe me an absolute Gentleman, full of most   110
excellent Differences, of very soft Society,
and great Showing. Indeed, to speak sellingly
of him, he is the Card or Calendar of Gentry:
for you shall find in him the Continent of what
Part a Gentleman would see.   115

HAMLET   Sir, his Definement suffers no Perdition
in you, though I know to divide him
inventorially would dazzy th' Arithmatic of
Memory; and yet but Raw neither in respect of
his quick Sale, but in the Verity of Extolment   120
I take him to be a Soul of great Article, and
his Infusion of such Dearth and Rareness as, to

123   make true Diction   *speak truly.*
      Semblable   *mirror image.*

124   who else would trace him   *and anyone else who would
      attempt to follow in his footsteps.*

125   Umbrage   *shadow.*

128   The Concernancy   *what is this all about?*

129   our more rawer Breath   *our crude, inadequate words.*

133– What . . . Gentleman?   *What is the significance of the
34   naming of this gentleman? Why are we talking about him
      now?*

141   much approve me   *prove much about me (go far toward
      proving it true that I am "not ignorant").*

145   compare   *appear to have the audacity to compare myself.*

147– in the Imputation laid on him   *in the reputation he bears.*
48

148   them in his Meed   *those of comparable merit.*

149   unfellowed   *unequaled.*

make true Diction of him, his Semblable is his
Mirror, and who else would trace him his
Umbrage, nothing more. 125
COURTIER   Your Lordship speaks most infallibly of
him.
HAMLET   The Concernancy, Sir? Why do we wrap the
Gentleman in our more rawer Breath?
COURTIER   Sir? 130
HORATIO   Is't not possible to understand in another
Tongue? You will do 't, Sir, really.
HAMLET   What imports the Nomination of this
Gentleman?
COURTIER   Of Laertes? 135
HORATIO   His Purse is empty already; all's Golden
Words are spent.
HAMLET   Of him, Sir.
COURTIER   I know you are not Ignorant—
HAMLET   I would you did, Sir; yet in faith if you 140
did, it would not much approve me. Well, Sir?
COURTIER   You are not Ignorant of what Excellence
Laertes is—
HAMLET   I dare not confess that, lest I should
compare with him in Excellence: but to know a 145
Man well were to know himself.
COURTIER   I mean, Sir, for his Weapon: but in the
Imputation laid on him, by them in his Meed,
he's unfellowed.
HAMLET   What's his Weapon? 150
COURTIER   Rapier and Dagger.
HAMLET   That's two of his Weapons, but well.
COURTIER   The King, Sir, hath wager'd with him six

307

155   impawn'd   *pledged, staked in equal wager.*

156   Poynards   *poniards (daggers). The spelling in the Quarto text probably reflects Elizabethan pronunciation.*
Assigns   *appurtenances.*
Girdle   *belt.*
Hanger   *the apparatus (usually one or two straps) attached to a courtier's girdle to hold his rapier and poniard.*

157   Carriages   *normally a term for gun-carriers, here used as an affected term for sword hangers*

158   dear to Fancy   *pleasing to the eye.*

158–59   responsive to the Hilts   *matching the sword hilts in design.*

160   liberal Conceit   *elaborate design.*

162   edified by the Margent   *informed by the explanatory notes in the margin (Horatio alludes to the glosses in weighty tomes).*

165   German   *germane, relevant; probably with an allusion to German cannons. In the opening scene Marcellus has referred to the "daily cost of Brazen Cannon / And foreign Mart for Implements of War" (I.i.68–69).*

168   Barbary Horses   *a breed known for its swiftness and quality.*

178   vouchsafe the Answer   *grant a response to the invitation.*

183–84   the Breathing . . . me   *the time of day when I ordinarily exercise.*

Barbary Horses, against the which he has
impawn'd, as I take it, six French Rapiers and   155
Poynards, with their Assigns, as Girdle, Hanger,
and so. Three of the Carriages in faith are
very dear to Fancy, very responsive to the
Hilts, most delicate Carriages, and of very
liberal Conceit.   160

HAMLET   What call you the Carriages?

HORATIO   I knew you must be edified by the Margent
ere you had done.

COURTIER   The Carriages, Sir, are the Hangers.

HAMLET   The Phrase would be more German to the   165
Matter if we could carry a Cannon by our sides.
I would it might be Hangers till then. But on,
six Barbary Horses against six French Swords,
their Assigns, and three liberal conceited
Carriages: that's the French Bet against the   170
Danish. Why is this all impawn'd, as you call
it?

COURTIER   The King, Sir, hath laid, Sir, that in
a dozen Passes between your self and him, he
shall not exceed you three Hits; he hath laid   175
on Twelve for Nine, and it would come to
immediate Trial if your Lordship would
vouchsafe the Answer.

HAMLET   How if I answer no?

COURTIER   I mean, my Lord, the Opposition of   180
your Person in Trial.

HAMLET   Sir, I will walk here in the Hall; if it
please his Majesty, it is the Breathing Time of
Day with me. Let the Foils be brought, the

186   and   *if.*

188   deliver you   *deliver this message from you.*

194   for's Turn   *who will speak for him, commending (praising) his duty.*

195–
96   This Lapwing . . . Head.   *Horatio compares Ostrick to a bird that was proverbially ludicrous and was said to run around with its eggshell on its head almost as soon as it was hatched.*

197   comply with his Dug   *compliment (bow politely to) his mother's nipple.*

198   Breed   *The Folio reads* Bevy, *a flock of birds.*

199   drossy   *worthless.*

199–
200   only got the Tune of the Time   *[have] only mastered the tune (without the words, the substance) of the time's fashions.*

200–1   an outward Habit of Encounter   *an outward manner of social interaction with no understanding of what society's customs really signify. Here* Habit *probably refers to a fashionable mode of dress that serves as a kind of uniform for members of the group.*

201   a kind of yeasty Collection   *a collection of superficial mannerisms that resembles the froth on a mug of beer or ale.*

202–3   fond and winnow'd Opinions   *foolish and winnowed-out (empty, chaff-like) opinions.*

203–4   and do . . . out   *so that if you try (test) them by blowing on them, all you get are frothy bubbles.*

Gentleman willing and the King hold his Purpose. 185
I will win for him and I can; if not, I will
gain nothing but my Shame and tl.e Odd Hits.

COURTIER   Shall I deliver you so?

HAMLET   To this Effect, Sir, after what Flourish
your Nature will. 190

COURTIER   I commend my Duty to your Lordship.

HAMLET   Yours.   *Exit Courtier.*
He dooes well to commend it himself:
there are no Tongues else for's Turn.

HORATIO   This Lapwing runs away with the Shell on 195
his Head.

HAMLET   'A did comply with his Dug before 'a suck'd
it: thus has he, and many more of the same Breed
that I know the drossy Age dotes on, only got
the Tune of the Time, an outward Habit of 200
Encounter, a kind of yeasty Collection, which
carries them through and through the most fond
and winnow'd Opinions; and do but blow them to
their Trial, the Bubbles are out.

Enter a Lord.

LORD   My Lord, his Majesty commended him to you 205
by young Ostrick, who brings back to him that
you attend him in the Hall; he sends to know if
your Pleasure hold to play with Laertes, or that
you will take longer Time.

HAMLET   I am constant to my Purposes: they follow 210
the King's Pleasure. If his Fitness speaks,

216– The Queen . . . Laertes *the Queen requests that you ex-*
17   *change some courteous words with Laertes.*

221– since . . . Practice *Whether Hamlet has been practicing*
22   *for the reasons the King suggested in his conversation with*
      Laertes (IV.vii.92–102) is impossible to determine. Hamlet
      has had better reasons to sharpen his skills with the rapier. But
      the Prince's words suggest that envy of Laertes' reputation
      may have been at least one motivating factor.

226   Foolery *something foolish, not to be taken seriously. What*
      Hamlet describes here is very similar to the "Fighting / That
      would not let [him] sleep" (V.ii.4–5) aboard the ship for
      England. That may have been a rash "Indiscretion," another
      kind of "Foolery," but his decision to act on it would probably
      have saved the Prince's life when he arrived in England.

227   Gaingiving *misgiving.*
      trouble a Woman *Elizabethans who had seen* Julius Cae-
      sar *would probably have recalled how the title character disre-*
      gards Calphurnia's fears, a series of omens, his well-wishers'
      warnings, and his own misgivings when he resolves to play the
      role of "mighty Caesar" and proceed to the Capitol.

228   If your Mind . . . obey it. *Horatio's words recall Ham-*
      let's observations about "God-like Reason" in IV.iv.33–36.

231   we defy Augury *I refuse to be guided by omens.*

231– There . . . Sparrow. *Hamlet alludes to Matthew 10:29–*
32   *31. But his words also recall* Julius Caesar, *II.ii.26–27,*
      where Caesar says "What can be avoided / Whose End is
      purpos'd by the mighty Gods?"

mine is ready; now or whensoever, provided I be
so able as now.

LORD   The King and Queen and all are coming down.

HAMLET   In happy Time.   215

LORD   The Queen desires you to use some gentle
Entertainment to Laertes before you fall to
play.

HAMLET   She well instructs me.   *Exit Lord.*

HORATIO   You will lose, my Lord.   220

HAMLET   I do not think so: since he went into France
I have been in continual Practice. I shall win
at the Odds. Thou would'st not think how ill
all's here about my Heart, but it is no matter.

HORATIO   Nay good my Lord—   225

HAMLET   It is but Foolery, but it is such a kind of
Gaingiving as would perhaps trouble a Woman.

HORATIO   If your Mind dislike any thing, obey it.
I will forestall their Repair hether, and say
you are not fit.   230

HAMLET   Not a whit: we defy Augury. There is special
Providence in the Fall of a Sparrow. If it be
now, 'tis not to come; if it be not to come, it
will be now; if it be not now, yet it will come:
the Readiness is all. Since no Man of ought he   235
leaves knows, what is't to leave betimes? Let
be.

A Table prepar'd, and Flagons of Wine on it;
Trumpets, Drums, and Officers with Cushions, Foils,
Daggers. King, Queen, and all the State.

238   this Hand   *Most interpreters infer that the King is speaking of Laertes' hand, and that he then places it in Hamlet's hand. Another possibility is that the King offers his own hand to Hamlet. If so, Hamlet ignores it and instead addresses Laertes.*

242   a sore Distraction   *a painful tendency to fall into fits of madness.*

244   Exception   *objection. Hamlet refers to an injury so severe that a man of honor would feel that he had no choice but to requite it.*

250   Faction   *party.*

252   in this Audience   *in the presence of all these noble witnesses.*

254   that   *as if.*

254–56   I . . . Brother   *The analogy Hamlet cites is one that would excuse what he did as a terrible accident: something for which he was the cause but not the willing agent, and something for which he is as sorry as he would be if he had shot his own brother.*

256–58   I am . . . Revenge   *you have satisfied the part of me that would most vigorously stir me to revenge: my human feelings.*

258–62   but . . . ungor'd   *but I am not prepared to say that the demands of my honor are satisfied until I have had an opportunity to submit the case to some venerable higher authorities in these matters and obtain their assurance that I can accept your apology without permanent injury to my good name.*

262   But all that Time   *but in the meantime.*

KING   Come, Hamlet, come and take this Hand from
       me.
HAMLET   —Give me your Pardon, Sir, I've done you
       Wrong.
       But pardon 't as you are a Gentleman.   240
       This Presence knows, and you must needs have
          heard,
       How I am punish'd with a sore Distraction.
       What I have done that might your Nature, Honor,
       And Exception roughly awake, I here
       Proclaim was Madness. Was't Hamlet wrong'd
          Laertes?   245
       Never Hamlet. If Hamlet from himself
       Be ta'en away, and when he's not himself
       Dooes wrong Laertes, then Hamlet dooes it not,
       Hamlet denies it. Who dooes it then? His
          Madness.
       If't be so, Hamlet is of the Faction   250
       That is wrong'd; his Madness is poor Hamlet's
       Enemy. Sir, in this Audience, let my
       Disclaiming from a purpos'd Evil free me
       So far in your most gen'rous Thoughts that I
       Have shot my Arrow o'er the House and hurt   255
       My Brother.
LAERTES   I am satisfied in Nature,
       Whose Motive in this Case should stir me most
       To my Revenge; but in my Terms of Honor
       I stand aloof, and will no Reconcilement
       Till by some elder Maisters of known Honor   260
       I have a Voice and President of Peace
       To keep my Name ungor'd. But all that Time

315

263   receive . . . like Love   *accept your offer of reconciliation in the spirit in which it is tendered.*

265   And . . . play   *Hamlet says that he will now treat Laertes as he would a brother;* frankly *means "freely," generously trusting, taking Laertes' word that he'll not "wrong" Hamlet.*

266   Foils   *fencing swords.*

267   your Foil   *Hamlet plays on another sense of* Foil, *a dull background to set off the bright luster of a precious gem.*
    Ignorance   *lack of skill and knowledge in the art of the rapier.*

269   Stick   *stand out. Hamlet puns on the kind of "sticking" (piercing) a sword does. The wit of his jest derives from the fact that a sporting foil (with its point blunted or dulled) will not stick. What Hamlet is saying, in other words, is that he will be the kind of foil that permits Laertes' foil to be the opposite of a normal fencing foil: a foil that sticks. As it happens, Hamlet's wit unwittingly points back to the Prince himself as target. The "foil" that Laertes uses* will *"Stick fiery off indeed," and Hamlet will fall victim to it because "He, being Remiss, / Most Generous, and Free from all Contriving, / Will not peruse the Foils" (IV.vii.131–33).*

273   laid the Odds   *staked the higher wager (the Barbary Horses).*

277   likes   *pleases.*
    have all a Length   *are all the same length.*

281   quit . . . Exchange   *requite (return a hit) in the third bout (having lost the first two).*

284   Union   *a large pearl of the most exquisite quality.*

I do receive your offer'd Love like Love,
And will not wrong it.

HAMLET   I embrace it freely,
And will this Brother's Wager frankly play.   265
—Give us the Foils, come on.

LAERTES   Come, one for me.

HAMLET   I'll be your Foil, Laertes; in mine
   Ignorance
Your Skill shall like a Star i' th' darkest
   Night
Stick fiery off indeed.

LAERTES   You mock me, Sir.

HAMLET   No, by this Hand.   270

KING   Give them the Foils, young Ostrick. —Cousin
   Hamlet,
You know the Wager.

HAMLET   Very well, my Lord.
Your Grace has laid the Odds a' th' Weaker Side.

KING   I do not fear it: I have seen you both.
But since he is better, we have therefore
   Odds.   275

LAERTES   —This is too heavy: let me see another.

HAMLET   —This likes me well. —These Foils have
   all a Length?

LAERTES   Ay my good Lord.   *They prepare to play.*

KING   Set me the stoups of Wine upon that Table.
If Hamlet give the first or second Hit,   280
Or quit in Answer of the third Exchange,
Let all the Battlements their Ordnance fire:
The King shall drink to Hamlet's better Breath
And in the Cup an Union shall he throw,

287   **Kettle** *kettledrum.*

293   **Judgment.** *Hamlet is appealing to the judges for a ruling.*

S.D.   **a Piece goes off** *a cannon fires.*

300   **Fat** *The Queen probably means "sweating." But she may also be saying that Hamlet is overweight and therefore not a match for Laertes' stamina.*

302   **carouses** *offers a toast and then drinks a full cup without pausing to breathe.*

Richer than that which four successive Kings   285
In Denmark's Crown have worn. Give me the Cups,
And let the Kettle to the Trumpet speak,
The Trumpet to the Cannoneer without,
The Cannons to the Heav'ns, the Heav'n to Earth:
"Now the King drinks to Hamlet." —Come begin.   290

Trumpets the while.

—And you the Judges bear a wary Eye.

HAMLET   Come on, Sir.

LAERTES   Come, my Lord.   *They play.*

HAMLET   One.

LAERTES   No.

HAMLET   —Judgment.

OSTRICK   A Hit, a very palpable Hit.

LAERTES   Well, again.

KING   Stay, give me Drink. Hamlet, this Pearl is
thine: 295
Here's to thy Health. —Give him the Cup.

Drum, Trumpets, and Shot.
Flourish: a Piece goes off.

HAMLET   I'll play this Bout first, set it by a while.

They play again.

—Come, another Hit. What say you?

LAERTES   A Touch,
A Touch, I do confess 't.

KING   —Our Son shall win.

QUEEN   He's Fat and scant of Breath.   300
—Here Hamlet, take my Napkin; rub thy Brows.
The Queen carouses to thy Fortune, Hamlet.

HAMLET   Good Madam.

KING   Gertrard, do not drink.

308   I do not think 't.   *This line would appear to be a reply to what Laertes has just said to the King. But another, equally likely possibility is that the playwright wrote these words to be spoken as an indication that the King is still reacting to what the Queen has done a moment earlier: "I can't bring myself to believe what has just happened: I've lost my beloved Queen."*

311   pass   *thrust.*

312   make a Wanton of me   *indulge me by toying with me.*

316   incens'd   *enflamed with rage. During this bout, Laertes has wounded Hamlet.*

317   how   *ho. So also in line 324.*

319   Springe   *snare. Earlier in the play, Laertes' father has employed the same proverb when warning Ophelia to avoid Hamlet (I.iii.114).*

321   s'ounds   *swoons.*

322   O my dear Hamlet   *The Queen realizes what has happened to her, who was responsible for it, and who the intended victim was to be; then, significantly, she turns away from her husband to address herself to her son.*

QUEEN   I will, my Lord: I pray you pardon me.
KING   —It is the poison'd Cup, it is too late.   305
HAMLET   I dare not drink yet, Madam; by and by.
QUEEN   Come, let me wipe thy Face.
LAERTES   My Lord, I'll hit him now.
KING   I do not think 't.
LAERTES   —And yet 'tis almost 'gainst my Conscience.
HAMLET   Come for the third, Laertes: you do but
    dally.   310
    I pray you pass with your best Violence:
    I am sure you make a Wanton of me.
LAERTES   Say you so? Come on.   *They play again.*
OSTRICK   Nothing neither way.
LAERTES   Have at you now!   *They play again.*   315
KING   Part them: they are incens'd.
                        In scuffling, they change Rapiers.
HAMLET   Nay come again!
                  They play again. The Queen falls down.
OSTRICK   Look to the Queen there, how!
HORATIO   They bleed on both sides!
    —How is it, my Lord?
OSTRICK   —How is't, Laertes?
LAERTES   Why as a Woodcock to mine own Springe,
    Ostrick:
    I am justly kill'd with mine own Treachery.   320
HAMLET   —How dooes the Queen?
KING   She s'ounds to see them bleed.
QUEEN   No, no, the Drink, the Drink! —O my dear
    Hamlet,
    The Drink, the Drink: I am poisoned.
HAMLET   O Villainy! How, let the Door be lock'd!

330   Unbated and envenom'd   *unprotected and poisoned.*

333   can   *am able to say.*

335   Treason   *What the onlookers appear to mean is that Hamlet is committing treason in attacking the King. Only Hamlet and Horatio know how Claudius obtained his throne and maintained his hold on it. And, apart from Horatio, there is no one else in the Castle with any reason to feel loyal to Hamlet rather than to the man they regard as their duly anointed Sovereign.*

340   temper'd   *mixed, prepared.*

341   Exchange Forgiveness   *This exchange concludes the cycle initiated by Hamlet at the beginning of the scene when he requested pardon of Laertes. It seals the bond between two would-be brothers, and it completes the transfer of Laertes' loyalty from Claudius to Hamlet.*

345   Wretched Queen, adieu.   *The early texts do not specify when the Queen dies. It may be that she expires only now, as Hamlet bids farewell.*

346   Chance   *mischance, catastrophe.*

347   Mutes   *unspeaking actors. Within the play-world, Hamlet is speaking metaphorically; but in the theatre imitating that play-world, the actor playing Hamlet is speaking literally to his mute fellow actors who are pretending to be "Audience to this Act."*

348   as   *since, now that.*

351   Cause   *both case and cause (Hamlet's justification for "this Act").*

Treachery: seek it out!   *Exit Ostrick.*   325
LAERTES   It is here, Hamlet: thou art slain.
   No Med'cine in the World can do thee good:
   In thee there is not half an hour's Life.
   The Treach'rous Instrument is in thy Hand,
   Unbated and envenom'd: the foul Practice   330
   Hath turn'd it self on me. Lo here I lie,
   Never to rise again. Thy Mother's poison'd.
   I can no more. The King, the King's too blame.
HAMLET   The Point envenom'd too!
   —Then Venom to thy work!   *He attacks the King.*
ALL   Treason, Treason!   335
KING   O yet defend me, Friends: I am but hurt.
HAMLET   Here, thou incestious, murd'rous, damned
      Dane:
   Drink off this Potion. Is thy Union here?
   Follow my Mother!   *The King dies.*
LAERTES   He is justly serv'd:
   It is a Poison temper'd by himself.   340
   Exchange Forgiveness with me, Noble Hamlet:
   Mine and my Father's Death come not upon thee,
   Nor thine on me.
HAMLET   Heav'n make thee free of it: *Laertes dies.*
                              I follow thee.
   —I am dead, Horatio. —Wretched Queen, adieu.   345
   —You that look pale and tremble at this Chance,
   That are but Mutes or Audience to this Act,
   Had I but Time, as this fell Sergeant Death
   Is strict in his Arrest, O I could tell you—
   But let that be. —Horatio, I am dead,   350
   Thou livest: report me and my Cause aright

323

352   the Unsatisfied *those who will believe that Hamlet committed treason unless they hear his "Cause aright."*

353   antique Roman *Horatio wishes to depart in what a later Shakespearean character calls "the high Roman Fashion." Horatio bears the name of an ancient Roman, so there is a special appropriateness to his words.*

359   Felicity *escape from "this harsh World" (line 360).*

S.D.   Osrick *Here, for the first time in the Second Quarto, this courtier bears the name he is given consistently in the First Folio. It is conceivable that at this point Shakespeare simply decided to change the character's name to something more noble (Osric is a name with dignified Anglo-Saxon roots). But it is also possible that the name change is meant to signal a stage metamorphosis in which a character who exits as a foppish youth (probably at line 325) re-enters as a stately messenger to announce the arrival of another young man who appears to have matured into a more august role. Since the name is never spoken in its new form, the change would be registered solely in manner and perhaps costume.*

365   o'er-crows *crows over (like a triumphant cock).*

367   Election *selection as Denmark's next King. Hamlet's "dying Voice" (recommendation) will probably assure that the Crown "lights" (alights) on Fortinbrasse.*

369–70   th' Occurrants . . . solicited *the occurrences, great and small, that have urged us to this pass.*

371   Good night *This farewell recalls the play's earlier "good nights" (among them Hamlet's in III.iv and Ophelia's IV.v), and it also echoes "To die to sleep, / To sleep, perchance to dream" (III.i.61–62).*

To the Unsatisfied.

HORATIO   Never believe it:
I am more an antique Roman than a Dane;
Here's yet some Liquor left.

HAMLET   As th' art a Man,
Give me the Cup! Let go, by Heav'n I'll ha't!   355
O God, Horatio: what a wounded Name,
Things standing thus unknown, shall live
    behind me!
If thou did'st ever hold me in thy Heart,
Absent thee from Felicity a while
And in this harsh World draw thy Breath in Pain   360
To tell my Story.   *A March afar off, and shout within.*
                    What warlike Noise is this?

                    Enter Osrick.

OSRICK   Young Fortinbrasse, with Conquest come
    from Poland,
To the Embassadors of England gives
This warlike Volley.

HAMLET   O I die, Horatio:
The potent Poison quite o'er-crows my Spirit.   365
I cannot live to hear the News from England,
But I do prophesy th' Election lights
On Fortinbrasse: he has my dying Voice.
So tell him, with th' Occurrants more and less
Which have solicited. The Rest is Silence.   370
                                        He dies.

HORATIO   Now cracks a Noble Heart. —Good night,
    sweet Prince,

372   And . . . Rest   *Horatio's benediction is in a very different mode from the "Roman" sentiments he uttered a moment earlier.*

S.D.   the Embassadors   *the ambassadors from England. It is only by coincidence that they arrive at the same time that Fortinbrasse returns from his expedition to Poland.*

375   ought   *anything.*
        Woe or Wonder   *events evoking pity or amazement.*

376   This Quarry . . . Havoc.   *Fortinbrasse combines a hunting metaphor (*Quarry *usually refers to a heap of deer or other game killed in a hunt) with a military one (*Havoc *is a warcry signaling slaughter without mercy), and what he means is "this pile of corpses proclaims that someone cried havoc."*

377   toward   *in the offing.*

378   Princes   *persons of princely rank.*

381   senseless   *without sense, unable to function.*

382   his Commandment   *The ambassadors assume, of course, that "his" refers to Claudius.*

387   jump   *simultaneously.*
        this bloody Question   *the carnage that has resulted from the "Question" (issue) debated here. Horatio's phrasing recalls Hamlet's earlier references to "some necessary Question" (III.ii.49) and "the Question of this Straw" (IV.iv.23).*

390   Stage   *Within the play-world, Horatio means "platform." But within the Elizabethan theatre, the character playing Horatio refers literally to a part of the Globe stage.*

And flights of Angels sing thee to thy Rest.
Why dooes the Drum come hether?

Enter Fortinbrasse, with the Embassadors,
with Drum, Colors, and Attendants.

FORTINBRASSE   Where is this Sight?
HORATIO   What is it you would see?
   If ought of Woe or Wonder, cease your Search.   375
FORTINBRASSE   This Quarry cries on Havoc.
   —O proud Death,
   What Feast is toward in thine eternal Cell,
   That thou so many Princes at a Shot
   So bloodily hast strook?
EMBASSADORS   The Sight is dismal,
   And our Affairs from England come too late;   380
   The Ears are senseless that should give us
      Hearing
   To tell him his Commandment is fulfill'd,
   That Rosencrans and Guildenstern are dead.
   Where should we have our Thanks?
HORATIO   Not from his Mouth,
   Had it th' Ability of Life to thank you: 385
   He never gave Commandment for their Death.
   But since so jump upon this bloody Question
   You from the Polack Wars—and you from England—
   Are here arriv'd, give Order that these Bodies
   High on a Stage be placed to the View,   390
   And let me speak to th' yet unknowing World
   How these things came about. So shall you hear
   Of carnal, bloody, and unnat'ral Acts,

394   accidental Judgments   *judgments guided by miscalculations or chance.*
       casual Slaughters   *deaths resulting from chance or from mis-readings of the circumstances.*

395   put on by Cunning   *incited by deviousness.*
       forc'd Cause   *circumstances imposed upon the agent.*

396   this Upshot   *the outcome you see here.*

396–   Purposes mistook . . . Heads   *Horatio probably means*
97   *plans mis-taken (not only mistakenly conceived, but conceived out of evil intent) that have boomeranged on the perpetrators: Claudius and Laertes in particular. But to a lesser degree, Horatio's words can be applied to Hamlet's "rough-hewn" purposes too, and most especially to the way the Prince disregarded his intuition that he was likely to be walking into an ambush when he accepted a wager proposed by the same King who had already made one attempt to kill him by treacherous means.*

401   some Rights of Mem'ry   *Fortinbrasse's words remind us that the wheel has now come full circle: like Hamlet, and like Laertes, Fortinbrasse has had a father's honor to reinstate, and he now claims not only the Norwegian territory the elder Fortinbrasse had lost to the elder Hamlet, but the elder Hamlet's kingdom in its entirety.*

409   put on   *placed on the throne.*

410   for his Passage   *to honor his passing (death). Line 412 is probably to be followed by a pause for "the Soldier's Music."*

414   Becomes the Field   *would be appropriate for the battlefield.*

Of accidental Judgments, casual Slaughters,
Of Deaths put on by Cunning and forc'd Cause, 395
And in this Upshot, Purposes mistook
Fall'n on th' Inventors' Heads. All this can I
Truly deliver.
FORTINBRASSE   Let us haste to hear it,
And call the Noblest to the Audience.
For me, with Sorrow I embrace my Fortune: 400
I have some Rights of Mem'ry in this Kingdom,
Which now to claim my Vantage doth invite me.
HORATIO   Of that I shall have also cause to speak,
And from his Mouth whose Voice will draw no
   more.
But let this same be presently perform'd 405
Ev'n while Men's Minds are wild, lest more
   Mischance
On Plots and Errors happen.
FORTINBRASSE   Let four Captains
Bear Hamlet like a Soldier to the Stage,
For he was likely, had he been put on,
To have prov'd most Royal; and for his Passage, 410
The Soldier's Music and the Rite of War
Speak loudly for him.
Take up the Bodies: such a Sight as this
Becomes the Field, but here shows much amiss.
Go bid the Soldiers shoot. 415

Exeunt marching: after the which a Peal of
Ordnance are shot off.

FINIS

329

TROILUS AND CRESSIDA

NAMES OF THE ACTORS

PRIAM, King of Troy

HECTOR
PARIS
DEIPHOBUS   Sons to Priam
HELENUS
TROILUS

CASSANDRA, Daughter to Priam

MARGARELON, a Bastard Son of Priam

ANDROMACHE, Wife to Hector

AENEAS
ANTENOR   Trojan Commanders

CALCHAS, a Trojan Seer who has joined the Greeks

PANDARUS, Uncle to Cressida

CRESSIDA, Daughter to Calchas

MAN (ALEXANDER), Servant to Cressida
BOY, Servant to Troilus
SERVANT to Paris

AGAMEMNON, Commander-in-Chief of the Greeks
MENELAUS, King of Sparta, Agamemnon's Brother

NESTOR
ULYSSES
ACHILLES
AIAX   Greek Commanders
DIOMEDES
PATROCLUS

THERSITES, a deformed Greek

SERVANT to Diomedes

TROJAN and GREEK SOLDIERS and ATTENDANTS

THE EPISTLE   *This foreword prefaced the second issue of the First Quarto of* Troilus and Cressida *in 1609. Who the "Never Writer" of it was is a matter of conjecture. And whether the Epistle is to be relied upon in its assertion that the play was never performed on the public stage is also a matter of uncertainty. The original title-page advertises "The Historie of Troylus and Cresseida" as a play that "was acted by the Kings Maiesties servants at the Globe." It is possible that the play was offered at the Globe and failed there because it "pleas'd not the Million"* (Hamlet, *II.ii.468). It is also possible that the play was designed for a more sophisticated audience, such as those to be found at the universities or at London's four Inns of Court.*

2   stal'd   *made stale.*
     clapper-claw'd   *pawed over, soiled (with applause).*

3   the Vulgar   *the common people.*
     passing   *surpassingly.*

4   the Palm Comical   *the palm branch awarded to an outstanding comedy. Whether* Troilus and Cressida *is to be classified as a comedy is one of the ongoing debates about its nature and atmosphere.*

6   chang'd   *both (a) exchanged, and (b) altered.*

7   titles of Commodities   *things to be commended for their monetary value.*
     Pleas   *probably a reference to attorneys' pleas or cases.*

8   Censors   *judges, critics.*

11   fram'd to the Life   *realistic in their portrayals of humanity.*

The Epistle

A Never Writer, to an ever Reader. News.

Eternal Reader, you have here a new Play, never
stal'd with the Stage, never clapper-claw'd with
the Palms of the Vulgar, and yet passing full of
the Palm Comical; for it is a Birth of your Brain,
that never undertook any thing comical vainly. And   5
were but the vain Names of Comedies chang'd for the
titles of Commodities, or of Plays for Pleas, you
should see all those grand Censors, that now style
them such Vanities, flock to them for the main
Grace of their Gravities: especially this Author's   10
Comedies, that are so fram'd to the Life that they
serve for the most common Commentaries of all the
Actions of our Lives, showing such a Dexterity and
Power of Wit that the most displeased with Plays
are pleas'd with his Comedies.   15

17   capable of   *able to appreciate.*

18   Representations   *dramatic works.*

24   borne   *probably both (a) carried, and (b) born.*

28   Testern   *sixpence.*

31   Terence or Plautus   *two Roman writers celebrated for their works in comedy. Plautus (254–184 B.C.) and Terence (190–150 B.C.) were both included in the Latin curriculum that Elizabethan boys studied in grammar school.*

34   Inquisition   *The Spanish Inquisition was a time of persecutions and book-banning. In lines 32–34 the writer implies that, because of their scarcity, copies of Shakespeare's comedies will eventually require a different kind of inquisition: an avid inquiry (search) for copies of these rare masterworks.*

38   scape   *escape. In lines 34–39 the writer implies that the play has been rescued from the "Multitude" and preserved in its chaste purity for the elite reader flattered in the Epistle.*

39   the grand Possessors   *The writer probably refers to the owners of the copyright for the play, presumably the acting company that had finally been persuaded to publish rather than perform it.*

40   pray'd   *begged (to buy).*
      them   *copies of the author's "Comedies" (line 33).*

43   Vale   *farewell (Latin).*

336

And all such dull and heavy-witted Worldlings
as were never capable of the Wit of a Comedy, coming
by Report of them to his Representations, have found
that Wit there that they never found in themselves,
and have parted better wittied than they came: 20
feeling an edge of Wit set upon them, more than ever
they dream'd they had Brain to grind it on. So much
and such savored Salt of Wit is in his Comedies that
they seem (for their height of Pleasure) to be borne
in that Sea that brought forth Venus. Amongst all   25
there is none more witty than this. And had I time
I would comment upon it, though I know it needs not
(for so much as will make you think your Testern
well bestow'd) but for so much worth as even poor I
know to be stuff'd in it. It deserves such a Labor   30
as well as the best Comedy in Terence or Plautus.
And believe this, that when he is gone, and his
Comedies out of Sale, you will scramble for them,
and set up a new English Inquisition. Take this for
a Warning, and at the peril of your Pleasure's Loss   35
and Judgments, refuse not, nor like this the less
for not being sullied with the smoky Breath of the
Multitude; but thank Fortune for the scape it hath
made amongst you. Since by the grand Possessors'
Wills I believe you should have pray'd for them   40
rather than been pray'd. And so I leave all such to
be pray'd for (for the states of their Wits' Healths)
that will not praise it.

                                          Vale.

PROLOGUE   *The Prologue does not appear in either issue of the 1609 Quarto; it was first printed in the Folio.*

2   Orgillous   *proud, enraged; a variant of* orgulous.
high   *both (a) noble, and (b) haughty.*
chaf'd   *heated from irritation.*

4   Fraught   *freighted, laden.*
Ministers and Instruments   *soldiers and weapons.*

6   Crownets   *coronets (small crowns).*

7   Phrygia   *the land of which Troy was the capital.*

8   Emures   *walls.*

9   ravish'd Helen   *The Greeks launched the Trojan War to avenge Paris' rape (abduction) of Helen, the wife of King Menelaus of Sparta.*

10   Quarrel   *basis of the conflict.*

11   Tenedos   *an island off the coast of Asia Minor, from which the Greeks mounted their assault on Troy.*

12   deep-drawing Bark   *ships lying low in the water because of their heavy cargo. Here* Bark *is to be regarded as plural.*

13   Frautage   *freight (soldiers and implements of war).*
Dardan Plains   *the plains surrounding Troy (named for Dardanus, an ancestral Trojan king).*

15   brave Pavilions   *bold, splendid tents.*
Priam's six-gated City   *Troy, here designated by the name of its King.*

Prologue

In Troy there lies the Scene: from Isles of
  Greece
The Princes Orgillous, their high Blood chaf'd,
Have to the Port of Athens sent their Ships
Fraught with the Ministers and Instruments
Of cruel War. Sixty and nine that wore   5
Their Crownets Regal, from th' Athenian Bay
Put forth toward Phrygia, and their Vow is made
To ransack Troy, within whose strong Emures
The ravish'd Helen, Menelaus' Queen,
With wanton Paris sleeps, and that's the
  Quarrel.   10
               To Tenedos they come,
And the deep-drawing Bark do there disgorge
Their warlike Frautage. Now on Dardan Plains
The fresh and yet unbruised Greeks do pitch
Their brave Pavilions. Priam's six-gated City,   15

339

16–17   Dardan . . . Antenonidus   *the names of Troy's six gates.*

17   Staples   *large slots or sockets.*

18   corresponsive . . . Bolts   *snug-fitting bolts.*

20   skittish   *high-strung, trigger-happy.*

21   Troian   *Trojan; normally spelled either* Troian *or* Troyan *in the early texts, and almost certainly so pronounced.*

22   on Hazard   *both (a) at stake, and (b) at odds.*

23   in Confidence   *in an aloof, assured manner. This description is likely to be an allusion to the similarly "armed Prologue" of Ben Jonson's* Poetaster *(1601), one of the plays involved in the so-called "War of the Theatres." Shakespeare also alludes to the controversy in II.ii of* Hamlet.

25   In like Conditions as our Argument   *in the same manner as the characters in the story to be dramatized.*

27   Vaunt   *both (a) vanguard (beginnings or "Firstlings"), and (b) vaunting defiance.*
   Broils   *conflicts.*

28   Beginning in the Middle   *picking up the story well after its beginning. Shakespeare alludes to the epic formula,* in medias res *(Latin for "in the middle of things"), initiated by Homer in the* Iliad, *the ultimate source for "the matter of Troy," and followed by Vergil in the* Aeneid.
   starting thence away   *proceeding from that point.*

29   digested   *dealt with, treated in an economical fashion.*

Dardan and Timbria, Helia, Chetas, Troien,
And Antenonidus, with massy Staples
And corresponsive and fulfilling Bolts,
Stir up the Sons of Troy.
Now Expectation, tickling skittish Spirits   20
On one and other side, Troian and Greek,
Sets all on Hazard. And hither am I come,
A Prologue arm'd, but not in Confidence
Of Author's Pen, or Actor's Voice, but suited
In like Conditions as our Argument,   25
To tell you, fair Beholders, that our Play
Leaps o'er the Vaunt and Firstlings of those
   Broils,
Beginning in the Middle: starting thence away
To what may be digested in a Play.
Like or find Fault, do as your Pleasures are;   30
Now Good or Bad, 'tis but the Chance of War.

341

I.i   *The opening scene takes place in Troy, probably near Priam's Palace.*

1   Varlet   *valet, servant boy.*

2   without   *outside.*

3   Battle here within   *Troilus refers to a conflict within the "walls" of his own breast (a* psychomachia, *or "battle for the soul"). Troilus draws an analogy between his own internal "war" and the external struggle to determine the fate of Troy.*

4   Maister   *master (from Latin* magister*).*

5   to field   *to the battlefield.*
    hath none   *has no such mastery.*

6   Gear   *matter, business; but with an allusion to the kind of gear (armor) Troilus is eager to have removed from his body.*

7   Skillful to their Strength   *with skill to match their strength. The phrases that follow are based on a similar grammatical construction.*

10   fonder   *more foolish.*

12   unpractic'd   *inexperienced, with no prior practice.*

Scene 1

Enter Pandarus and Troilus.

TROILUS   Call here my Varlet, I'll unarm again.
  Why should I war without the Walls of Troy
  That find such cruel Battle here within?
  Each Troian that is Maister of his Heart,
  Let him to field; Troilus alas hath none.   5
PANDARUS   Will this Gear ne'er be mended?
TROILUS   The Greeks are Strong, and Skillful to
    their Strength,
  Fierce to their Skill, and to their Fierceness
    Valiant;
  But I am weaker than a Woman's Tear,
  Tamer than Sleep, fonder than Ignorance,   10
  Less Valiant than the Virgin in the Night,
  And Skilless as unpractic'd Infancy.
PANDARUS   Well, I have told you enough of this; for

343

14   meddle nor make   *a proverbial expression meaning "involve myself." Here* make *means "attempt or undertake."*

16   tarry the Grinding   *wait till the wheat has been ground. As with the other stages of cake-preparation Pandarus describes in the lines that follow, the name he gives the procedure enumerated here could also be applied to sexual activity.*

19   Boulting   *sifting (of the flour).*

22   Leavening   *fermenting, to make the dough rise.*

30   blench   *flinch.*
       at Suff'rance   *at having to suffer (put up with) trials to test her tolerance and endurance.*

33   then . . . thence   *Troilus plays on the similar sounds of "then she" and "thence" to make the point that whenever Cressida is present in his thoughts, she is frustratingly absent ("thence").*

34   yesternight   *last night.*

37   wedged   *driven into with a wedge. Here* wedged *is a two-syllable word.*
       rive   *split.*
       twain   *two.*

39   light a Scorn   *cast its light upon a scornful expression, thereby making it appear more like a smile than a frown. Many editions follow the Folio here and read* a-scorn.

41   couch'd   *laid low, hidden away.*

my part, I'll not meddle nor make no farther.
He that will have a Cake out of the Wheat must   15
tarry the Grinding.

TROILUS   Have I not tarried?

PANDARUS   Ay the Grinding; but you must tarry the
Boulting.

TROILUS   Have I not tarried?   20

PANDARUS   Ay the Boulting; but you must tarry the
Leavening.

TROILUS   Still have I tarried.

PANDARUS   Ay, to the Leavening; but here's yet in
the word "Hereafter" the Kneading, the Making   25
of the Cake, the Heating the Oven, and the
Baking; nay you must stay the Cooling too, or
ye may chance burn your Lips.

TROILUS   Patience her self, what Goddess ere she be,
Doth lesser blench at Suff'rance than I do: 30
At Priam's royal Table do I sit,
And when fair Cressid comes into my Thoughts,
So, Traitor, then she comes when she is thence.

PANDARUS   Well she look'd yesternight Fairer than
ever I saw her look, or any Woman else.   35

TROILUS   I was about to tell thee when my Heart,
As wedged with a Sigh, would rive in twain
Lest Hector or my Father should perceive me.
I have (as when the Sun doth light a Scorn)
Buri'd this Sigh in Wrinkle of a Smile;   40
But Sorrow that is couch'd in seeming
    Gladness
Is like that Mirth Fate turns to sudden
    Sadness.

345

43   And   *if; so also in line 69.*

43–44 darker than Helen's   *Pandarus' point is that Cressida is somewhat less "fair" (blonde, conventionally beautiful) than Helen.*

44   go to   *enough said.*

52   Fadoms   *fathoms (nautical measures of six feet).*

53   indrench'd   *submerged.*

55   Pour'st in . . . Heart   *Troilus' image suggests that Pandarus is pouring salt water into an open wound, thereby increasing rather than relieving the pain.*

57   Handlest in thy Discourse   *[you] discuss in your conversation.*

58   are Ink   *are as black as ink.*

59   Writing their own Reproach   *inscribing their own dispraise.*
       Seizure   *grasp.*

60   Cygnet's Down   *fluff of the infant swan.*
       Spir't of Sense   *vapors transmitting the sensations of perception through the nerves.*

63   in steed   *instead.*
       Balm   *a soothing, healing ointment.*

69   Mends   *means to improve her situation.*

PANDARUS   And her Hair were not somewhat darker
        than Helen's—well go to, there were no more
        Comparison between the Women! But for my part   45
        she is my Kinswoman, I would not (as they term
        it) praise her, but I would somebody had heard
        her talk yesterday as I did. I will not dispraise
        your sister Cassandra's Wit, but—
TROILUS   O Pandarus, I tell thee, Pandarus,   50
        When I do tell thee there my Hopes lie drown'd,
        Reply not in how many Fadoms deep
        They lie indrench'd. I tell thee I am mad
        In Cressid's Love; thou answer'st she is Fair,
        Pour'st in the open Ulcer of my Heart;   55
        Her Eyes, her Hair, her Gait, her Voice,
        Handlest in thy Discourse. O, that her Hand
        (In whose Comparison all Whites are Ink
        Writing their own Reproach), to whose soft
          Seizure
        The Cygnet's Down is harsh, and Spir't of Sense   60
        Hard as the Palm of Plowman! This thou tell'st
          me,
        As true thou tell'st me, when I say I love her;
        But saying thus, in steed of Oil and Balm,
        Thou lay'st in ev'ry Gash that Love hath given me
        The Knife that made it.
PANDARUS   I speak no more than Truth.   65
TROILUS   Thou dost not speak so much.
PANDARUS   Faith I'll not meddle in it; let her be
        as she is. If she be Fair, 'tis the better for
        her; and she be not, she has the Mends in her
        own Hands.   70

347

72 Travel *travail, pains. In Shakespeare's time,* travail *and* travel *tended to be used interchangeably. Here the playwright is punning on Pandarus' role as a go-between (line 74), the archetypal traveling salesman.*

73 on *of.*

79 and *if; so also in line 81.*

80 a' Friday *on Friday; that is, in her ordinary workaday apparel, as opposed to Helen's Sunday best.*

82 all one *all the same. In many contexts this phrase has sexual connotations in Shakespeare, ultimately deriving from the teaching that when a man and a woman join together they become "one flesh" (Genesis 2:24).*

85 to stay behind her Father *Cressida's father, Calchas, has defected to the Greek camp, leaving his daughter in Troy.*

87–88 meddle . . . matter *have nothing more to do with the affair. Once again Pandarus' phrasing is sexually suggestive.*

91 all *Elsewhere Shakespeare plays on* awl, *a boring instrument, as a figure for the male member. See* Julius Caesar, *I.i.25–27.*

there an end *that's all I have to say on the subject. But* an end *can also mean "on end," and thus remind us of Troilus' plight.*

95 upon this Argument *for this cause. In* Romeo and Juliet, *II.iv.107, an* Argument *is a woman's "case," and that sense is pertinent to a play that focuses on the relationships between different types of "sword" (line 96).*

348

TROILUS   Good Pandarus, how now, Pandarus?

PANDARUS   I have had my Labor for my Travel, ill
thought on of her, and ill thought of you;
gone between and between, but small Thanks
for my Labor.   75

TROILUS   What, art thou angry, Pandarus? What,
with me?

PANDARUS   Because she's kin to me therefore she's
not so Fair as Helen; and she were not kin to
me, she would be as Fair a' Friday as Helen is   80
on Sunday. But what I? I care not and she were
a Blackamoor; 'tis all one to me.

TROILUS   Say I she is not Fair?

PANDARUS   I do not care whether you do or no,
she's a Fool to stay behind her Father; let   85
her to the Greeks, and so I'll tell her the
next time I see her; for my part, I'll meddle
nor make no more i' th' matter.

TROILUS   Pandarus—

PANDARUS   Not I.

TROILUS   Sweet Pandarus—

PANDARUS   Pray you speak no more to me: I will   90
leave all as I found it, and there an end.

Exit. Sound Alarum.

TROILUS   —Peace, you ungracious Clamors; peace,
rude Sounds!
Fools on both sides; Helen must needs be Fair
When with your Blood you daily paint her thus.
I cannot fight upon this Argument: 95
It is too starv'd a Subject for my Sword.
—But Pandarus! —O Gods! How do you plague me!

349

99   teachy   *tetchy, touchy, like an irritable schoolteacher.*
         woe   *woo. The ambiguity in the original spelling proves prophetic.*

100   against all Suit   *unwilling to entertain any suitors.*

101   Tell . . . Love   *Troilus invokes the counsel of Apollo, the God of Healing. Daphne, a nymph pursued by the love-afflicted Apollo in Book I of Ovid's* Metamorphoses, *sought help from her father's river-spirit and escaped Apollo's advances by being transformed into a laurel.*

102   we   *I. Troilus uses the royal "we."*

104   Ilium   *Priam's palace, the capitol of Troy; here disyllabic.*

105   Flood   *ocean.*

106   Marchant   *merchant (here one of the traders who ventured their fortunes on ships to carry merchandise).*
         Sailing   *Troilus compares Pandarus to a "selling" Bark (boat), line 107.*

107   doubtful Hope   *both (a) hope against doubt, and (b) dubious source of hope.*
         Convoy   *escort, with wordplay on a convoy of merchant ships.*

109   Woman's Answer   *an answer that is not an answer. This phrase frequently refers to a woman's coy "no" when she really means "yes" (an implication Troilus hints at in line 117).*

114   a Scar to Scorn   *a fit punishment for the scorn he has shown to Menelaus, giving "the Bull" the horns of a cuckold by stealing his wife.*

I cannot come to Cressid but by Pandar,
And he's as teachy to be woo'd to woe
As she is stubborn, chaste, against all Suit.   100
—Tell me, Apollo, for thy Daphne's Love,
What Cressid is, what Pandar, and what we.
Her Bed is India, there she lies, a Pearl;
Between our Ilium and where she resides
Let it be call'd the wild and wand'ring Flood,   105
Our Self the Marchant, and this Sailing Pandar
Our doubtful Hope, our Convoy, and our Bark.

Alarum. Enter Aeneas.

AENEAS   How now, Prince Troilus, wherefore not
    a-field?
TROILUS   Because not there; this Woman's Answer
    sorts,
    For Womanish it is to be from thence.   110
    What News, Aeneas, from the Field today?
AENEAS   That Paris is returned home and hurt.
TROILUS   By whom, Aeneas?
AENEAS   Troilus, by Menelaus.
TROILUS   Let Paris bleed: 'tis but a Scar to Scorn.
    Paris is gor'd with Menelaus' Horn.   *Alarum.* 115
AENEAS   Hark what good Sport is out of Town today.
TROILUS   Better at Home, if "Would I Might" were
    "May."
    But to the Sport abroad, are you bound thither?
AENEAS   In all swift Haste.
TROILUS   Come go we then together.
                                            Exeunt.

I.ii   *This scene takes place on a street in Troy.*

2   wheth'r   *whither (to where).*

3   Vale   *valley.*

5   mov'd   *angered. Here the word is used in contrast with* fix'd
         (unmoveable).

7   like as   *as if.*
         Husbandry   *industry and thriftiness. Husbandry also refers to
         farming, however, and there is wordplay on that sense in the
         words* harness'd *(both "armed" and "yoked") and* Field
         (both a battlefield and a plot of tilled land) in lines 8–9.

8   lyte   *light. Here the word plays on at least three meanings: (a)
         quickly, (b) lightly, and (c) a source of light "Before the Sun
         rose." The unusual spelling may also be intended to suggest
         (d) lithe, a word meaning "gentle, supple, and athletic."*

9–11   ev'ry Flow'r . . . Wrath   *These lines imply that the flowers
         are weeping for those who will fall victim to Hector's wrath.
         But another implication, relating to Hector's habitual defi-
         ciency in wrath, is also hinted at in what will prove a pro-
         phetic image.*

14   Aiax   *Ajax; probably pronounced "Ayax" (from* Aias *in
         Greek).*

15   per se   *in himself (in a class all his own).*

16   stands alone   *is unique. But in line 17 Cressida takes the
         phrase in a more literal sense, with reference to men's "Legs."*

Scene 2

Enter Cressida and her Man.

CRESSIDA Who were those went by?
MAN   Queen Hecuba, and Helen.
CRESSIDA And wheth'r go they?
MAN   Up to th' Eastern Tower,
    Whose Height commands as Subject all the Vale,
    To see the Battle. Hector, whose Patience
    Is as a Virtue fix'd, today was mov'd: 5
    He chid Andromache and strook his Armorer,
    And like as there were Husbandry in War;
    Before the Sun rose he was harness'd lyte,
    And to the Field goes he, where ev'ry Flow'r
    Did as a Prophet weep what it foresaw   10
    In Hector's Wrath.
CRESSIDA   What was his Cause of Anger?
MAN The Noise goes this: there is among the Greeks
    A Lord of Troian Blood, Nephew to Hector;
    They call him Aiax.
CRESSIDA   Good, and what of him?
MAN They say he is a very Man *per se*   15
    And stands alone.
CRESSIDA   So do all Men unless
    Th' are Drunk, Sick, or have no Legs.

19   their particular Additions   *the attributes that distinguish them from other beasts. In the context of Cressida's wordplay in line 17, this term picks up a bawdy "addition" of its own. For similar wordplay on "particular," see II.ii.9.*

20   churlish   *surly.*

22   Humours   *psychological perturbations, resulting from imbalances or excesses of one or more of the four humours (deriving from the four elements, Earth, Water, Air, and Fire) that make up a person's "complexion" (composition or disposition).*

23   sauced with Discretion   *mixed with reason and judgment.*

25   glimpse   *trace.*
        Attaint   *taint, blemish.*

26   Melancholy   *depressed, despondent.*

27   without Cause   *with no objective reason for it. The Man's point is that Aiax's melancholy is a humour resulting from an excess of black bile in his system.*
        against the Hair   *contrary to circumstances. The image refers to rubbing an animal's fur the wrong way.*

29–30   a gouty Briareus   *a man like the giant Briareus, with his hundred hands all swollen with gout (a condition caused by an excess of uric acid).*

30–31   purblind Argus   *the hundred-eyed monster who was slain by Hermes after the piping God charmed all his eyes to sleep.*

34   cop'd   *encountered.*

MAN   This Man, Lady, hath robb'd many Beasts of
        their particular Additions. He is as valiant
        as the Lion, churlish as the Bear, slow as   20
        the Elephant: a Man into whom Nature hath so
        crowded Humours that his Valor is crush'd into
        Folly, his Folly sauced with Discretion. There
        is no Man hath a Virtue that he hath not a
        glimpse of, nor any Man an Attaint but he   25
        carries some Stain of it. He is Melancholy
        without Cause, and Merry against the Hair; he
        hath the Joints of every thing, but every
        thing so out of joint that he is a gouty
        Briareus (many Hands and no Use), or purblind   30
        Argus (all Eyes and no Sight).
CRESSIDA   But how should this Man, that makes me
        smile, make Hector angry?
MAN   They say he yesterday cop'd Hector in the
        Battle and stroke him down, the Disdain and   35
        Shame whereof hath ever since kept Hector
        fasting and waking.

Enter Pandarus.

CRESSIDA   Who comes here?
MAN   Madam, your Uncle Pandarus.
CRESSIDA   Hector's a gallant Man.   40
MAN   As may be in the World, Lady.
PANDARUS   What's that, what's that?
CRESSIDA   Good morrow, Uncle Pandarus.
PANDARUS   Good morrow, Cousin Cressid. What do
        you talk of? —Good morrow, Alexander. —How do   45

355

46   at Ilium   *at the Palace.*

57   lay about him   *lay corpses around him (because of the fury of his fighting).*

67   Ay . . . knew him.   *Cressida is probably playing on a sexual sense of* knew; *she may also be having fun with the phrase* saw him before *(saw his "manliness" before—in front of— him).*

71–72   in some Degrees   *both (a) in some respects, and (b) by some ways of measuring manly stature.*

73   to each of them he is Himself   *as for either of them, he is uniquely himself. Cressida is probably thinking back to Alexander's comment about another man who "stands alone" (line 16).*

you, Cousin? When were you at Ilium?

CRESSIDA This morning, Uncle.

PANDARUS What were you talking of when I came?
Was Hector arm'd and gone ere ye came to Ilium?
Helen was not up, was she?   50

CRESSIDA Hector was gone, but Helen was not up.

PANDARUS E'en so, Hector was stirring early.

CRESSIDA That were we talking of, and of his Anger.

PANDARUS Was he angry?

CRESSIDA So he says here.   55

PANDARUS True he was so; I know the Cause too.
He'll lay about him today, I can tell them
that; and there's Troilus will not come far
behind him. Let them take heed of Troilus, I
can tell them that too.   60

CRESSIDA What, is he angry too?

PANDARUS Who, Troilus? Troilus is the better Man
of th' two.

CRESSIDA O Jupiter, there's no Comparison.

PANDARUS What, not between Troilus and Hector?   65
Do you know a Man if you see him?

CRESSIDA Ay, if I ever saw him before and knew him.

PANDARUS Well I say Troilus is Troilus.

CRESSIDA Then you say as I say, for I am sure he
is not Hector.   70

PANDARUS No, nor Hector is not Troilus in some
Degrees.

CRESSIDA 'Tis just: to each of them he is Himself.

PANDARUS Himself: alas poor Troilus, I would he
were.   75

CRESSIDA So he is.

357

77   Condition . . . India. *Pandarus' implication is that to make Troilus' condition more like that of his true self, his faithful go-between would walk barefoot all the way to India.*

81   friend or end *befriend him or destroy him.*

84   Excuse me. *Cressida is probably saying "Please forgive me if I differ from what you say." Another possibility, however, is that she is either expressing incredulity or pretending not to have understood her uncle's meaning: "Excuse me: did I hear you correctly?"*

85   He is elder. *Pandarus is conceding that Hector is indeed older, but with the implication that he is not therefore better.*

87   Th' other's not come to 't *Troilus is not yet grown to his full stature as a man. But* come to 't *can also carry several erotic senses.*

87–88   you shall tell me another Tale *you'll have a different story (your attitude will be quite different).*

89   his Will *his way, his continued superiority. In the next line Cressida gives the phrase a bawdy implication.* Will *can refer to the genitalia, and Cressida probably uses the term to refer both to Hector's own "will" and that of the women whose "will" and will power he masters. She may also be picking up on a bawdy meaning for* Tale *("tail").*

93   No matter. *it makes no difference. Cressida is probably using* matter *with genital innuendo, as does Pandarus in I.i.87–88.*

97–98   for a Brown Favor *for a man of dark complexion.*

358

PANDARUS Condition I had gone barefoot to India.

CRESSIDA He is not Hector.

PANDARUS Himself? No, he's not Himself; would 'a
were Himself. Well the Gods are above; Time   80
must friend or end. —Well Troilus, well, I
would my Heart were in her Body. —No, Hector
is not a better Man than Troilus.

CRESSIDA Excuse me.

PANDARUS He is elder.   85

CRESSIDA Pardon me, pardon me.

PANDARUS Th' other's not come to 't; you shall
tell me another Tale when th' other's come
to 't; Hector shall not have his Will this
year.   90

CRESSIDA He shall not need it if he have his own.

PANDARUS Nor his Qualities.

CRESSIDA No matter.

PANDARUS Nor his Beauty.

CRESSIDA 'Twould not become him; his own's better.   95

PANDARUS You have no Judgment, Niece: Helen her
self swore th' other day that Troilus for a
Brown Favor (for so 'tis, I must confess), not
Brown neither—

CRESSIDA No, but Brown.   100

PANDARUS Faith to say truth, Brown and not Brown.

CRESSIDA To say the truth, True and not True.

PANDARUS She prais'd his Complexion above Paris'.

CRESSIDA Why Paris hath Color enough.

PANDARUS So he has.   105

CRESSIDA Then Troilus should have too much, if
she prais'd him above; his Complexion is higher

109　　too flaming a Praise　*Cressida is punning on* Color *(line 108) and* Choler *(anger), a humour thought to result from an excess of the element Fire in the system. She is alluding to the red color of a choleric person's face.*

110　　Complexion　*Cressida uses this term in two senses: (a) skin color, and (b) psychological disposition.*
　　　　lieve　*lief, gladly.*

111　　Copper Nose　*a nose red from excessive drinking.*

114　　a Merry Greek　*a loose, wanton person.*

115　　dooes　*does. Here and elsewhere the spelling in the Quarto printing appears likely to reflect Shakespeare's own.*

116　　compass'd Window　*bay window.*

117　　past　*more than.*

119　　a Tapster's Arithmetic　*a bartender's ability to calculate sums.*

124　　Lifter　*Cressida is probably referring to at least two senses in addition to Pandarus' literal one: (a) a thief, and (b) a man who can "stand to thee Proof" of his masculinity (line 137).*

127　　Cloven　*cleft, dimpled.*

134　　a Cloud in Autumn　*a dark, ominous cloud.*

137　　stand to thee Proof　*stand up as a witness for you to help you prove your case. Cressida uses a legal metaphor, and one with an obvious additional sense in this instance.*

than his; he having Color enough, and the
other higher, is too flaming a Praise for a
good Complexion. I had as lieve Helen's Golden   110
Tongue had commended Troilus for a Copper Nose.

PANDARUS   I swear to you I think Helen loves him
better than Paris.

CRESSIDA   Then she's a Merry Greek indeed.

PANDARUS   Nay I am sure she dooes; she came to him   115
th' other day into the compass'd Window, and
you know he has not past three or four Hairs
on his Chin.

CRESSIDA   Indeed a Tapster's Arithmetic may soon
bring his Particulars therein to a Total, I.   120

PANDARUS   Why he is very Young, and yet will he
within three Pound lift as much as his brother
Hector.

CRESSIDA   Is he so Young a Man and so Old a Lifter?

PANDARUS   But to prove to you that Helen loves him,   125
she came and puts me her white Hand to his
Cloven Chin.

CRESSIDA   Juno have mercy, how came it Cloven?

PANDARUS   Why, you know 'tis Dimpled; I think his
Smiling becomes him better than any Man in all   130
Phrygia.

CRESSIDA   O he smiles valiantly.

PANDARUS   Dooes he not?

CRESSIDA   O yes, and 'twere a Cloud in Autumn.

PANDARUS   Why go to then, but to prove to you that   135
Helen loves Troilus—

CRESSIDA   Troilus will stand to thee Proof if you'll
prove it so.

361

140   **Addle**   *addled, rotten.*

142   **Idle**   *empty, addled (impaired).*

145   **marvel's**   *marvelous.*

147   **Without the Rack.**   *Cressida picks up on the word* confess, *alluding to an instrument of torture to extract confessions from prisoners by stretching them unmercifully.*

153   **Millstones**   *Those too unemotional to shed tears were said to drop millstones (large, flat stones for grinding wheat and other grains) from their eyes.*

155   **a more temperate Fire**   *a fire less likely to cause liquid to boil over from the pot above it.*

162   **Green Hair**   *Cressida means "a hair of a truly extraordinary color." But* **Green** *is also appropriate here because of its association with youthfulness.*

165   **pretty**   *cute, charming.*

PANDARUS   Troilus, why he esteems her no more
    than I esteem an Addle Egg.   140
CRESSIDA   If you love an Addle Egg as well as you
    love an Idle Head, you would eat Chickens
    i' th' Shell.
PANDARUS   I cannot choose but laugh to think how
    she tickled his Chin; indeed she has a marvel's   145
    white Hand, I must needs confess.
CRESSIDA   Without the Rack.
PANDARUS   And she takes upon her to spy a White
    Hair on his Chin.
CRESSIDA   Alas poor Chin, many a Wart is richer.   150
PANDARUS   But there was such laughing, Queen
    Hecuba laugh'd that her Eyes ran o'er.
CRESSIDA   With Millstones.
PANDARUS   And Cassandra laugh'd.
CRESSIDA   But there was a more temperate Fire   155
    under the Pot of her Eyes; did her Eyes run
    o'er too?
PANDARUS   And Hector laugh'd.
CRESSIDA   At what was all this Laughing?
PANDARUS   Marry at the White Hair that Helen spied   160
    on Troilus' Chin.
CRESSIDA   And 't had been a Green Hair I should
    have laugh'd too.
PANDARUS   They laugh'd not so much at the Hair as
    at his pretty Answer.   165
CRESSIDA   What was his Answer?
PANDARUS   Quoth she, "Here's but two and fifty
    Hairs on your Chin, and one of them is White."
CRESSIDA   That is her Question.

174   **Hairs** *There is wordplay on* **heirs.** *Queen Hecuba bore fifty sons to King Priam.*

175   **The Forked One** *This phrase is bawdy in several related ways. Here as elsewhere in Shakespeare,* **fork** *refers to the crotch area, and thus to the genitalia. In this connection, like* **firk, fut, foot, foutre,** *and similar sounding words, it has bawdy connotations. Like* **horn,** *however (which can refer either to a man's erect member or to the horns on the forehead of a frustrated cuckold),* **fork** *is also a word that frequently applies to a man's brows. Here Helen's blushes and Paris' chafing (irritation) suggest that both of them take Troilus' phrase to imply that Paris is a cuckolder whose "Merry Greek" wife keeps him anxious too.*

178   **pass'd** *surpassed all description. In line 179, Cressida plays on two other senses: passed by (a) in time, and (b) in a procession.*

181   **Cousin** *a word that could be applied to any kind of blood relative.*
        a thing *something, with a hint at another implication.*

184–   **he will weep . . . April** *he will weep over you (long for you*
85   *and care tenderly for you) as if he were a man borne in the time of the year most frequently associated with budding love. Here* **borne** *probably has at least three meanings: (a) borne by his pregnant mother, (b) born (given birth to), and (c) borne sexually by a woman like Cressida.*

187   **against May** *in anticipation of May (to achieve full growth).*

190   **Ilion** *Ilium, the palace.*

PANDARUS   That's true, make no question of that.   170
  "Two and fifty Hairs," quoth he, "and one
  White; that White Hair is my Father, and all
  the rest are his Sons." "Jupiter," quoth she,
  "which of these Hairs is Paris my Husband?"
  "The Forked One," quoth he, "pluck 't out and   175
  give it him." But there was such Laughing, and
  Helen so blush'd, and Paris so chaf'd, and
  all the rest so laugh'd, that it pass'd.
CRESSIDA   So let it now, for it has been a great
  While going by.   180
PANDARUS   Well, Cousin, I told you a thing
  yesterday; think on 't.
CRESSIDA   So I do.
PANDARUS   I'll be sworn 'tis true, he will weep
  you an' 'twere a Man borne in April.   185

                                    Sound a Retreat.

CRESSIDA   And I'll spring up in his Tears an'
  'twere a Nettle against May.
PANDARUS   Hark, they are coming from the Field;
  shall we stand up here and see them as they
  pass toward Ilion? Good Niece, do, sweet Niece   190
  Cressida.
CRESSIDA   At your Pleasure.
PANDARUS   Here, here, here's an excellent place;
  here we may see most bravely. I'll tell you
  them all by their Names as they pass by; but   195
  mark Troilus above the rest.

                    Enter Aeneas.

198   Brave   *bold, splendid, handsome.*

200   anon   *shortly.*

202   shrow'd   *sharp-tongued, biting. This adjective derives from* shrew, *and its spelling indicates the way both words were normally pronounced.*

205   Proper Man of Person   *a handsome man in appearance.*

208   give you the Nod   *Cressida's primary implication is "give you a nod of recognition that classifies you as a Noddy, a fool." But* nod *is also a word that frequently carries sexual innuendo, (a) as a sign of assent, (b) as a male's "standing offer" to a woman who arouses his interest, and (c) as a word that sounds like* naught *and* nada *(Spanish for "nothing"), and can thus have "naughty" meanings related to the notion that a woman, having "no thing," desires one.*

210   the Rich shall have more   *Cressida's point is that Pandarus, already well endowed with folly, will be made even wealthier. She is probably referring primarily to his silliness. But folly was also a concept with sexual dimensions in Shakespeare's time. Sexual license is often referred to as "folly." A sexual tool (both a person and a person's "equipment") is frequently referred to as a "fool." And the word* fool *often denotes a deceived victim of sexual exploitation.*

212   Go thy way   *a term of encouragement, roughly equivalent to "fare you well" or "keep up the good work."*

220   laying on   *laying on of blows, leaving hack-marks and dents.*

CRESSIDA Speak not so loud.

PANDARUS That's Aeneas: is not that a Brave Man?
  He's one of the Flowers of Troy, I can tell
  you. But mark Troilus; you shall see anon.   200

CRESSIDA Who's that?

Enter Antenor.

PANDARUS That's Antenor; he has a shrow'd Wit,
  I can tell you, and he's Man good enough;
  he's one o' th' soundest Judgments in Troy
  whosoever, and a Proper Man of Person. When   205
  comes Troilus? I'll show you Troilus anon; if
  he see me, you shall see him nod at me.

CRESSIDA Will he give you the Nod?

PANDARUS You shall see.

CRESSIDA If he do, the Rich shall have more.   210

Enter Hector.

PANDARUS That's Hector, that, that, look you:
  that, there's a Fellow! —Go thy way, Hector.
  —There's a Brave Man, Niece. O brave Hector,
  look how he looks: there's a Countenance! Is't
  not a Brave Man?   215

CRESSIDA O a Brave Man.

PANDARUS Is 'a not? It dooes a man's Heart good.
  Look you what Hacks are on his Helmet; look
  you yonder, do you see? Look you there; there's
  no Jesting; there's laying on, take 't off who   220
  will, as they say; there be Hacks.

367

224 all one *all the same, a matter of indifference.*
     Lid *eyelid.*

234 he *Troilus. In this and in his following speech, Pandarus is so
     intent on locating Troilus that he is paying only half attention
     to the soldier who is parading in front of the viewing stand at
     the present moment.*

237 indifferent *as well as the next man. In Shakespeare's time*
     indifferent *normally means "not different," with more neu-
     tral connotations than is usually the case today.*

241 sneaking *the antithesis of brave and upright. Cressida knows
     that this "Fellow" is Troilus, and she teasingly describes him
     in a way that will deflate all her uncle's efforts to advertise him
     as the noblest Trojan of them all.*

243 hem *This throat-clearing utterance is frequently associated
     with the pledging of toasts, where it means something like
     "Down the hatch!" Here Pandarus probably uses it to attract
     Cressida's full attention and to say with pride "See, he's just
     as wonderful as I told you he would be!"*

CRESSIDA Be those with Swords?

Enter Paris.

PANDARUS Swords, any thing: he cares not. And the
Divel come to him it's all one. By God's Lid,
it dooes one's Heart good. Yonder comes Paris,   225
yonder comes Paris; look ye yonder, Niece. Is't
not a Gallant Man too, is't not? Why this is
Brave now: who said he came Hurt home today?
He's not Hurt; why this will do Helen's Heart
good now, ha? Would I could see Troilus now;   230
you shall see Troilus anon.
CRESSIDA Who's that?

Enter Helenus.

PANDARUS That's Helenus; I marvel where Troilus
is; that's Helenus; I think he went not forth
today; that's Helenus.   235
CRESSIDA Can Helenus fight, Uncle?
PANDARUS Helenus, no; yes, he'll fight indifferent.
Well, I marvel where Troilus is; hark, do you
not hear the People cry "Troilus"? Helenus is
a Priest.   240
CRESSIDA What sneaking Fellow comes yonder?

Enter Troilus.

PANDARUS Where? Yonder? That's Deiphobus. 'Tis
Troilus! There's a Man, Niece, hem! Brave

369

250 goes *walks.*
   admirable *wondrous.*

250– he never saw three and twenty *he is not yet twenty-three*
51 *years old.*

252 a Grace *one of the three Graces—Aglaia (Brilliance), Eu-*
   phrosyne (Joy), and Thalia (Bloom)—who brought pleasure
   and beauty into the world. Daughters of Zeus, they were the
   most benign of Goddesses.

254 to him *compared to him. In the first scene, Pandarus has*
   commended Cressida to Troilus by praising her more highly
   than Helen; now he commends Troilus by rating him more
   highly than Paris.

255 warrant *guarantee, assure you.*
   change *both (a) change men, and (b) exchange [Paris for*
   Troilus].

258 Chaff and Bran *the husks (rather than kernels) that remain*
   after grain has been sifted.

259 Porridge after Meat *soup, following a course of solid food.*

260– Ne'er . . . Daws. *Pandarus' point is that after the noblest*
62 *of birds have passed by, there is no reason to keep looking; only*
   such base fowl as crows and jackdaws (types of crows) remain.

266 Dray-man *the driver of a dray (brewer's cart).*
   Porter *a man who ports (carries) heavy objects. Pandarus*
   implies that Achilles is all brawn and no brain or grace.

269 Discretion *judgment, intelligence.*

370

Troilus, the Prince of Chivalry.

CRESSIDA   Peace for shame, peace!   245

PANDARUS   Mark him, note him. O brave Troilus,
look well upon him, Niece; look you how his
Sword is bloodied, and his Helm more hack'd
than Hector's, and how he looks, and how he
goes. O admirable Youth, he never saw three   250
and twenty. —Go thy way, Troilus, go thy way.
—Had I a Sister were a Grace, or a Daughter
a Goddess, he should take his Choice. O
admirable Man! Paris? Paris is Dirt to him,
and I warrant Helen to change would give an   255
Eye to boot.

Enter Common Soldiers.

CRESSIDA   Here comes more.

PANDARUS   Asses, Fools, Dolts; Chaff and Bran,
Chaff and Bran; Porridge after Meat. I could
live and die in the Eyes of Troilus. Ne'er   260
look, ne'er look: the Eagles are gone; Crows
and Daws, Crows and Daws. I had rather be such
a Man as Troilus than Agamemnon and all Greece.

CRESSIDA   There is amongst the Greeks Achilles, a
better Man than Troilus.   265

PANDARUS   Achilles? A Dray-man, a Porter, a very
Camel!

CRESSIDA   Well, well.

PANDARUS   Well, well, why have you any Discretion?
Have you any Eyes? Do you know what a Man is?   270
Is not Birth, Beauty, good Shape, Discourse,

371

272   **Gentleness**   *the arts and manners of a man of gentle birth.*

273   **Liberality**   *a generosity of spirit.*

275   **a Minc'd Man**   *a man chopped into tiny pieces and baked in a pie. Cressida alludes to all the "ingredients" Pandarus has listed as Troilus' attributes. She is also suggesting that a man so constituted would walk with the "mincing" (effeminate) steps of one who is too refined.*

277   **Date is out**   *Cressida plays on the idea of a pie with no dates in it for seasoning; she goes on to imply that Troilus, as Pandarus describes him, would quickly become stale and useless.*

279   **Ward**   *posture of defense.*

280   **Upon my Back**   *Cressida describes her posture in deliberately ambiguous terms. She is on her back, presumably, because that is where her attacker would force her to "lie"; but her "Ward" also suggests a willingness to have her resistance overcome.*

281   **Wit**   *cunning, intelligence. But like* **Will,** **Wit** *could also refer to sexual desire and to the genitalia of either gender.*

282   **Honesty**   *honor. Cressida's phrasing suggests that she is less concerned about real chastity than about a respectable reputation.*
       Mask   *Cressida probably refers to the kind of silk mask Elizabethan ladies wore to shield their delicate faces from the sun and wind.*

289–   **unless . . . hiding**   *Cressida refers to a "Blow" whose*
90   *swelling extends for nine months.*

295   **doubt**   *fear.*

Manhood, Learning, Gentleness, Virtue, Youth,
Liberality, and such like the Spice and Salt
that seasons a Man?

CRESSIDA   Ay a Minc'd Man, and then to be bak'd   275
with no Date in the Pie: for then the Man's
Date is out.

PANDARUS   You are such a Woman a Man knows not
at what Ward you lie.

CRESSIDA   Upon my Back to defend my Belly, upon   280
my Wit to defend my Wiles, upon my Secrecy to
defend mine Honesty, my Mask to defend my
Beauty, and you to defend all these: and at
all these Wards I lie, at a thousand Watches.

PANDARUS   Say one of your Watches.   285

CRESSIDA   Nay I'll watch you for that; and that's
one of the chiefest of them too. If I cannot
ward what I would not have hit, I can watch
you for telling how I took the Blow unless it
swell past hiding, and then it's past watching.   290

PANDARUS   You are such another.

Enter Boy.

BOY   Sir, my Lord would instantly speak with you.

PANDARUS   Where?

BOY   At your own House; there he unarms him.

PANDARUS   Good Boy, tell him I come; I doubt he   295
be hurt.   *Exit Boy.*
—Fare ye well, good Niece.

CRESSIDA   Adieu, Uncle.

PANDARUS   I will be with you, Niece, by and by.

373

302   **Bawd**   *pimp, go-between. But it is clear from line 300 that Cressida is more than willing to avail herself of Pandarus' services, however much she teases him and pretends to be uninterested in the man he is commending to her.*

303   **Sacrifice**   *Cressida alludes to the notion that love's "rites" are analogous to those of a religion. As she describes them, Pandarus' efforts on behalf of his "friends" are a parody of the self-sacrifice associated with a very different kind of go-between (John 15:13).*

306   **Glass**   *mirror.*

307   **are Angels wooing**   *both (a) act like angels while being wooed, and (b) are treated with the reverence reserved for angels while being wooed.*

308   **woon**   *both (a) successfully wooed, and (b) won.*
       Done   *over and done with; spent; of no further interest or value.*
       Doing   *Here Cressida refers to the act of wooing.*

310   **price**   *hold at a price; prize.*

314   **Achievement . . . Beseech.**   *What Cressida means here is that the woman who has been achieved (won) no longer has any control over her man; he may command her at will. The woman who remains "ungain'd," on the other hand, must be beseeched (begged) for any favors she deigns to bestow. The moral of Cressida's soliloquy is that even though she may be in love with Troilus, she is not yet ready to surrender herself to him and lose the advantage she enjoys while he remains her suitor.*

374

CRESSIDA   To bring, Uncle—   300
PANDARUS   Ay, a Token from Troilus.
CRESSIDA   By the same Token you are a Bawd.
                                        Exit Pandarus.
   —Words, Vows, Gifts, Tears, and Love's full
      Sacrifice,
   He offers in another's Enterprise;
   But more in Troilus thousand-fold I see   305
   Than in the Glass of Pandar's Praise may be.
   Yet hold I off. Women are Angels wooing;
   Things woon are Done; Joy's Soul lies in the
      Doing.
   That She Belov'd knows Naught that knows not
      this:
   Men price the thing ungain'd more than it is.   310
   That She was never yet that ever knew
   Love Got so Sweet as when Desire did sue.
   Therefore this Maxim out of Love I teach:
   "Achievement is Command; ungain'd, Beseech."
   Then though my Heart's Content firm Love doth
      bear,   315
   Nothing of that shall from mine Eyes appear.   *Exit.*

I.iii   *This scene provides us our first glimpse of the Greek camp.*

S.D.   Sennet   *a trumpet fanfare to signal a ceremonial entrance.*

2   these Jaundies   *this jaundice (a yellow complexion).*

3   The . . . makes   *the high optimism that hope encourages.*

5   Fails . . . Largeness   *falls short of expectation in what it delivers.*
        Checks and Disasters   *obstacles and "star-crossings" ("Disasters" are misfortunes brought about by adverse astral influences).*

7   As   *just as, in the same way that.*
        by . . . Sap   *by the convergence of sap that causes blockages (Knots) in a tree's veins. In line 6* Vains *refers to various kinds of* veins *(including those in fleshly "Actions highest rear'd") whose "promis'd Largeness" proves both "vain" (empty, overreaching) and "in vain" (frustrated).*

9   Tortive and errant   *twisting and diverted away.*

11   our Suppose   *our expectations, what we supposed possible.*

13   Sith ever   *since (a) always, and (b) every.*

14–15   Trial . . . thwart   *circumstances frustrated the original plan.*

15–17   not . . . Shape   *not responding (or corresponding) to the aim and the hypothetical plan that charted its intended course. Agamemnon's metaphor derives from the game of bowls, where one rolled a ball (bowl) weighted on one side so that its bias would cause it to curve as it approached its destination.*

Scene 3

· *Sennet. Enter Agamemnon, Nestor, Ulysses, Diomedes,*
Menelaus, with Others.

AGAMEMNON Princes:
What Grief hath set these Jaundies o'er your
    Cheeks?
The ample Proposition that Hope makes
In all Designs begun on Earth below
Fails in the promis'd Largeness; Checks and
    Disasters   5
Grow in the Vains of Actions highest rear'd
As Knots, by the Conflux of meeting Sap,
Infects the sound Pine and diverts his Grain
Tortive and errant from his Course of Growth.
Nor, Princes, is it Matter new to us   10
That we come short of our Suppose so far
That after sev'n years Siege yet Troy Walls
    stand,
Sith ever Action that hath gone before,
Whereof we have Record, Trial did draw
Bias and thwart, not answering the Aim   15
And that unbodi'd Figure of the Thought
That gave 't surmised Shape. Why then, you
    Princes,

18   abash'd   *embarrassed, ashamed.*
          Works   *endeavors, accomplishments.*

20   protractive Trials   *long-drawn-out tests.*

21   To find . . . Men   *to find out which men can persist (persevere) while remaining constant in their resolve.*

22   Metal   *both (a) a metal that is made durable by extremes of heat and cold, and (b) true mettle (virtue) in men.*

23   In Fortune's Love   *when Fortune is too kind.*

24   the Artist and Unread   *the expert and the amateur.*

25   seem . . . kin   *all seem to have an affinity (kinship) with one another, which makes it impossible to distinguish them.*

28   winnows the Light away   *blows away all the lightweight husks.*

30   unmingled   *pure, separated from "the Light"; here a four-syllable word.*

31   With . . . Seat   *with due respect for the divine throne you occupy.*

33   the Reproof of Chance   *the buffetings of Fortune.*

35   shallow Bauble-boats   *flat-bottomed, toy-like boats.*

38   Boreas   *the north wind.*

39   Thetis   *a sea-nymph; here personifying the sea itself.*

42   Perseus' Horse   *Pegasus, an extraordinary winged creature.*

Do you with Cheeks abash'd behold our Works
And call them Shames which are indeed naught
   else
But the protractive Trials of great Jove,   20
To find persistive Constancy in Men,
The Fineness of which Metal is not found
In Fortune's Love? For then the Bold and
   Coward,
The Wise and Fool, the Artist and Unread,
The Hard and Soft, seem all affyn'd and kin;   25
But in the Wind and Tempest of her Frown,
Distinction with a broad and pow'rful Fan,
Puffing at All, winnows the Light away,
And what hath Mass or Matter by it self
Lies rich in Virtue and unmingled.   30
NESTOR   With due Observance of the Godlike Seat,
Great Agamemnon, Nestor shall apply
Thy latest Words. In the Reproof of Chance
Lies the true Proof of Men: the Sea being
   smooth,
How many shallow Bauble-boats dare sail   35
Upon her ancient Breast, making their way
With those of nobler Bulk?
But let the ruffian Boreas once enrage
The gentle Thetis, and anon behold
The strong-ribb'd Bark through liquid Mountains
   cut,   40
Bounding between the two moist Elements
Like Perseus' Horse. Where's then the saucy
   Boat
Whose weak untimber'd Sides but even now

44   Co-rival'd Greatness   *rashly sought to compete with their betters.*

45   a Toast for Neptune   *like a piece of toasted bread floated on top of an alcoholic drink. Neptune is the Roman name for the God of the Sea.*

46   Doth Valor's Show . . . divide   *does the mere appearance of Valor become sorted out from true Valor.*

48   Bryze   *breese, the gadfly that pesters cattle in the summer.*

49   splitting Wind   *Here the wind is called "splitting" not only because of its power to split oaks, but also because of its role as a winnower (divider or sorter).*

52   with . . . sympathize   *rages in accord with Rage itself.*

54   Retires to chiding Fortune   *rages at Fortune in reply.*

56   Spright   *spirit.*

58   shut up   *both (a) contained, embodied, and (b) controlled.*

60   thy Place and Sway   *Agamemnon's position and power.*

61   thou   *the aged Nestor.*

65   hatch'd in Silver   *covered with white hair. Here* hatch'd *can refer both to (a) the lines in an engraving, and (b) the hatch door to a ship's hold; the image also suggests (c) a silver bird's nest in which white eggs are hatched.*

66   Axle-tree   *axle or axis, here the one by which the Heavens revolve around the Earth.*

Co-rival'd Greatness? Either to Harbor fled
Or made a Toast for Neptune. Even so   45
Doth Valor's Show and Valor's Worth divide
In Storms of Fortune: for in her Ray and
   Brightness
The Herd hath more Annoyance by the Bryze
Than by the Tiger; but when the splitting Wind
Makes flexible the Knees of knotted Oaks,   50
And Flies fled under Shade, why then the thing
   of Courage,
As rous'd with Rage, with Rage doth sympathize,
And with an Accent tun'd in self-same Key
Retires to chiding Fortune.
ULYSSES   Agamemnon,
Thou great Commander, Nerves and Bone of
   Greece,   55
Heart of our Numbers, Soul and only Spright,
In whom the Tempers and the Minds of all
Should be shut up, hear what Ulysses speaks,
Besides th' Applause and Approbation,
The which, most mighty for thy Place and Sway,   60
And thou, most Rev'rend for thy stretch'd-out
   Life,
I give to both your Speeches, which were such
As Agamemnon and the Hand of Greece
Should hold up high in Brass, and such again
As venerable Nestor, hatch'd in Silver,   65
Should with a Bond of Air strong as the Axle-
   tree
On which Heav'n rides knit all the Greekish Ears

69   Great and Wise   *Agamemnon and Nestor, respectively.*

70   be 't of less Expect   *and let it be with less expectation.*

71   of importless Burthen   *of no import (importance).*

73   rank   *foul, disgusting, gross, licentious.*
Mastic   *both (a) masticating (grinding), and (b) abusive (from* mastix, *Greek for "whip" or "scourge").*

75   Bases   *foundations.*
had been down   *would have been overthrown by now.*

78   The Specialty of Rule   *the unique authority of the established ruler.*
neglected   *disregarded, held in disrespect.*

79   look how many   *however many.*

80   so . . . Factions   *there are that many empty mini-kingdoms.*

81   the Hive   *the central gathering place, the home, of a kingdom of bees.*

83   Degree being vizarded   *when the symbols of hierarchy are covered with masks (visors) that obscure the ranks of those ordained to rule.*

84   shows as fairly   *appears just as beautiful and powerful.*

85   this Center   *the Earth, at the center of Ptolemaic cosmology.*

87   In Sisture   *in consistency or constancy (evidently a Shakespearean coinage).*

89   Planet Sol   *the Sun, here depicted as a healing King whose beneficent "Eye" (radiating light) overrules the malign sway of all lesser planets.*

To his experienc'd Tongue; yet let it please
   both,
Thou Great and Wise, to hear Ulysses speak.
AGAMEMNON   Speak, Prince of Ithaca, and be 't of
   less Expect   70
That Matter needless, of importless Burthen,
Divide thy Lips than we are confident
When rank Thersites opes his Mastic Jaws
We shall hear Music, Wit, and Oracle.
ULYSSES   Troy, yet upon his Bases, had been down,   75
And the great Hector's Sword had lack'd a
   Master,
But for these Instances:
The Specialty of Rule hath been neglected,
And look how many Grecian Tents do stand
Hollow upon this Plain, so many hollow
   Factions.   80
When that the Gen'ral is not like the Hive
To whom the Foragers shall all repair,
What Honey is expected? Degree being vizarded,
Th' Unworthiest shows as fairly in the Mask.
The Heav'ns themselves, the Planets and this
   Center,   85
Observe Degree, Priority, and Place,
In Sisture, Course, Proportion, Season, Form,
Office and Custom in all line of Order;
And therefore is the glorious Planet Sol
In noble Eminence enthron'd and spher'd   90
Amidst the oth'r; whose med'cinable Eye
Corrects the Influence of evil Planets
And posts like the Commandment of a King,

94 Sans Check *without resistance.*

95 in evil Mixture *without retaining their assigned positions within the cosmic order.*

96 Portents *omens of disaster; here pronounced "por-ténts".*
Mutiny *rebellion.*

99 Divert *turn into unnatural courses.*
rend and deracinate *tear and uproot.*

101 Quite from their Fixure *completely away from their fixed places.*

105 Peaceful . . . Shores *harmonious trading and communication between countries divided from each other by seas or other boundaries.*

106 Primogenity and Due of Birth *the rights of succession and inheritance that descend to the eldest son in every family.*

107 Prerogative *privilege, authority.*

108 stand in authentic Place *maintain their authorized positions.*

111 mere Oppugnancy *absolute discord, conflict.*

113 a Sop *a piece of soggy toast in a cup of liquor.*

114 Imbecility *feebleness, impotence (not mental debilitation).*

117 Jar *conflict, opposition.*
recides *falls down, recedes. Most editors emend to* resides.

119 include it self in Power *[would] become an aspect of the tyranny of force.*

Sans Check, to Good and Bad. But when the
    Planets
In evil Mixture to Disorder wander,   95
What Plagues and what Portents, what Mutiny?
What raging of the Sea, shaking of Earth?
Commotion in the Winds, Frights, Changes,
    Horrors,
Divert and crack, rend and deracinate
The Unity and marri'd Calm of States   100
Quite from their Fixure. O when Degree is
    shak'd,
Which is the Ladder of all high Designs,
The Enterprise is sick. How could Communities,
Degrees in Schools, and Brotherhoods in Cities,
Peaceful Commerce from divid'ble Shores,   105
The Primogenity and Due of Birth,
Prerogative of Age, Crowns, Scepters, Laurels,
But by Degree stand in authentic Place?
Take but Degree away, untune that String,
And hark what Discord follows. Each thing melts   110
In mere Oppugnancy: the bounded Waters
Should lift their Bosoms higher than the Shores,
And make a Sop of all this solid Globe;
Strength should be Lord of Imbecility,
And the rude Son should strike his Father dead.   115
Force should be Right, or rather Right and
    Wrong
(Between whose endless Jar Justice recides)
Should lose their Names, and so should Justice
    too.
Then ev'ry thing include it self in Power,

120   Power into Will   *power becomes an aspect of unbridled will.*
       Appetite   *brute desire and uncontrolled voraciousness.*

123   Must . . . Prey   *must of necessity make everything in the*
       world its prey (since the only way to survive is to devour others
       before they can devour you).

125   suffocate   *suffocated, strangled.*

127   Neglection of   *disregard of, contempt for.*

128–   by a Pace . . . climb   *step by step descends the ladder as*
 29   *those on the upper rungs are successively challenged by those*
         just below them whose "Purpose" is to "climb."

129   disdain'd   *held in contempt.*

133   an envious Fever   *a malicious disease, fed by "Emulation"*
       (envy, rivalry).

135   on foot   *standing, unfallen.*

136   Sinews   *muscles, strength.*

138   discover'd   *disclosed, diagnosed.*

143   Sinow   *sinew.*

145   dainty of his Worth   *too vain about his own dignity.*

146   Designs   *plans and efforts.*

148   scurril   *scurrilous; contemptuous, demeaning.*

Power into Will, Will into Appetite,   120
And Appetite, an universal Wolf
(So doubly seconded with Will and Power),
Must make perforce an universal Prey
And last eat up himself. Great Agamemnon,
This Chaos, when Degree is suffocate,   125
Follows the Choking,
And this Neglection of Degree it is
That by a Pace goes backward with a Purpose
It hath to climb. The General's disdain'd
By him one step below, he by the next,   130
That next by him beneath: so ev'ry Step,
Exampl'd by the first Pace that is sick
Of his Superior, grows to an envious Fever
Of pale and bloodless Emulation.
And 'tis this Fever that keeps Troy on foot,   135
Not her own Sinews. To end a Tale of Length,
Troy in our Weakness stands, not in her Strength.
NESTOR   Most wisely hath Ulysses here discover'd
The Fever whereof all our Pow'r is sick.
AGAMEMNON   The Nature of the Sickness found,
    Ulysses,   140
    What is the Remedy?
ULYSSES   The great Achilles, whom Opinion crowns
The Sinow and the Forehand of our Host,
Having his Ear full of his airy Fame,
Grows dainty of his Worth, and in his Tent   145
Lies mocking our Designs. With him Patroclus
Upon a lazy Bed the live-long Day
Breaks scurril Jests,
And with ridiculous and silly Action,

387

151 pageants *represents, as in a crude dramatic pageant.*

152 Topless Deputation *position as God's highest deputy.*

153 Conceit *wit, cleverness, intelligence (related to* concept*).*

154 Hamstring *thigh sinews; a reference to his "strutting" (line 153).*

156 Scaffolage *scaffolding, here referring to the stage itself. Ulysses' choice of words is probably meant to echo the scoffing manner of the Player's exaggerated strides ("stretch'd Footing").*

157 o'er-rested *over-wrested; far-fetched, strained. The spelling is a reminder that this indulgence results from too much rest.*

159 a Chime a-mending *the cacophony of a set of bells being repaired.*
Terms unsquare *unfitting, discordant expressions.*

160 Tiphon *Typhon, a giant with a hundred heads and mouths.*

161 fusty *both (a) stale, and (b) fustian (overblown, bombastic).*

167– as near . . . Parallels *with an accuracy as near as are the*
68 *two ends of a pair of parallel straight lines (infinitely apart).*

168 Vulcan and his Wife *Vulcan, a lame, deformed blacksmith, was married to Venus, the Goddess of Beauty and Love.*

174 Gorget *a piece of armor to protect the throat.*

175 Rivet *the metal bolt to fasten the gorget.*

178 Spleen *the seat of the impulsive emotions, including mirth.*

Which (Slanderer) he Imitation calls,   150
He pageants us. Sometime, great Agamemnon,
Thy Topless Deputation he puts on,
And like a strutting Player whose Conceit
Lies in his Hamstring and doth think it rich
To hear the wooden Dialogue and Sound   155
'Twixt his stretch'd Footing and the Scaffolage,
Such to-be-piti'd and o'er-rested Seeming
He acts thy Greatness in. And when he speaks,
'Tis like a Chime a-mending, with Terms unsquare
Which, from the Tongue of roaring Tiphon
    dropp'd,   160
Would seem Hyperboles. At this fusty Stuff
The large Achilles on his press'd Bed lolling,
From his deep Chest laughs out a loud Applause,
Cries "Excellent! 'Tis Agamemnon right!
Now play me Nestor: hem and stroke thy Beard,   165
As he, being dress'd to some Oration."
That's done as near as the extremest Ends
Of Parallels, as like as Vulcan and his Wife;
Yet God Achilles still cries "Excellent!
'Tis Nestor right; now play him me, Patroclus,   170
Arming to answer in a Night Alarm."
And then forsooth the faint Defects of Age
Must be the Scene of Mirth, to cough and spit
And, with a palsy Fumbling on his Gorget,
Shake in and out the Rivet; and at this Sport   175
Sir Valor dies, cries "O enough, Patroclus,
Or give me Ribs of Steel; I shall split all
In pleasure of my Spleen!" And in this Fashion
All our Abilities, Gifts, Natures, Shapes,

180   Severals . . . exact   *individual and collective virtues.*

181   Preventions   *defenses, precautions.*

182   Excitements to the Field   *incitements to action in battle.*

184   Paradoxes   *jests reducing us to absurdity.*

188   self-wild   *a force unto himself. The Folio reads* self-will'd.

189   Reyne   *both (a) reign, and (b) rein.*

191   Makes factious Feasts   *provides hospitality in order to gather
       men into insubordinate factions.*
       rails on our State of War   *assails the way we conduct the
       war.*

193   Gall   *rancor, bitterness (from bile, a secretion of the liver).*

195   weaken our Discredit   *further downgrade our present inepti-
       tude.*
       our Exposure   *our exposure to danger from the enemy.*

196   rank   *thickly (as in a garden overwhelmed with weeds).*

197   tax our Policy   *criticize our strategic maneuvers, our attempts
       to use our minds as well as their brute strength.*

199   Forestall Prescience   *proceed without the benefit of plan-
       ning; pronounced "pre-scí-ence."*

203   Observant Toil   *efforts to obtain military intelligence.*

207   for . . . Poise   *because of its overwhelmingly heavy thrust.*

208   They . . . Engine   *they value more highly than the intelli-
       gence and skill required to devise such a weapon.*

Sev'rals and Generals of Grace exact,   180
Achievements, Plots, Orders, Preventions,
Excitements to the Field, or Speech for Truce,
Success or Loss, what is or is not, serves
As Stuff for these two to make Paradoxes.

NESTOR   And in the Imitation of these Twain,   185
Who, as Ulysses says, Opinion crowns
With an imperial Voice, many are infect;
Aiax is grown self-wild, and bears his Head
In such a Reyne, in full as proud a Place,
As broad Achilles; keeps his Tent like him,   190
Makes factious Feasts, rails on our State of
    War
Bold as an Oracle, and sets Thersites,
A Slave whose Gall coins Slanders like a Mint,
To match us in Comparisons with Dirt,
To weaken our Discredit, our Exposure   195
How rank so ever rounded in with Danger.

ULYSSES   They tax our Policy, and call it Cowardice,
Count Wisdom as no member of the War,
Forestall Prescience and esteem no Act
But that of Hand. The Still and Mental Parts   200
That do contrive how many Hands shall strike,
When Fitness calls them on, and know by Measure
Of their Observant Toil the En'my's Weight,
Why this hath not a Finger's Dignity:
They call this Bed-work, Mapp'ry, Closet War;   205
So that the Ram that batters down the Wall
For the great Swinge and Rudeness of his Poise
They place before his Hand that made the Engine,
Or those that with the Fineness of their Souls

391

210   guide his Execution   *direct the use of it in battle. Here and frequently elsewhere,* his *means "its." In Shakespeare's time, "his" and "it" were the normal forms for the neuter possessive pronoun.*

212   Makes many Thetis' Sons   *is worth many times what Achilles (the son of Thetis) is worth.*

S.D.   Tucket   *a brief series of notes on a trumpet, normally to signal the advance of military forces.*

219   fair   *peaceful, non-threatening.*

220–   With Surety . . . General.   *Given what we have just*
22   *heard about "Achilles' Arm" and the supposed unity of "the Greekish Heads" under Agamemnon, this remark reverberates with a hollow irony the speaker doesn't intend.*

223   Leave   *permission.*
      Security   *guarantee of safety. But* Security *often refers to unwarranted self-confidence, and Aeneas is probably implying that Agamemnon is overly self-assured.*

224   A Stranger . . . Looks   *one who has never seen the mighty Agamemnon and doesn't know what he looks like. Aeneas' overblown rhetoric parodies Agamemnon's own hyperbole and satirizes the General by bestowing on him a dignity ludicrously in excess of what his merits and his present situation justify.*

229   The youthful Phoebus   *the rising son. Phoebus was one of the names of the Sun God.*

230   God   *Aeneas goes well beyond the commonplace that a ruler was to be regarded as God's deputy in relation to his subjects.*
      in Office   *in his position, responsible for.*

234   debonair   *courteous, gentle in manner.*

By Reason guide his Execution.   210
NESTOR   Let this be granted, and Achilles' Horse
    Makes many Thetis' Sons—   *Tucket.*
AGAMEMNON   What Trumpet? Look, Menelaus.
MENELAUS   From Troy.

Enter Aeneas.

AGAMEMNON   What would you 'fore our Tent?   215
AENEAS   Is this great Agamemnon's Tent, I pray you?
AGAMEMNON   Ev'n this.
AENEAS   May one that is a Herald and a Prince
    Do a fair Message to his Kingly Eyes?
AGAMEMNON   With Surety stronger than Achilles' Arm   220
    'Fore all the Greekish Heads which with one Voice
    Call Agamemnon Head and General.
AENEAS   Fair Leave and large Security; how may
    A Stranger to those most Imperial Looks
    Know them from Eyes of other Mortals?
AGAMEMNON   How?   225
AENEAS   Ay, I ask that I might waken Reverence,
    And bid the Cheek be ready with a Blush
    Modest as Morning when she coldly eyes
    The youthful Phoebus,
    Which is that God, in Office guiding Men,   230
    Which is the high and mighty Agamemnon?
AGAMEMNON   This Troian scorns us, or the Men of
    Troy
    Are ceremonious Courtiers.
AENEAS   Courtiers as free, as debonair, unarm'd,
    As bending Angels: that's their Fame in Peace.   235

393

236   Galls   *the bitter bile in their stomachs to make them fierce.*

237   great Jove's Accord   *Aeneas probably means "such a unity of heart and spirit that they have the power of great Jove himself." If so, he is probably alluding to the absence of such* esprit de corps *in the Greek ranks. Aeneas may also be asserting that Jove is in accord with the Trojans (fighting on their side). In this line* and *is probably glided over and merged with* great *so that the two words form a single syllable metrically. Most editors follow the Folio and omit* great.

238   Nothing so full of Heart.   *There is nothing else so full of courage [as this spirited corps of warriors]. Here* Heart (cor *or* cordis *in Latin) is a virtual translation of* Accord *in line 237.*

240   distains   *stains, detracts from.*

242   what th' repining Enemy commends   *what the envious (complaining) enemy praises.*

243   sole pure transcends   *rises above all other commendations in its purity (because praise from enemies is either disinterested or grudging).*

248   naught   *either (a) no one, or (b) nothing.*

251   To set . . . Bent   *to make him sit up and pay full attention.*

252   frankly   *both (a) freely, and (b) openly, uninhibitedly.*

257   Mettle   *worthiness, spirit. In Shakespeare's time* mettle *and* metal *were so closely linked as to be all but indistinguishable. Here the playwright puns on "Brass Voice" in line 256.*

394

But when they would seem Soldiers, they have
   Galls,
Good Arms, strong Joints, true Swords, and
   great Jove's Accord:
Nothing so full of Heart. —But peace, Aeneas,
Peace, Troian, lay thy Finger on thy Lips.
The worthiness of Praise distains his Worth   240
If that the Prais'd himself bring the Praise forth;
But what th' repining Enemy commends,
That Breath Fame blows, that Praise sole pure
   transcends.
AGAMEMNON   Sir, you of Troy, call you your self
   Aeneas?
AENEAS   Ay Greek, that is my Name.   245
AGAMEMNON   What's your Affairs, I pray you?
AENEAS   Sir, pardon, 'tis for Agamemnon's Ears.
AGAMEMNON   He hears naught privately that comes
   from Troy.
AENEAS   Nor I from Troy come not to whisper with
   him;
I bring a Trumpet to awake his Ear,   250
To set his Seat on that Attentive Bent,
And then to speak.
AGAMEMNON   Speak frankly as the Wind:
It is not Agamemnon's Sleeping-hour.
That thou shalt know, Troian, he is awake,
He tells thee so himself.
AENEAS   —Trumpet blow aloud;   255
Send thy Brass Voice through all these lazy
   Tents,
And ev'ry Greek of Mettle let him know

258   fairly   *gently, peacefully. Here the placement of the adverb
         allows it to modify both what precedes it and what follows.*

261   his   *Most editors adopt the Folio's* this. *But the implication of
         the Quarto reading seems equally likely: that with so many of
         his Greek counterparts keeping to their "lazy Tents" (line
         256), Hector has taken himself out of action. Whether a
         formal truce has been called by the two armies is unclear.*

262   resty   *This adjective probably combines several senses: (a)
         over-rested and sluggish, (b) restless, and (c) rusty (the word
         in the Folio).*

266   feeds his Praise   *nourishes those qualities in himself that will
         result in his being honored for his valor.*

269   truant Vows   *idle, empty professions of love.*

270   avow   *uphold, maintain.*

271   In other Arms   *that is, in the arms and armor of a soldier.*

272   in view of   *in the presence of.*

273   make it good   *maintain it in combat.*

275   couple   *embrace; with wordplay on military arms and on the
         conjoining of insignia in a coat of arms.*

279   honor him   *do him the honor of fighting him.*

281   Sunburnt   *In Shakespeare's time, a dark or sunburnt skin was
         not considered a sign of beauty. Women shielded their faces to
         ward off the sun.*

282   Launce   *What Hector proposes is a chivalric joust, a tourna-
         ment.*

What Troy means fairly shall be spoke aloud.

Sound Trumpet.

—We have, great Agamemnon, here in Troy
A Prince call'd Hector (Priam is his Father),   260
Who in his dull and long continu'd Truce
Is resty grown. He bade me take a Trumpet
And to this Purpose speak: "Kings, Princes,
    Lords,
If there be one among the Fair'st of Greece
That holds his Honor higher than his Ease,   265
And feeds his Praise more than he fears his
    Peril,
That knows his Valor and knows not his Fear,
That loves his Mistress more than in Confession
With truant Vows to her own Lips he loves,
And dare avow her Beauty and her Worth   270
In other Arms than hers, to him this Challenge.
Hector in view of Troians and of Greeks
Shall make it good, or do his best to do it:
He hath a Lady wiser, fairer, truer,
Than ever Greek did couple in his Arms,   275
And will tomorrow with his Trumpet call
Midway between your Tents and Walls of Troy
To rouse a Grecian that is true in Love.
If any come, Hector shall honor him;
If none, he'll say in Troy when he retires,   280
The Grecian Dames are Sunburnt and not worth
The Splinter of a Launce." Ev'n so much.
AGAMEMNON   This shall be told our Lovers, Lord
    Aeneas;
If none of them have Soul in such a kind,

286   a mere Recreant   *an absolute traitor.*

287   means not   *means not to be in love.*
hath not   *hath not been in love.*

288   or hath . . . be   *or has a lady to whom he could pledge his love. Most editors adopt the Folio's "or hath, or means to be."*

295   Beaver   *the part of the head armor that protected the mouth and chin.*

296   Vambrace   *vantbrace, armor for the arm.*
Brawns   *muscles.*

298   Grandam   *grandmother.*

299   His Youth in Flood   *even though he will meet me while his youth is at the full (like the sea at high tide).*

300   prove this Troth   *both (a) make this pledge good, and (b) prove the truth of the woman to whom I vow continued fidelity.*

301   forfend   *defend against.*
Men   *Most editors adopt the Folio's* youth *here. That is Aeneas' implication: that it would be regrettable if an aged man like Nestor (upholding the honor of a wife long dead) were the only champion the Greeks could muster. Ulysses'* Amen *(so be it) in the next line would seem to be a play on* Men, *the word in the Quarto text.*

304   our Pavilion   *my tent (the "capitol" of the Greek camp).*

311   young Conception   *newly conceived thought.*

312   Time   *occasion.*

We left them all at home. But we are Soldiers, 285
And may that Soldier a mere Recreant prove
That means not, hath not, or is not in love:
If then one is, or hath a means to be,
That one meets Hector; if none else, I am he.
NESTOR   Tell him of Nestor, one that was a Man 290
When Hector's Grandsire suck'd. He is old now,
But if there be not in our Grecian Host
A Noble Man that hath no spark of Fire
To answer for his Love, tell him from me,
I'll hide my Silver Beard in a Gold Beaver, 295
And in my Vambrace put my wither'd Brawns
And, meeting him, tell him that my Lady
Was Fairer than his Grandam, and as Chaste
As may be in the World. His Youth in Flood,
I'll prove this Troth with my three drops of Blood. 300
AENEAS   Now Heav'ns forfend such Scarcity of Men.
ULYSSES   Amen.
AGAMEMNON   Fair Lord Aeneas, let me touch your
   Hand.
To our Pavilion shall I lead you, Sir.
Achilles shall have word of this Intent; 305
So shall each Lord of Greece from Tent to Tent.
Your self shall feast with us before you go,
And find the Welcome of a Noble Foe.
                    Exeunt Agamemnon and Aeneas.
ULYSSES   Nestor.
NESTOR   What says Ulysses? 310
ULYSSES   I have a young Conception in my Brain;
Be you my Time to bring it to some Shape.
NESTOR   What is't?

315   rive hard Knots   *split knots that are too hard for sharper wedges to open. Ulysses' image echoes line 7.*
seeded   *gone to seed through uncontrolled growth.*

316   blown up   *both (a) reached full bloom, and (b) become puffed up, proud.*

317   rank   *both (a) overgrown (like weeds), and (b) coarse, vile.*
or   *either.*

318   shedding   *dropping its seed to generate more plants.*

319   overbulk   *both (a) outgrow, and (b) overwhelm.*

321   spread in Gen'ral Name   *delivered to us as a general challenge. Ulysses' verb continues the agricultural metaphor.*

323   perspicuous as Substance   *as obvious as if its substance were made explicit (completely open to view).*

324   Whose Grossness . . . up   *whose overall import is clearly present in the small letters that add up to communicate the message.*

325   And in the Publication . . . Strain   *and require no straining at interpretation to be understood when made public.*

327   Banks of Libya   *that is, desert sands where seeds cannot sprout.*

329   Celerity   *speed and ease.*

334   Opinion   *reputation, honor.*

335   taste   *both (a) taste, and (b) test.*
dear'st Repute   *most highly regarded soldier.*

ULYSSES   This 'tis.
  Blunt Wedges rive hard Knots; the seeded
    Pride   315
  That hath to this Maturity blown up
  In rank Achilles must or now be cropp'd
  Or, shedding, breed a Nursery of like Evil
  To overbulk us all.
NESTOR   Well, and how?
ULYSSES   This Challenge that the gallant Hector
    sends,   320
  How ever it is spread in Gen'ral Name,
  Relates in Purpose only to Achilles.
NESTOR   True, the Purpose is perspicuous as
    Substance,
  Whose Grossness little Characters sum up
  And in the Publication make no Strain,   325
  But that Achilles, were his Brain as barren
  As Banks of Libya (though Apollo knows
  'Tis dry enough), will with great speed of
    Judgment,
  Ay with Celerity, find Hector's Purpose
    pointing on him.
ULYSSES   And wake him to the Answer, think you?   330
NESTOR   Why 'tis most meet: who may you else
    oppose
  That can from Hector bring those Honors off
  If not Achilles? Though 't be a sportful Combat,
  Yet in the Trial much Opinion dwells:
  For here the Troians taste our dear'st Repute   335
  With their fin'st Palate; and trust to me,
    Ulysses,

401

337   Our Imputation . . . pois'd   *our reputation shall be challenged by an adversary who carries great odds.*

338   vild   *vile.*
      Success   *outcome (not limited to success in the modern sense).*

339   Particular   *individual (pertaining to the combatants).*
      Scantling   *small (scant) measure.*

340   the General   *the armies as a whole.*

341   Indexes   *prefatory summaries (as on title-pages), tables of contents.*

341–42   although . . . Volumes   *though they may seem like tiny prick-marks in comparison to the huge volumes that follow.*

343   Baby Figure . . . Mass   *epitome or digest of the whole volume.*

347   Makes Merit her Election   *selects the best on the basis of merit.*

349–51   who . . . themselves   *who, if he fails, will give to the hearts of the victors a taste of conquest that will strengthen their opinion of their own power and ability.*

352–54   Which . . . Limbs   *which, reflected upon, will instill strength ("Limbs" and their muscles) in their hearts and stomachs ("Instruments") that will prove no less effectual than the weapons wielded by their arms and legs.*

355   Therefore   *for this reason.*

358–59   the Luster . . . first   *the attractiveness of the better wares shall be all the greater if we display the lesser ones first.*

Our Imputation shall be oddly pois'd
In this vild Action; for the Success,
Although Particular, shall give a Scantling
Of Good or Bad unto the General; 340
And in such Indexes (although small Pricks
To their subsequent Volumes) there is seen
The Baby Figure of the Giant Mass
Of things to come at large. It is suppos'd
He that meets Hector issues from our Choice, 345
And Choice (being mutual Act of all our Souls)
Makes Merit her Election and doth boil
(As 'twere from forth us all) a Man distill'd
Out of our Virtues; who, miscarrying,
What Heart receives from hence a conqu'ring
    Part 350
To steel a strong Opinion to themselves;
Which entertained, Limbs are in his Instruments,
In no less working than are Swords and Bows
Directive by the Limbs.
ULYSSES   Give pardon to my Speech. Therefore 'tis
    meet 355
Achilles meet not Hector. Let us like Marchants
First show Foul Wares and think perchance
    they'll sell;
If not, the Luster of the Better shall exceed
By showing the Worse first. Do not consent
That ever Hector and Achilles meet: 360
For both our Honor and our Shame in this
Are dogg'd with two strange Followers.
NESTOR   I see them not with my old Eyes; what are
    they?

364   shares from Hector   *derives from victory over Hector (by adding to his own glory the shares of glory that Hector has accumulated).*

368   salt   *Ulysses is referring to the salt of eye-brine, but he may also be thinking of a desert salt flat.*

370   our Main Opinion crush   *reduce our general reputation.*

372   by Device   *by rigging the outcome.*
        blockish   *blockheaded.*

374   Give him Allowance for   *credit him with being, pretend that he is.*

375   physic   *provide medicine for.*
        the great Myrmidon   *Achilles. His soldiers were known as Myrmidons.*

376   broils in   *enjoys the warmth of. Ulysses probably uses this verb as a reminder that Achilles is so caught up in the glow of his own reputation that he is broiling (quarreling) with his fellow Greeks rather than with the Trojans.*
        fall   *lower, drop.*

377   Crest   *the plume at the top of his helmet (analogous to the comb, plume, or mane of a proud cock, bird, or stallion).*
        blue Iris   *probably both the blue flower and the rainbow (whose Goddess was Iris, like Mercury a messenger of the Gods).*

388   arre   *the snarling sound of two fierce mastiffs (ferocious dogs). Most editors adopt the Folio's* tarre, *incite. Preceded by* Must, *the two words would be virtually indistinguishable when spoken in the theatre.*

ULYSSES   What Glory our Achilles shares from
            Hector,
        Were he not Proud, we all should share with
            him.   365
        But he already is too Insolent,
        And it were better parch in Afric Sun
        Than in the Pride and salt Scorn of his Eyes
        Should he scape Hector fair. If he were foil'd,
        Why then we do our Main Opinion crush   370
        In Taint of our Best Man. No, make a Lott'ry
        And by Device let blockish Aiax draw
        The Sort to fight with Hector; among our selves
        Give him Allowance for the Better Man,
        For that will physic the great Myrmidon,   375
        Who broils in loud Applause, and make him fall
        His Crest, that prouder than blue Iris bends.
        If the dull brainless Aiax come safe off,
        We'll dress him up in Voices; if he fail,
        Yet go we under our Opinion still   380
        That we have Better Men. But hit or miss,
        Our Project's Life this Shape of Sense assumes:
        Aiax employ'd plucks down Achilles' Plumes.
NESTOR   Now Ulysses, I begin to relish thy Advice,
        And I will give a Taste thereof forthwith   385
        To Agamemnon. Go we to him straight.
        Two Curs shall tame each other; Pride alone
        Must arre the Mastiffs on, as 'twere a Bone.
                                            Exeunt.

II.i	*This scene takes place elsewhere in the Greek camp.*
2	**Biles** *boils, but with wordplay on* **bile**, *bitterness.* **full** *loaded with pus.*
7	**botchy** *ulcerous, lumpy with sores.* **Core** *a pun on (a) the hard center of a boil, (b)* **corps**, *French for body, and (c) corpse.*
9	**Matter** *substance, here referring to (a) pus, rather than (b) intelligent discourse.*
14	**Mongrel** *Thersites probably alludes to the fact that Aiax was half Greek and half Trojan.* **Beef-witted** *as stupid as an ox. It was a commonplace, moreover, that eating too much beef resulted in dull wits.*
15	**unsalted Leaven** *tasteless, fermenting dough. Three Biblical passages may be relevant here. In Matthew 5:13 Jesus tells his disciples "Ye are the salt of the earth: but if the salt have lost his savour, wherewith shall it be salted? it is thenceforth good for nothing but to be cast out, and to be trodden under foot of men." In Matthew 16:13 Jesus says to "beware of the leaven [doctrine] of the Pharisees and Sadducees." And in 1 Corinthians 5:8, Paul says "let us keep the feast, not with the old leaven, neither with the leaven of malice and wickedness, but with the unleavened bread of sincerity and truth."*

Scene 1

Enter Aiax and Thersites.

AIAX   Thersites!

THERSITES   Agamemnon, how if he had Biles, full,
   all over, generally—

AIAX   Thersites!

THERSITES   And those Biles did run. Say so: did   5
   not the General run then, were not that a
   botchy Core?

AIAX   Dog!

THERSITES   Then there would come some Matter
   from him: I see none now.   10

AIAX   Thou Bitch-wolf's Son, canst thou not hear?
   Feel then!   *He strikes him.*

THERSITES   The Plague of Greece upon thee, thou
   Mongrel Beef-witted Lord!

AIAX   Speak then, thou unsalted Leaven, speak; I   15

407

16   beat . . . Handsomeness   *Aiax continues the dough metaphor, promising now to beat (not knead) Thersites until he becomes suitable for baking.*

19   cun   *con; memorize, learn by heart ("without Book").*

21   Murrion   *murrain, plague.*
        Jade's Tricks   *the stubbornness of a worthless horse.*

22   Toadstool   *probably a reference to Thersites' deformed shape and poisonous disposition, with a pun on toad's stool (dung).*
        Learn me   *teach me, inform me about.*
        Proclamation   *Aiax has heard rumors about Hector's challenge and is now frantic to learn more about it.*

27   Do not   *don't provoke me.*
        Porpentine   *porcupine.*
        itch   *itch to strike you (see III.v.165 of* Romeo and Juliet*).*

31   Incursions   *battles.*

32   as slow as another   *Thersites is calling Aiax a cowardly bully: his point is that Aiax's fingers do not "itch" when he is confronted with an adversary who could strike him back.*

34   gromblest   *grumblest.*

36   Cerberus   *the ugly dog who guarded the entrance to Hades.*
        Proserpina   *the beautiful Queen of the Underworld.*

40   Cobloaf   *a small loaf with a big, lumpy top.*

41   pun   *pound.*

46   sodden-witted   *boiled-brained.*

will beat thee into Handsomeness.

THERSITES   I shall sooner rail thee into Wit and
Holiness; but I think thy Horse will sooner
cun an Oration without Book than thou learn
Prayer without Book. Thou canst strike, canst   20
thou? A red Murrion 'a thy Jade's Tricks.

AIAX   Toadstool! Learn me the Proclamation.

THERSITES   Doost thou think I have no Sense, thou
strikest me thus?

AIAX   The Proclamation.   25

THERSITES   Thou art proclaim'd Fool, I think.

AIAX   Do not, Porpentine, do not; my Fingers itch.

THERSITES   I would thou didst itch from Head to
Foot, and I had the Scratching of thee; I
would make thee the loathsomest Scab in   30
Greece. When thou art forth in the Incursions,
thou strikest as slow as another.

AIAX   I say the Proclamation!

THERSITES   Thou gromblest and railest every hour
on Achilles, and thou art as full of Envy at   35
his Greatness as Cerberus is at Proserpina's
Beauty; ay that thou bark'st at him—

AIAX   Mistress Thersites!

THERSITES   Thou should strike him.

AIAX   Cobloaf!   40

THERSITES   He would pun thee into Shivers with
his Fist, as a Sailor breaks a Biscuit.

AIAX   You whoreson Cur!

THERSITES   Do! Do!

AIAX   Thou Stool for a Witch!   45

THERSITES   Ay, do, do, thou sodden-witted Lord!

409

48   Asinico   *bastard Spanish for "little ass."*

50   bought and sold   *Thersites' implication is that Aiax is all brawn and no brain, and that he is treated like little more than a useful beast by his masters. There may also be a suggestion that Aiax is a mercenary whose mixed blood would make him as suitable for the Trojans as for the Greeks.*

53   by Inches   *in detail, inch by inch.*

54   Bowels   *tenderness, human feeling.*

58   Mars his Idiot   *the brainless tool of the God of War. Here as elsewhere* Mars his *is an early form of* Mars's.

62   You see him there?   *The implication of Thersites' reply is that Aiax is "the matter" (line 61), an insentient lump of brutish flesh. In view of line 69, Thersites is probably also implying that Aiax is a piece of excrement.*

69   Aiax   *Thersites is probably punning on "A Iakes" (a jakes or privy).*

71   that Fool   *Thersites gives a derogatory twist to Achilles' previous line.*

72   Therefore I beat thee.   *For that reason I beat you [since I know you are a fool].*

74   Evasions   *replies, responses in defense of his honor.*
        Ears thus long   *Thersites probably gestures in such a way as to indicate that Aiax has the ears of an ass.*

Thou hast no more Brain than I have in mine
Elbows. An Asinico may tutor thee, you scurvy
valiant Ass; thou art here but to thrash
Troians, and thou art bought and sold among 50
those of any Wit like a Barbarian Slave. If
thou use to beat me, I will begin at thy Heel
and tell what thou art by Inches, thou thing
of no Bowels thou!

AIAX You Dog! 55

THERSITES You scurvy Lord!

AIAX You Cur!

THERSITES Mars his Idiot! Do, Rudeness! Do, Camel,
do, do!

Enter Achilles and Patroclus.

ACHILLES Why how now, Aiax, wherefore do ye thus? 60
—How now, Thersites, what's the matter, man?

THERSITES You see him there? Do you?

ACHILLES Ay what's the matter?

THERSITES Nay look upon him.

ACHILLES So I do, what's the matter? 65

THERSITES Nay but regard him well.

ACHILLES Well, why so I do.

THERSITES But yet you look not well upon him,
for whosomever you take him to be, he is Aiax.

ACHILLES I know that, Fool. 70

THERSITES Ay but that Fool knows not himself.

AIAX Therefore I beat thee.

THERSITES Lo, lo, lo, lo, what modicums of Wit
he utters! His Evasions have Ears thus long. I

75   bobb'd   *knocked, bopped.*

77   Pia Mater   *brain; actually one of the membranes enclosing it.*

79–80   who wears . . . Head   *Thersites implies that there is no difference between Aiax's pia mater and the matter he excretes from his "Guts."*

84   —Nay good Aiax—   *Achilles restrains Aiax's "itch."*

87   the Eye . . . Needle   *As Thersites points out in line 88, "the Eye of Helen's Needle" is what the war is ultimately about. Shakespeare engages in similar wordplay in* Henry V, *II.i.34–38, where the Hostess complains that "we cannot lodge and board a dozen or fourteen Gentlewomen that live honestly by the prick of their Needles but it will be thought we keep a Bawdy-house straight." In this context* Wit *(line 85) refers to both a brain and the kind of male "I" that will "stop" (stuff or prick) Helen's "Eye."*

94   Will . . . Fool's?   *Thersites functions as a kind of court fool, and Achilles asks Aiax why he is contending with a person so far below him in station.*

97   Good words   *Patroclus probably means "speak politely"; the expression derives from* bona verba, *a Latin phrase originating with Plautus.*

99   tenor   *import.*

102   go to   *so what? The expression "go to" is a form of dismissal.*

104   Suff'rance   *(a) suffering and (b) involuntary endurance.*

have bobb'd his Brain more than he has beat 75
my Bones; I will buy nine Sparrows for a
Penny, and his Pia Mater is not worth the
ninth part of a Sparrow. This Lord, Achilles—
Aiax, who wears his Wit in his Belly and his
Guts in his Head—I tell you what I say of 80
him.

ACHILLES   What?

THERSITES   I say this Aiax—

ACHILLES   —Nay good Aiax—

THERSITES   Has not so much Wit— 85

ACHILLES   —Nay I must hold you—

THERSITES   As will stop the Eye of Helen's Needle,
for whom he comes to fight.

ACHILLES   Peace, Fool!

THERSITES   I would have Peace and Quietness, but 90
the Fool will not: he there, that he, look you
there!

AIAX   O thou damned Cur, I shall—

ACHILLES   Will you set your Wit to a Fool's?

THERSITES   No I warrant you, the Fool's will 95
shame it.

PATROCLUS   Good words, Thersites.

ACHILLES   What's the Quarrel?

AIAX   I bade the vile Owl go learn me the tenor
of the Proclamation, and he rails upon me. 100

THERSITES   I serve thee not.

AIAX   Well, go to, go to.

THERSITES   I serve here Voluntary.

ACHILLES   Your last Service was Suff'rance: 'twas
not Voluntary; no man is beaten voluntary. 105

413

107   under an Impress   *both (a) impressed (involuntarily con-*
       scripted) into military service, and (b) imprinted by the im-
       press (stamp) of Aiax's blows.

110   and 'a   *if he.*

112   fusty   *stale, musty.*

116   draught Oxen   *oxen to draw (draught) or pull loads or*
       ploughs.

126   Brooch   *ornament. Thersites is probably alluding to Patro-*
       clus' role as a hanger-on who serves Achilles in any way he
       desires. Most editors emend to brach *(bitch).*

128   Clatpoles   *clodheads.*

134   first   *The Folio prints* fift. *Most editors follow suit, citing*
       Thersites' remark in III.iii.290–91 that he expects the issue
       with Hector to be resolved "by eleven of the Clock." When the
       Greeks sound the first trumpet in IV.v, however, the absence of
       an immediate reply from the Trojan side is explained by Achil-
       les' observation that " 'Tis but Early Days" (IV.v.12), a
       statement that would seem to support the notion that the
       Greeks were expecting the match to occur "by the first hour of
       the Sun."

Aiax was here the Voluntary, and you are as
under an Impress.

THERSITES   E'en so; a great deal of your Wit too
lies in your Sinews, or else there be Liars.
Hector shall have a great Catch and 'a knock   110
out either of your Brains; 'a were as good
crack a fusty Nut with no Kernel.

ACHILLES   What, with me too, Thersites?

THERSITES   There's Ulysses and old Nestor, whose
Wit was mouldy ere their Grandsires had Nails   115
on their Toes, yoke you like draught Oxen, and
make you plough up the Wars.

ACHILLES   What? What?

THERSITES   Yes good sooth; to Achilles, to Aiax,
to—   120

AIAX   I shall cut out your Tongue.

THERSITES   'Tis no matter, I shall speak as much
as thou afterwards.

PATROCLUS   No more words, Thersites, peace!

THERSITES   I will hold my Peace when Achilles'   125
Brooch bids me, shall I?

ACHILLES   There's for you, Patroclus.

THERSITES   I will see you hang'd like Clatpoles
ere I come any more to your Tents; I will
keep where there is Wit stirring, and leave   130
the Faction of Fools.   *Exit.*

PATROCLUS   A good Riddance.

ACHILLES   Marry this, Sir, is proclaim'd through
all our Host,
That Hector by the first hour of the Sun
Will with a Trumpet 'twixt our Tents and Troy   135

415

137   **a Stomach** *more or less equivalent to "guts" in modern parlance. The stomach was considered the seat of both appetite and valor.*

II.ii   *This Trojan Council scene is probably to be thought of as taking place in Ilium, the Palace of Troy.*

3   **Domage** *a variant of* **damage.** *Here the Quarto spelling may be intended to pick up some of the implications of* **doom** *and hint both at judgment and at the fate awaiting those who fail to change their ways before it is too late.*

4   **As** *such as. Here* as *serves to introduce an itemized list.*
       Travel *both (a) travel, and (b) travail (effort and pain). In this line the accent falls on the second syllable, with the consequence that the stress is more on* travail *(as the word is spelled in the Folio and in most modern editions) than on* travel.

6   **Corm'rant** *a voracious seabird. In* Love's Labor's Lost, *I.i.4, Shakespeare applies the same adjective to Time.*

7   **stroke** *struck. In this play as in others,* stroke *and* strook *are the usual Shakespearean spellings.*

9   **as toucheth my Partic'lar** *as concerns me personally. Although Hector doesn't intend it, his phrasing suggests another kind of "part-tickler" (hinted at in line 52) that plays a larger role in Trojan political affairs than it should. Other references to "tickling" occur in III.i.126 and V.ii.45–47.*
       dread *revered.*

10   **Bowels** *the seat of compassion.*

11   **spungy** *sponge-like in absorbency.*

Tomorrow morning call some Knight to Arms
That hath a Stomach, and such a one that dare
Maintain I know not what: 'tis Trash. Farewell.

AIAX   Farewell. Who shall answer him?

ACHILLES   I know not: 'tis put to Lott'ry. Otherwise   140
He knew his Man.   *Exit, with Patroclus.*

AIAX   O meaning you? I will go learn more of it.   *Exit.*

Scene 2

Enter Priam, Hector, Troilus, Paris, and Helenus.

PRIAM   After so many Hours, Lives, Speeches spent,
Thus once again says Nestor from the Greeks:
"Deliver Helen, and all Domage else,
As Honor, loss of Time, Travel, Expense,
Wounds, Friends, and what else dear that is
consum'd   5
In hot Digestion of this Corm'rant War,
Shall be stroke off." —Hector, what say you
to 't?

HECTOR   Though no man lesser fears the Greeks
than I
As far as toucheth my Partic'lar, yet, dread Priam,
There is no Lady of more softer Bowels,   10
More spungy to suck in the sense of Fear,
More ready to cry out "Who knows what follows?"

13   The Wound of Peace is Surety   *the injury that peace inflicts is a sense of overconfidence, Hector's comment is similar to that in* Julius Caesar, *II.ii.49, where Calphurnia tells Caesar "Your Wisdom is consum'd in Confidence," and* Macbeth, *III.v.32–33, where the Witches note that "Security / Is Mortals' chiefest Enemy."*

14   modest Doubt   *rational fear, prudent caution.*

15   Tent   *medical probe (such as a strip of gauze) to search a wound.*

18   tithe   *tenth.*
      Dismes   *tenths, "dimes" (Old French, from Latin* decimus).

19   Hath . . . Helen   *has been paid as the price for Helen.*

22   one Ten   *either (a) one life (one lot of ten tithes), or ten lives.*

27   Common Ounces   *the same weight in ordinary human flesh.*
      Compters   *counters; both (a) accountants, and (b) tokens, worthless coins.*

28   The . . . Infinite   *his immeasurable value.*

29   Waste   *waist, but with reminders of (a) vast (a related word), and (b) waste (profligate expenditure, such as the thousands now dead).*

30   Spanes   *The Quarto spelling conveys both (a) spangs (buckles), and (b) spans. A span could be either the width of an outstretched hand or the circumference of the waist.*

34   with Reason   *with sufficient justification (with reasons of his own).*

Than Hector is. The Wound of Peace is Surety,
Surety secure; but modest Doubt is call'd
The Beacon of the Wise, the Tent that searches   15
To th' Bottom of the Worst. Let Helen go:
Since the first Sword was drawn about this
    Question,
Ev'ry tithe Soul 'mongst many thousand Dismes
Hath been as dear as Helen. I mean of ours:
If we have lost so many Tenths of Ours,   20
To guard a thing Not Ours, not worth to us
(Had it our Name) the Value of one Ten,
What Merit's in that Reason which denies
The yielding of her up?
TROILUS   Fie, fie, my Brother,
Weigh you the Worth and Honor of a King   25
So great as our dread Father's in a Scale
Of Common Ounces? Will you with Compters sum
The past-Proportion of his Infinite,
And buckle in a Waste most fathomless
With Spanes and Inches so diminutive   30
As Fears and Reasons? Fie, for Godly Shame!
HELENUS   No marvel though you bite so sharp of
    Reasons,
You are so empty of them. Should not our Father
Bear the great Sway of his Affairs with Reason
Because your Speech hath none that tell him so?   35
TROILUS   You are for Dreams and Slumbers, brother
    Priest:
You fur your Gloves with Reason. Here are your
    Reasons:
You know an Enemy intends you Harm;

419

44   fly like chidden Mercury   *Mercury, the chief messenger of the Gods, was traditionally depicted with wings on his heels (line 43). Here* fly *means both (a) flee, and (b) take wing. Shakespeare alludes to an incident in which Mercury was "chidden" (rebuked) by Jove for stealing Apollo's cattle. Since Paris' theft of Helen is the matter at issue, the example Troilus cites is quite apt.*

45   Star disrob'd   *a shooting star whose clothing (sphere) has been stolen. Again the imagery is pertinent.*

46   Gates   *both (a) our eyelids, and (b) the gates of Troy.*
     sleep   *another reference to Helenus' effeminate lethargy (lines 36–37).*

47   Hare Hearts   *Fleet-footed rabbits were symbols of cowardice.*
     fat   *associated with sloth and irresolution, as in* Hamlet, *I.v.30–33.*

48–49   Reason . . . deject.   *Reason and consideration (prudence) turn pale the source of courageous passion and cast down the spirit of lusty vigor. Compare* Hamlet, *III.i.80–85.*

51   aught   *anything. Troilus defines value subjectively, as something that lies solely in the eyes of the beholder. In lines 52–59, Hector defines it objectively, as something that resides in the "Merit" of the thing prized.*

57   is attributive   *pays tribute, is subject.*

58   affects   *desires, holds in affection, dotes on.*

63   traded Pilots   *captains conducting sea trade. But* traded *can mean "bought, corrupted, compromised."*

You know a Sword employ'd is perilous;
And Reason flies the Object of all Harm.   40
Who marvels then, when Helenus beholds
A Grecian and his Sword, if he do set
The very Wings of Reason to his Heels
And fly like chidden Mercury from Jove,
Or like a Star disrob'd? Nay if we talk of
   Reason,   45
Let's shut our Gates and sleep. Manhood and
   Honor
Should have Hare Hearts would they but fat their
   Thoughts
With this cramm'd Reason. Reason and Respect
Make Livers pale and Lustihood deject.
HECTOR   Brother, she is not worth what she doth cost   50
   The Keeping.
TROILUS   What's aught but as 'tis valued?
HECTOR   But Value dwells not in partic'lar Will;
   It holds his Estimate and Dignity
   As well wherein 'tis precious of it self
   As in the Prizer. 'Tis mad Idolatry   55
   To make the Service greater than the God,
   And the Will dotes that is attributive
   To what infectiously it self affects
   Without some Image of th' affected Merit.
TROILUS   I take today a Wife, and my Election   60
   Is led on in the conduct of my Will,
   My Will enkindl'd by mine Eyes and Ears,
   Two traded Pilots 'twixt the dang'rous Shores
   Of Will and Judgment. How may I avoid,
   Although my Will distaste what it elected,   65

421

67   **blench** *flinch, shrink from, turn aside.*
         and *and at the same time.*

69   **remainder Viands** *uneaten food.*

70   **unrespective Sieve** *undiscriminating waste-basket. Troilus says that the garbage should receive only inedible scraps, not edible food whose only fault lies in the satiety of the disposer.*

73   **Your . . . Sails** *Troilus conflates (combines) the breath with which his fellow Greeks consented to Paris' mission and the wind that made the sails of his ships resemble pregnant women. His point is that the plan was judged to be rational and honorable at the time it was approved "with full Consent"; it should thus seem equally rational and honorable now.*

74   **old Wranglers** *traditional adversaries.*

76   **from** *in retaliation for.*
         an old Aunt *King Priam's sister Hesione, whom the Greeks had taken captive and refused to return to the Trojans.*

78   **Wrinkles Apollo's** *makes the youthful Apollo's look old.*

81   **above** *more than.*

82   **Marchants** *merchants, traders (because they have sailed to Troy to regain the priceless "Pearl" that is no longer theirs). Paris' image suggests that, like Pandarus' "trading," the ventures of these "Marchants" are of questionable honor and merit.*

88   **proper** *both (a) own, personal, and (b) working properly.*
         rate *berate (estimating it now at a lower rate than before).*

The Wife I choose? There can be no Evasion,
To blench from this and to stand firm by Honor.
We turn not back the Silks upon the Marchant
When we have soil'd them, nor the remainder
    Viands
We do not throw in unrespective Sieve   70
Because we now are full. It was thought meet
Paris should do some Vengeance on the Greeks;
Your Breath with full Consent belli'd his Sails;
The Seas and Winds, old Wranglers, took a Truce
And did him Service; he touch'd the Ports
    desir'd,   75
And from an old Aunt whom the Greeks held
    Captive
He brought a Grecian Queen whose Youth and
    Freshness
Wrinkles Apollo's and makes pale the Morning.
Why keep we her? The Grecians keep our Aunt.
Is she worth keeping? Why she is a Pearl   80
Whose Price hath launch'd above a thousand
    Ships
And turn'd crown'd Kings to Marchants.
If you'll avouch 'twas Wisdom Paris went
(As you must needs, for you all cried "Go,
    go!"),
If you'll confess he brought home worthy Prize   85
(As you must needs, for you all clapp'd your
    Hands
And cried "Inestimable!"), why do you now
The Issue of your proper Wisdoms rate
And do a Deed that never Fortune did,

90–91 **Beggar . . . Land** *reduce to beggary (value as worthless) the object you prized above everything else in the world. Troilus finds such a prospect unthinkable, something that even so capricious a power as Fortune has never done (line 89).*

93 **But** *only, no better than.*

94–95 **That . . . Place** *that in the Greeks' country did them a disgrace that we are afraid to own up to in our own country.*

96 **Shrike** *shriek. The Shakespearean word suggests a more strident sound than is conveyed by the modern spelling and pronunciation.*

103 **Mid-age** *middle-aged men.*

104 **canst** *can do.*

105 **betimes** *early, while there is still time.*

106 **Moi'ty** *portion.*

109 **Fire-brand Brother Paris** *According to Vergil's* Aeneid, *Books VII and X, when Queen Hecuba was pregnant with Paris, she dreamed that she gave birth to a firebrand (a flaming ember) that burnt Troy to the ground. The firebrand is an appropriate symbol for the passions that initiated, and now sustain, the Trojan War.*

112 **these high Strains** *Hector refers to Cassandra's high-pitched ravings, which he interprets as well-timed admonitions, solemn warnings, from the Gods. For him, Cassandra's entry is a Providential warning, and one the Council should heed in its deliberations.*

Beggar the Estimation which you priz'd   90
Richer than Sea and Land? O Theft most base,
That we have stol'n what we do fear to keep!
But Thieves unworthy of a thing so stol'n,
That in their Country did them that Disgrace
We fear to warrant in our Native Place.   95
CASSANDRA [*Within*] Cry, Troians, cry!
PRIAM   What Noise? What Shrike is this?
TROILUS 'Tis our mad Sister, I do know her Voice.
CASSANDRA Cry, Troians!

Enter Cassandra raving.

HECTOR   It is Cassandra!
CASSANDRA   Cry, Troians, cry! Lend me ten
        thousand Eyes,   100
    And I will fill them with prophetic Tears.
HECTOR   Peace, Sister, peace!
CASSANDRA   Virgins and Boys, Mid-age, and
        wrinkled Elders,
    Soft Infancy, that nothing canst but cry,
    Add to my Clamors: let us pay betimes   105
    A Moi'ty of that mass of Moan to come.
    Cry, Troians, cry; practice your Eyes with
        Tears.
    Troy must not be, nor goodly Ilion stand;
    Our Fire-brand Brother Paris burns us all.
    Cry, Troians, cry, a Helen and a Woe!   110
    Cry, cry, Troy burns, or else let Helen go.   *Exit.*
HECTOR   Now youthful Troilus, do not these
        high Strains

113   Divination   *divinely inspired prophecy.*

115   discourse of Reason   *rational consideration. The same phrase occurs in the Prince of Denmark's first soliloquy (Hamlet, I.ii.150).*

116   Success   *outcome, issue (not* success *in the modern sense).*

118–   We may . . . it   *we should not assume that the justness of an*
19   *act is determined by and only by its outcome.*

120   deject   *cast down.*

121   Raptures   *seizures of mad ecstasy (when she is beside herself).*

122   distaste   *give a bad taste to, make unpalatable.*
        Quarrel   *dispute.*

124   For my Private Part   *as far as I am concerned personally. Troilus' phrasing offers an unwitting reminder that his judgment, like that of Paris, may be guided by his private parts to a greater degree than he recognizes.*

127   Spleen   *the seat of the impulsive emotions and passions.*

129   Levity   *lightness, irresponsibility, frivolity.*

130   Undertakings   *endeavors. Like a number of other words in this speech (among them* Consent, cut, stand, Push, *ex-cite, retract, faint, and* Pursuit*),* Undertakings *hints at the erotic aspect of Paris' "Project."*

132   Propension   *inclination. One meaning of* Pro- *is "thrusting forward." This speech is replete with "pro-fixes."*

135   Propugnation   *protection, defense (from* propugn, *go forth and fight).*

Of Divination in our Sister work
Some touches of Remorse? Or is your Blood
So madly Hot that no discourse of Reason,   115
Nor fear of Bad Success in a Bad Cause
Can qualify the same?

TROILUS   Why brother Hector,
We may not think the Justness of each Act
Such and no other than Event doth form it,
Nor once deject the Courage of our Minds   120
Because Cassandra's mad; her Brain-sick
    Raptures
Cannot distaste the Goodness of a Quarrel
Which hath our sev'ral Honors all engag'd
To make it Gracious. For my Private Part,
I am no more touch'd than all Priam's Sons;   125
And Jove forbid there should be done amongst us
Such things as might offend the weakest Spleen
To fight for and maintain.

PARIS   Else might the World convince of Levity
As well my Undertakings as your Counsels;   130
But I attest the Gods your full Consent
Gave Wings to my Propension and cut off
All Fears attending on so dire a Project.
For what, alas, can these my single Arms?
What Propugnation is in one man's Valor   135
To stand the Push and Enmity of those
This Quarrel would excite? Yet I protest
Were I alone to pass the Difficulties,
And had as ample Pow'r as I have Will,
Paris should ne'er retract what he hath done,   140
Nor faint in the Pursuit.

142   besotted on   *doting on, made irrational by.*

143   Gall   *bitter bile, vinegar; the antithesis of sweetness.*

147   fair Rape   *Paris regards the rape as "fair" in two senses: (a) it was an act of just retaliation, and (b) it brought to Troy a lady who is the epitome of "fairness" (blond beauty).*

149   Treason   *treachery, breach of loyalty.*
      ransack'd   *stolen, plundered.*

150   Worths   *reputations, honors.*

152   terms of Base Compulsion   *terms that would force us to demean ourselves as if we were no better than base slaves.*

154   gen'rous   *noble (from Latin* generosus*), here used in contrast with* degenerate *in line 153.*

155   meanest Spirit   *basest courage.* Spirit *is often associated with the "Sword" (line 156) of love as well as with the weapons of war.*
      on our Party   *in our company.*

158   bestow'd   *employed.*
      unfam'd   *unworthy of being recorded by fame.*

164   gloz'd   *glossed, interpreted (here with an implication of questionable, self-serving "logic").*

167   conduce   *lead on, lend support.*

168   distemper'd Blood   *uncontrolled, overheated desire (rather than reason).*

169   free Determination   *rational discrimination (unswayed by passion).*

PRIAM   Paris, you speak
    Like one besotted on your sweet Delights;
    You have the Honey still, but these the Gall;
    So to be Valiant is no Praise at all.
PARIS   Sir, I propose not merely to my self   145
    The Pleasures such a Beauty brings with it,
    But I would have the Soil of her fair Rape
    Wip'd off in honorable keeping her.
    What Treason were it to the ransack'd Queen,
    Disgrace to your great Worths, and Shame to me,   150
    Now to deliver her Possession up
    On terms of Base Compulsion? Can it be
    That so degenerate a Strain as this
    Should once set footing in your gen'rous
        Bosoms?
    There's not the meanest Spirit on our Party   155
    Without a Heart to dare, or Sword to draw,
    When Helen is defended; nor none so Noble,
    Whose Life were ill bestow'd, or Death unfam'd,
    Where Helen is the Subject. Then, I say,
    Well may we fight for her whom we know well   160
    The World's large Spaces cannot parallel.
HECTOR   Paris and Troilus, you have both said well,
    And on the Cause and Question now in hand
    Have gloz'd but superficially, not much
    Unlike Young Men, whom Aristotle thought   165
    Unfit to hear Moral Philosophy.
    The Reasons you allege do more conduce
    To the hot Passion of distemp'red Blood
    Than to make up a free Determination

171 Adders *small poisonous snakes, proverbial for their deafness. Shakespeare's audience would have been familiar with a passage from Psalm 58, included in* The Book of Common Prayer, *that compared the wicked to "the deaf adder that stoppeth her ear."*

172 true Decision *decision made on just and rational grounds.*

176 Affection *desire.*

177– And . . . same *and the minds of important people, because*
78 *of their self-indulgent submission to their dulled (adder-like) wills, resist this law.*

181 refractory *uncooperative, stubborn.*

186 extenuates *excuses, lessens in intensity. Hector plays paradoxically on the original Latin meaning of the word: to stretch out (as in* persist*) and thereby make thin (as opposed to making something "more Heavy").*

188 in way of Truth *as regards the truth of the matter (what reason and justice would dictate as our course of action at this juncture). Hector goes on to contrast* Truth *with* Resolution, *the course dictated by "Honor" (line 198) and "Courage" (line 200).*

189 spritely *spirited, lusty.*
   propend *incline. Hector's use of this "projecting" term (a Shakespearean coinage that literally means "jut or hang forward") is one of several linguistic signals that he, too, is now submitting his Will to the promptings, not of Reason, but of "Blood" (passion, impulse, unreason).*

192 joint . . . Dignities *collective and individual standings.*

'Twixt Right and Wrong. For Pleasure and
   Revenge   170
Have Ears more deaf than Adders to the Voice
Of any true Decision. Nature craves
All Dues be rend'red to their Owners. Now
What nearer Debt in all Humanity
Than Wife is to the Husband? If this Law   175
Of Nature be corrupted through Affection,
And that great Minds of partial Indulgence
To their benumbed Wills resist the same,
There is a Law in each well-order'd Nation
To curb those raging Appetites that are   180
Most disobedient and refractory;
If Helen then be Wife to Sparta's King,
As it is known she is, these Moral Laws
Of Nature and of Nations speak aloud
To have her back return'd. Thus to persist   185
In doing Wrong extenuates not Wrong
But makes it much more Heavy. Hector's Opinion
Is this in way of Truth; yet ne'er the less,
My spritely Brethren, I propend to you
In Resolution to keep Helen still,   190
For 'tis a Cause that hath no mean Dependance
Upon our joint and sev'ral Dignities.
TROILUS   Why there you touch'd the Life of our
   Design:
Were it not Glory that we more affected
Than the Performance of our heaving Spleens,   195
I would not wish a drop of Troian Blood
Spent more in her Defense. But worthy Hector,
She is a Theme of Honor and Renown,

199   Magnan'mous   *magnanimous; literally, great-spirited.*

200   present Courage   *Here* present *probably means both (a) at present, and (b) resident, active (as opposed to* absent*).* Courage *derives from the Latin word for "heart" (*cor, cordis*), and is strongly linked with such words as* Blood *(lines 168, 196),* Heart *(lines 47, 156),* Manhood *(line 46), and* Resolution *(line 190). The same complex of meanings occurs in several of Hamlet's soliloquies (see especially III.i.80–85). What has happened in this scene is that the forces of hot Resolution have beaten down the objections of cool Reason: the Trojans will do the "manly" thing with no further regard to the consequences.*

201   canonize   *glorify, memorialize; here accented on the second syllable.*

203   Advantage   *a favorable opportunity.*

204   Forehead   *forefront, onset.*

207   roisting   *rousing, boisterous.*

209   Will shrike Amazement   *that will shriek and thus startle into wide-eyed astonishment. The Folio prints* strike.

210   advertis'd   *informed; accented on the second syllable.*

211   Emulation   *rivalrous insubordination.*

II.iii   *This scene begins with Thersites outside the tent of Achilles.*

6   'Sfoot   *God's foot.*
        Divels   *devils (a common Shakespearean spelling).*

A Spur to Valiant and Magnan'mous Deeds,
Whose present Courage may beat down our Foes   200
And Fame in Time to Come canonize us;
For I presume brave Hector would not lose
So rich Advantage of a promis'd Glory
As smiles upon the Forehead of this Action
For the wide World's Revenue.
HECTOR   I am yours,   205
You valiant Offspring of great Priamus;
I have a roisting Challenge sent amongst
The dull and factious Nobles of the Greeks
Will shrike Amazement to their drowsy Spirits;
I was advertis'd their great Gen'ral slept   210
Whilst Emulation in the Army crept:
This I presume will wake him.   *Exeunt.*

Scene 3

Enter Thersites solus.

THERSITES   How now, Thersites? What, lost in the
Labyrinth of thy Fury? Shall the Elephant Aiax
carry it thus? He beats me, and I rail at him.
O worthy Satisfaction! Would it were otherwise:
that I could beat him whilst he rail'd at me.   5
'Sfoot, I'll learn to conjure and raise Divels
but I'll see some Issue of my spiteful

8   Execrations   *curses.*

9   Enginer   *miner; one who digs tunnels under enemy defenses.*

14   Caduceus   *the snake-entwined staff that symbolized Mercury's magical powers, including his capacity to settle disputes.*

16   short-arm'd   *impotent, unable to reach even the nearest object. Here Thersites contrasts Ignorance with the long-armed omnipotence of Thunder-darting Jove (Zeus).*

17   aboundant scarce   *abundantly scarce. Thersites resorts to paradox to describe Aiax's and Achilles' ignorance.*

18   in Circumvention   *with the forethought of reason.*

21–22   Neapolitan Bone-ache   *syphilis, assumed to have originated in Naples.*

23   depending on   *hanging from, attached to.*
         a Placket   *This word had a cluster of related meanings: (a) a petticoat or skirt, (b) a slit in such a garment, (c) the female genitalia, and (d) a whore.*

28–29   gilt Counterfeit   *spurious gold coin (also called a "slip"). Thersites is noting that it somehow slipped his mind to include Patroclus in his list of Greeks to be cursed.*

30   my Contemplation   *the curses I have just invoked.*

33   Heaven bless thee from   *may Heaven keep you away from.*

34   Discipline   *proper tutoring, and the self-control that would result if you rid yourself of the "Blood" (vice) that now directs your life.*

434

Execrations. Then there's Achilles, a rare
Enginer. If Troy be not taken till these two
undermine it, the Walls will stand till they   10
fall of themselves. —O thou great Thunder-
darter of Olympus, forget that thou art Jove
the King of Gods, and Mercury, loose all the
Serpentine Craft of thy Caduceus, if ye take
not that little little, less than little Wit   15
from them that they have: which short-arm'd
Ignorance it self knows is so aboundant scarce
it will not in Circumvention deliver a Fly
from a Spider without drawing their massy Irons
and cutting the Web. After this the Vengeance   20
on the whole Camp, or rather the Neapolitan
Bone-ache: for that me thinks is the Curse
depending on those that war for a Placket.
—I have said my Prayers, and divel Envy say
"Amen." —What ho, my Lord Achilles!   25
PATROCLUS [*Within*]   Who's there? Thersites?

Enter Patroclus.

Good Thersites, come in and rail.
THERSITES   —If I could 'a rememb'red a gilt
Counterfeit, thou couldst not have slipp'd
out of my Contemplation; but it is no matter,   30
thy self upon thy self. The Common Curse of
Mankind, Folly and Ignorance, be thine in
great Revenue. Heaven bless thee from a Tutor,
and Discipline come not near thee. Let thy
Blood be thy Direction till thy Death; then   35

435

36 she that lays thee out *the woman who prepares your "Corse" (corpse) for burial.*

37 fair *Thersites uses this term sarcastically, with the implication that Patroclus' body will be what the Gravedigger in* Hamlet *calls a "pocky" (disease-rotted) corpse.*

38 shrouded *wrapped in a burial shroud (cloth).*
Lazars *lepers, here referring to victims of the "pox" (syphilis).*

42 the Heavens hear me *Thersites means "may the Heavens heed my prayer."*

47 my Cheese, my Digestion *Cheese was traditionally served at the end of a meal to aid the digestive process.*

48 so many Meals *for such a long time.*

58 decline *state in order, as in the declining of noun and pronoun forms in the study of a language and its grammar. Thersites treats this "Question" (topic, issue) as if it were a logical syllogism leading to the conclusion that "Patroclus is a Fool." He uses a pseudo-logic that aptly ridicules the ignorance he is satirizing in Achilles and Patroclus.*

if she that lays thee out says thou art not a
fair Corse, I'll be sworn and sworn upon 't,
she never shrouded any but Lazars. Amen.
—Where's Achilles?

PATROCLUS   What, art thou devout? Wast thou in   40
Prayer?

THERSITES   Ay, the Heavens hear me.

PATROCLUS   Amen.

Enter Achilles.

ACHILLES   Who's there?

PATROCLUS   Thersites, my Lord.   45

ACHILLES   Where? Where? O where? Art thou come?
Why my Cheese, my Digestion, why hast thou not
served thy self into my Table so many Meals?
Come, what's Agamemnon?

THERSITES   Thy Commander, Achilles. —Then tell me,   50
Patroclus, what's Achilles?

PATROCLUS   Thy Lord, Thersites. Then tell me, I
pray thee, what's Thersites?

THERSITES   Thy Knower, Patroclus; then tell me
Patroclus, what art thou?   55

PATROCLUS   Thou must tell that knowest.

ACHILLES   O tell, tell.

THERSITES   I'll decline the whole Question:
Agamemnon commands Achilles, Achilles is my
Lord, I am Patroclus' Knower, and Patroclus   60
is a Fool.

PATROCLUS   You Rascal!

THERSITES   Peace, Fool, I have not done.

437

64   Privileg'd Man   *Here* Privileg'd *means "protected, immune from punishment," as with the licensed fools who were maintained in Renaissance courts for the amusement of royalty. Achilles probably addresses this sentence to Patroclus, restraining him from striking Thersites; but it is also possible that he speaks it to Thersites, with the implication that if Patroclus is a Fool, he is thereby privileged.*

74   Positive   *absolute, without any qualifying circumstances that make him a fool only in certain respects.*

76   Make that Demand   *demand the answer to that question.*
of the Prover   *from the one who proves it so: either (a) Patroclus himself, or (b) the ultimate logician, God. The Folio reads "to the Creator."*

81   Patchery   *folly. Thersites alludes to the patched (particolored) suit of the traditional court fool.*
Juggling   *cheating, hypocrisy, irrationality.*

82   Knavery   *villainy, vice.*

82–83   All . . . Cuckold   *The whole basis for the war is a Whore (Helen) and a Cuckold (Menelaus). Here* Argument *means both "theme" and "dispute" (*Quarrel*), with a bawdy implication hinted at in I.i.95 and spelled out in IV.v.26–31. Thersites speaks these lines as an aside to the audience.*

83   emulous   *rivalrous, envious (like two male beasts fighting over a female in heat).*

85   Suppeago   *serpigo, any of several loathsome skin diseases.*
the Subject   *both (a) the argument, and (b) the participants.*

ACHILLES   He is a Privileg'd Man. —Proceed,
   Thersites.   65
THERSITES   Agamemnon is a Fool, Achilles is a Fool,
   Thersites is a Fool, and, as aforesaid, Patroclus
   is a Fool.
ACHILLES   Derive this: come!
THERSITES   Agamemnon is a Fool to offer to   70
   command Achilles, Achilles is a Fool to be
   commanded of Agamemnon, Thersites is a Fool
   to serve such a Fool, and this Patroclus is
   a Fool Positive.
PATROCLUS   Why am I a Fool?   75
THERSITES   Make that Demand of the Prover: it
   suffices me thou art. Look you, who comes
   here?

   Enter Agamemnon, Ulysses, Nestor, Diomed, Aiax,
   and Calcas.

ACHILLES   Come, Patroclus, I'll speak with no body.
   —Come in with me, Thersites.   *Exit.*   80
THERSITES   Here is such Patchery, such Juggling,
   and such Knavery! All the Argument is a Whore
   and a Cuckold, a good Quarrel to draw emulous
   Factions and bleed to death upon. Now the dry
   Suppeago on the Subject, and War and Lechery   85
   confound all.   *Exit.*
AGAMEMNON   Where is Achilles?
PATROCLUS   Within his Tent, but ill dispos'd, my
   Lord.
AGAMEMNON   Let it be known to him that we are here;

439

90   sate   *perhaps a variant of* set *(set aside). The Folio reads* sent *(refused).*
       lay by   *set aside.*

91   Our Appertainings   *the dignities that go with our august position. Agamemnon means "I" here.*

93   move . . . Place   *assert the prerogatives of a monarch (and demand obeisance rather than politely request cooperation).*

97   Lion-sick   *"sick" in the sense that he thinks he is really a lion (the king of beasts) rather than a lesser, humbler creature.*

99   by my Head   *Aiax's use of this oath is ironic, (a) in that a man with so little in his head swears by his head, and (b) in that a man criticizing another's pride uses a word that is often symbolic of ambition and insubordination (as in raising one's head in rebellion).*

101   bay   *bark, like a hunting dog with its prey cornered.*

102   inveigled   *enticed, lured.*

105–6 lost his Argument   *both (a) been cheated out of the chief object of his abuse, and (b) lost out in his dispute with Achilles.*

107   Argument   *both (a) subject of his interest, and (b) adversary in dispute.*

109   their Fraction   *their division, their being in opposition.*

110   their Faction   *their unity as allies.*

111   Composure   *bond of unity, alliance.*

112   Amity   *friendship, partnership.*

He sate our Messengers, and we lay by   90
Our Appertainings, visiting of him.
Let him be told so, lest perchance he think
We dare not move the Question of our Place,
Or know not what we are.
PATROCLUS   I shall say so to him.   *Exit.*
ULYSSES   We saw him at   95
The op'ning of his Tent: he is not Sick.
AIAX   Yes, Lion-sick, Sick of Proud Heart; you may
call it Melancholy if you will favor the Man,
but by my Head 'tis Pride. But why, why? Let
him show us a Cause. —A word, my Lord.   100
                          Aiax draws Agamemnon aside.
NESTOR   What moves Aiax thus to bay at him?
ULYSSES   Achilles hath inveigled his Fool from him.
NESTOR   Who, Thersites?
ULYSSES   He.
NESTOR   Then will Aiax lack Matter, if he have lost   105
his Argument.
ULYSSES   No, you see he is his Argument that has
his Argument, Achilles.
NESTOR   All the better: their Fraction is more our
Wish than their Faction. But it was a strong   110
Composure a Fool could disunite.
ULYSSES   The Amity that Wisdom knits not, Folly
may easily untie.

Re-enter Patroclus.

Here comes Patroclus.
NESTOR   No Achilles with him.   115

441

116   Elephant   *Ulysses calls Achilles an elephant (a) to indicate the size to which he has now grown in his gigantic, stubborn pride, and (b) to allude to the common belief that the elephant lacked knee joints.*

118   Flexure   *bending, in "Courtesy" (obeisance).*

121   your Greatness   *Agamemnon.*
       this Noble State   *the General's entourage of Grecian princes.*

124   Breath   *walk for air; light aerobic exercise.*

127   Apprehensions   *both (a) understandings (the power to reach out and seize), and (b) concerns (for his well-being).*

128   Attribute   *both prowess and reputation.*

130   beheld   *both (a) viewed, and (b) held, maintained.*

131   Gloss   *sheen. Agamemnon is also playing on another sense of Gloss: interpretation, comment (like the marginal notes in a large tome). His point is that because Achilles is allowing his attractive qualities to grow stale, he is also beginning to lose the interest of those who have been accustomed to noting his deeds. This implication is continued in lines 137 and 140.*

136   Honest   *virtuous, right-thinking, modest.*

137   the Note of Judgment   *the opinions of judicious observers.*

138   tend . . . on   *tolerate the uncivilized aloofness he adopts.*

140–   under-write . . . Predominance   *note and indulge in a*
41   *knowing way the humour (ungoverned pride) of his lordly manner ("Predominance").*

ULYSSES   The Elephant hath Joints, but none for
      Courtesy. His Legs are Legs for Necessity, not
      for Flexure.
PATROCLUS   Achilles bids me say he is much sorry
      If anything more than your Sport and Pleasure   120
      Did move your Greatness, and this Noble State,
      To call upon 'im. He hopes it is no other
      But for your Health and your Digestion' sake,
      An after-Dinner's Breath.
AGAMEMNON   Hear you, Patroclus:
      We are too well acquainted with these Answers.   125
      But his Evasion, wing'd thus swift with Scorn,
      Cannot out-fly our Apprehensions.
      Much Attribute he hath, and much the Reason
      Why we ascribe it to him; yet all his Virtues,
      Not virtuously on his own Part beheld,   130
      Do in our Eyes begin to lose their Gloss;
      Yea, like fair Fruit in an unwholesome Dish,
      Are like to rot untasted. Go and tell him
      We come to speak with him; 'nd you shall not
         sin
      If you do say we think him over-Proud   135
      And under-Honest, in Self-assumption greater
      Than in the Note of Judgment. And worthier
         than himself
      Here tend the savage Strangeness he puts on,
      Disguise the holy Strength of their Commaund,
      And under-write in an observing kind   140
      His humourous Predominance; yea watch
      His Course and Time, his Ebbs and Flows, as if
      The Passage and whole Carriage of this Action

443

144   his Tide   *Agamemnon implies that Achilles thinks himself the sea that keeps the whole Greek enterprise ("Action") afloat.*

145   over-hold his Price so much   *keep his price too high and for too long.*

146   Engine   *here, a cumbersome, overly heavy instrument of warfare.*

147   portable   *movable.*

149   stirring Dwarf   *a smaller "engine" that moves easily or of its own accord.*
       Allowance give   *hold in esteem, value highly.*

150   Before   *in preference to, ahead of.*

152   second Voice   *an intermediary who repeats Achilles' words (Patroclus).*

153   Ulysses entertain   *[therefore] receive Ulysses into your tent [and let him speak directly to Achilles on our behalf].*

159   subscribe   *underwrite, endorse.*

162   Tractable   *cooperative, compliant.*

167   Glass   *mirror.*

168   Chronicle   *reporter, historian.*

169   but   *except.*

169–70   devours . . . Praise   *undoes the credit the deed would otherwise earn by boasting about it.*

Rode on his Tide. Go tell him this, and add
That if he over-hold his Price so much   145
We'll none of him, but let him, like an Engine
Not portable, lie under this Report:
"Bring Action hither, this cannot go to War."
A stirring Dwarf we do Allowance give
Before a sleeping Giant. Tell him so.   150
PATROCLUS   I shall, and bring his Answer presently.
AGAMEMNON   In second Voice we'll not be satisfied;
We come to speak with him: Ulysses entertain.
                    Exeunt Patroclus and Ulysses.
AIAX   What is he more than another?
AGAMEMNON   No more than what he thinks he is.   155
AIAX   Is he so much? Do you not think he thinks
himself a Better Man than I am?
AGAMEMNON   No Question.
AIAX   Will you subscribe his Thought and say he is?
AGAMEMNON   No, noble Aiax, you are as Strong, as   160
Valiant, as Wise, no less Noble, much more
Gentle, and altogether more Tractable.
AIAX   Why should a Man be Proud? How doth Pride
grow? I know not what Pride is.
AGAMEMNON   Your Mind is the clearer, Aiax, and   165
your Virtues the fairer; he that is Proud eats
up Himself. Pride is his own Glass, his own
Trumpet, his own Chronicle; and what ever
praises it self but in the Deed devours the
Deed in the Praise.   170

                    Re-enter Ulysses.

445

172   engend'ring   *copulation.*

176   carries . . . Dispose   *maintains the current of his disposition. Ulysses continues the sea-tide imagery introduced in line 142.*

177   Observance . . . any   *considering or respecting anyone else.*

178   Peculiar   *individual, arbitrary; peculiar to himself.*
        in Self-admission   *completely content with his own company and desirous of no views other than his own.*

179   fair   *uncoercive, peaceful.*

181   for Request's sake only   *merely because they are requested.*

182   Possess'd . . . Greatness   *Ulysses' phrasing suggests that "Greatness" is like a demonic spirit that has taken possession of Achilles. Achilles' condition recalls that of Malvolio, who needs to have his "Greatness" exorcised in* Twelfth Night.

184   Imagin'd Worth   *the esteem he imagines himself to deserve.*

186   his Mental and his Active Parts   *his mind and his body.*

187   Kingdom'd Achilles   *the little kingdom that constitutes the man Achilles.*

189   He is so Plaguy Proud   *his pride is so much like a seizure of the plague.*
        Death-tok'ns   *ominous spots (tokens) on a plague victim's body.*

195   consecrate   *set aside as holy shrines.*

AIAX   I do hate a Proud Man as I do hate the
      engend'ring of Toads.
NESTOR   —And yet he loves himself: is't not Strange?
ULYSSES   Achilles will not to the Field tomorrow.
AGAMEMNON   What's his Excuse?
ULYSSES   He doth rely on none,   175
      But carries on the Stream of his Dispose
      Without Observance or Respect of any,
      In Will Peculiar and in Self-admission.
AGAMEMNON   Why will he not upon our fair Request
      Untent his Pers'n and share the Air with us?   180
ULYSSES   Things small as nothing, for Request's
         sake only,
      He makes important. Possess'd he is with
         Greatness,
      And speaks not to Himself but with a Pride
      That quarrels at Self-breath. Imagin'd Worth
      Holds in his Blood such swoll'n and hot
         Discourse   185
      That 'twixt his Mental and his Active Parts
      Kingdom'd Achilles in Commotion rages
      And batters down Himself. What should I say?
      He is so plaguy Proud that th' Death-tok'ns
         of 't
      Cry "No Recovery."
AGAMEMNON   Let Aiax go to him.   190
      —Dear Lord, go you and greet him in his Tent;
      'Tis said he holds you well, and will be led,
      At your Request, a little from Himself.
ULYSSES   O Agamemnon, let it not be so:
      We'll consecrate the Steps that Aiax makes   195

447

197   Seam   *fat. The Prince of Denmark refers to "the rank Sweat of an enseamed Bed" in III.iv.90 of* Hamlet.

198   suffers   *permits.*

200   ruminate   *ponder.*

203   staule   *probably both (a) stall, stable, and (b) stale (the word in the Folio text). The spelling to be found in the Quarto is a variant of both words, and both are pertinent to the context. One of the meanings of* stale *is horse or cattle urine.*
       Palm   *palm branch, a symbol of worthiness and triumph.*

204   assubjugate   *subjugate, probably with a pun on* ass *to reinforce the implications of* staule *in the previous line.*

205   liked   *admired; here to be pronounced as a two-syllable word. Modern editors normally adopt the Folio's* titled. *But* liked *offers Ulysses the opportunity for additional wordplay on* ass *(*as*), suggesting that Achilles too is "like an ass."*

207   enlard   *further fatten.*

208   Cancer   *the Zodiacal sign that initiates the hottest season of the year, when the Sun ("great Hyperion") enters Cancer (the Crab) to mark the summer solstice (June 21–22).*

212   Vain   *vein (humour, disposition). The Quarto spelling anticipates the modern sense of* vain *(vanity, emptiness). Aiax's vein is to be vain.*

215   push   *shove. The Folio reads* pash.

216   pheeze   *fix.*

When they go from Achilles; shall the proud
    Lord,
That bastes his Arrogance with his own Seam
And never suffers Matter of the World
Enter his Thoughts, save such as doth revolve
And ruminate Himself, shall he be worshipp'd   200
Of that we hold an Idol more than he?
No, this thrice-worthy and right valiant Lord
Shall not so staule his Palm nobly acquir'd,
Nor by my Will assubjugate his Merit,
As amply liked as Achilles' is,   205
By going to Achilles.
That were t' enlard his Fat-already Pride
And add more Coals to Cancer when he burns
With entertaining great Hyperion.
This Lord go to him? Jupiter forbid,   210
And say in Thunder, "Achilles go to him!"
NESTOR —O this is well, he rubs the Vain of him.
DIOMED —And how his Silence drinks up his
    Applause!
AIAX If I go to him, with my armed Fist
    I'll push him o'er the Face!
AGAMEMNON   O no, you shall not go.   215
AIAX And he be Proud with me, I'll pheeze his
    Pride!
    Let me go to him.
ULYSSES Not for the Worth that hangs upon our
    Quarrel.
AIAX A paltry insolent Fellow!
NESTOR —How he describes himself.   220
AIAX Can he not be sociable?

222   The Raven . . . Blackness. *Ulysses quotes a proverb with implications similar to those of "The Pot calling the Kettle black." From here to line 235 Ulysses, Agamemnon, and Nestor speak privately among themselves while the asinine Aiax fulminates against Achilles.*

225   And *if.*

228   carry it *prevail, carry the day. In the next line Nestor gives Aiax's verb a literal meaning.*

230   ten Shares *all ten shares (the entire lot).*
        knead *work, twist, as a baker does with a lump of soft dough.*

231   through *thoroughly.*

233   Force *stuff, force-feed.*

235   My Lord *Ulysses addresses Agamemnon, as do Nestor and Diomed in the following lines. All three speak loudly.*

239   Here is a Man *Ulysses refers to Aiax.*
        before his Face *in his presence (so that he can hear how he is praised).*

241   Wherefore *why.*
        emulous *proud, ambitious, insubordinate.*

244   A whoreson Dog *Aiax refers to Achilles.*
        palter *toy, trifle, treat contemptuously.*

247   covetous of *enviously desirous of.*

248   Surly borne *haughty and disagreeable in his bearing.*
        Strange *aloof, distant (estranged).*

ULYSSES —The Raven chides Blackness.

AIAX I'll tell his humourous Blood!

AGAMEMNON —He will be th' Physician that should be
The Patient.

AIAX   And all Men were of my Mind— 225

ULYSSES —Wit would be out of Fashion.

AIAX He should not bear it so, 'a should eat Swords first! Shall Pride carry it?

NESTOR —And 'twould, you'd carry Half.

ULYSSES —'A would have ten Shares. I will knead 230
him; I'll make him supple; he's not yet through Warm.

NESTOR —Force him with Praises; pour in, pour in; his Ambition is dry.

ULYSSES My Lord, you feed too much on this Dislike. 235

NESTOR Our noble General, do not do so.

DIOMED You must prepare fight without Achilles.

ULYSSES Why 'tis the naming of him does him Harm.
Here is a Man—but 'tis before his Face, I will
be silent. 240

NESTOR Wherefore should you so? He is not emulous
as Achilles is.

ULYSSES Know the whole World he is as Valiant—

AIAX A whoreson Dog that shall palter with us
thus; would he were a Troian! 245

NESTOR What a Vice were it in Aiax now—

ULYSSES If he were Proud—

DIOMED   Or covetous of Praise—

ULYSSES Ay, or Surly borne—

DIOMED   Or Strange, or Self-affected.

451

249   sweet Composure   *Aiax's affable, peaceful disposition.*

250   gat   *begot, conceived, fathered.*

252   beyond all Erudition   *above all learning (here, all fame).*

254   Mars   *a God eternally famed for his military discipline.*

256   Bull-bearing Milo   *Milo was an athlete who carried a bull for forty yards on his shoulders; he then killed it with a single punch and ate it.*
Addition   *title, reputation. But Ulysses is probably also making a bawdy reference to a bull's "Addition" (either his "horn" or his horns, proverbially associated with the "addition" of a cuckold). In* 1 Henry IV *(II.iv.268) Falstaff calls Prince Hal a "Bull's-pizzle." Compare I.ii.19.*

257   I will not praise thy Wisdom   *Ulysses uses a rhetorical formula whose implication is that "It is not necessary for me to praise a virtue too obvious to require mention." The usual meaning of the formula heightens the audience's amusement that in this case there is literally nothing to praise.*

258   Bourn   *boundary, border.*
Pale   *fence.*

259   spacious . . . Parts   *plenteous and extended qualities.*

260   Antiquary Times   *period of the ancients, good old days.*

264   the Eminence of him   *superiority over him.*

268   Keeps Thicket   *remains hidden (like a "Hart," deer).*

271   our Main of Pow'r   *our mightiest forces.*

ULYSSES   Thank the Heavens, Lord, thou art of
        sweet Composure.
      Praise him that gat thee, she that gave thee
        suck;   250
      Fam'd be thy Tutor, and thy Parts of Nature
      Thrice fam'd beyond, beyond all Erudition;
      But he that disciplin'd thine Arms to fight,
      Let Mars divide Eternity in Twain
      And give him Half; and for thy Vigor,   255
      Bull-bearing Milo his Addition yield
      To sinowy Aiax. I will not praise thy Wisdom,
      Which like a Bourn, a Pale, a Shore, confines
      Thy spacious and dilated Parts. Here's Nestor,
      Instructed by the Antiquary Times;   260
      He must, he is, he cannot be but Wise.
      —But pardon, Father Nestor, were your Days
      As green as Aiax', and your Brain so temper'd,
      You should not have the Eminence of him,
      But be as Aiax.
AIAX   Shall I call you Father?   265
NESTOR   Ay my good Son.
DIOMED   Be rul'd by him, Lord Aiax.
ULYSSES   There is no tarrying here; the Hart
        Achilles
      Keeps Thicket. Please it our great General
      To call together all his State of War;
      Fresh Kings are come to Troy. Tomorrow   270
      We must with all our Main of Pow'r stand fast.
      And here's a Lord: come Knights from East to
        West,

453

274   cull their Flow'r   *pick their choicest warrior.*
        cope   *match, compete successfully with.*

276   Light Boats sail swift   *boats that skim over the water without drawing deeply (displacing large volumes with their bulk) sail more swiftly. Agamemnon's nautical imagery recalls the reference to Achilles' "Ebbs and Flows" in line 142.*

        greater Hulks   *slower, more cumbersome vessels with weighty cargoes. Agamemnon's point is that the Greek forces will be lighter without Achilles, and may well find that they are better off without him. In Shakespeare's time as in ours,* hulk *was a word that could be applied to a huge, brawny character with little or no intelligence. What Agamemnon is not saying is that in many ways Aiax (the newly designated Greek champion) is even more of a hulk than the "greater" one [Achilles] for whom he will be serving as a stand-in.*

454

And cull their Flow'r, Aiax shall cope the Best.

AGAMEMNON   Go we to Council; let Achilles sleep.
Light Boats sail swift, though greater Hulks
draw deep.   *Exeunt.*   275

III.i   *This scene returns us to Troy, in or near the Palace.*

3   goes before me   *walks in front of me. The Servant takes*
          follow *literally rather than as a verb meaning "serve."*

5   depend upon the Lord   *The Servant's reply is deliberately*
          ambiguous: as an answer to Pandarus' question, it can mean
          "I draw my support from serving Lord Paris," but its more
          obvious implication is "My faith and trust is in God." The
          Servant plays on the same two senses of Lord *in line 8.*

11   know me better   *Pandarus means (a) know me to be your*
          better, and (b) start acting better (more respectfully) as a result
          of your better knowledge.

13   know your Honor better   *In addition to its obvious mean-*
          ing, this phrase can be interpreted as an implied admonition:
          "know you to be a better (more honorable) man [than you are
          at present]." The Servant speaks as if he were a pious Puritan,
          one who knows Pandarus to be a man who could be "better"
          (more virtuous) than he is.

15   the State of Grace   *a spiritual condition that would result in*
          your going to Heaven if you were to die at this moment. The
          Servant picks up on Pandarus' I do desire it, *which he*
          pretends to understand as a pious statement that "I do desire
          to be better than I am" [being humbly aware of my spiritual
          deficiencies and praying for grace to grow more godly].

456

Scene 1

Music sounds within. Enter Pandarus and a Servant.

PANDARUS Friend you, pray you a word: do you not
    follow the young Lord Paris?
MAN Ay Sir, when he goes before me.
PANDARUS You depend upon him, I mean.
MAN Sir, I do depend upon the Lord.   5
PANDARUS You depend upon a notable Gentleman;
    I must needs praise him.
MAN The Lord be praised!
PANDARUS You know me, do you not?
MAN Faith Sir, superficially.   10
PANDARUS Friend, know me better: I am the Lord
    Pandarus.
MAN I hope I shall know your Honor better.
PANDARUS I do desire it.
MAN You are in the State of Grace?   15

457

16   Grace? Not so   *Pandarus takes the Servant to be attributing to him a title reserved for royalty (Dukes and Princes).*

18–19 Music in Parts   *music with different scorings for different voices or instruments. The Servant puns on* partly, *partially.*

21   Wholly   *another play on* partly, *but also a continuation of the Servant's "holy" discourse. With pretended naivete, his phrasing also hints at holes and parts that relate to Pandarus' kind of "Music."*

24   At whose Pleasure   *under whose commission (pay).*

29   Courtly   *Pandarus refers to the indirect, complimentary discourse of the courtly classes.*
          Cunning   *both (a) clever, and (b) evasive (like a fox).*

33   mortal Venus   *Helen, the earthly embodiment of the Goddess of Beauty and Love.*

36   find out that   *figure that out.*

41   Complemental Assault   *attack of compliments (complying with all the forms of courtly persuasion).*

41–42 my Business seethes   *I come on urgent matters.*

43   Sodden Business . . . Stew'd Phrase   *The Servant plays on* seethes *as a word meaning "boiling";* Sodden *and* Stew'd *both mean "boiled." He also picks up on at least two bawdy meanings for* Business: *(a) the male member (a sense alluded to in* Hamlet, *I.v.126–27), and (b) any form of sexual activity, including that of a go-between.* Stew'd *alludes to a common name for brothels: "stews."*

PANDARUS   Grace? Not so, Friend: Honor and
        Lordship are my Titles. What Music is this?
MAN   I do but partly know, Sir: it is Music in
        Parts.
PANDARUS   Know you the Musicians?   20
MAN   Wholly, Sir.
PANDARUS   Who play they to?
MAN   To the Hearers, Sir.
PANDARUS   At whose Pleasure, Friend?
MAN   At mine, Sir, and theirs that love Music.   25
PANDARUS   Command, I mean, Friend.
MAN   Who shall I command, Sir?
PANDARUS   Friend, we understand not one another:
        I am too Courtly, and thou too Cunning. At
        whose Request do these Men play?   30
MAN   That's to 't indeed, Sir. Marry Sir, at the
        Request of Paris, my Lord, who is there in
        person; with him the mortal Venus, the Heart-
        blood of Beauty, Love's invisible Soul.
PANDARUS   Who, my Cousin Cressida?   35
MAN   No Sir, Helen; could not you find out that
        by her Attributes?
PANDARUS   It should seem, Fellow, thou hast not
        seen the Lady Cressid; I come to speak with
        Paris, from the Prince Troilus. I will make a 40
        Complemental Assault upon him, for my
        Business seethes.
MAN   Sodden Business: there's a Stew'd Phrase
        indeed.

            Enter Paris and Helen.

459

45   Fair   *Pandarus probably means "fair fortune," with wordplay on "fare you well."*

51   Broken Music   *another reference to music in parts, and presumably to the "Music" and the musicians first alluded to in line 17.*

52   broke   *interrupted.*

53–54   piece it out   *make it whole, repair it.*

54   Piece   *piece of music. But in all likelihood Paris speaks with bawdy innuendo. In* Romeo and Juliet *(I.i.31–32) Sampson refers to his "pretty piece of Flesh," and in* Titus Andronicus *(I.i.313), Saturninus calls Lavinia a "Changing Piece."*

58   Rude   *unskilled.*
       sooth   *truth.*

59–60   in Fits   *(a) in fits and starts (alluding to Pandarus' repetitions in the previous speech), with wordplay on (b) in brief strains (as with music for dancing), and (c) in fits (both "fittings" and spasms) of copulation.*

61   to   *to conduct with. Pandarus is politely requesting that Helen leave him and Paris to speak privately.*

63   hedge us out   *both (a) shove me aside, and (b) keep me from hearing you sing. Helen is using the royal plural.*

65   Pleasant   *teasing, merry.*

72   bob   *fob, cheat.*

73   our . . . Head   *you'll be to blame for my despondency.*

PANDARUS   Fair be to you, my Lord, and to all this   45
   Fair Company. Fair Desires in all Fair Measure
   fairly guide them, especially to you, Fair
   Queen. Fair Thoughts be your Fair Pillow.
HELEN   Dear Lord, you are full of Fair Words.
PANDARUS   You speak your Fair Pleasure, sweet Queen.   50
   —Fair Prince, here is good Broken Music.
PARIS   You have broke it, Cousin; and by my Life
   you shall make it Whole again; you shall piece
   it out with a Piece of your Performance.
   —Nell, he is full of Harmony.   55
PANDARUS   Truly, Lady, no.
HELEN   O Sir.
PANDARUS   Rude, in sooth; in good sooth, very Rude.
PARIS   Well said, my Lord, well; you say so in
   Fits.   60
PANDARUS   I have Business to my Lord, dear Queen.
   —My Lord, will you vouchsafe me a word?
HELEN   Nay this shall not hedge us out: we'll
   hear you sing certainly.
PANDARUS   Well, sweet Queen, you are Pleasant   65
   with me. —But marry thus, my Lord, my dear
   Lord, and most esteemed Friend, your brother
   Troilus—
HELEN   My Lord Pandarus, honey sweet Lord—
PANDARUS   Go to, sweet Queen, go to! —commends   70
   himself most affectionately to you—
HELEN   You shall not bob us out of our Melody;
   if you do, our Melancholy upon your Head.
PANDARUS   Sweet Queen, sweet Queen, that's a
   sweet Queen. —I' faith—   75

461

78   serve your Turn   *get you what you want.*

79–80 care not for   *am not moved by.*

82   make his Excuse   *explain why he is absent.*

86   Exploit   *This term normally refers to heroic adventures or
       military engagements. From Paris' next question it is clear that
       he believes Troilus to be plotting a different kind of encounter.*

90   fall out with you   *be annoyed with you.*

92   my Disposer   *Paris probably means "the woman at whose
       disposal Pandarus places himself." The phrase* my Disposer
       *is probably meant to parallel and echo "my Lady." Since the
       word* dispose *literally means "put apart," Paris' phrase* I'll
       lay my life *is erotically suggestive as well.*

93   you are wide   *you are wide of the mark; you miss with that
       guess.* Wide *can also mean "naughty."*

98   I spy.   *Paris alludes to the game of this name; his implication is
       that he has spotted what Pandarus is trying to keep hidden.*

103   thing you have   *Pandarus probably refers to one of Helen's
       trinkets, which remains unspecified because of the interrup-
       tions that follow. The phrase also carries bawdy potential, and
       Helen picks up on it in her next line, where* Paris *could also be
       rendered* Paris'. *At the time when Shakespeare's plays were
       printed, the apostrophe was yet to come into common use as the
       way to indicate possession; as a consequence, words that take
       plural forms in Shakespeare can often be interpreted as posses-
       sives rather than, or as well as, plurals.*

HELEN   And to make a sweet Lady sad is a sour
   Offense.
PANDARUS   Nay that shall not serve your Turn,
   that shall it not, in truth la! Nay I care not
   for such words, no, no. —And my Lord, he   80
   desires you that if the King call for him at
   Supper, you will make his Excuse.
HELEN   My Lord Pandarus?
PANDARUS   What says my sweet Queen, my very
   very sweet Queen?   85
PARIS   What Exploit's in hand? Where sups he
   tonight?
HELEN   Nay but my Lord—
PANDARUS   What says my sweet Queen? My Cousin
   will fall out with you.   90
HELEN   You must not know where he sups.
PARIS   I'll lay my Life, with my Disposer Cressida.
PANDARUS   No, no! No such matter; you are wide.
   Come, your Disposer is sick.
PARIS   Well I'll make 's Excuse.   95
PANDARUS   Ay, good my Lord. Why should you say
   Cressida? No, your poor Disposer's sick.
PARIS   I spy.
PANDARUS   You spy? What do you spy? —Come,
   give me an Instrument. —Now, sweet Queen.   100
HELEN   Why this is kindly done!
PANDARUS   My Niece is horribly in love with a
   thing you have, sweet Queen.
HELEN   She shall have it, my Lord, if it be not
   my Lord Paris.   105
PANDARUS   He? No, she'll none of him; they two

107   Twain   *two, at odds with one another.*

108–9   Falling . . . Three.   *Helen means that if they patch up their quarrel and Paris "falls in" with Cressida, the end result may be a third party to their reunion (a child).*

113   fine Forehead   *Helen probably alludes to a song about cuckoldry. As she speaks these lines she no doubt caresses Pandarus' forehead, a handsome setting for a pair of horns.*

115–16   This Love will undo us all.   *Helen jests, of course, but what she says is what* Troilus and Cressida *is largely about.*

116   Cupid   *the God who initiates love with his golden arrow.*

122   Love's   *Cupid's.*

123   Buck and Doe   *male and female.* Buck *is another name for "Hart," stag, so there is implicit wordplay on* heart *(the organ that Cupid's arrow wounds). But* Buck *is also a word associated with cuckoldry (because of the buck's horns).*

124   Shaft   *both (a) Cupid's arrow, and (b) the male member.*
    confounds   *overwhelms, destroys, kills.*

126   Sore   *both (a) the wound made by Cupid, and (b) the place that is "tickled" by the shaft.* Sore *is a word that could also refer to a fourth-year buck.*

128   die   *Pandarus refers to the throes of orgasm; but this line also hints at the overtones of lines 115–16.*

136   Nose   *In* Antony and Cleopatra *(I.ii.56) the nose is associated with another appendage.*

are Twain.

HELEN   Falling in after falling out may make them
Three.

PANDARUS   Come, come, I'll hear no more of this: 110
I'll sing you a Song now.

HELEN   Ay, I prethee now, by my troth, "Sweet Lad,
thou hast a fine Forehead."

PANDARUS   Ay, you may, you may.

HELEN   Let thy Song be Love: "This Love will undo   115
us all." O Cupid, Cupid, Cupid!

PANDARUS   Love? Ay, that it shall i' faith.

PARIS   Ay, good now, "Love, Love, nothing but Love."

PANDARUS   In good troth, it begins so:

"Love, Love, nothing but Love,   *Song*   120
    Still love still more;
        For O Love's Bow
        Shoots Buck and Doe;
            The Shaft confounds
            Not that it wounds,   125
        But tickles still the Sore.
        These Lovers cry,
        O ho, they die,
    Yet that which seems the Wound to kill
        Doth turn 'O ho' to 'Ha ha he';   130
    So dying Love lives still,
        'O ho' a while, but ha ha ha,
        'O ho' groans out for 'ha ha ha'—
            Hey ho."

HELEN   In love i' faith, to the very tip of the   135
Nose.

PARIS   He eats nothing but Doves, Love, and that

465

141   Generation *genesis, origin. But* generation *could also mean "copulation" (compare* engend'ring, *II.iii.172).*

143   Generation of Vipers *Pandarus alludes to Matthew 23:33, where Jesus rebukes the Scribes and Pharisees as "serpents," a "generation of vipers." There* generation *means "offspring," "race." As poisonous snakes, vipers are an apt symbol of (a) the phallus, (b) the workings of lust, and (c) the dangers involved in what might appear to be idle play.*

144   a-field *engaged in battle.*

146   fain *gladly.*

147   Nell *Helen.*

149   He hangs the Lip at something. *He pouts over something. Helen is probably using* Lip *and* something *with additional implications; so also with* all *in line 150, which may allude to what* Awl *implies in I.i.26 of* Julius Caesar.

154   To a Hair *to the smallest detail. Further meanings are suggested by* Romeo and Juliet, *II.iv.102–3, 140–48.*

S.D.   Retreat *a trumpet call to signal a withdrawal.*

162   enchaunting *charming, forcing obedience.*

164–   Island Kings *the Greek generals.*
65

166   proud *This adjective often meant "wanton or lustful." Clearly this "Merry Greek" (I.ii.114) is willing to "disarm great Hector" on behalf of the warrior's generous younger brother.*

466

breeds Hot Blood, and Hot Blood begets Hot
Thoughts, and Hot Thoughts beget Hot Deeds,
and Hot Deeds is Love. 140

PANDARUS   Is this the Generation of Love? Hot
Blood, Hot Thoughts, and Hot Deeds? Why they
are Vipers: is Love a Generation of Vipers?
Sweet Lord, who's a-field today?

PARIS   Hector, Deiphobos, Helenus, Antenor, and 145
all the Gallantry of Troy; I would fain have
arm'd today, but my Nell would not have it so.
How chance my brother Troilus went not?

HELEN   He hangs the Lip at something. —You know
all, Lord Pandarus. 150

PANDARUS   Not I, honey-sweet Queen; I long to hear
how they sped today. —You'll remember your
Brother's Excuse?

PARIS   To a Hair.

PANDARUS   Farewell, sweet Queen. 155

HELEN   Commend me to your Niece.

PANDARUS   I will, sweet Queen.   *Sound a Retreat.*

PARIS   They're come from the Field. Let us to
Priam's Hall to greet the Warriors. Sweet
Helen, I must woo you to help unarm our Hector: 160
his stubborn Buckles with these your white
enchaunting Fingers touch'd shall more obey
than to the edge of Steel or force of Greekish
Sinews. You shall do more than all the Island
Kings: disarm great Hector. 165

HELEN   'Twill make us proud to be his Servant,
Paris.
Yea, what he shall receive of us in Duty

168   **Palm** *glory.*

170   **her** *The Quarto reading, followed here, would suggest that Paris addresses this line to Pandarus, which seems altogether appropriate in view of the role that Paris appears to be playing for his wife and brother. Most editors adopt the Folio's* **thee,** *on the assumption that Paris is speaking to Helen.*

III.ii   *This scene opens in the garden of Cressida's house.*

6   **Sirrah** *a term normally reserved for social inferiors, such as servants.*

9   **strange Soul** *a newcomer to the Underworld.*
    Stygian Banks *the shore of the Styx, one of the four rivers of Hades.*

10   **Waftage** *passage.*
    Charon *the boatman who ferried souls across Styx to the Elysian Fields. Troilus thinks of himself as a man about to receive his heavenly reward (line 13); but the figures and locales he alludes to were also associated with other destinies in the classical underworld.*

12   **wallow in the Lily Beds** *The incompatibility between Troilus' verb and the setting he envisions (linked with Paradise in both Biblical and Classical imagery) epitomizes the the tension between his bestial desire and his romantic idealism.*

13   **Propos'd** *held in prospect, said to lie in wait.*

14   **painted Wings** *the colored wings represented by artists who have painted pictures of Cupid.*

Gives us more Palm in Beauty than we have,
Yea, overshines our self.

PARIS —Sweet, above Thought I love her!   *Exeunt.*   170

Scene 2

Enter Pandarus, Troilus' Man, meeting.

PANDARUS   How now, where's thy Maister, at my
   Cousin Cressida's?
MAN   No Sir, he stays for you to conduct him
   thether.

Enter Troilus.

PANDARUS   O here he comes. —How now, how now?   5
TROILUS   —Sirrah, walk off.   *Exit Man.*
PANDARUS   Have you seen my Cousin?
TROILUS   No, Pandarus, I stalk about her Door
   Like to a strange Soul upon the Stygian Banks
   Staying for Waftage. O be thou my Charon,   10
   And give me swift Transportance to these
      Fields
   Where I may wallow in the Lily Beds
   Propos'd for the Deserv'r. O gentle Pandar,
   From Cupid's Shoulder pluck his painted Wings
   And fly with me to Cressid.

469

18   imaginary   *imagined, anticipatory.*

21   thrice-repured   *most refined, quintessentially pure.*
      Nectar   *the drink of the Olympian Gods.*

22   Sounding   *swounding, swooning.*
      Destruction   *collapse.*

24   ruder Powers   *cruder senses. Troilus fears that he, a mere
            "earthen vessel" (2 Corinthians 4:7), will not be able to hold
            such nectar.*

26   lose Distinction   *lose all powers of discrimination, become
            over-eager.*

27   Battail   *battalion, army.*

30   Witty   *sensitive and tactful, keeping your wits about you and
            putting her at ease with charming small talk.*

31   fetches . . . short   *draws her breath in excited pants.*

32   fraid   *frightened, apprehensive.*
      with a Spirit   *either (a) by a ghost she has seen, or (b) by a
            demon that possesses her.*

33   It is the prettiest Villain   *she is the most delicate thing. Here
            Villain is used as a term of endearment.*

36   thicker   *more rapidly.*

37   their Bestowing lose   *lose control of themselves.*

38–39 Like Vassalage . . . Majesty   *like a servant unexpectedly
            finding himself in the presence of his monarch.*

PANDARUS   Walk here i' th' Orchard: 15
    I'll bring her straight.   *Exit.*
TROILUS   I'm Giddy: Expectation whirls me round;
    Th' imaginary Relish is so Sweet
    That it enchaunts my Sense. What will it be
    When that the wat'ry Palates taste indeed   20
    Love's thrice-repured Nectar? Death, I fear me
    Sounding Destruction, or some Joy too fine,
    Too subtle, potent, tun'd too sharp in Sweetness,
    For the Capac'ty of my ruder Powers;
    I fear it much, and I do fear besides   25
    That I shall lose Distinction in my Joys
    As doth a Battail when they charge on heaps
    The En'my flying.

                Re-enter Pandarus.

PANDARUS   She's making her ready, she'll come
    straight. You must be Witty now: she does so   30
    blush, and fetches her Wind so short, as if
    she were fraid with a Spirit. I'll fetch her.
    It is the prettiest Villain; she fetches her
    Breath as short as a new ta'en Sparrow.   *Exit.*
TROILUS   Ev'n such a Passion doth embrace my
    Bosom: 35
    My Heart beats thicker than a fev'rous Pulse,
    And all my Pow'rs do their Bestowing lose
    Like Vassalage at unawares encount'ring
    The Eye of Majesty.

                Re-enter Pandar with Cressid.

471

40–41 Shame's a Baby. *Blushing is for babies; you're too old.*

43 watch'd *kept under close observation (so you don't escape).*

46 Fills *thills, the shafts between which a horse is hitched to a wagon or cart to pull it.*

47 Curtain *veil hiding Cressida's face* (Picture, *line 48*).

49 close *come together.*

50 rub on . . . Mistress *Pandarus compares Troilus to the bowl (the large off-center ball) as it rolls over any "rub" (impediment) in its course to the smaller ball (the "Mistress"), which the bowler hopes to make it "kiss" (touch).*

51 in Fee-farm *held in perpetuity (a legal term for the acquisition of real property), here referring to a long kiss.*

51–52 Build there, Carpenter *Pandarus implies that, having purchased a piece of land, the "Carpenter" should now erect a dwelling on it. In his next speech Pandarus puns on* Deeds *(both contracts and acts),* Activity *(both building and sexual "doing"), and* Billing *(both calling in debts and kissing like doves) to encourage the parties' "interchange" (line 61).*

53 fight your Hearts out *"wrestle" ardently, like male and female falcons.*

58 bereave you *deprive you of, take from you.*

69 Abruption *abrupt interruption.*
too curious Dreg *too-scrupulously-noted piece of refuse (dregs).*

PANDARUS   Come, come, what need you blush? Shame's   40
a Baby. —Here she is now; swear the Oaths now
to her that you have sworn to me. —What, are
you gone again? You must be watch'd ere you be
made tame, must you? Come your ways, come your
ways; and you draw backward, we'll put you i'   45
th' Fills. —Why do you not speak to her?
—Come draw this Curtain, and let's see your
Picture. Alas the Day, how loath you are to
offend Daylight; and 'twere Dark you'd close
sooner! —So, so, rub on and kiss the Mistress.   50
How now, a Kiss in Fee-farm? Build there,
Carpenter: the Air is sweet. —Nay, you shall
fight your Hearts out ere I part you. The
Falcon as the Tercel, for all the Ducks i' th'
River: go to, go to.   55
TROILUS   You have bereft me of all Words, Lady.
PANDARUS   Words pay no Debts: give her Deeds.
But she'll bereave you a' th' Deeds too if she
call your Activity in Question. What, Billing
again? Here's in witness whereof the Parties   60
interchangeably— —Come in, come in, I'll go
get a Fire.   *Exit.*
CRESSIDA   Will you walk in, my Lord?
TROILUS   O Cressid, how often have I wish'd me
thus!   65
CRESSIDA   Wish'd, my Lord? The Gods graunt—
O my Lord!
TROILUS   What should they graunt? What makes this
pretty Abruption? What too curious Dreg espies
my sweet Lady in the Fountain of our Love?   70

473

71–72 if my Tears have Eyes *if the tears in my Fountain (watery eye) have Eyes (are trying to show me something they see). The Folio prints* Fears *instead of* Tears, *and that word captures the implication of the more subtle Quarto phrasing.*

73 Cherubins *angels. Troilus' point in this speech is that Fears (or tears) distort one's perception so much that even angels can appear to be devils (things to fear rather than welcome).*

77 stumbling without Fear *falling because of a lack of caution. Cressida's remarks recall Hector's comments about "Surety" in II.ii.13–15. Her phrasing also echoes what Friar Lawrence says in* Romeo and Juliet *(II.iii.94): "Wisely and slow: they stumble that run fast."*

80 Cupid's Pageant *any play or symbolic procession based on Cupid's doings.*
   Monster *object to fear. The word* monster *derives from the Latin* monstrare, *to show, warn, or foretell. Troilus is saying that Cressida's fears can be dismissed as idle anxieties.*

82 our own Undertakings *what lovers pledge themselves to do for their ladies.*

90 the Act a slave to Limit *the performance limited to what life in a finite world permits a lover of infinite Will to do to prove his devotion. In the next speech Cressida attributes the disparity not to Ability but to Will (the fact that men swear to do more than they intend to fulfill).*

101 in Reversion *held as a promissory note (promised but not delivered). In this speech* we *means "I."*

CRESSIDA   More Dregs than Water, if my Tears have
    Eyes.
TROILUS   Fears make Divels of Cherubins: they never
    see truly.
CRESSIDA   Blind Fear, that seeing Reason leads,   75
    finds safer Footing than blind Reason,
    stumbling without Fear. To fear the Worst oft
    cures the Worse.
TROILUS   O let my Lady apprehend no Fear; in all
    Cupid's Pageant there is presented no Monster.   80
CRESSIDA   Nor nothing monstrous neither?
TROILUS   Nothing but our own Undertakings, when
    we vow to weep Seas, live in Fire, eat Rocks,
    tame Tigers, thinking it harder for our
    Mistress to devise Imposition enough than   85
    for us to undergo any Difficulty imposed.
    This is the Monstruosity in Love, Lady, that
    the Will is infinite and the Execution
    confin'd, that the Desire is boundless, and
    the Act a slave to Limit.   90
CRESSIDA   They say all Lovers swear more Performance
    than they are able, and yet reserve an Ability
    that they never perform: Vowing more than the
    Perfection of Ten, and Discharging less than
    the Tenth Part of One. They that have the Voice   95
    of Lions and the Act of Hares, are they not
    Monsters?
TROILUS   Are there such? Such are not we. Praise
    us as we are tasted; allow us as we prove. Our
    Head shall go bare till Merit crown it: no   100
    Perfection in Reversion shall have a Praise in

102–3   We . . . Birth   *I will not make any claims about what I deserve until I have given birth to deeds that justify such claims.*

103–4   and . . . humble   *Here* borne *can mean either (a) carried, like a burden or a fetus, or (b) born. If the first meaning applies, Troilus is saying "and, being carried, Merit's addition shall be of humble weight." If the second applies, Troilus is saying "and, being new-born, his addition shall be as humble as an infant." One meaning of* Addition *is "title" or claim for credit and recognition. Here* borne *can also mean "borne sexually," and* Addition *can refer to the male member, as in I.ii.19 and II.iii.256.*

104   Few . . . Faith.   *Few words are needed to prove true fidelity.*

104–6   Troilus . . . his Truth   *Troilus shall be so faithful to Cressida that the worst that Malice can say shall be mocked [shown to be ridiculous] by Troilus' fidelity.*

111   Folly   *foolishness, act to be regretted later.*

115   flinch   *deviate from his pledge of fidelity.*

116   your Hostages   *the pledges you can call in if you feel betrayed.*

119   wooed   *won by wooing.*

121–22   they'll stick . . . thrown   *Pandarus' phrasing plays on erotic senses for* stick *and* thrown *(another term for a woman's being "tumbled" or "undertaken").*

125   Moneths   *months (a common spelling).*

128   That   *Cressida refers to what she has just blurted out.*

476

Present. We will not name Desert before his
Birth; and, being borne, his Addition shall be
humble. Few Words to Fair Faith. Troilus shall
be such to Cressid as what Envy can say worst   105
shall be a Mock for his Truth, and what Truth
can speak truest no truer than Troilus.

CRESSIDA   Will you walk in, my Lord?

Re-enter Pandarus.

PANDARUS   What, blushing still? Have you not done
     talking yet?   110
CRESSIDA   Well, Uncle, what Folly I commit I
     dedicate to you.
PANDARUS   I thank you for that: if my Lord get a
     Boy of you, you'll give him me. Be true to my
     Lord; if he flinch, chide me for it.   115
TROILUS   You know now your Hostages; your Uncle's
     Word and my firm Faith.
PANDARUS   Nay I'll give my Word for her too. Our
     Kindred, though they be long ere they be wooed,
     they are Constant being won. They are Burs,   120
     I can tell you: they'll stick when they are
     thrown.
CRESSIDA   Boldness comes to me now, and brings
     me Heart. —Prince Troilus, I have loved you
     Night and Day for many weary Moneths.   125
TROILUS   Why was my Cressid then so hard to win?
CRESSIDA   Hard to seem won; but I was won, my Lord,
     With the first Glance. That ever pardon me:
     If I confess much, you will play the Tyrant.

477

135   unsecret to our selves   *unable to keep our own secrets.*

140   Rapture   *ecstasy, seizure by a force (Love) beyond my control.*

142   Dumbness   *speechlessness.*

142–   draws . . . Counsel   *prompts my heart to empty out all her*
43   *secrets.*

144   thence   *from there.*

I love you now, but till now not so much   130
But I might maister it. In faith I lie:
My Thoughts were like unbridl'd Children grown
Too headstrong for their Mother. See we Fools,
Why have I blabb'd? Who shall be true to us
When we are so unsecret to our selves?   135
But though I lov'd you well, I woo'd you not;
And yet good faith I wish'd my self a Man,
Or that we Women had Men's Privilege
Of speaking first. Sweet, bid me hold my
    Tongue,
For in this Rapture I shall surely speak   140
The thing I shall repent. See, see, your Silence,
Coming in Dumbness, from my Weakeness draws
My very Soul of Counsel. Stop my Mouth.
TROILUS   And shall, albeit sweet Music issues
    thence.   *He kisses her.*
PANDARUS   Pretty, i' faith.   145
CRESSIDA   My Lord, I do beseech you pardon me:
    'Twas not my Purpose thus to beg a Kiss.
    I am asham'd; O Heav'ns, what have I done?
    For this time will I take my Leave, my Lord.
TROILUS   Your Leave, sweet Cressid?   150
PANDARUS   Leave, and you take Leave till tomorrow
    morning—!
CRESSIDA   Pray you content you.
TROILUS   What offends you, Lady?
CRESSIDA   Sir, mine own Company.
TROILUS   You cannot shun your Self.   155
CRESSIDA   Let me go and try:

159   Fool   *plaything.*

160   Wit   *judgment, self-possession, common sense. But* Wit *could also refer to the cunning (*Craft, *line 162) a woman used to attain the object of her desire, and Troilus suggests in his next line that in that sense Cressida's wit is by no means deficient.*

163   roundly   *openly, freely.*
       large Confession   *full disclosure of my thoughts and fears.*

164   angle   *fish. But* angle *can also refer to other ways of approaching a matter at an angle, using "Indirections" to "find Directions out" (*Hamlet, *II.i.63).*
       Wise   *prudent, reserving your judgment and refusing to commit yourself to anything that might involve risk.*

165   and love   *and love at the same time.*

169   feed for Age   *supply for old age. The Folio prints* aye *(forever).*

170   To keep . . . Youth   *to maintain forever the constancy (fidelity) she plighted (vowed) in the ardor of youth.*

171   Beauty's Outward   *external beauty.*

175   affronted   *set over against (as on balance scales).*
       the Match and Weight   *the equal in gravity and solidity.*

176   winnow'd   *separated from the light husks whose lack of weight will not withstand the winnower's fan. Compare I.iii.26–30.*

180   war   *compete.*

182   Swains   *simple, innocent youths (such as pastoral shepherds).*

I have a kind of Self resides with you;
But an unkind Self that it self will leave
To be another's Fool. I would be gone;
Where is my Wit? I know not what I speak.   160

TROILUS   Well know they what they speak that
    speak so wisely.

CRESSIDA   Perchance, my Lord, I show more Craft
    than Love,
And fell so roundly to a large Confession
To angle for your Thoughts; but you are Wise,
Or else you love not. For to be Wise and love   165
Exceeds Man's Might: that dwells with Gods
    above.

TROILUS   O that I thought it could be in a Woman,
As if it can I will presume in you,
To feed for Age her Lamp and Flames of Love;
To keep her Constancy in Plight and Youth,   170
Out-living Beauty's Outward with a Mind
That doth renew swifter than Blood decays;
Or that Persuasion could but thus convince me
That my Integrity and Truth to you
Might be affronted with the Match and Weight   175
Of such a winnow'd Purity in Love;
How were I then uplifted! But alas,
I am as true as Truth's Simplicity,
And simpler than the Infancy of Truth.

CRESSIDA   In that I'll war with you.

TROILUS   O virtuous Fight,   180
When Right with Right wars who shall be most
    Right!
True Swains in Love shall in the World to Come

183   Approve *prove, validate (by citing an irrefutable instance).*
        Troilus *Here* Troilus' *would be an equally defensible reading of what appears in the original texts.*

184   Protest *protestations (professions) of love.*
        big Compare *grandiose comparisons.*

185   Iteration *repetition.*

186   as Plantage to the Moon *either (a) as the proverbial fruitfulness of crops planted when the moon is full, or (b) as the inseparable relationship between fruitful vegetation and the lunar cycle.*

187   Turtle *turtledove, proverbial for its faithfulness.*

188   Adamant *lodestone, magnet.*

190   authentic Author *true originator.*

192   sanctify the Numbers *consecrate the meters (making them holy).*

193   swear a Hair from Truth *vow anything that deviates from the truth by so much as a hair. For audiences who knew the outcome of Cressida's story, her reference to* Hair *at this moment would probably have carried ironic overtones of a similar-sounding word (as illustrated by the wordplay on* Hare *and* Hoar *in* Romeo and Juliet, *II.iv.140–48).*

196   Oblivion *forgetfulness, erasure of memory.*

197   characterless *without inscriptions or engraved marks of themselves; here pronounced "char-ác-ter-lèss."*

203   Pard to the Hind *panther or leopard to the doe.*

Approve their Truth by Troilus. When their
  Rimes,
Full of Protest, of Oath and big Compare,
Wants Similes, Truth tir'd with Iteration   185
("As true as Steel," "as Plantage to the Moon,"
"As Sun to Day," "as Turtle to her Mate,"
"As Iron to Adamant," "as Earth to th'
  Center"),
After all Comparisons of Truth,
As Truth's authentic Author to be cited,   190
"As True as Troilus" shall crown up the Verse
And sanctify the Numbers.
CRESSIDA   Prophet may you be.
If I be False, or swear a Hair from Truth,
When Time is old, or hath forgot it self,
When Water-drops have worn the Stones of Troy,   195
And blind Oblivion swallow'd Cities up,
And mighty States characterless are grated
To dusty Nothing, yet let Memory
From False to False among False Maids in Love
Upbraid my Falsehood, when th' have said "as
  False   200
As Air, as Water, Wind, or Sandy Earth,"
"As Fox to Lamb," or "Wolf to Heifer's Calf,"
"Pard to the Hind," or "Stepdame to her Son,"
Yea let them say, to stick the Heart of
  Falsehood,
"As False as Cressid."   205
PANDARUS   Go to, a Bargain made: seal it, seal it;
I'll be the Witness. Here I hold your Hand.
Here, my Cousins, if ever you prove false one

212   **call them all Panders** *By the time Shakespeare dramatized the story, of course, Pandarus' words had proven prophetic.*

218–   **which Bed . . . death** *Pandarus' joke derives from the*
19   *practice of pressing to death a person accused of crime who refused to speak when asked to plead innocent or guilty. The bed "shall not speak" in the sense that it will keep the lovers' use of it secret.* Encounters *is one of many military terms employed by Shakespeare to describe engagements of a more friendly nature. Given the playwright's frequent wordplay on* count *(as in "Country Matters,"* Hamlet, *III.ii.122), it seems to have struck him as a particularly apt word for the kind of coming together described in this line.*

221   **Tongue-tied Maidens** *maidens reluctant or unable to express their desires openly (and thus in need of a go-between like Pandarus to arrange a meeting for them). Here* Maidens *refers primarily to bashful women, but the term could also be applied to male virgins. Pandarus addresses the audience.*

222   **Gear** *equipment, arrangements.*

III.iii   *This scene returns us to the Greek camp for our first meeting with Cressida's father, Calchas.*

1   **the Service I have done** *Calchas, a Trojan seer, has gone over to the Greeks and has provided them with intelligence and "Sight" (prophecies) about the future (line 4).*

4   **in things to love** *with respect to things I hold dear.*

5   **Possession** *the house in which the previous scene took place.*

to another, since I have taken such Pain to
bring you together, let all pitiful Goers-   210
between be call'd to the World's End after my
Name: call them all Panders. Let all Constant
Men be Troiluses; all False Women Cressids,
and all Brokers-between Panders. Say "Amen."
TROILUS   Amen.   215
CRESSIDA   Amen.
PANDARUS   Amen. Whereupon I will show you a
Chamber, which Bed, because it shall not speak
of your pretty Encounters, press it to death.
Away.   *Exeunt Troilus and Cressida.*   220
—And Cupid grant all Tongue-tied Maidens here
Bed, Chamber, Pander, to provide this Gear.   *Exit.*

Scene 3

*Enter Ulysses, Diomed, Nestor, Agamemnon,
Menelaus, Aiax, and Calchas. Flourish.*

CALCHAS   Now Princes, for the Service I have done,
Th' Advantage of the Time prompts me aloud
To call for Recompense. Appear 't to Mind
That through the Sight I bear, in things to
    love
I have abandon'd Troy, left my Possession,   5
Incurr'd a Traitor's Name, expos'd my self,

8   sequest'ring   *separating; probably pronounced "squést-ring" here.*

9   Condition   *position, station in Trojan society.*

10   tame   *domesticated, mine without effort.*

12   strange   *a stranger.*

13   as in way of Taste   *as a foretaste of the rewards I have coming to me.*

15   regist'red in Promise   *formally pledged.*

19   dear   *valuable.*

20   therefore   *for which.*

22   still   *always.*

23   Wrest   *Calchas' metaphor relates to several instruments for turning or tightening things to make them taut: (a) a tuning-key, (b) a peg for a surgical ligature, and (c) a wrench.*

25   Wanting his Manage   *without him to manage (direct) some of their key military operations.*

27   change   *exchange.*

29   strike . . . done   *strike from the ledger all you owe me for the services I have rendered thus far.*

30   most accepted Pain   *efforts most willingly undertaken.*

34   Withal   *with all, in addition [to carrying out this mission].*

From certain and possess'd Conveniences,
To doubtful Fortunes, sequest'ring from me all
That Time, Acquaintance, Custom, and Condition
Made tame and most familiar to my Nature;   10
And here to do you Service am become
As new into the World, strange, unacquainted.
I do beseech you, as in way of Taste,
To give me now a little Benefit
Out of those many regist'red in Promise   15
Which you say live to come in my behalf.

AGAMEMNON   What wouldst thou of us, Troian? Make
    Demand.

CALCHAS   You have a Troian Pris'ner call'd Antenor,
    Yesterday took; Troy holds him very dear.
    Oft have you (often have you Thanks therefore)   20
    Desir'd my Cressid in right great Exchange,
    Whom Troy hath still denied; but this Antenor
    I know is such a Wrest in their Affairs
    That their Negotiations all must slack
    Wanting his Manage, and they will almost   25
    Give us a Prince of Blood, a Son of Priam,
    In change of him. Let him be sent, great
        Princes,
    And he shall buy my Daughter; and her presence
    Shall quite strike off all Service I have done
    In most accepted Pain.

AGAMEMNON   Let Diomedes bear him   30
    And bring us Cressid hither; Calchas shall have
    What he requests of us. —Good Diomed,
    Furnish you fairly for this Interchange;
    Withal bring word, if Hector will tomorrow

39 Please it   *if it please him, let.*
    strangely   *as if a stranger, not acknowledging him.*

41 negligent   *careless, unnoticing.*

42 like   *likely.*

43 unplausive   *unpleased, disapproving.*

44 Derision med'cinable   *a scornful manner that will prove to
    be good medicine.*

47 Glass   *mirror. What Ulysses proposes is a form of homeopathic
    medicine (fighting fire with fire).*

48 supple Knees   *knees that bow to his whims.*

49 Fees   *rewards (positive reinforcements for his haughty behav-
    ior).*

57 ought   *anything.*

Be answer'd in his Challenge, Aiax is ready.   35
DIOMED   This shall I undertake, and 'tis a Burthen
    Which I am proud to bear.   *Exit with Calchas.*

    Achilles and Patroclus stand in their Tent.

ULYSSES   Achilles stands i' th' entrance of his
    Tent.
    Please it our General pass strangely by him,
    As if he were forgot; and Princes all,   40
    Lay negligent and loose Regard upon him.
    I will come last; 'tis like he'll question me
    Why such unplausive Eyes are bent, why turn'd
        on him.
    If so, I have Derision med'cinable
    To use between your Strangeness and his Pride,   45
    Which his own Will shall have desire to drink.
    It may do good: Pride hath no other Glass
    To show it self but Pride. For supple Knees
    Feed Arrogance and are the Proud Man's Fees.
AGAMEMNON   We'll execute your Purpose and put on   50
    A Form of Strangeness as we pass along;
    So do each Lord, and either greet him not
    Or else disdainf'lly, which shall shake him
        more
    Than if not look'd on. I will lead the way.
ACHILLES   What, comes the General to speak with me?   55
    You know my Mind: I'll fight no more 'gainst
        Troy.
AGAMEMNON   —What says Achilles? Would he ought
        with us?

489

61 What, does the Cuckold scorn me? *The force of Achilles'*
   remark derives from the fact that a cuckold was himself a
   proverbial object of scorn: a man who was either too stupid to
   realize that his wife was cheating on him or too weak to do
   anything about it. Although the Greeks are fighting a costly,
   bloody war to avenge an injury to one of their Kings, they all
   feel free to laugh openly at the cuckolded King himself. Mene-
   laus gets no respect, even from the friends who are besieging
   Troy to defend his honor.

65 they were us'd to bend *they used to bow respectfully.*

73 mealy Wings *wings with a texture like that of meal or flour.*

NESTOR —Would you, my Lord, ought with the
    General?
ACHILLES No.
NESTOR   —Nothing, my Lord.
AGAMEMNON   The better.
                    Exeunt Agamemnon and Nestor.
ACHILLES Good day, good day.
MENELAUS   How do you? How do you?   60
                                        Exit.
ACHILLES What, does the Cuckold scorn me?
AIAX How now, Patroclus?
ACHILLES   Good morrow, Aiax.
AIAX   Ha?
ACHILLES Good morrow.
AIAX   Ay and good next day too.   *Exit.*
ACHILLES What mean these Fellows? Know they not
    Achilles?
PATROCLUS They pass by strangely; they were us'd
    to bend,   65
  To send their Smiles before them to Achilles,
  To come as humbly as they us'd to creep
  To holy Alt'rs.
ACHILLES   What, am I poor of late?
  'Tis certain: Greatness, once fall'n out with
    Fortune,
  Must fall out with Men too. What the Declin'd
    is   70
  He shall as soon read in the Eyes of Others
  As feel in his own Fall: for Men, like
    Butterflies,
  Show not their mealy Wings but to the Summer.

491

76   That are without him   *both (a) that exist apart from him,
      and (b) that are outside him, not essential to his own being.*

77   Accident   *random chance, circumstances unrelated to merit.*

78   slipp'ry Standers   *things that stand on slippery surfaces and
      are thus subject to unexpected falls.*

83   At ample Point   *to the height.*

85   rich Beholding   *favorable regard.*

89   A strange Fellow   *either (a) a fellow who's a stranger to me,
      or (b) a fellow with ideas that are strange (new) to me.*

90   Writes me   *It is not clear whether what Ulysses is pretending
      to read is a letter or a book. If the latter, Ulysses is using the
      "ethic dative," a construction that Shakespeare often employs
      to convey a more colloquial mode of address.*
      how dearly ever parted   *no matter how well endowed with
      good parts (attributes, accomplishments).*

91   having   *possessions.*
      or without or in   *whether without or with good fortune.*

93   owes   *owns.*

94   aiming upon others   *directed toward others (like the Sun's
      rays).*

95   retort   *return.*

97   borne   *carried.*

98   but commends   *but it offers, recommends.*

And not a Man for being simply Man
Hath any Honor, but Honor for those Honors   75
That are without him: as Place, Riches, and
   Favor,
Prizes of Accident as oft as Merit,
Which when they fall, as being slipp'ry
   Standers,
The Love that lean'd on them, as slipp'ry too,
Doth one pluck down another, and together   80
Die in the Fall. But 'tis not so with me:
Fortune and I are Friends. I do enjoy
At ample Point all that I did possess
Save these Men's Looks, who do me thinks find
   out
Something not worth in me such rich Beholding   85
As they have often giv'n. Here is Ulysses:
I'll interrupt his Reading.
—How now, Ulysses?

ULYSSES   Now great Thetis' Son—

ACHILLES   What are you reading?

ULYSSES   A strange Fellow here
Writes me that Man, how dearly ever parted,   90
How much in having, or without or in,
Cannot make Boast to have that which he hath,
Nor feels not what he owes, but by Reflection:
As when his Virtues, aiming upon others,
Heat them, and they retort that Heat again   95
To the first Giver's.

ACHILLES   This is not strange, Ulysses:
The Beauty that is borne here in the Face
The Bearer knows not, but commends it self

101   Not going from it self   *without stepping outside itself and seeing itself through the eyes of others.*

103   Speculation   *seeing, the operations of vision.*

104   marri'd there   *joined there, united with the eye of the beholder. Modern editors normally adopt the Folio's* mirror'd, *which offers a slightly different, though not incompatible, sense.*

106   strain at   *have difficulty accepting.*

110   much consisting   *a good deal of substance.*

112   know them for aught   *know them for what they are; know them to be anything.*

114   where th' are extended   *where an extension of themselves is recognized [after they have been communicated to others].*
       reverb'rate   *echo, bounce back.*

115   like   *as.*

117   Figure   *image (as seen in a mirror).*
       rapt   *transported, wrapped up.*

119   unknown   *unfamed, unrecognized.*

122   abject in Regard   *cast down in reputation, held in low esteem.*
       dear in Use   *valuable (appreciated) when employed.*

125   very Chance   *something so trifling as Chance (as opposed to the agency of men such as the sage Greek generals).*

To Others' Eyes; nor doth the Eye it self,
That most pure Spir't of Sense, behold it self   100
Not going from it self, but Eye to Eye oppos'd
Salutes each Other with each Other's Form.
For Speculation turns not to it self
Till it hath travel'd and is marri'd there
Where it may see it self. This is not strange
    at all.   105

ULYSSES   I do not strain at the Position
   (It is familiar), but at the Author's Drift,
   Who in his Circumstance expressly proves
   That no Man is the Lord of any thing,
   Though in and of him there be much consisting,   110
   Till he communicate his Parts to Others;
   Nor doth he of himself know them for aught
   Till he behold them form'd in the Applause
   Where th' are extended, who, like an Arch
      reverb'rate
   The Voice again, or like a Gate of Steel   115
   Fronting the Sun receives and renders back
   His Figure and his Heat. I was much rapt in
      this,
   And apprehended here immediately
   Th' unknown Aiax: Heav'ns, what a Man is there!
   A very Horse, that has he knows not what!   120
   Nature, what things there are
   Most abject in Regard, and dear in Use!
   What things again most dear in the Esteem,
   And poor in Worth! Now shall we see tomorrow
   An Act that very Chance doth throw upon him.   125
   Aiax renown'd? O Heav'ns, what some Men do,

495

127   leave to do   *leave undone, or leave yet to be done.*

128   creep   *move slowly or in a lowly manner.*
       skittish   *fickle, changeable.*

129   play the Idiots   *display themselves ostentatiously and thereby
       make fools of themselves.*

130–   How . . . Wantonness!   *Here Ulysses touches Achilles
31   closer to home. Whatever else he means, he alludes to what
       Aiax is doing to erode Achilles' reputation (his "Pride" as
       reflected in the eyes of others) while Achilles allows his "Pride"
       (the military valor that is the basis for his reputation) to fast
       and famish (as a result of his refusal to feed it with battlefield
       exploits) in his wanton (self-indulgent) withdrawal to his
       tent.*

135   shriking   *shrieking with lamentation.*

140   Alms   *offerings. Ulysses picks up on the reference to beggars.*

143   made   *completed, done.*

146   Mail   *suit of armor.*

147   In monumental Mock'ry   *as a monument (memorial) to the
       scorn a knight earns by allowing his honor to grow rusty
       through disuse.*
       Take th' Instant Way   *both (a) take the way now offered, and
       (b) keep pace with the present traffic on the narrow "Strait"
       (passageway).*

149   one but goes abreast   *only one goes at a time (in single file).*

150   Emulation   *rivalry.*

While some Men leave to do!
How some Men creep in skittish Fortune's Hall,
While others play the Idiots in her Eyes!
How one Man eats into another's Pride, 130
While Pride is fasting in his Wantonness!
To see these Grecian Lords, why ev'n already
They clap the Lubber Aiax on the Shoulder
As if his Foot were on brave Hector's Breast
And great Troy shriking.
ACHILLES   I do believe it, for 135
They pass'd by me as Misers do by Beggars:
Neither gave to me good Word nor Look.
What, are my Deeds forgot?
ULYSSES   Time hath, my Lord, a Wallet at his Back
Wherein he puts Alms for Oblivion, 140
A great-siz'd Monster of Ingratitudes:
Those Scraps are Good Deeds past, which are
    devour'd
As fast as they are made, forgot as soon
As done. Persev'rance, dear my Lord,
Keeps Honor bright: to have done is to hang 145
Quite out of Fashion like a rusty Mail
In monumental Mock'ry. Take the Instant Way,
For Honor travels in a Strait so narrow
Where one but goes abreast: keep then the
    Path,
For Emulation hath a thousand Sons 150
That one by one pursue if you give way
Or turn aside from the direct Forthright.
Like to an ent'red Tide, they all rush by,
And leave you hindmost;

497

155   in first Rank   *while running at the head of the pack.*

156   the Abject   *those in its rear (those it had formerly scorned).*

159   a fashionable Host   *a host whose welcome is dictated by fashion.*

160   slightly   *perfunctorily, with little attention or feeling.*

161   as he would fly   *This phrase can mean either (a) as if he [the Host] would use his arms as wings and fly, or (b) as if he [the newly arrived Guest] would flee rather than enter unless the Host reached out and pulled him in the door.*

162   The Welcome   *the person being welcomed.*

163   Farewell   *the person being told farewell.*

164   Remuneration   *payment, reward.*

165   Vigor of Bone   *physical strength.*

167   calumniating   *scandalizing, reputation-destroying.*

168   one Touch of Nature . . . kin   *all human beings share the same nature.*

169   new-born Gauds   *fresh trifles, novelties.*

171–72   that is a little Gilt . . . o'er-dusted   *which in turn is only a little gilt [gold coating], indeed more praise for gilt than true gilt, that has now been turned to dust itself. Ulysses' point is that nothing is proof against Time's unrelenting tendency to reduce everything to Dust. His moral is an echo of Genesis 3:19.*

177   Cry   *acclaim.*

Or like a gallant Horse fall'n in first Rank, 155
Lie there for Pavement to the Abject, near
O'er-run and trampl'd on. Then what they do in
    Present,
Though less than yours in Past, must o'ertop
    yours.
For Time is like a fashionable Host
That slightly shakes his parting Guest by th'
    Hand, 160
And with his Arms out-stretch'd, as he would
    fly,
Grasps in the Comer. The Welcome ever smiles,
And Farewell goes out sighing. Let not Virtue
    seek
Remuneration for the thing it was: for Beauty,
    Wit,
High Birth, Vigor of Bone, Desert in Service, 165
Love, Friendship, Charity, are Subjects all
To envious and calumniating Time.
One Touch of Nature makes the whole World kin,
That all with one Consent praise new-born
    Gauds,
Though they are made and moulded of things
    past 170
And go to Dust, that is a little Gilt,
More Laud than Gilt, o'er-dusted.
The present Eye praises the present Object:
Then marvel not, thou Great and Complete Man,
That all the Greeks begin to worship Aiax, 175
Since Things in Motion sooner catch the Eye
Than what stirs not. The Cry went once on thee,

178   And still it might   *and even yet it might have.*

180   case   *encase, close up.*

182   Made . . . themselves   *caused the Gods themselves to enter the fray because of their envy of your prowess.*

183   drave great Mars to Faction   *drove even the God of War to join a side.*
    Of this my Privacy   *for this my withdrawal into privacy.*

185   Heroical   *pertaining to your reputation as a hero.*

188   Providence   *foresight, provision for its own security (and hence its intelligence about what most affects its security).*

190   Finds Bottom . . . Depth   *is able to plumb the depths of even the most unfathomable bodies of water (here metaphorical for other mysteries that the State is able to penetrate).*

191   Keeps . . . Thought   *keeps pace with even the fleetest thought.*

192   Do . . . Cradles   *uncovers thoughts in their silent cribs.*

193–94   with whom Relation . . . meddle   *into which Report is afraid to intrude itself.*

196   Expressure   *expression.*

200   throw down   *Ulysses uses this term in both military and sexual senses, the latter to refer to the Trojan "daughter."*

201   Pyrrhus   *Achilles' son (the warrior depicted in* Hamlet, *II.ii.485–532).*

And still it might; and yet it may again,
If thou wouldst not entomb thy self alive
And case thy Reputation in thy Tent, 180
Whose glorious Deeds but in these Fields of
    late
Made emulous Missions 'mongst the Gods
    themselves
And drave great Mars to Faction.
ACHILLES   Of this my Privacy
I have strong Reas'ns.
ULYSSES   But 'gainst your Privacy
The Reasons are more Potent and Heroical: 185
'Tis known, Achilles, that you are in love
With one of Priam's Daughters.
ACHILLES   Ha? Known?
ULYSSES   Is that a Wond'r? The Providence that's in
A watchful State knows almost ev'ry thing,
Finds Bottom in th' uncomprehensive Depth, 190
Keeps Place with Thought, and almost like the
    Gods
Do Thoughts unvail in their dumb Cradles.
There is a Mystery (with whom Relation
Durst never meddle) in the Soul of State,
Which hath an Operation more Divine 195
Than Breath or Pen can give Expressure to.
All the Commerce that you have had with Troy
As perfectly is ours as yours, my Lord,
And better would it fit Achilles much
To throw down Hector than Polyxena. 200
But it must grieve young Pyrrhus now at home,
When Fame shall in our Islands sound her Trump

501

203   tripping   *teasingly, tauntingly, as children do.*

205   him   *Hector.*

206   your Lover   *one who loves you and looks after your interests.*

207   The Fool . . . break.   *Ulysses' image is complex and probably has several implications. One reading is that the "Ice" he refers to is Achilles' aloof isolation, which smooths the way for a lightweight fool like Aiax to skate his way to fame as a hero.*

210   an Effem'nate Man   *a man who refuses to play the role expected of him.*

212   Stomach to   *both (a) appetite for, and (b) guts for.*

215   am'rous Fold   *loving embrace (that which induces love for Polyxena).*

220   shrowdly   *sharply, severely.*

223   Seals . . . Danger   *provides a sealed warrant, a blank check, for Danger to use as it will.*

224   an Ague   *a shivering fever.*
        taints   *infects, makes ill.*

225   Ev'n . . . Sun   *so that they [men who wound themselves] shake with chills even when they sit in the direct sunlight.*

226   hether   *hither, here.*

And all the Greekish Girls shall tripping sing
"Great Hector's Sister did Achilles win,
But our great Aiax bravely beat down him."   205
Farewell, my Lord. I as your Lover speak:
The Fool slides o'er the Ice that you should
   break.   *Exit.*
PATROCLUS   To this effect, Achilles, have I mov'd
   you:
A Woman Impudent and Mannish grown
Is not more loath'd than an Effem'nate Man   210
In Time of Action. I stand condemn'd for this;
They think my little Stomach to the War,
And your great Love to me, restrains you thus.
Sweet, rouse your self, and the weak Wanton Cupid
Shall from your Neck unloose his am'rous Fold,   215
And like a Dewdrop from the Lion's Mane,
Be shook to Air.
ACHILLES   Shall Aiax fight with Hector?
PATROCLUS   Ay, and perhaps receive much Honor
   by him.
ACHILLES   I see my Reputation is at Stake;
My Fame is shrowdly gor'd.
PATROCLUS   O then beware: 220
Those Wounds heal ill that Men do give
   themselves.
Omission to do what is necessary
Seals a Commission to a Blank of Danger,
And Danger, like an Ague, subtly taints
Ev'n then when they sit idly in the Sun.   225
ACHILLES   Go call Thersites hether, sweet
   Patroclus:

229   a Woman's Longing   *an uncontrollable and inexplicable craving, like those that women develop during pregnancy.*

230   withal   *with.*

231   Weeds   *garments.*

233   full of View   *fill of viewing.*

241   heroical Cudgeling   *Thersites deliberately combines two words that don't belong together. Cudgeling, a beating with crude clubs, is normally associated not with heroic endeavors but with the feuding of country bumpkins. The phrasing is ambiguous, conveying the suggestion that Aiax believes that he is going to cudgel Hector, whereas in reality he is more likely to become Hector's victim.*

241–
42   raves in saying nothing   *This is another oxymoron (contradiction in terms). Thersites means that Aiax's manner resembles a dumb-show (pantomime) of a man in a raving fit.*

245   a-stride and a-stand   *alternating between striding and standing.*
      ruminates   *contemplates deeply.*

246   Arithmatic   *means of calculation, such as a tablet.*

248   a politic Regard   *a manner calculated to suggest grave thought on important matters of state. This phrase recalls Malvolio's resolve to "read Politic Authors" when he is gulled into a state similar to Aiax's in II.v of* Twelfth Night.

249   and 'twould out   *if it would only come out.*

252   undone   *brought to ruin.*

I'll send the Fool to Aiax and desire him
T' invite the Troian Lords after the Combat
To see us here unarm'd. I have a Woman's
   Longing,
An Appetite that I am Sick withal,   230
To see great Hector in his Weeds of Peace,
To talk with him, and to behold his Visage,
Ev'n to my full of View.

Enter Thersites.

                 A Labor sav'd.
THERSITES   A Wonder.
ACHILLES   What?   235
THERSITES   Aiax goes up and down the Field
   asking for himself.
ACHILLES   How so?
THERSITES   He must fight singly tomorrow with
   Hector, and is so prophetically proud of an   240
   heroical Cudgeling that he raves in saying
   nothing.
ACHILLES   How can that be?
THERSITES   Why 'a stalks up and down like a
   Peacock, a-stride and a-stand; ruminates like   245
   an Hostess that hath no Arithmatic but her
   Brain to set down her Reckoning; bites his Lip
   with a politic Regard, as who should say there
   were Wit in this Head and 'twould out; and so
   there is, but it lies as coldly in him as Fire   250
   in a Flint, which will not show without
   knocking. The Man's undone for ever: for if

258 **Land-fish** *a monstrosity, a fish out of water.*

258– **a Plague of Opinion** *something to be pointed at in horror,*
59 *like a visitation of the plague.*

263 **professes Not Answering** *makes a profession of being too*
  aloof to condescend and answer a question.

265 **put on his Presence** *impersonate his manner.*

266 **Pageant** *dramatic representation, brief play. The "Pageant"*
  that Thersites is putting on in imitation of Achilles and Patro-
  clus recalls the presentation of Achilles and Patroclus that
  Ulysses provided for the Greek Council in I.iii.142–84.

271 **Safe-conduct** *an escort to convey him safely through the*
  Greek army (so that he will not be attacked as an enemy
  attempting to infiltrate the ranks or conduct a raid).
  of *from (as in line 282).*

Hector break not his Neck i' th' Combat, he'll
break 't himself in Vain-glory. He knows not
me. I said "Good morrow, Aiax," and he replies   255
"Thanks Agamemnon." What think you of this Man
that takes me for the General? He's grown a
very Land-fish: Language-less, a Monster, a
Plague of Opinion; a Man may wear it on both
sides like a leather Jerkin.   260

ACHILLES   Thou must be my Ambassador, Thersites.

THERSITES   Who, I? Why he'll answer no body: he
professes Not Answering. Speaking is for
Beggars. He wears his Tongue in's Arms. I will
put on his Presence. Let Patroclus make   265
Demands to me: you shall see "The Pageant of
Aiax."

ACHILLES   To him, Patroclus: tell him I humbly
desire the valiant Aiax to invite the valorous
Hector to come unarm'd to my Tent, and to   270
procure Safe-conduct for his Person of the
magnanimous and most illustrious six- or
seven-times honor'd Captain General of the
Army, Agamemnon. Do this.

PATROCLUS   "Jove bless great Aiax."   275

THERSITES   "Hum."

PATROCLUS   "I come from the worthy Achilles—"

THERSITES   "Ha?"

PATROCLUS   "Who most humbly desires you to invite
Hector to his Tent—"   280

THERSITES   "Hum."

PATROCLUS   "And to procure safe Conduct from
Agamemnon."

507

288   buy   *be with.*

292   howsoever . . . me   *however it goes, he will have to pay a price for victory over me before he has defeated me.*

295   in this Tune   *in this mode of behavior.*

299   Fiddler Apollo   *Thersites reduces the God of Music to a common fiddler.*
        his Sinews   *Aiax's tendons.*

300   Catlings on   *lute strings of. Lute strings were made of catgut.*

303   capable   *capable of reason and discourse.*

304   Fountain stirr'd   *muddied spring.*

307   water an Ass   *bring an ass (Aiax) to drink from it.*

309   Valiant Ignorance   *vainglorious ignoramus.*

THERSITES   "Agamemnon."
PATROCLUS   "Ay my Lord."   285
THERSITES   "Ha?"
PATROCLUS   "What say you to 't?"
THERSITES   "God buy you with all my Heart."
PATROCLUS   "Your Answer, Sir?"
THERSITES   "If tomorrow be a fair Day, by eleven   290
   of the Clock it will go one way or other;
   howsoever he shall pay for me ere he has me."
PATROCLUS   "Your Answer, Sir?"
THERSITES   "Fare ye well with all my Heart."
ACHILLES   Why, but he is not in this Tune, is he?   295
THERSITES   No, but out of Tune thus. What Music
   will be in him when Hector has knock'd out his
   Brains I know not; but I am sure none, unless
   the Fiddler Apollo get his Sinews to make
   Catlings on.   300
ACHILLES   Come, thou shalt bear a Letter to him
   straight.
THERSITES   Let me bear another to his Horse, for
   that's the more capable Creature.
ACHILLES   My Mind is troubled like a Fountain
   stirr'd,
   And I my self see not the Bottom of it.   305

                                        Exit with Patroclus.

THERSITES   Would the Fountain of your Mind were
   clear again, that I might water an Ass at it;
   I had rather be a Tick in a Sheep than such a
   Valiant Ignorance.   *Exit.*

IV.i   *This scene returns us to a street in Troy. Diomed has come from the Greek camp to exchange Antenor (a Trojan recently captured by the Greeks) for Cressida. Diomed and Antenor are being escorted (provided "Safe-conduct," III.iii.271) by Paris and Deiphobus, and the four of them meet Aeneas.*

4   lie long   *stay in bed.*

9   Witness the process of your Speech   *lay your eyes on the subject of your earlier comments.*

10   a whole Week by Days   *every day for a week.*

11   haunt   *pursue.*

Scene 1

Enter at one Door Aeneas, at another Paris,
Deiphobus, Antenor, Diomed the Grecian, with Torches.

PARIS See ho! Who is that there?
DEIPHOBUS It is the Lord Aeneas.
AENEAS Is the Prince there in person?
　　—Had I so good Occasion to lie long
　　As you, Prince Paris, nothing but Heav'nly
　　　　Bus'ness　　　　　　　　　　　　　　　　　　　　　5
　　Should rob my Bed-mate of my Company.
DIOMED That's my Mind too. Good morrow, Lord
　　Aeneas.
PARIS A valiant Greek: Aeneas, take his Hand.
　　Witness the process of your Speech, wherein
　　You told how Diomed a whole Week by Days　　10
　　Did haunt you in the Field.
AENEAS　　　　　　　　　Health to you, valiant Sir,

12   **During . . . Truce**   *during all the discourse we have while we are at truce with one another. Such a truce exists now while Diomed is on a mission to exchange a prisoner of war.*

16   **and so long Health**   *and for so long as they are [calm], they are also in health.*

19   **Policy**   *the strategy and tactics of combat.*

21   **With his Face backward**   *facing his adversary (that is, not flying at all). Aeneas is speaking with magnanimous understatement.*
            Humane   *In Shakespeare's time this spelling conveyed the meanings of both "human" and "humane."*

22   **Anchises' Life**   *the life of Aeneas' father.*

23   **Venus**   *Goddess of Love and Beauty, and Aeneas' mother.*

26   **sympathize**   *are in accord in our pledges of future discord.*

27   **his Fate**   *his fated death.*

29   **emulous**   *rivalrous; here, as frequently elsewhere, to be treated as a two-syllable word.*

38   **render**   *give, surrender to.*

39   **enfreed**   *ransomed, freed.*

During all Question of the gentle Truce;
But when I meet you arm'd, as black Defiance
As Heart can think or Courage execute.

DIOMED   The one and other Diomed embraces.   15
Our Bloods are now in calm, and so long
    Health;
But when Contention and Occasion meet,
By Jove, I'll play the Hunter for thy Life
With all my Force, Pursuit, and Policy.

AENEAS   And thou shalt hunt a Lion that will fly   20
With his Face backward, in Humane Gentleness.
Welcome to Troy. Now by Anchises' Life,
Welcome indeed. By Venus' Hand I swear,
No Man alive can love in such a sort
The thing he means to kill, more excellently.   25

DIOMED   We sympathize. Jove let Aeneas live,
If to my Sword his Fate be not the Glory,
A thousand complete Courses of the Sun;
But in mine emulous Honor let him die,
With ev'ry Joint a Wound, and that tomorrow.   30

AENEAS   We know each other well.

DIOMED   We do, and long to know each other worse.

PARIS   This is the most despiteful gentle Greeting,
The noblest hateful Love that e'er I heard of.
—What Bus'ness, Lord, so early?

AENEAS   I was sent   35
For to the King, but why I know not.

PARIS   His Purpose meets you: 'twas to bring this
    Greek
To Calchas' House, and there to render him,
For the enfreed Antenor, the fair Cressid.

513

41   constantly   *firmly (with no waverings of doubt).*

45   With . . . wherefore   *with a full accounting of the reasons why.*

48   Help   *remedy, alternate solution.*

49   The bitter . . . Time   *the bitterness and pain that the present time imposes upon us.*

57   Not making any Scruple of her Soil   *not raising the slightest objection to the blemish she now bears. A* scruple *was a tiny unit of weight in apothecary's measure.*

58   Pain   *both (a) trouble, and (b) suffering.*
Charge   *expenditure.*

60   palating   *tasting (literally, allowing the taste to reach your palate).*

62   puling   *whimpering.*

63   flat tamed Piece   *Diomed compares Helen to a stale, pierced cask of wine. In Shakespeare's time as in ours, however,* piece *was also a derogatory term for a woman who was regarded as little more than a piece of flesh. Paris has hinted at that sense in III.i.54.*

64   Loins   *here, the genital region of the body.*

Let's have your company; or if you please,   40
Haste there before 's. I constantly believe
(Or rather call my Thought a certain Knowledge)
My brother Troilus lodges there tonight:
Rouse him and give him note of our Approach
With the whole Quality wherefore. I fear   45
We shall be much unwelcome.
AENEAS   That I assure you:
Troilus had rather Troy were borne to Greece
Than Cressid borne from Troy.
PARIS   There is no Help.
The bitter Disposition of the Time
Will have it so. —On, Lord, we'll follow you.   50
AENEAS   Good morrow all.   *Exit.*
PARIS   And tell me, noble Diomed, faith tell me
    true,
Ev'n in Soul of sound good Fellowship,
Who in your Thoughts deserves fair Helen best,
My self or Menelaus?
DIOMED   Both alike.   55
He merits well to have her, that doth seek her,
Not making any Scruple of her Soil,
With such a Hell of Pain and World of Charge;
And you as well to keep her, that defend her,
Not palating the Taste of her Dishonor,   60
With such a costly Loss of Wealth and Friends.
He, like a puling Cuckold, would drink up
The Lees and Dregs of a flat tamed Piece;
You, like a Lecher, out of whorish Loins
Are pleas'd to breed out your Inheritors.   65

66   pois'd   *set on opposite sides of a pair of balance scales.*
      nor . . . nor   *neither . . . nor.*

67   he as he   *the one side as the other (that is, both men equally).*
      the heavier for a Whore   *both (a) weighing the more because
      of the extra burden of carrying a whore, and (b) the less to be
      admired because of his association with a whore.*

69   bitter   *a bitter pill, something that leaves a bitter taste.*

70   bawdy   *whorish.*

71   Scruple   *tiny portion.*

72   carrion   *rotting (like a carcass).*

73   Since she could speak   *for as long as she has had the ability
      to talk.*

75   for her   *both (a) on her behalf, and (b) because of her.*

76   Chapmen   *wholesale buyers, accustomed to haggling over the
      price.*

79   We'll . . . sell.   *This sentence is puzzling. It would appear
      to depict the Trojans as clever merchants who figure that they
      will get the highest price for an object of inestimable value by
      disdaining to advertise it. But there is no indication that the
      Trojans plan to sell Helen at any price. What Paris probably
      means, then, is that "We'll not commend Helen as if we
      intended to sell her."*

80   Here lies our Way.   *This is a polite way of saying "The way
      lies before you: please proceed."*

IV.ii   *This scene takes place in Cressida's house.*

Both Merits pois'd, each weighs nor less nor
    more,
But he as he, the heavier for a Whore.
PARIS   You are too bitter to your Countrywoman.
DIOMED   She's bitter to her Country. Hear me,
    Paris:
For ev'ry false Drop in her bawdy Veins,   70
A Grecian's Life hath sunk; for ev'ry Scruple
Of her contaminated carrion Weight,
A Troian hath been slain. Since she could speak,
She hath not giv'n so many good Words breath
As for her Greeks and Troians suff'red Death.   75
PARIS   Fair Diomed, you do as Chapmen do,
Dispraise the thing that they desire to buy.
But we in silence hold this Virtue well:
We'll not commend what we intend to sell.
Here lies our Way.   *Exeunt.*   80

Scene 2

Enter Troilus and Cressida.

TROILUS   Dear, trouble not your self: the Morn is
    cold.
CRESSIDA   Then sweet my Lord, I'll call mine
    Uncle down:
He shall unbolt the Gates.

4   pritty   *This spelling, to be found in both early texts, is probably meant to indicate an affectionately diminutive pronunciation of* pretty.

5   Attachment   *arrest, imprisonment. It is early morning, and Troilus is telling Cressida to go back to sleep rather than trouble herself with unbolting the gates for Troilus to leave.*

10   ribald Crows   *disrespectful, cawing birds who seem to be mocking at the lovers. One of Troilus' concerns is that other kinds of "Crows" (gossips) will learn where he has spent the night if he doesn't leave before people are up and about.*

12   from   *be away from.*

13   ven'mous Wights   *evil people. Troilus is probably thinking of thieves and other venomous types who do evil under cover of darkness.*
         stays   *remains (like a whorish witch who shares the bed of "ven'mous Wights").*

14   tediously   *with unending monotony.*

15   momentary swift   *as swift as the passing of a brief moment.*

18   held off   *It is not clear whether Cressida means (a) remained unwon (in accordance with the sentiments expressed in I.ii.307–16), or (b) delayed sexually.*

21   mocking   *teasing.*

22   I shall have such a Life!   *Cressida means "What I'll have to put up with!" But in view of what is about to happen, her words are prophetic in ways that she is unable to anticipate.*

TROILUS   Trouble him not.
To Bed, to Bed: Sleep kill those pritty Eyes,
And give as soft Attachment to thy Senses   5
As Infants empty of all Thought.
CRESSIDA   Good morrow then.
TROILUS   I prithee now to Bed.
CRESSIDA   Are you a-weary of me?
TROILUS   O Cressida! But that the busy Day
Wak'd by the Lark hath rous'd the ribald Crows,   10
And dreaming Night will hide our Joys no longer,
I would not from thee.
CRESSIDA   Night hath been too brief.
TROILUS   Beshrew the Witch! With ven'mous Wights
     she stays
As tediously as Hell, but flies the grasps of Love
With Wings more momentary swift than Thought.   15
You will catch cold and curse me.
CRESSIDA   Prithee tarry; you Men will never tarry.
—O foolish Cresseid! —I might have still held off,
And then you would have tarri'd. Hark, there's
     one up.
PANDARUS   [Within]
What's all the Doors op'n here?
TROILUS   It is your Uncle.   20
CRESSIDA   A Pest'lence on 'im: now will he be
     mocking.
I shall have such a Life!

Enter Pandarus.

24   **Here . . . Cresseid?** *Pandarus implies that if the woman he is speaking to is a "Maid" (virgin), she cannot be "my Cousin Cresseid." Here and at places elsewhere, the spelling of Cressida's name echoes that in Robert Henryson's* Testament of Cresseid, *a sequel to Chaucer's* Troilus and Criseyde *in which Cressida degenerates into a leprous beggar.*

26   **do** *a common euphemism for sexual activity.*

30   **suffer others** *allow others to "be good." Cressida probably means at least two things here: (a) remain pure, and (b) retain a reputation for purity ("be good" in name if not in fact).*

31   **Chipochia** capocchia, *Italian for "head" (here implying a dimunitive, innocent one).*

33   **Bug-bear** *hobgoblin.*

34   **knock'd i' th' Head** *The knocking at the door that follows immediately (and with ironic juxtaposition) upon this jest signals an abrupt shift in key. Shakespeare frequently employs knocks on the door to effect sudden alterations in the mood of a scene. The most famous instance occurs in II.ii of* Macbeth.

40   **Pray you come in** *Cressida addresses this line to Troilus, not to the person knocking. Pandarus has already moved across the stage to see who is at the door.*

PANDARUS How now, how now, how go Maidenheads?
  Here, you Maid; where's my Cousin Cresseid?
CRESSIDA Go hang your self, you naughty mocking
  Uncle!   25
  You bring me to do, and then you flout me too.
PANDARUS To do what? To do what? —Let her say
  what. —What have I brought you to do?
CRESSIDA Come, come, beshrew your Heart, you'll
  ne'er be good,
  Nor suffer others!
PANDARUS   Ha ha, alas poor Wretch,   30
  A poor Chipochia! Hast not slept tonight?
  Would he not (ah Naughty Man) let 't sleep?
  A Bug-bear take him!
CRESSIDA Did not I tell you? Would he were
  knock'd i' th' Head.   *One knocks.*
  Who's that at Door? —Good Uncle, go and see.   35
  —My Lord, come you again into my Chamber.
  You smile and mock me, as if I meant
  naughtily!
TROILUS Ha ha.
CRESSIDA Come, you are deceiv'd: I think of no
  such thing.   *Knock.*
  How earnestly they knock! Pray you come in: 40
  I would not for half Troy have you seen here.
                                Exit, with Troilus.
PANDARUS Who's there? What's the matter? Will
  you beat down the Door?
  How now? What's the matter?
AENEAS [*Within*] Good morrow, Lord, good morrow.   45
PANDARUS Who's there?

46   troth   *faith.*

51   It doth import him much   *it is very important to him. Here import is used with all the force of the original Latin for two related words: (a)* in + portus *(whence* importunity*), which relates to entering a portal (as Aeneas has just done, and as Troilus has earlier done in another sense) and (b)* in + portare *(whence* import*), which relates to carrying something through a portal (in this case the bad news Aeneas has for his friend Troilus).*

54   What . . . here?   *What business would he have here?*

56   ware   *both (a) aware [of what you are doing], and (b) wary [of what you should avoid doing].*

56–57   you'll . . . him   *you'll be so loyal to him that you'll end up hurting him.*

57–58   Do . . . him   *maintain your pretense that you do not know where he is.*

61   rash   *urgent, something to be rushed.*

64   forthwith   *without delay.*

68   gen'ral State   *chief counselors (in this case the ruling generals).*

He opens the Door, and Aeneas enters.

                   My Lord Aeneas. By my troth,
    I knew you not. What News with you so early?
AENEAS   Is not Prince Troilus here?
PANDARUS   Here, what should he do here?
AENEAS   Come, he is here, my Lord; do not deny him;   50
    It doth import him much to speak with me.
PANDARUS   Is he here, say you? 'Tis more than I
    know, I'll be sworn. For my own part, I came
    in late. What should he do here?
AENEAS   Who, nay then! Come, come, you'll do him   55
    wrong ere you are ware: you'll be so true to
    him to be false to him. Do not you know of
    him, but yet go fetch him hither; go.

Enter Troilus.

TROILUS   How now, what's the matter?
AENEAS   My Lord, I scarce have Leisure to salute
    you,   60
    My Matter is so rash. There is at hand
    Paris your Brother, and Deiphobus,
    The Grecian Diomed, and our Antenor
    Deliver'd to us, and for him forthwith,
    Ere the first Sacrifice, within this Hour,   65
    We must give up to Diomedes' hand
    The Lady Cresseida.
TROILUS   Is 't so concluded?
AENEAS   By Priam and the gen'ral State of Troy;
    They are at hand, and ready to effect it.

70 **my Achievements** *what I have labored so hard to achieve. Troilus is probably thinking of all the effort he has expended to woo Cressida. He may also be recalling his role in the Trojan Council (II.ii), where he helped persuade his fellow Trojans to continue the war by refusing to return Helen to the Greeks. If the Trojans had ended the war then, Troilus would not be forced to surrender Cressida to the Greeks now. From this point on in the play, both Troilus and Cressida are required to make their choices in a political context that puts individuals largely at the mercy of forces beyond their control.*

72 **We met by chance** *What Troilus means is that Aeneas is to provide corroboration for Troilus' alibi.*

74 **Gift in Taciturnity** *talent for keeping silent.*

76 **the young Prince** *The only person Pandarus seems to be concerned about is his client Troilus. Neither here nor elsewhere in the scene does he indicate any understanding of or sympathy for his Niece and the plight she faces.*

92 **chang'd** *exchanged. But the more usual meaning of* chang'd *will also prove applicable.*

94 **Bane** *poison.*

TROILUS   How my Achievements mock me!   70
     I will go meet them. And, my Lord Aeneas,
     We met by chance: you did not find me here.
AENEAS   Good, good, my Lord: the Secrets of
     neighbor Pandar
     Have not more Gift in Taciturnity.   *Exit with Troilus.*
PANDARUS   Is't possible? No sooner got but lost!   75
     The Divel take Antenor; the young Prince will
     go mad; a Plague upon Antenor! I would they
     had broke 's Neck!

                    Enter Cressida.

CRESSIDA   How now? What's the matter? Who was
     here?
PANDARUS   Ah, ah!   80
CRESSIDA   Why sigh you so profoundly? Where's my
     Lord?
     Gone? Tell me, sweet Uncle, what's the matter?
PANDARUS   Would I were as deep under the Earth
     as I am above.
CRESSIDA   O the Gods! What's the matter?   85
PANDARUS   Pray thee get thee in: would thou hadst
     ne'er been born! I knew thou would'st be his
     Death! O poor Gentleman! A Plague upon Antenor!
CRESSIDA   Good Uncle, I beseech you on my Knees,
     what's the matter?   90
PANDARUS   Thou must be gone, Wench; thou must be
     gone. Thou art chang'd for Antenor. Thou must
     to thy Father and be gone from Troilus: 'twill
     be his Death, 'twill be his Bane; he cannot

99   I know . . . Consanguinity   *I feel no sense of blood relationship with him.*

107   Drawing all things to it   *Cressida appears to be referring to gravity. The laws of universal gravitation were not formulated until the 1660s, when Isaac Newton made the great discoveries that established his name in the annals of science, but a less systematic understanding of magnetic forces was available to Shakespeare and his contemporaries. What Cressida means here is that the foundations of her love are so deep that they go to the very core of the globe.*

111   sounding   *speaking the name of. But Cressida may also be playing on two other meanings: (a) sounding the depth of (a nautical term, and here one that relates to lines 106–7), and (b) swooning over the loss of (*swounding, *swooning, is often spelled* sounding *in Shakespeare's texts).*

		95
CRESSIDA	O you immortal Gods, I will not go!	
PANDARUS	Thou must.	
CRESSIDA	I will not, Uncle. I have forgot my	

Father;

I know no touch of Consanguinity;

No Kin, no Love, no Blood, no Soul so near me   100

As the sweet Troilus. —O you Gods divine,

Make Cresseid's Name the very Crown of

Falsehood

If ever she leave Troilus. —Time, Force, and

Death,

Do to this Body what Extremes you can;

But the strong Base and Building of my Love   105

Is as the very Center of the Earth,

Drawing all things to it. I'll go in and weep.

PANDARUS   Do, do.

CRESSIDA   Tear my bright Hair, and scratch my

praised Cheeks;

Crack my clear Voice with Sobs, and break my

Heart   110

With sounding "Troilus": I will not go from

Troy!   *Exeunt.*

IV.iii *This brief scene takes place just outside the house of Cressida.*

1 great Morning *full day (compare the French* grand jour*).*

3 Comes fast upon *comes quickly, is now upon us.*

11 as I shall Pity *as much as I shall commiserate.*

Scene 3

Enter Paris, Troilus, Aeneas, Deiphobus,
Antenor, Diomedes.

PARIS   It is great Morning, and the Hour prefix'd
For her Deliv'ry to this valiant Greek
Comes fast upon. —Good my brother Troilus,
Tell you the Lady what she is to do,
And haste her to the Purpose.
TROILUS   Walk into her House.   5
I'll bring her to the Grecian presently;
And to his Hand when I deliver her,
Think it an Altar, and thy brother Troilus
A Priest there off'ring to it his own Heart.
PARIS   I know what 'tis to love,   10
And would, as I shall Pity, I could help.
—Please you walk in, my Lords?   *Exeunt.*

IV.iv *This scene returns us to the Cressida's chamber within the house.*

1 Be moderate *moderate your emotions; exercise self-control to keep your passions from going to extremes.*

3 fine *pure, refined.*

4 violenteth in a Sense *rages in a manner, and with a feeling.*

6 temporize with *temper, control.*
Affections *emotions.*

7 brew it to *mix it for. Here* it *refers back to* Affections *(line 6). In Shakespeare's time the treatment of number (whether in terms of pronoun reference, as here, or in terms of subject-verb agreement, as frequently elsewhere) was much looser than in modern grammar.*
a weak and colder Palate *a less intense and more dispassionate sense of taste.*

8 Allayment *reduction in intensity, mitigation.*

9 qualifying Dross *diluting impurities.*

10 precious Loss *loss of something precious.*

13 Spectacles *sights, with wordplay on* eyeglasses.

Scene 4

Enter Pandarus and Cressida.

PANDARUS   Be moderate, be moderate.
CRESSIDA   Why tell you me of Moderation?
    The Grief is fine, full, perfect that I taste,
    And violenteth in a Sense as strong
    As that which causeth it. How can I moderate
      it?   5
    If I could temporize with my Affections,
    Or brew it to a weak and colder Palate,
    The like Allayment could I give my Grief:
    My Love admits no qualifying Dross,
    No more my Grief in such a precious Loss.   10

Enter Troilus.

PANDARUS   Here, here, here he comes. —Ah sweet
    Ducks!
CRESSIDA   O Troilus, Troilus!   *She embraces him.*
PANDARUS   What a pair of Spectacles is here:
    Let me embrace too.
      "O Heart,"   15
    as th' goodly Saying is,
                "O Heart, heavy Heart,

19   he answers again   *the Heart replies.*

20   Smart   *pain.*

24   We see it   *we see the truth of it.*

25   strain'd   *both (a) refined, and (b) intense.*

26   as angry with my Fancy   *as if in revenge against the depth of my affection.*

34   Injury of Chance   *the injury inflicted by cruel Chance.*

35   justles roughly by   *shoves rudely aside.*

36   beguiles   *cheats.*

37   Rejoindure   *both (a) rejoinder (reply or rebuttal to Chance), and (b) rejoining (with each other) in a sustained kiss.*

38   Embrasures   *(a) embraces, (b) windows (in the locked position), and (c) "burnings" (from* embrase, *to set fire or enflame with passion). Like* Rejoindure, *this appears to be a Shakespearean nonce-word (coined for a single occasion) to depict the heated embraces of passionate lovers.*

39   lab'ring Breath   *both (a) the pangs of childbirth, and (b) the pants of lovemaking.*

41   poorly   *both (a) at a low price, and (b) pitiably.*

42   Discharge of one   *exhalation of one sigh. But Troilus' phrasing is a reminder that it is for the "Discharge of one" prisoner of war that this love affair must now be discharged (stolen away).*

Why sigh'st thou without breaking?"
where he answers again
   "Because thou canst not ease thy Smart   20
     By Friendship, nor by Speaking."
There was never a truer Rime. Let us cast away
nothing, for we may live to have need of such
a Verse. We see it, we see it, how now, Lambs?

TROILUS   Cressid, I love thee in so strain'd a
   Purity   25
   That the blest Gods, as angry with my Fancy,
   More bright in Zeal than the Devotion which
   Cold Lips blow to their Deities, take thee
     from me.

CRESSIDA   Have the Gods Envy?

TROILUS   Ay, ay, ay, ay, 'tis too plain a Case.   30

CRESSIDA   And is it true that I must go from Troy?

TROILUS   A hateful Truth.

CRESSIDA   What, and from Troilus too?

TROILUS   From Troy and Troilus.

CRESSIDA   Is't possible?

TROILUS   And suddenly, where Injury of Chance
   Puts back Leave-taking, justles roughly by   35
   All time of Pause, rudely beguiles our Lips
   Of all Rejoindure, forcibly prevents
   Our lock'd Embrasures, strangles our dear Vows
   Ev'n in the Birth of our own lab'ring Breath.
   We two, that with so many thousand Sighs   40
   Did buy each other, must poorly sell our
    selves
   With the rude Brev'ty and Discharge of one.
   Injurious Time now with a Robber's Haste

44   Crams his rich Thiev'ry up   *roughly shoves his stolen goods into a bag. Troilus' image recalls Ulysses' earlier portrayal of Time as an ungrateful "Monster" with "a Wallet at his Back" (III.iii.139–44).*

46   consign'd . . . them   *kisses for each one of them.*

47   fumbles . . . Adieu   *fumblingly ties together a loose grab-bag that constitutes a clumsy, hasty gesture of farewell.*

49   Distasted   *its sweet taste spoiled.*
       broken Tears   *both (a) tears of heartbreak, and (b) tears that result from Time's tearing us apart.*

51   Genius   *a person's guardian spirit.*

54   lay this Wind   *allay this wind (comparing the lovers' sighs to the gales that precede a rainstorm).*

55   blown up by my Throat   *blown by windy sighs until it threatens to come out at my throat. Here* by *can mean either "near" or "through."*

57   Merry Greeks   *Cressida is contrasting the Greeks' joviality with her sadness. But they are also "merry" in another sense (I.iii.114) that will make this line prophetic.*

60   Deem   *assumption, opinion, suspicion.*

61   use Expostulation kindly   *be kind to earnest Protestation (personified).*

65   Maculation   *spot, stain of infidelity.*

66–67   fashion . . . Protestation   *lead into my following pledge.*

Crams his rich Thiev'ry up he knows not how.
As many Farewells as be Stars in Heav'n,   45
With distinct Breath and consign'd Kisses to
    them,
He fumbles up into a loose Adieu,
And scants us with a single famish'd Kiss,
Distasted with the Salt of broken Tears.
AENEAS   [*Within*] My Lord, is the Lady ready?   50
TROILUS   —Hark, you are call'd. Some say the
    Genius so
Cries "Come" to him that instantly must die.
—Bid them have Patience: she shall come anon.
PANDARUS   Where are my Tears? Rain to lay this
    Wind,
Or my Heart will be blown up by my Throat.   *Exit.*   55
CRESSIDA   I must then to the Grecians.
TROILUS   No Remedy.
CRESSIDA   A Woeful Cressid 'mongst the Merry
    Greeks.
When shall we see again?
TROILUS   Hear me, Love: be thou but true of Heart—
CRESSIDA   I true? How now? What wicked Deem is
    this?   60
TROILUS   Nay we must use Expostulation kindly,
For it is parting from us.
I speak not "Be thou true" as fearing thee,
For I will throw my Glove to Death himself
That there's no Maculation in thy Heart,   65
But "Be thou true" say I to fashion in
My sequent Protestation: "Be thou true,
And I will see thee."

535

69–70   **O you . . . imminent.** *Cressida is referring to the dangers Troilus will incur if he arranges to visit ("see") her in the Greek camp. Her remarks recall Juliet's concerns about Romeo's safety in the Balcony Scene of* Romeo *and* Juliet *(II.ii.64–66).*

73   **corrupt** *pay bribes to.*

78   **compos'd** *combined, mixed.*

79   **Flawing and swelling o'er** *Here* flawing *is a variant of* flowing. *But at least two meanings of* flawing *are also pertinent to the fears that Troilus' sexual imagination suggests to him: (a) gusting (as with a sudden rush of wind), and (b) cracking open. Meanwhile* swelling *suggests tumescence.*

80   **Parts, with Person** *attractive gifts combined with handsome features.*

86   **mainly** *strongly.*

87   **heel the high Lavolt** *leap with abandon when dancing the lavolta (a bounding dance for two persons).*
      sweeten Talk *fill my conversation with sweet compliments.*

89   **prompt and pregnant** *apt and ready. The word* prompt *derives from the Latin* promptus, *one of whose meanings is "brought out" or "brought forward." The word* pregnant *(which literally refers to a pre-birthing condition) could relate both to the abdominal swelling of women with child and to a variety of other protuberances. The two words convey Troilus' anxiety with an almost visceral vividness.*

91   **dumb-discoursive** *unspeaking but nevertheless communicating a form of discourse.*

CRESSIDA   O you shall be expos'd, my Lord, to
      Dangers
      As infinite as imminent. But I'll be true.   70
TROILUS   And I'll grow Friend with Danger. Wear
      this Sleeve.
CRESSIDA   And you this Glove. When shall I see you?
TROILUS   I will corrupt the Grecian Sentinels
      To give thee nightly Visitation.
      But yet be true.
CRESSIDA   O Heav'ns: "be true" again?   75
TROILUS   Hear why I speak it, Love.
      The Grecian Youths are full of Quality,
      Their Loving well compos'd with Gift of Nature,
      Flawing and swelling o'er with Arts and
         Exercise;
      How Novelty may move, and Parts, with Person—   80
      Alas a kind of Godly Jealousy,
      Which I beseech you call a virtuous Sin,
      Makes me afeard.
CRESSIDA   O Heav'ns, you love me not!
TROILUS   Die I a Villain then!
      In this I do not call your Faith in question   85
      So mainly as my Merit. I cannot sing,
      Nor heel the high Lavolt, nor sweeten Talk,
      Nor play at subtle Games: fair Virtues all,
      To which the Grecians are most prompt and
         pregnant.
      But I can tell that in each Grace of these   90
      There lurks a still and dumb-discoursive Divel
      That tempts most cunningly. But be not tempted.
CRESSIDA   Do you think I will?

537

94   something . . . not   *something may happen to us that carries us beyond what we consciously will ourselves to do. Troilus echoes Romans 7:19–20.*

97   Presuming . . . Potency   *Troilus talks about yet another kind of "Surety" (II.ii.13), that which results from a person's presumption that he or she is strong enough to resist temptation. Members of Shakespeare's audience would have heard in his words an echo of the Lord's Prayer: "lead us not into temptation, but deliver us from evil" (Matthew 6:13). The phrase* changeful Potency *probably means "variable strength" (subject to periods of weakness).*

102   Fault   *flaw, weakness.*

104   mere Simplicity   *pure innocence (the opposite of "Craft," deviousness, cunning).*

105   gild their Copper Crowns   *coat copper coins with gold to make them appear to be French crowns.*

106   wear mine bare   *wear my crown (head) without a hat.*

107   Fear not   *have no concerns about.*
       my Wit   *my verbal cleverness. But in combination with words like "Fault," "Crowns," "bare," and "Reach,"* Wit *is probably meant to remind us of another male attribute that could also be said to "fish" (line 103).*

111   Port   *Troy's principal gate.*

112   by the way   *as we walk along.*
       possess   *inform.*

113   Entreat   *both (a) treat, and (b) entreat (be solicitous of her wishes).*

TROILUS   No,
    But something may be done that we will not,
    And sometimes we are Divels to our selves   95
    When we will tempt the Frailty of our Powers,
    Presuming on their changeful Potency.
AENEAS [*Within*]   Nay good my Lord!
TROILUS   —Come kiss, and let us part.
PARIS [*Within*]   Brother Troilus!
TROILUS   Good Brother, come you hither,
    And bring Aeneas and the Grecian with you.   100
CRESSIDA   My Lord, will you be true?
TROILUS   Who, I? Alas it is my Vice, my Fault.
    Whiles others fish with Craft for great
      Opinion,
    I with great Truth catch mere Simplicity;
    Whilst some with Cunning gild their Copper
      Crowns,   105
    With Truth and Plainness I do wear mine bare.
    Fear not my Truth: the Moral of my Wit
    Is "Plain and True." There's all the Reach of it.

    Enter Aeneas, Paris, Deiphobus, and Diomedes.

    —Welcome, Sir Diomed; here is the Lady
    Which for Antenor we deliver you.   110
    At the Port, Lord, I'll give her to thy Hand,
    And by the way possess thee what she is.
    Entreat her fair, and by my Soul, fair Greek,
    If e'er thou stand at mercy of my Sword,
    Name Cressid and thy Life shall be as safe   115

116   Fair Lady Cressid   *Diomed ignores Troilus and addresses Cressida directly.*

121   use   *treat.*

122   To shame the Seal of my Petition   *to scorn my request and refuse to seal it with an acknowledgment or acceptance.*

126   charge   *command.*
       e'en for my Charge   *precisely because of my command.*

127   Pluto   *God of the Underworld (here depicted as more or less equivalent to Satan in his role in the Hell of Christian theology).*

129   mov'd   *moved to anger.*

132   I'll answer to my Lust   *I'll please myself. Here* Lust *means "pleasure or will." But of course it also carries a not-very-subtle sexual threat.*

133   on Charge   *on demand.*
       To her own Worth   *in accordance with her own value.*

137   Brave   *vaunting defiance.*
       hide thy Head   *Troilus probably means both (a) in fear of reprisal, and (b) in shame and regret once that reprisal has been rendered.*

As Priam is in Ilion.

DIOMEDES   —Fair Lady Cressid,
   So please you save the Thanks this Prince
      expects:
   The Lustre in your Eye, Heav'n in your Cheek,
   Pleads your Fair Usage, and to Diomed
   You shall be Mistress and command him wholly.   120
TROILUS   Grecian, thou dost not use me courteously,
   To shame the Seal of my Petition to thee
   In praising her. I tell thee, Lord of Greece,
   She is as far high soaring o'er thy Praises
   As thou unworthy to be call'd her Servant.   125
   I charge thee use her well, ev'n for my Charge:
   For by the dreadful Pluto, if thou dost not,
   Though the great Bulk Achilles be thy Guard,
   I'll cut thy Throat.
DIOMEDES   O be not mov'd, Prince Troilus;
   Let me be privileg'd by my Place and Message   130
   To be a Speaker free. When I am hence
   I'll answer to my Lust; and know you, Lord,
   I'll nothing do on Charge. To her own Worth
   She shall be priz'd; but that you say "Be't
      so,"
   I speak it in my Spir't and Honor, "No."   135
TROILUS   Come to the Port. I'll tell thee, Diomed,
   This Brave shall oft make thee to hide thy
      Head.
   —Lady give me your Hand, and as we walk
   To our own selves bend we our needful Talk.
                  Exeunt Troilus, Cressida, and Diomedes.
                                Sound Trumpet.

140   How . . . Morning!   *How the time has flown this morning!*

141   remiss   *neglectful, irresponsible.*

143   'Tis Troilus' Fault.   *In view of all that Troilus has sacrificed for him, Paris' comment here is appallingly insensitive.*

146   tend on Hector's Heels   *wait on Hector as his faithful servants.*

148   single Chivalry   *the man-to-man combat resulting from Hector's challenge to the Greeks in I.iii.*

IV.v   *We now move to the Greek camp for the long-awaited joust between Hector and Aiax.*

1   Appointment   *knightly accoutrements.*

2   Anticipating Time   *ahead of schedule.*
   With starting Courage   *with a spirit that will rouse the Trojans.*

4   appauled   *appalled; terrified, made pale.*

6   hale   *both (a) call, and (b) haul.*
   Trumpet   *trumpeter.*
   my Purse   *Aiax hands him a bag of money.*

7   brazen   *both (a) brass, and (b) defiant.*

8   sphered Bias Cheek   *Aiax compares the trumpeter's cheek to a bowl, a bowling ball with a bias (off-center weight) to make it curve as it rolls toward its destination.*

PARIS   Hark, Hector's Trumpet!

AENEAS   How have we spent this Morning!   140
  The Prince must think me tardy and remiss,
  That swore to ride before him to the Field.

PARIS   'Tis Troilus' Fault. Come, come to Field
    with him.

DIEPHOBUS   Let us make ready straight.

AENEAS   Yea, with a Bridegroom's fresh Alacrity,   145
  Let us address to tend on Hector's Heels.
  The Glory of our Troy doth this Day lie
  On his fair Worth and single Chivalry.   *Exeunt.*

Scene 5

Enter Aiax armed, Achilles, Patroclus, Agamemnon,
Menelaus, Ulysses, Nestor, Calchas, etc.

AGAMEMNON   Here art thou, in Appointment fresh
    and fair,
  Anticipating Time. With starting Courage
  Give with thy Trumpet a loud Note to Troy,
  Thou dreadful Aiax, that th' appauled Air
  May pierce the Head of the great Combatant   5
  And hale him hither.

AIAX   Thou Trumpet, there's my Purse:
  Now crack thy Lungs and split thy brazen Pipe.
  Blow, Villain, till thy sphered Bias Cheek

543

9   Colic of puff'd Aquilon   *the flatulent cheeks of the swelled-up God of the North Wind (the Greek deity corresponding to Boreas, the same God in the Roman Pantheon).*

12   Early Days   *early in the morning. Achilles' line would seem to support the Quarto reading for II.i.134, "That Hector by the first hour of the Sun" will summon the Greeks with a trumpet.*

14   ken   *recognize.*

16   Aspiration   *Ulysses' description of Diomed's "Aspiration" (ascending ambition) suggests that his lifting "Spir't" is not limited to his rising "Toe."*

20   Particular   *singular, individual; literally, limited to but one part (member) of the council of generals. But compare II.ii.9 for an additional implication.*

21   in General   *both (a) generally, and (b) by all the generals.*

24   Winter   *Achilles alludes to Nestor's frosty (white-haired) age; his implication is that after kissing Nestor, Cressida's lips are covered with icicles.*

26   Argument   *case, justification. But in line 29 Patroclus uses the word to refer to a more physical kind of "case." For similar implications, compare I.i.95 and II.iii.82.*

28   Hardiment   *a medieval term for a chivalric deed of daring (hardihood), and here a reference as well to the tumescent "weapon" that Paris used to "pop" into the breach of Menelaus' "Argument."*

29   parted   *separated, but with wordplay on (a) private parts, and (b) partitions (formal divisions of a rhetorical argument).*

544

Out-swell the Colic of puff'd Aquilon.
Come stretch thy Chest, and let thy Eyes spout
    Blood: 10
Thou blowest for Hector. *Sound Trumpet.*
ULYSSES No Trumpet answers.
ACHILLES   'Tis but Early Days.

Enter Diomed and Cressida.

AGAMEMNON Is not yond Diomed with Calchas'
    Daughter?
ULYSSES 'Tis he, I ken the manner of his Gait:
He rises on the Toe. That Spir't of his 15
In Aspiration lifts him from the Earth.
AGAMEMNON Is this the Lady Cressid?
DIOMED   Even she.
AGAMEMNON Most dearly welcome to the Greeks,
    sweet Lady. *He kisses her.*
NESTOR Our Gen'ral doth salute you with a Kiss.
ULYSSES Yet is the Kindness but Particular: 20
'Twere better she were kiss'd in General.
NESTOR And very courtly Counsel. I'll begin;
He kisses her.   So much for Nestor.
ACHILLES I'll take that Winter from your Lips,
    fair Lady:
Achilles bids you welcome. *He kisses her.* 25
MENELAUS I had good Argument for Kissing once.
PATROCLUS But that's no Argument for Kissing now.
For thus popp'd Paris in his Hardiment
And parted thus you and your Argument.
                     He kisses her.

31   to gild his Horns   *to coat the horns of this cuckold with gold.*

33   Trim   *fine, dandy (spoken with sarcasm).*

34   Paris . . . him.   *Just as Paris kisses Helen for Menelaus, so I now kiss Cressida.*

37   Both take and give.   *Patroclus answers for Menelaus, indicating that, as befits a cuckold, he both takes what Paris dishes out to him and gives Helen to another man. This is not strictly true, of course (Menelaus has an entire army fighting to win back his wife), but Patroclus obviously feels that he can jest freely.*
      I'll . . . live.   *Cressida seems to be saying that she will wager her life on her "Match." In the following lines she also appears to imply that she will offer herself only to someone who is man enough to win, hold, and defend her.*

38   The Kiss you take   *Cressida probably means Paris' kiss (taking Helen).*

40   I'll . . . One.   *Menelaus boasts that he will give Cressida a bonus for a kiss: a child to result from the proposed union of two into one.*

41   Odd Man   *Cressida refers to Menelaus' play on* One *(with phallic innuendo) and* Three, *both odd numbers. But she probably also uses* Odd *to mean "deformed" (horned) and "at odds" (as yet unavenged for an injury).*
      give Even   *This probably means "give as good as you get, get even" (as explained in line 44), or "start acting like a man."*

45   fillip me a' th' Head   *flip your fingernail against my head.*

ULYSSES   O deadly Gall, and Theme of all our
          Scorns,   30
     For which we lose our Heads to gild his Horns!
PATROCLUS   The first was Menelaus' Kiss, this mine;
     Patroclus kisses you.   *He kisses her.*
MENELAUS   O this is Trim.
PATROCLUS   Paris and I kiss evermore for him.
MENELAUS   I'll have my Kiss, Sir. —Lady, by your
     Leave.   35
CRESSIDA   In Kissing do you render or receive?
PATROCLUS   Both take and give.
CRESSIDA   I'll make my Match to live.
     The Kiss you take is better than you give:
     Therefore no Kiss.
MENELAUS   I'll give you Boot, I'll give you Three
     for One.   40
CRESSIDA   You are an Odd Man: give Even or give
     None.
MENELAUS   An Odd Man, Lady? Ev'ry Man is Odd.
CRESSIDA   No, Paris is not: for you know 'tis true
     That you are Odd, and he is Ev'n with you.
MENELAUS   You fillip me a' th' Head.
CRESSIDA   No, I'll be sworn.   45
ULYSSES   It were no Match, your Nail against his
     Horn.
     —May I, sweet Lady, beg a Kiss of you?
CRESSIDA   You may.
ULYSSES   I do desire it.
CRESSIDA   Why beg then.
ULYSSES   Why then for Venus' sake give me a Kiss
     When Helen is a Maid again and his—   50

547

52 **Never's my Day** *Ulysses' conditions, impossible to fulfill, make it clear that he has no interest in participating in this wanton piece of "Match-making" other than as a cynical observer with contempt for a woman who would act so "merry" on her first introduction to a group of randy Greek officers.*

54 **quick Sense** *Nestor probably means both (a) lively wit, and (b) an active sensual appetite.*

55 **Language** *nonverbal communication.*

57 **Motive** *motion, moving part.*

58 **Encounterers** *"greeters" (with the same innuendo as in the reference to* **Encounters** *in III.ii.219).*

59 **a Coasting** *an accosting, a cruising approach (as from a ship that sidles up and would "fain lay Knife aboard," as the Nurse puts it in* **Romeo and Juliet,** *II.iv.211).*

60 **unclasp the Tables** *open the tablets.*

61 **ticklish** *both (a) readily aroused, and (b) eager to arouse. Ulysses' adjective picks up on the implications in Pandarus' song about tickling (III.i.120–34).*

62 **Spoils of Opportunity** *almost literally, pickups (like the spoils of a battle or hunt); women who are available for any occasion.*

65 **State of Greece** *commanding leaders.*

67 **A Victor shall be known** *one knight shall be determined to be the victor (as opposed to the lone survivor of a fight to the death).*

69 **divided** *separated; required to cease fighting.*

CRESSIDA   I am your Debtor, claim it when 'tis Due.
ULYSSES   Never's my Day, and then a Kiss of you.
DIOMEDES   Lady, a word: I'll bring you to your
    Father.   *Exit, with Cressida.*
NESTOR   A Woman of quick Sense.
ULYSSES   Fie, fie upon her,
   There's Language in her Eye, her Cheek, her
     Lip;   55
   Nay her Foot speaks, her wanton Spir'ts look
     out
   At ev'ry Joint and Motive of her Body.
   O these Encounterers, so glib of Tongue,
   That give a Coasting welcome ere it comes
   And wide unclasp the Tables of their Thoughts   60
   To ev'ry ticklish Reader; set them down
   For sluttish Spoils of Opportunity
   And Daughters of the Game.

*Flourish. Enter all of Troy: Hector, Paris,
Aeneas, Helenus, Troilus, and Attendants.*

ALL   The Troians' Trumpet.
AGAMEMNON   Yonder comes the Troop.
AENEAS   —Hail all the State of Greece. What shall
    be done   65
   To him that Victory commands? Or do you purpose
   A Victor shall be known? Will you the Knights
   Shall to the Edge of all Extremity
   Pursue each other, or shall they be divided
   By any Voice or Order of the Field?   70
   Hector bade ask.

72   **obey Conditions**   *abide by the terms agreed upon.*

73   **securely**   *overconfidently, with a false sense of invulnerability.*

74   **misprizing**   *underestimating.*

78   **In the Extremity of Great and Little**   *at the extreme ends of the spectrum extending from the largest to the smallest. Hector's image recalls Ulysses' figure of speech in I.iii.167–68.*

80   **The one**   *Valor.*

87   **Maiden Battle**   *Achilles probably means a sportive combat without rancor or bloodshed, like a fight between two maidens. His words imply scorn for a combat he regards as a frivolous game for sissies.*

90   **the Order of their Fight**   *the nature of the combat and the rules to be applied to it.*

91   **to the Uttermost**   *to the death.*

AGAMEMNON   Which way would Hector have it?
AENEAS   He cares not; he'll obey Conditions.
AGAMEMNON   'Tis done like Hector, but securely
      done,
   A little proudly, and great deal misprizing
   The Knight oppos'd.
AENEAS   —If not Achilles, Sir,   75
   What is your Name?
ACHILLES   If not Achilles, nothing.
AENEAS   Therefore Achilles. But what e'er, know
      this:
   In the Extremity of Great and Little,
   Valor and Pride excel themselves in Hector,
   The one almost as Infinite as All,   80
   The other Blank as Nothing. Weigh him well,
   And that which looks like Pride is Courtesy.
   This Aiax is half made of Hector's Blood,
   In love whereof half Hector stays at home:
   Half Heart, half Hand, half Hector comes to
      seek   85
   This blended Knight, half Troian and half
      Greek.
ACHILLES   A Maiden Battle then: O I perceive you.

Re-enter Diomedes.

AGAMEMNON   Here is Sir Diomed. —Go, gentle
      Knight,
   Stand by our Aiax. As you and Lord Aeneas
   Consent upon the Order of their Fight,   90
   So be it, either to the Uttermost

92   a Breath   *a competition for exercise and sport.*

93   stints   *impedes, stops.*

94   oppos'd   *in their positions facing one another in the lists (the area enclosed for a tilting tournament).*

98   Speaking . . . Tongue   *allowing his deeds to speak for him, and not speaking defiantly and boastfully.*

100   Free   *frank, honest, generous.*

103   impare   *unconsidered or unworthy.*

105–6   subscribes / To Tender Objects   *allows himself to be swayed by feelings of tenderness. Once again Hector is faulted for his lack of what today would be called the killer instinct.*

107   Vindicative   *vindictive, vengeful.*

111   to his Inches   *to the last detail. Whether this phrase and "erect" (line 108) are meant to relate to Troilus' manhood in a sense having to do with his "Jealous Love" (line 107) is not clear.*
        with private Soul   *confidentially, privately.*

112   translate him to me   *communicate (interpret) to me his virtues.*

115   well dispos'd   *well placed, to good effect.*

Or else a Breath; the Combatants being kin
Half stints their Strife before their Strokes
   begin.

ULYSSES   They are oppos'd already.

AGAMEMNON   What Troian is that same that looks so
   heavy?   95

ULYSSES   The youngest Son of Priam; a true Knight,
Not yet mature, yet matchless firm of Word;
Speaking Deeds, and Deedless in his Tongue;
Not soon provok'd, nor, being provok'd, soon
   calm'd;
His Heart and Hand both Open and both Free;   100
For what he has he gives; what thinks, he shows;
Yet gives he not till Judgment guide his Bounty,
Nor dignifies an impare Thought with Breath;
Manly as Hector, but more Dangerous,
For Hector in his Blaze of Wrath subscribes   105
To Tender Objects, but he in Heat of Action
Is more Vindicative than Jealous Love.
They call him Troilus, and on him erect
A second Hope as fairly built as Hector.
Thus says Aeneas, one that knows the Youth   110
Ev'n to his Inches, and with private Soul
Did in great Ilion thus translate him to me.

Alarum. Hector and Aiax fight.

AGAMEMNON   They are in Action.

NESTOR   —Now Aiax, hold thine own!

TROILUS   Hector, thou sleep'st; awake thee!

AGAMEMNON   His Blows are well dispos'd: there
   Aiax!   115

S.D.   Trumpets cease.   *Trumpets signal an end to the combat.*

120   Cousin German   *first cousin.*
Seed   *offspring.*

122   a gory Emulation   *a bloody battle motivated by mutual rivalry and hate.*

123   Commixtion   *mixture.*
so   *such, in such a way.*

124   Grecian all   *entirely Grecian.*

127   dexter   *right.*
sinister   *left. It is perhaps significant that Hector attributes the sinister side to Aiax's Greek patrimony. In addition to its root meaning,* sinister *also meant "evil" or "ill-omened." In this line the word is to be accented on the second syllable.*

128   multipotent   *all-powerful.*

130   Impressure   *impression.*

131   rank Feud   *uncontrolled combat.*

132   Drop   *drop of blood.*

135   him that thunders   *Zeus, Jove.*

138   Free   *generous, magnanimous.*

140   Addition   *title, addition to my honor.*

DIOMEDES   You must no more.
AENEAS   Princes, enough so please you.
AIAX   I am not warm yet: let us fight again.
DIOMEDES   As Hector pleases.
HECTOR   Why then will I no more.
   —Thou art, great Lord, my Father's Sister's Son,
   A Cousin German to great Priam's Seed.   120
   The Obligation of our Blood forbids
   A gory Emulation 'twixt us Twain.
   Were thy Commixtion Greek and Troian, so
   That thou couldst say "This Hand is Grecian all
   And this is Troian, the Sinews of this Leg   125
   All Greek, and this all Troy, my Mother's Blood
   Runs on the dexter Cheek, and this sinister
   Bounds in my Father's," by Jove multipotent,
   Thou shouldst not bear from me a Greekish
     Member
   Wherein my Sword had not Impressure made   130
   Of our rank Feud. But the just Gods gainsay
   That any Drop thou borrow'dst from thy Mother,
   My sacred Aunt, should by my mortal Sword
   Be drain'd. Let me embrace thee, Aiax.
                        He embraces him.
   By him that thunders, thou hast lusty Arms!   135
   Hector would have them fall upon him thus.
   Cousin, all Honor to thee.
AIAX   I thank thee, Hector.
   Thou art too Gentle and too Free a Man;
   I came to kill thee, Cousin, and bear hence
   A great Addition earned in thy Death.   140

555

141   Neoptolymous   *possibly a reference to Achilles' as-yet-young
       son Pyrrhus Neoptolemus (prophesied to be the key to a Greek
       victory over the Trojans). But it has also been suggested that
       the name was applied to Achilles himself, on the assumption
       that Neoptolemus was a family name.*
       mirable   *admirable, to be marveled at.*

142   O yes   *acclaim. Hector echoes* oyez *(hear ye!), the call of the
       town crier and the court bailiff.*

145   Expectance   *expectation, an eagerness to learn the outcome
       ("Issue").*

149   seld   *seldom.*
       desire   *invite, request a visit from.*

154   this Loving Interview   *this friendly conversation.*

156   Desire them home   *request that they depart.*

160   for   *as concerns.*

161   portly   *imposing. The word was yet to be limited to its present
       meaning (overweight).*

162   Worthy all Arms   *worthy to be embraced by all who bear
       arms.*

162–   as welcome . . . Enemy   *This greeting can be interpreted
63   in various ways, among them (a) as welcome as is possible for
       one (Agamemnon) who would have so formidable an enemy
       killed, and (b) as welcome as would be a warrior on our side
       who pledged himself to rid us of an enemy such as yourself.*

HECTOR   Not Neoptolymous so mirable,
    On whose bright Crest Fame with her loud'st
        "O yes"
    Cries "This is he," could promise to himself
    A thought of added Honor torn from Hector.
AENEAS   There is Expectance here from both the
        Sides: 145
    What further will you do?
HECTOR   We'll answer it:
    The Issue is Embracement. —Aiax, farewell.
AIAX   If I might in Entreaties find Success,
    As seld I have the Chance, I would desire
    My famous Cousin to our Grecian Tents.   150
DIOMEDES   'Tis Agamemnon's Wish, and great
        Achilles
    Doth long to see unarm'd the valiant Hector.
HECTOR   Aeneas, call my brother Troilus to me,
    And signify this Loving Interview
    To the Expecters of our Troian part;   155
    Desire them home. —Give me thy Hand, my Cousin:
    I will go eat with thee, and see your Knights.

Agamemnon and the rest step forward.

AIAX   Great Agamemnon comes to meet us here.
HECTOR   The Worthiest of them tell me Name by
        Name:
    But for Achilles, my own searching Eyes   160
    Shall find him by his large and portly Size.
AGAMEMNON   Worthy all Arms, as welcome as to one
    That would be rid of such an Enemy!

557

166 formless Ruin of Oblivion *a shapeless heap of things for-gotten.*

167 extant *standing, present.*

168 Strain'd . . . drawing *sorted out from all the hollow husks that might bias one's judgment. Compare I.iii.26–30 and III.ii.176.*

169 Integrity *oneness, unadulterated sincerity.*

171 imperious *imperial, kingly.*

174 Brace *pair, couple (referring to Hector and Aiax).*

175 Who must we answer? *To whom am I speaking now?*

176 By Mars his Gauntlet *by the glove of the God of War. Hector hints at a famous episode in which Mars and Venus, the adulterous wife of Vulcan, were caught in a net and displayed to all the Gods by Venus' angry cuckold. Ovid told the story in* Metamorphoses, *Book IV.*

177 affect . . . Oath *use an oath that is not yet overworn.*

178 Your . . . Glove *your former wife is still a devotee of Venus.* Quondom *(by its sound) and* Venus' Glove *(by its shape) allude to the "Argument" (line 29) at the root of the war.*

183 Destiny *immortal fame.*

185 Perseus *a mythical hero who slew the snake-haired Medusa.*

186 Despising . . . Subduements *disdaining the chance to kill or capture many warriors who have been subdued by your sword in battle.*

558

But that's no Welcome: understand more clear,
What's past and what's to come is strew'd with
   Husks 165
And formless Ruin of Oblivion;
But in this extant Moment, Faith and Troth,
Strain'd purely from all hollow Bias drawing,
Bids thee with most Divine Integrity,
From Heart of very Heart, great Hector,
   Welcome. 170
HECTOR   I thank thee, most imperious Agamemnon.
AGAMEMNON   —My well-fam'd Lord of Troy, no less
   to you.
MENELAUS   Let me confirm my princely Brother's
   Greeting:
You Brace of warlike Brothers, welcome hether.
HECTOR   Who must we answer?
AENEAS   The noble Menelaus. 175
HECTOR   O you, my Lord. By Mars his Gauntlet,
   thanks.
Mock not that I affect th' untraded Oath:
Your quondam Wife swears still by Venus' Glove,
She's well, but bade me not commend her to you.
MENELAUS   Name her not now, Sir: she's a deadly
   Theme. 180
HECTOR   O pardon, I offend.
NESTOR   I have, thou gallant Troian, seen thee oft,
Laboring for Destiny, make cruel Way
Through ranks of Greekish Youth, and I have
   seen thee,
As hot as Perseus, spur thy Phrygian Steed, 185
Despising many Forfeits and Subduements,

187   advanced   *poised, uplifted. Compare the description of "Pyrrhus' Pause" in the Player's Speech of* Hamlet *(II.ii.513–27).*

188   decline on the Declined   *fall on the fallen.*

189   some my Standers-by   *some of those who stood by me.*

190   Lo Jupiter . . . Life   *Behold, Jupiter the thunder-bearer is there meting out mercy rather than judgment (death).*

192   shrupp'd   *a variant of* shraped, *enclosed, trapped. Most editors follow the Folio and print* hemm'd.

193   Like an Olympian Wrastling   *as in an Olympian wrestling match.*

194   Countenance   *face.*
       still lock'd in Steel   *heretofore always enclosed in armor.*

195   Grandsire   *Laodemon.*

198   like thee   *It is not clear whether Nestor means "as valiant as thee" or "as civilized (magnanimous and merciful) as thee"; both would fit the context, and both may be implicit in his remarks.*

201   Chronicle   *Once Hector learns Nestor's identity from Aeneas (line 200), he embraces him as if he were the very embodiment of history, the past personified.*

208   I have seen the Time   *Nestor means "I have seen the time when I could have contended with you in battle." But here his words also have a more general application: "I have seen the glory days of old, and I live to bear witness to them."*

When thou hast hung thy advanced Sword i' th'
    Air,
Not letting it decline on the Declined,
That I have said to some my Standers-by,
"Lo Jupiter is yonder dealing Life."   190
And I have seen thee pause and take thy Breath
When that a Ring of Greeks have shrupp'd thee
    in
Like an Olympian Wrastling. This have I seen,
But this thy Countenance, still lock'd in Steel,
I never saw till now. I knew thy Grandsire   195
And once fought with him; he was a Soldier
    good,
But by great Mars the Captain of us all,
Never like thee. O let an Old Man embrace
    thee,
And worthy Warrior, welcome to our Tents.
AENEAS   'Tis the old Nestor.   200
HECTOR   Let me embrace thee, good old Chronicle,
    That hast so long walk'd Hand in Hand with
        Time:
    Most rev'rend Nestor, I am glad to clasp thee.
NESTOR   I would my Arms could match thee in
        Contention
    As they contend with thee in Courtesy.   205
HECTOR   I would they could.
NESTOR   Ha?
    By this White Beard, I'd fight with thee
        tomorrow.
    Well, welcome, welcome; I have seen the Time.

210 Base *foundation.*

211 Favor *here, both (a) face, and (b) favorable manner.*

214 your Greekish Embassy *Hector alludes to an occasion near the beginning of the war when, after capturing Tenedos from the Trojans, the Greeks sent Ulysses and Diomedes to Troy to offer peace if the Trojans would surrender Helen.*

217 pertly front *cheekily (over-confidently) stand in front of.*

218 wanton *heedlessly secure.*
buss *kiss. Ulysses' image carries the suggestion that Troy's proud "Tow'rs" are symbolic embodiments of another kind of wanton erection that will prove to be the city's undoing.*

219 must not *am unable to.*

220 modestly *in all modesty (trying not to be boastful).*

222 The End crowns all *a proverb more or less equivalent to "Time will tell." End and all are words that frequently have genital implications in Shakespeare (as in Sir Toby Belch's promise "if thou hast her not i' th' End, call me Cut," in* Twelfth Night, *II.iii.202–3), and it may well be that members of Shakespeare's audience would have found Hector's phrasing ironically pertinent, coming as it does from the champion of a city distinguished for its "wanton Tops" (line 218).*

228 forestall *intercept, prevent.*

231 quoted *noted; often spelled, and probably pronounced, coted.*

ULYSSES   I wonder now how yonder City stands
      When we have here her Base and Pillar by us?   210
HECTOR   I know your Favor, Lord Ulysses, well.
      Ah Sir, there's many a Greek and Troian dead
      Since first I saw your self and Diomed
      In Ilion on your Greekish Embassy.
ULYSSES   Sir, I foretold you then what would ensue.   215
      My Proph'cy is but half his Journey yet,
      For yonder Walls that pertly front your Town,
      Yon Tow'rs, whose wanton Tops do buss the
         Clouds,
      Must kiss their own Feet.
HECTOR   I must not believe you:
      There they stand yet, and modestly I think   220
      The Fall of ev'ry Phrygian Stone will cost
      A Drop of Grecian Blood. The End crowns all,
      And that old common Arbitrator Time
      Will one Day end it.
ULYSSES   So to him we leave it.
      Most gentle and most valiant Hector, welcome.   225
      After the Gen'ral, I beseech you next
      To feast with me, and see me at my Tent.
ACHILLES   I shall forestall thee, Lord Ulysses,
         thou.
      —Now Hector, I have fed mine Eyes on thee,
      I have with exact View perus'd thee, Hector,   230
      And quoted Joint by Joint.
HECTOR   Is this Achilles?
ACHILLES   I am Achilles.
HECTOR   Stand fair, I pray thee: let me look on
         thee.

236   Lim   *both (a) limb, member (with particular reference to the arms and legs), and (b) line, countour (as it might be depicted by an artist limning—drawing or painting—a human form).*

237   a Book of Sport   *either (a) a book to be read for sport, pleasure, or (b) a book explaining the rules of a sport (such as the fencing manuals that were so popular in the Renaissance).*

239   oppress me   *press in upon me.*

242   give . . . Name   *Achilles' phrasing recalls Duke Theseus' definition of the Poet as a person who gives "to airy Nothing / A local Habitation and a Name"* (A Midsummer Night's Dream, *V.i.16–17*).

243   make distinct   *define with precision.*

243–   the very Breach . . . flew   *the exact wound from out of*
44   *which Hector's life fled his body. This sentence echoes Mark Antony's funeral oration, where he links each stab mark to a particular conspirator in* Julius Caesar, *III.ii.176–92.*

246   Stand again   *This probably means "stand back again." Apparently Achilles has moved in on Hector to point to particular spots as potential wounds.*

247   pleasantly   *pleasurably (sportingly, without effort).*

248   prenominate   *identify in advance.*
        in nice Conjecture   *with fastidious precision, as if with a detailed blueprint.*

253   stithi'd Mars his Helm   *forged Mars's helmet. Hector audaciously (and perhaps hubristically) swears by the forge of Vulcan, blacksmith of the Gods and prototype of cuckolds.*

ACHILLES   Behold thy fill.

HECTOR   Nay I have done already.

ACHILLES   Thou art too brief: I will the second
    time,   235
  As I would buy thee, view thee Lim by Lim.

HECTOR   O like a Book of Sport thou'lt read me
    o'er.
  But there's more in me than thou understand'st.
  Why doost thou so oppress me with thine Eye?

ACHILLES   —Tell me, you Heav'ns, in which part of
    his Body   240
  Shall I destroy him? Whether there, or there, or
    there,
  That I may give the local Wound a Name,
  And make distinct the very Breach whereout
  Hector's great Spirit flew. Answer me, Heavens.

HECTOR   It would discredit the blest Gods, Proud
    Man,   245
  To answer such a Question. Stand again:
  Think'st thou to catch my Life so pleasantly
  As to prenominate in nice Conjecture
  Where thou wilt hit me dead?

ACHILLES   I tell thee Yea.

HECTOR   Wert thou an Oracle to tell me so,   250
  I'd not believe thee. Henceforth guard thee
    well,
  For I'll not kill thee there, nor there, nor
    there,
  But by the Forge that stithi'd Mars his Helm,
  I'll kill thee ev'ry where, yea o'er and o'er.
  —You wisest Grecians, pardon me this Brag: 255

565

256   Folly   *Hector dimly recognizes that he may have overstepped his bounds with this "Brag."*

258   chafe   *fret with irritation.*

259   let these Threats alone   *set those threats aside.*

260   Accident   *the chance of battle.*

262   If you have Stomach   *Aiax is reminding Achilles that he will have plenty of opportunity to fight Hector if he will simply return to action. Here* Stomach *probably means "appetite" primarily, though it is conceivable that Aiax is also calling Achilles' courage into question.*
     The Gen'ral State   *the council of generals.*

263   entreat   *beg, persuade.*
     be odd with him   *oppose him, be at odds with him. Compare Cressida's comments to Menelaus in lines 41–44.*

265   pelting   *paltry, insignificant.*
     refus'd   *renounced, trashed.*

267   fell   *fierce, terrifying.*

270   convive   *feast and carouse (literally, live) together.*

272   entreat   *both (a) invite, and (b) treat (to hospitality).*

273   Tab'rins   *taborins, drums.*

280   bent   *inclining of the eyes.*

His Insolence draws Folly from my Lips,
But I'll endeavor Deeds to match these Words,
Or may I never—
AIAX   Do not chafe thee, Cousin.
—And you, Achilles, let these Threats alone
Till Accident or Purpose bring you to 't.   260
You may have ev'ry Day enough of Hector
If you have Stomach. The Gen'ral State, I fear,
Can scarce entreat you to be odd with him.
HECTOR   I pray you, let us see you in the Field:
We have had pelting Wars since you refus'd   265
The Grecians' Cause.
ACHILLES   Dost thou entreat me, Hector?
Tomorrow do I meet thee fell as Death,
Tonight all Friends.
HECTOR   Thy Hand upon that Match.
AGAMEMNON   First, all you Peers of Greece, go to
    my Tent;
There in the full convive we. Afterwards   270
As Hector's Leisure and your Bounties shall
Concur together, sev'rally entreat him.
—Beat loud the Tab'rins, let the Trumpets
    blow,
That this great Soldier may his Welcome know.
                    Exeunt all but Troilus and Ulysses.
TROILUS   My Lord Ulysses, tell me, I beseech you,   275
In what place of the Field doth Calchas keep?
ULYSSES   At Menelaus' Tent, most princely Troilus.
There Diomed doth feast with him tonight,
Who neither looks upon the Heav'n nor Earth
But gives all gaze and bent of Am'rous View   280

567

282   **bound**   *indebted, pledged.*

285   **gentle**   *courteously, in keeping with the behavior expected of a man of gentle birth.*

289   **A Mock is due**   *ridicule is the deserved reward. Troilus declines to claim Cressida as his lover, implying that it is modesty that prevents him from displaying his "Scars" in the way a boastful soldier would brag about the wounds he has suffered in battle. His words echo the exchange we have just heard, with Troilus taking care not to tempt "Fortune's Tooth" in the way that Achilles and Hector have done.*

290   **she is, and dooth**   *she is loved, and doth still love.*

291   **still**   *always.*
    Food for Fortune's Tooth   *subject to the whims of Fortune, which can devour one's happiness in a single instant.*

On the fair Cresseid.

TROILUS   Shall I, sweet Lord, be bound to you so
        much,
    After we part from Agamemnon's Tent,
    To bring me theth'r?

ULYSSES   You shall command me, Sir.
    But gentle tell me of what Honor was   285
    This Cressida in Troy? Had she no Lover there
    That wails her Absence?

TROILUS   O Sir, to such as boasting show their
        Scars
    A Mock is due. Will you walk on, my Lord?
    She was belov'd, she lov'd; she is, and dooth;   290
    But still sweet Love is Food for Fortune's
        Tooth.   *Exeunt.*

V.i   *This scene takes place at Achilles' tent in the Greek camp.*

2   **Cemitar**   *scimitar. It is conceivable that the unusual spelling is designed to distinguish this kind of Greek sword from the Oriental blade that Shakespeare associates with Moors in two other plays (*Titus Andronicus *and* The Merchant of Venice*). There may also be wordplay on* cemetery, *a word which originally referred to the cool, damp Roman catacombs and which derived from a Greek word meaning "sleeping place."*

4   **Cur of Envy**   *malicious, envious dog. Most editors adopt the Folio reading,* core, *and it is conceivable that Shakespeare intended a pun on the two words.*

5   **Batch of Nature**   *loaf of humanity. A "Crusty Batch" of bread could readily be likened to a scabby botch (sore), and it may be that Shakespeare intended to allude to two forms of crustiness.*

7   **Idol of Idiot-worshippers**   *Thersites manages to insult both Achilles and his admirers with this epithet.*

9   **Fragment**   *Achilles is probably calling Thersites a piece of broken crust.*

10   **Dull**   *both (a) stupid, and (b) stale and tasteless.*

Scene 1

Enter Achilles and Patroclus.

ACHILLES   I'll heat his Blood with Greekish Wine
     tonight,
   Which with my Cemitar I'll cool tomorrow.
   Patroclus, let us feast him to the height.
PATROCLUS   Here comes Thersites.

Enter Thersites.

ACHILLES   —How now, thou
     Cur of Envy,
   Thou Crusty Batch of Nature, what's the News?   5
THERSITES   Why, thou Picture of what thou seem'st,
   and Idol of Idiot-worshippers, here's a Letter
   for thee.
ACHILLES   From whence, Fragment?
THERSITES   Why, thou Dull Dish of Fool, from Troy.   10

12–13 **The Surgeon's Box or the Patient's Wound.** *Thersites mis-takes* Tent *to refer to the surgical gauze used to tent (search) a patient's wound. He says that the doctor's tent is either in his box of medical supplies or in the wound being treated. There is probably a second pun on* Box *as a word meaning "buffet" or "blow" (as in boxing), with the surgeon as the one inflicting the wound on the "Patient" (a submissive, unretaliating victim).*

14 **Adversity** *adversary, one who speaks in rebuttal.*

15 **Box** *Most editors adopt the Folio's* boy *here. But the Quarto's* Box *continues the wordplay initiated in line 12. Here it probably relates to a* Box *as a "case" or sexual receptacle.*

17 **Varlot** *A variant of* varlet *(valet), suggesting that in this case the servant also functions as a harlot (line 19).*

20–27 **Diseases . . . Discoveries** *Thersites invokes a number of afflictions he connects with "preposterous Discoveries," the licentious exploration of "the South" (the nether regions). The word* preposterous *literally means "placing what should be behind (*post, posterior*) in the front (*pre*) position." Among other things, Thersites curses Patroclus with colic and hernia, mucus infections, kidney-stones, apoplexy (stroke), paralysis, eye disease, hepatitis, asthma, cystitis, neuritis, psoriasis, syphilis, and a body totally given over to skin diseases.*

31 **Butt** *both (a) a wine cask, and (b) a buttock.*

34–36 **Skein . . . Purse** *Thersites calls Patroclus a spool of silk thread, a taffeta handkerchief, and a decorative purse tassel.*

PATROCLUS   Who keeps the Tent now?

THERSITES   The Surgeons's Box or the Patient's
   Wound.

PATROCLUS   Well said, Adversity, and what needs
   these Tricks?

THERSITES   Prithee be silent, Box: I profit not by   15
   thy Talk. Thou art said to be Achilles' male
   Varlot.

PATROCLUS   Male Varlot, you Rogue? What's that?

THERSITES   Why his masculine Whore. Now the
   rotten Diseases of the South, the Guts-griping   20
   Ruptures, Catarrhs, Loads a' Gravel in the
   Back, Lethargies, cold Palsies, raw Eyes,
   dirt-rotten Livers, whissing Lungs, Bladders
   full of Impostume, Sciaticas, Lime-kills i' th'
   Palm, incurable Bone-ache, and the rivel'd   25
   Fee-simple of the Tetter, take and take again
   such preposterous Discoveries!

PATROCLUS   Why, thou damnable Box of Envy, thou,
   what means thou to curse thus?

THERSITES   Do I curse thee?   30

PATROCLUS   Why no, you ruinous Butt, you whoreson
   indistinguishable Cur, no.

THERSITES   No? Why art thou then exasperate, thou
   idle, immaterial Skein of Sleave-silk, thou
   green Sarcenet-flap for a sore Eye, thou   35
   Tossel of a Prodigal's Purse, thou! Ah how the
   poor World is pest'red with such Water-flies,
   Diminutives of Nature.

PATROCLUS   Out, Gall!

THERSITES   Finch Egg!   40

573

44   her Daughter   *Polyxena, the maiden for whom Achilles pines.*

45   taxing   *tasking, charging.*
        gaging   *engaging, pledging.*

47   or go   *either go.*

48   major Vow   *foremost commitment.*

49   trim   *prepare.*

52   Blood   *base appetites and drives of the flesh.*

56   Honest   *decent, ordinary.*

57   Quails   *wenches, whores.*

59   the Bull   *Menelaus, so called because of his horns. Jupiter had taken on the form of a bull to seduce Europa, a story told in Book II of Ovid's* Metamorphoses.
        primitive   *prime, archetype, original of the type.*

61   Shoeing-horn in a Chain   *serviceable tool. Men of the Renaissance sometimes wore shoehorns attached to their legs by chains.*

63   larded   *interlarded (mingling beef with strips of bacon for cooking).*

67   Moil   *mule.*
        Fitchock   *fitchew (skunk).*

68   Puttock   *chicken-hawk, kite.*
        without a Roe   *without eggs or sperm (spent, shotten, worthless).*

ACHILLES   My sweet Patroclus, I am thwarted quite
From my great Purpose in tomorrow's Battle.
Here is a Letter from Queen Hecuba,
A Token from her Daughter, my fair Love,
Both taxing me and gaging me to keep   45
An Oath that I have sworn. I will not break it.
Fall Greeks, fail Fame, Honor or go or stay,
My major Vow lies here: this I'll obey.
—Come, Thersites, help to trim my Tent:
This night in banqueting must all be spent.   50
—Away, Patroclus.   *Exit with Patroclus.*

THERSITES   With too much Blood and too little
Brain, these two may run mad; but if with too
much Brain and too little Blood they do, I'll
be a Curer of Mad-men. Here's Agamemnon,   55
an Honest Fellow enough, and one that loves
Quails, but he has not so much Brain as Ear-
wax. And the goodly Transformation of Jupiter
there, his Brother the Bull, the primitive
Statue and oblique Memorial of Cuckolds, a   60
thrifty Shoeing-horn in a Chain, hanging at
his Brother's Leg: to what Form but that he is
should Wit larded with Malice, and Malice
faced with Wit, turn him to? To an Ass were
nothing: he is both Ass and Ox. To an Ox were   65
nothing: he's both Ox and Ass. To be a Dog, a
Moil, a Cat, a Fitchock, a Toad, a Lizard, an
Owl, a Puttock, or a Herring without a Roe, I
would not care; but to be Menelaus, I would
conspire against Destiny. Ask me not what I   70
would be if I were not Thersites, for I care

575

71–72   I care not . . . Lazar   *I don't care if I become no better than a parasitic louse on a leper.*

73   Hey-day, Sprites and Fires!   *Thersites pretends to be excited by the approach of spirits and fires. He implicitly compares the approaching party to a manifestation of the* ignis fatuus, *the "false fire" or will-o'-the-wisp sometimes seen in swampy areas and thought to result from inflammations of combustible marsh gas.*

74   We go wrong   *we are lost, we're headed in the wrong direction. Apparently Agamemnon has had a lot to drink.*

78   God night   *God give you good night.*

79   Aiax . . . you.   *Aiax is in charge of the soldiers who will provide you escort while you are in the Greek camp.*

82   Draught   *both (a) drink, and (b) latrine, privy.*

83   Sink   *cesspool.*

86   Old Nestor . . . Diomed.   *Old Nestor is going to stay awhile, so you do the same, Diomed.*

not to be the Louse of a Lazar, so I were not
Menelaus. Hey-day, Sprites and Fires!

Enter Agamemnon, Ulysses, Nestor, Aiax, Diomed,
Hector, and Troilus with Lights.

AGAMEMNON We go wrong, we go wrong.
AIAX   No, yonder 'tis:
    There where we see the Lights.
HECTOR   I trouble you.   75
AIAX No, not a whit.

Enter Achilles.

ULYSSES   Here comes himself to guide you.
ACHILLES Welcome, brave Hector. —Welcome,
    Princes all.
AGAMEMNON So now, fair Prince of Troy, I bid
    God night;
    Aiax commands the Guard to tend on you.
HECTOR Thanks, and good night to the Greeks'
    General.   80
MENELAUS Good night, my Lord.
HECTOR   Good night, sweet Lord Menelaus.
THERSITES Sweet Draught: "Sweet," quoth 'a! Sweet
    Sink, Sweet Sewer!
ACHILLES Good night and welcome, both at once,
    to those
    That go or tarry.
AGAMEMNON   Good night.   *Exit with Menelaus.*   85
ACHILLES Old Nestor tarries, and you too, Diomed:

577

88   important Bus'ness   *Diomed refers to his assignation with Cressida. Here* important *probably means both (a) weighty, significant, and (b) urgent, "importunate" (a word that literally refers to a demand that a portal be opened). Meanwhile,* Bus'ness *almost certainly has the same sense it has in III.i.41, 43 (and by contrasting implication in IV.i.5).*

89   Tide   *both (a) time, and (b) high tide, full flood.*

96   leers   *smiles seductively.*
        Serpent   *proverbial for deceptiveness, owing primarily to its role in bringing about the Fall of Eve (Genesis 3), an archetypal event about to be reenacted.*

97   spend his Mouth   *speak freely.*

98   promise like Brabbler the Hound   *Here Thersites combines two ideas: (a) the barking of a hound who promises thereby that he is on the scent of real prey, and (b) the licking and fawning of a dog that flatters his master with an abundance of obsequious affection.*

99   Astronomers   *astrologers.*

100   prodigious   *an event so extraordinary that it is taken to be a prodigy, a sign from Heaven that some great "Change" (momentous, disastrous event) is about to occur.*

100–1   The Sun borrows of the Moon   *The Sun reflects light from the Moon, rather than vice-versa.*

102–3   I . . . him   *I would rather miss the chance to see Hector than quit dogging Diomed.*

104   Drab   *whore.*

Keep Hector company an hour or two.

DIOMED   I cannot, Lord, I have important Bus'ness,
The Tide whereof is now. —Good night, great
Hector.

HECTOR   Give me your Hand.   90

ULYSSES   —Follow his Torch: he goes to Calchas'
Tent;
I'll keep you company.

TROILUS   Sweet Sir, you honor me.

HECTOR   And so good night.
                    Exit Diomedes, followed by Ulysses and Troilus.

ACHILLES   Come, come, enter my Tent.
                    Exeunt Achilles, Hector, Aiax, and Nestor.

THERSITES   That same Diomed's a false-hearted
Rogue, a most unjust Knave. I will no more   95
trust him when he leers than I will a Serpent
when he hisses. He will spend his Mouth and
promise like Brabbler the Hound; but when
he performs, Astronomers foretell it. It is
prodigious: there will come some Change. The   100
Sun borrows of the Moon when Diomed keeps his
Word. I will rather leave to see Hector than
not to dog him; they say he keeps a Troian
Drab, and uses the Traitor Calchas' Tent. I'll
after. Nothing but Lechery; all incontinent   105
Varlots!   *Exit.*

V.ii   *This scene takes place at Menelaus' tent, where Calchas and his daughter Cressida are staying. Diomed calls from outside the tent, and as he and Cressida converse, Troilus and Ulysses watch and comment from a hidden vantage point that allows them to hear but not be heard. Meanwhile Thersites watches from yet another vantage point that allows him to be a chorus to the events as they occur.*

2   I think   *as I presume. Diomed is trying to verify that the voice he hears is in fact that of Cressida's father.*

4   discover   *disclose.*

5   my Charge   *Diomed's title for Cressida means "my responsibility" (as the Greek soldier designated to tend to Cressida); but here it also takes on overtones of endearment similar to the same expression used by a parent to refer to a child.*

8   sing   *make invitingly erotic music to.*

10   Cliff   *This word combines at least three meanings: (a) clef (the lines on which the notes are arranged in a musical score, (b) cliff (a word that can refer either to a woman's breasts or to her "Mount of Venus"), and (c) cleft (a word that can refer to a woman's "fault," "cut," or "nothing").*
      noted   *This word here means (a) played upon, like a musical note, (b) played upon or with, like a musical instrument, (c) observed, known for what she is, and (d) recorded (noted down) for what she is (in terms of her reputation).*

11   remember   *remember what you said earlier.*

Scene 2

Enter Diomed.

DIOMED   What, are you up here, ho? Speak!

CALCHAS [*Within*]   Who calls?

DIOMED   Diomed. Calchas, I think, where's your
    Daughter?

CALCHAS [*Within*]   She comes to you.

*Enter Troilus and Ulysses to one side, and
behind them Thersites.*

ULYSSES   Stand where the Torch may not discover us.

Enter Cressid.

TROILUS   Cressid comes forth to him.

DIOMED   How now, my Charge?   5

CRESSIDA   Now my sweet Guardian, hark a word
    with you.

TROILUS   Yea so familiar?

ULYSSES   She will sing any Man at first Sight.

THERSITES   And any Man may sing her: if he can
    take her Cliff, she's noted.   10

DIOMEDES   Will you remember?

CRESSIDA   Remember? Yes.

DIOMEDES   Nay but do then,

12   coupl'd with   *made at one with, combined with.*

13   List.   *Listen.*

14   Folly   *What Cressida means is best captured by the modern phrase "fooling around."*

16   So . . . forsworn.   *This sentence is subject to varying interpretations. One possibility is that Diomed is expressing impatience: "So, that's all you have to say: you were only leading me on!" Another possibility is that he is saying that there is nothing for Cressida to be in conflict about: what she is about to do is of no more moment than a pin, since she is already pledged to bestow her favors on Diomed.*

18   A Juggling Trick   *an impossible feat (explained by the phrase that follows).*
       secretly open   *both (a) open while remaining closed, and (b) open in secret (private) situation.*

19   bestow on me   *give to me.*

22   How now, Troian?   *This can be read (a) "What do you make of that, Troian? What did I tell you about her?" or (b) "Are you all right, Troian? I'm worried about you." A third possibility is that it can be interpreted as an exclamation rather than a question, with the implication "Hold it, Troian, be patient!"*

23   Fool   *plaything, toy to trifle with.*

27   enlarge it self   *become so powerful that you lose control and endanger your life with an angry outburst. Ulysses' phrasing is a painful reminder that Troilus' "Displeasure" results from the fact that Diomed's pleasure is about to "enlarge it self."*

And let your Mind be coupled with your Words.

TROILUS   What shall she remember?

ULYSSES   List.

CRESSIDA   Sweet Honey Greek, tempt me no more to
　　Folly.

THERSITES   Roguery.

DIOMEDES   Nay then—

CRESSIDA   I'll tell you what—   15

DIOMEDES   So, so, come tell a Pin, you are forsworn.

CRESSIDA   In faith I cannot; what would you have me
　　do?

THERSITES   A Juggling Trick: to be secretly open.

DIOMEDES   What did you swear you would bestow on
　　me?

CRESSIDA   I prethee do not hold me to mine Oath: 20
　　Bid me do any thing but that, sweet Greek.

DIOMEDES   Good night.

TROILUS   Hold patience!

ULYSSES   How now, Troian?

CRESSIDA   Diomed.

DIOMEDES   No, no, good night: I'll be your Fool no
　　more.

TROILUS   Thy Better must.

CRESSIDA   Hark a Word in your Ear.

TROILUS   O Plague and Madness!   25

ULYSSES   You're moved, Prince: let us depart, I pray,
　　Lest your Displeasure should enlarge it self
　　To Wrathful Terms. This Place is dangerous,
　　The Time right deadly. I beseech you go.

TROILUS   Behold, I pray you.

ULYSSES   Now good my Lord, go off: 30

31   You flow to great Destruction.   *If you keep flowing in this direction, you will destroy yourself. The Folio prints* distraction *(disturbance), and most editors follow suit. Either reading implies the other, and Shakespeare may well have expected his audience to combine the two implications.*

36   withered   *probably to be treated here as a two-syllable word: either* wither'd *or* with'red.

38   palter   *equivocate, play games by sending incompatible messages.*

41   break out   *burst out in anger.*

43   my Will   *what I feel inclined to do.*
       all Offenses   *anything I might do that would get me in trouble.*

45   Luxury   *self-indulgent lechery and gluttony.*

46   Potato Finger   *This phrase has phallic implications, probably with reference to the long, pointed shape of a "sweet potato" (the kind of tuber that Thersites is almost certainly referring to) and perhaps also with reference to the fatness of a "Finger" that "Luxury" has swelled to the size of a potato. But the phrase is also related to the assumption that sweet potatoes (which were still regarded as exotic at this time) were aphrodisiacs to "tickle" (excite) desire.*

50   for the Surety of it   *to prove that you mean what you promise.*

You flow to great Destruction. Come, my Lord.

TROILUS I prethee stay.

ULYSSES You have not Patience, come.

TROILUS I pray you stay; by Hell and all Hell's
    Torments,
I will not speak a word.

DIOMEDES And so good night.

CRESSIDA Nay but you part in Anger.

DIOMEDES Doth that grieve thee? 35
    O withered Truth!

CRESSIDA How now, my Lord?

TROILUS By Jove,
  I will be Patient.

CRESSIDA Guardian? Why Greek!

DIOMEDES Fo, fo, adieu: you palter.

CRESSIDA In faith I do not: come hether once again.

ULYSSES You shake, my Lord, at something: will you
    go? 40
You will break out.

TROILUS She strokes his Cheek.

ULYSSES Come, come.

TROILUS Nay stay, by Jove I will not speak a word.
There is between my Will and all Offenses
A Guard of Patience. Stay a little while.

THERSITES How the Divel Luxury, with his Fat 45
Rump and Potato Finger, tickles these together!
Fry, Lechery, fry!

DIOMEDES But will you then?

CRESSIDA In faith I will lo, never trust me else.

DIOMEDES Give me some Token for the Surety of it. 50

CRESSIDA I'll fetch you one. *Exit.*

585

53–54   nor . . . feel   *nor allow my mind to register what my senses are telling me.*

57   O Beauty . . . Faith!   *Troilus' words echo Hamlet's observation "That if you be Honest and Fair, your Honesty should admit no Discourse to your Beauty"* (Hamlet, III.i.104–5).

60   O false Wench!   *Cressida reproaches herself. Then she takes back the sleeve she has given Diomed in line 56.*

65   Now . . . Whetstone!   *Thersites means "Now she sharpens his appetite: well done, Cressida!" A whetstone is an abrasive surface for the sharpening of cutting implements. Thersites assumes that Cressida is merely playing a game with Diomed, and his assumption is consistent with what Cressida has said about a woman's strategy for controlling a man in I.ii.307–16. But it seems equally likely that Cressida's soul really is divided at this point.*

67   Pledge   *Cressida addresses the sleeve as a token of Troilus' love for her. But it is soon to become a token of her willingness to give herself to Diomed, and thus a pledge of a very different character.*

70   memorial dainty Kisses   *delicate kisses to keep alive the memory of Cressida's love and faithfulness.*

71   Nay . . . me.   *Modern editors normally reassign this speech to Cressida. But both early texts give it to Diomed, who has probably put his hand back on the sleeve while saying "Ay, that" in line 66. Whether Cressida has surrendered it again or retained her grip on it while speaking lines 67–71, however, is unclear. The word* snatch *is used with crude innuendo in* Titus Andronicus, *II.i.95.*

ULYSSES   You have sworn Patience.

TROILUS   Fear me not, my Lord.
    I will not be my Self, nor have Cognition
    Of what I feel: I am all Patience.

Re-enter Cressida.

THERSITES   Now the Pledge: now, now, now!   55
CRESSIDA   Here, Diomed, keep this Sleeve.
TROILUS   O Beauty, where is thy Faith!
ULYSSES   My Lord.
TROILUS   I will be Patient: outwardly I will.
CRESSIDA   You look upon that Sleeve? Behold it
    well.
    He lov'd me. —O false Wench! —Give 't
    me again.   60
DIOMEDES   Whose was 't?
CRESSIDA   It is no matter now I ha't again.
    I will not meet with you tomorrow night.
    I prethee, Diomed, visit me no more.
THERSITES   Now she sharpens: well said, Whetstone!   65
DIOMEDES   I shall have it.
CRESSIDA   What, this?
DIOMEDES   Ay, that.
CRESSIDA   —O all you Gods! —O pretty pretty
    Pledge!
    Thy Maister now lies thinking on his Bed
    Of thee and me, and sighs, and takes my Glove,
    And gives memorial dainty Kisses to it,   70
    As I kiss thee.
DIOMEDES   Nay do not snatch it from me.

587

72   withal   *both (a) with it, and (b) with all. Shakespeare probably expected his audience to hear the accented -al as* all, *a syllable that echoes earlier uses of* all *with sexual implications, but here a word that goes beyond that to remind us that what is at stake at this moment is nothing less than all of Cressida and all that she symbolizes.*

76   I will have this   *Diomed snatches the sleeve for the last time.*
    It is no matter.   *both (a) it is of no consequence, and (b) it no longer matters, because the die is now cast.*

80   Diana's Waiting-women yond   *Cressida refers to the stars who "serve" the Moon (associated with the Goddess of Chastity, usually referred to as Cynthia in her celestial manifestation and as Diana in her role as the sylvan huntress on Earth). It is tragically ironic that Cressida now swears by the chaste maidens who wait on Diana. The word* yond *("out there") may be a signal that the heroine is dimly aware of having just crossed a great divide.*

82   Helm   *helmet.*

84   wor'st   *wore; here elided for metrical purposes.*
    Horn   *Troilus is thinking primarily of the Devil's horns, but two other meanings of the word are also pertinent: (a) the erect male member, and (b) the horns of a cuckold, a man whose woman has betrayed him.*

87   I'll not keep my Word.   *Here Cressida may be "Fooling" (line 90), or playing manipulative games. But once again it is also possible to see her as having genuine second thoughts.*

91   Pluto   *the God of the Underworld, here equivalent to the Devil.*

CRESSIDA   He that takes that doth take my Heart
    withal.
DIOMEDES   I had your Heart before, this follows it.
TROILUS   I did swear Patience.
CRESSIDA   You shall not have it, Diomed,
    Faith you shall not: I'll give you something
        else.   75
DIOMEDES   I will have this: whose was 't?
CRESSIDA   It is no matter.
DIOMEDES   Come tell me whose it was.
CRESSIDA   'Twas one's that lov'd me better than you
    will;
    But now you have it, take it.
DIOMEDES   Whose was it?
CRESSIDA   By all Diana's Waiting-women yond,   80
    And by her self, I will not tell you whose.
DIOMEDES   Tomorrow will I wear it on my Helm,
    And grieve his Spir't that dares not challenge it.
TROILUS   Wert thou the Div'l and wor'st it on thy
    Horn,
    It should be challeng'd.   85
CRESSIDA   Well, well, 'tis done, 'tis past. And yet
    it is not:
    I'll not keep my Word.
DIOMEDES   Why then farewell:
    Thou never shalt mock Diomed again.
CRESSIDA   You shall not go: one cannot speak a
    word
    But it straight starts you.
DIOMEDES   I do not like this Fooling.   90
THERSITES   Nor I, by Pluto; but that that likes not

94 plagu'd *Cressida probably means nothing more than (a) teased, or (b) pestered for sexual favors. But sophisticated members of Shakespeare's audience would have heard in her words an ironic reminder that in some versions of the story Cressida eventually degenerated into a leper and a beggar.*

97 other Eye *This phrase is probably meant to refer both to (a) Cressida's second instrument of sight, and to (b) the "other Eye" in her anatomy (see II.i.87).*

98 this Fault *Cressida means "this weakness." But* Fault *literally means "crack" or "fissure," and frequently refers to the female "eye."*

101 Turpitude *vile behavior (from the Latin* turpis, *base), depravity.*

102 A Proof of strength *Thersites refers to Cressida's "conclusion" (line 100). What he means is that (a) Cressida has arrived at a strong (irrefutable) demonstration of the proposition to be tested, and (b) she herself is strong "Proof" (evidence) of the validity of the statement she has just "published" (uttered).*

109– Sith . . . calumniate. *Since there is still a will to believe in*
13 *my heart, a hope so stubborn that it inverts the evidence brought to it by my eyes and ears, as if those organs were instruments of deception, created only to bear false witness.*

114 I cannot conjure *I can neither send back the spirit (Cressida) who was here nor raise up a new one more to your liking.*

you please me best.

DIOMEDES   What, shall I come? The Hour—

CRESSIDA   Ay come. —O Jove! —Do come. I shall
    be plagu'd.

DIOMEDES   Farewell till then.

CRESSIDA   Good night, I prethee come.   95

Exit Diomedes.

—Troilus, farewell. One Eye yet looks on thee,
But with my Heart the other Eye doth see.
—Ah poor our Sex, this Fault in us I find:
The Error of our Eye directs our Mind.
What Error leads must err. O then conclude,   100
"Minds sway'd by Eyes are full of Turpitude."

Exit.

THERSITES   A Proof of strength: she could not
    publish more
    Unless she said "My Mind is now turn'd Whore."

ULYSSES   All's done, my Lord.

TROILUS   It is.

ULYSSES   Why stay we then?

TROILUS   To make a Recordation to my Soul   105
    Of ev'ry Syllable that here was spoke.
    But if I tell how these two did coact,
    Shall I not lie in publishing a Truth?
    Sith yet there is a Credence in my Heart,
    An Esperance so obstinately strong   110
    That doth invert th' Attest of Eyes and Ears,
    As if those Organs were Deception's functions,
    Created only to calumniate.
    Was Cressid here?

ULYSSES   I cannot conjure, Troian.

115   sure *surely, certainly.*

118   for Womanhood *for the sake of Womanhood.*

120–   apt . . . Depravation *prone, even without a story of de-*
21   *pravity to point to as an object for their detraction.*

121–   to square . . . Rule *Here the primary meaning of* Rule *is*
22   *carpenter's square or ruler, with the implication that one*
       should not use Cressida as the instrument for defining or
       measuring women in general. But Rule *can also refer to (a) a*
       law or principle, and (b) the reign or sway that governs one's
       behavior. Troilus' inability to make sense of a world which has
       both mothers and unfaithful Cressidas is the obverse of Ham-
       let's skepticism that there can be faithful Ophelias in a world
       in which mothers prove so grossly unfaithful to their vows.

123   spoil our Mothers *turn our mothers rotten (or into spoils).*
       Most editors follow the Folio here and print soil.

125   Will . . . Eyes? *Will he sway so far in this vein that he loses*
       the use of what his eyes report to him?

129   Sanctimonies *things of sacred value.*

134   Bi-fold Author'ty *divided authority, whereby Reason works*
       both for and against the Truth.

137   conduce *occur.*

138   Insep'rate *"inseparatable," indivisible ("Unity it self").*

141   Orifex *orifice, opening; here disyllabic.*
       subtle *refined, tiny.*

TROILUS   She was not sure.

ULYSSES   Most sure she was.   115

TROILUS   Why my Negation hath no taste of Madness!

ULYSSES   Nor mine, my Lord: Cresseid was here but
   now.

TROILUS   Let it not be believ'd for Womanhood.
   Think we had Mothers: do not give Advantage
   To stubborn Critics, apt, without a Theme   120
   For Depravation, to square the gen'ral Sex
   By Cresseid's Rule. Rath'r think this is not
   Cresseid.

ULYSSES   What hath she done, Prince, that can
   spoil our Mothers?

TROILUS   Nothing at all, unless that this were she.

THERSITES   Will 'a swagger himself out on's own   125
   Eyes?

TROILUS   This she? No, this is Diomed's Cresseida.
   If Beauty have a Soul, this is not she.
   If Souls guide Vows, if Vows be Sanctimonies,
   If Sanctimony be the Gods' Delight,   130
   If there be Rule in Unity it self,
   This was not she. O Madness of Discourse,
   That Cause sets up with and against it self;
   Bi-fold Authority, where Reason can revolt
   Without Perdition, and Loss assume all Reason   135
   Without Revolt. This is and is not Cresseid.
   Within my Soul there doth conduce a Fight
   Of this strange Nature, that a Thing Inseparate
   Divides more wider than the Sky and Earth;
   And yet the spacious Breadth of this Division   140
   Admits no Orifex for a Point as subtle

593

142 Ariachne's broken Woof *a piece of broken spider web. Troilus alludes to Arachne (here spelled in such a way as to yield an additional syllable, probably for metrical purposes), a woman turned into a spider for challenging and defeating the Goddess Pallas Athena in a weaving contest.*

143 Pluto's Gates *the Gates of Hades (here equivalent to Hell).*

146 dissolv'd *untied.*

147 And . . . tied *and with another pledge of love (another bond) find their fingers tied. Most editors adopt the Folio's* five fingers.

148 Fractions *both (a) infractions (breaches of bonds), and (b) fractures.*

   Orts *scraps.*

150 o'er-eaten *gnawed upon and discarded.*

151 attach'd *seized upon, crazed.*

154 Mars his *Mars'.*

160 Cask *casque, helmet.*
   compos'd *formed, put together.*
   Vulcan *another reference to the blacksmith cuckolded by Mars and Venus.*

162 Hurricano *a cyclonic waterspout rather than a hurricane.*

163 Constring'd in Mass *drawn together into a dense tempest.*

167 Concupie *whore (referring to Cressida). Thersites coins a word that combines* concupiscent *and* concubine.

As Ariachne's broken Woof to enter.
Instance, O Instance strong as Pluto's Gates,
Cresseid is mine, tied with the Bonds of
    Heaven.
Instance, O Instance, strong as Heav'n it self,   145
The Bonds of Heav'n are slipp'd, dissolv'd,
    and loos'd,
And with another Knot find Finger tied.
The Fractions of her Faith, Orts of her Love,
The Fragments, Scraps, the Bits and greasy
    Relics
Of her o'er-eaten Faith, are giv'n to Diomed.   150
ULYSSES   May worthy Troilus be half attach'd
With that which here his Passion doth express?
TROILUS   Ay Greek, and that shall be divulged well
In Characters as red as Mars his Heart
Inflam'd with Venus. Nev'r did Young Man fancy   155
With so eternal and so fix'd a Soul.
Hark, Greek, as much as I do Cressid love,
So much by Weight hate I her Diomed.
That Sleeve is mine that he'll bear on his
    Helm.
Were it a Cask compos'd by Vulcan's Skill,   160
My Sword should bite it. Not the dreadful Spout
Which Shipmen do the Hurricano call,
Constring'd in Mass by the almighty Sun,
Shall dizzy with more clamor Neptune's Ear
In his Descent than shall my prompted Sword   165
Falling on Diomed.
THERSITES   He'll tickle it for his Concupie.

169   stand by   *be placed beside.*

173   by this   *by this time.*

174   Aiax your Guard   *Here the syntax hovers between "Aiax, your Guard," and "Aiax as your Guard."*

175   Have with you   *I'll join you.*

176   revolted Fair   *traitorous fair one. Troilus addresses this line to the absent Cressida.*

177   Castle   *Troilus probably uses this term figuratively, to refer to the proud projection (Troilus' sleeve) that Diomed will wear on the plumed crest of his helmet. But Troilus is probably also issuing a threat: "Diomed, even though your head is protected by a helmet as thick as a castle, I'll still break through it with 'my prompted [eager] Sword' " (line 165).*

180   a Raven   *a bird of ill omen, and frequently a symbol of vengeance. In III.ii.278–79 of* Hamlet *the Prince says "Come, the croaking Raven doth bellow for Revenge."*
              bode   *prophesy (as in the expression "bode ill").*

182   the intelligence of   *information about.*

184   commodious Drab   *accommodating whore.*
              still   *both (a) even now, and (b) always.*

185–
86   A burning Divel   *both (a) the burning inflammations of venereal disease, and (b) a minister of the fires of hell.*

TROILUS   —O Cresid, O false Cressid, false, false,
      false!
   Let all Untruths stand by thy stained Name
   And they'll seem glorious.
ULYSSES   O contain your self: 170
   Your Passion draws Ears hether.

                    Enter Aeneas.

AENEAS   I have been seeking you this hour, my
      Lord.
   Hector by this is arming him in Troy.
   Aiax your Guard stays to conduct you home.
TROILUS   Have with you, Prince. —My courteous
      Lord, adieu.   175
   —Farewell, revolted Fair. —And Diomed,
   Stand fast and wear a Castle on thy Head.
ULYSSES   I'll bring you to the Gates.
TROILUS   Accept distracted Thanks.
                    Exeunt Troilus, Aeneas, and Ulysses.
THERSITES   Would I could meet that Rogue Diomed!
   I would croak like a Raven; I would bode, I   180
   would bode. Patroclus will give me any thing
   for the intelligence of this Whore. The Parrot
   will not do more for an Almond than he for a
   commodious Drab. Lechery, Lechery: still Wars
   and Lechery! Nothing else holds Fashion. A   185
   burning Divel take them!   *Exit.*

597

V.iii   *This scene return us to Priam's Palace in Troy.*

1   ungently temper'd   *bearing an ungentle disposition.*

2   Admonishment   *warnings, cautionary urgings.*

4   train   *constrain, compel.*

6   om'nous   *ominous, the bearers of omens that will prove accu-*
        rate.

9   dear Petition   *loving pleas.*

13   my Trumpet   *the trumpet announcing Hector's readiness for*
        battle.

Scene 3

Enter Hector and Andromache.

ANDROMACHE   When was my Lord so much ungently
    temper'd
    To stop his Ears against Admonishment?
    Unarm, unarm, and do not fight today.
HECTOR   You train me to offend you: get you in.
    By all the everlasting Gods, I'll go!   5
ANDROMACHE   My Dreams will sure prove om'nous
    to the Day.
HECTOR   No more, I say.

Enter Cassandra.

CASSANDRA   Where is my brother Hector?
ANDROMACHE   Here, Sister, Arm'd and Bloody in
    Intent.
    Consort with me in loud and dear Petition;
    Pursue we him on Knees: for I have dreamt   10
    Of bloody Turbulence, and this whole Night
    Have nothing been but Shapes and Forms of
    Slaughter.
CASSANDRA   O 'tis true.
HECTOR   —Ho! Bid my Trumpet sound!

599

14   Sally   *sortie, skirmish.*

16   peevish   *foolish, prompted by passion.*

18   spotted   *tainted, impure (and thus unacceptable to the Gods).*

20–22   It is as lawful . . . Charity.   *These lines, which occur only in the Folio text, may be corrupt in some way. What Andromache appears to be saying is: "It is just as lawful, as we would account it, to commit thefts so violent, and to rob in the name of Love." Her point is that Hector's sense of duty and justice, which demands that he fulfill his vow even when to do so is harmful, makes no better sense than to commit robbery and call it an act of charity.*

26   keeps the Weather of my Fate   *stays to the windward of my concern for what might happen to me. Hector means that his sense of Honor takes precedence over such lesser considerations as whether others feel that it is wise to fight on a particular day.*

27   the Dear Man   *the man of highest worth (truest honor).*

32   i' th' Vain of Chivalry   *in the mood for chivalrous (single) combat. Hector is not only deaf to warnings that he should not enter the battle today; he is so supremely confident that he believes he can take on all the adversaries that two or more men would normally be required to defend against. Vain, derived from the spelling in both early texts, means* vein *(strain or mood), but it anticipates the modern sense of* vain *(a vanity that makes one unwarrantedly secure in his sense of prowess or invulnerability).*

CASSANDRA   No Notes of Sally, for the Heav'ns,
    sweet Brother—
HECTOR   Begone, I say! The Gods have heard me
    swear.   15
CASSANDRA   The Gods are deaf to hot and peevish
    Vows:
    They are polluted Off'rings, more abhorr'd
    Than spotted Livers in the Sacrifice.
ANDROMACHE   O be persuaded: do not count it holy
    To hurt by being just. It is as lawful,   20
    For we would count, give much, to as violent
        Thefts,
    And rob in the behalf of Charity.
CASSANDRA   It is the Purpose that makes strong the
        Vow,
    But Vows to ev'ry Purpose must not hold:
    Unarm, sweet Hector.
HECTOR   Hold you still, I say!   25
    Mine Honor keeps the Weather of my Fate.
    Life ev'ry Man holds dear, but the Dear Man
    Holds Honor far more precious dear than Life.

            Enter Troilus.

    —How now, Young Man? Mean'st thou to fight
        today?
ANDROMACHE   Cassandra, call my Father to persuade.   30
                                        Exit Cassandra.
HECTOR   No faith, young Troilus, doff thy Harness,
        Youth:
    I am today i' th' Vain of Chivalry.

    601

34   tempt . . . War   *don't put yourself at the mercy of the encounters the war will throw your way. Ironically, Hector is telling his younger brother almost precisely the same thing that Hector's wife and sister are telling him.*

37   Vice of Mercy   *a fatal tendency to be magnanimous when you should go for the kill.*

38   Which . . . Man   *which is more suitable for the king of beasts than for a man of much less imposing strength. According to Pliny's* Natural History *(an ancient text that remained a standard reference work in the Renaissance), the lion would spare any foe that submitted to it.*

41   Fan and Wind   *Troilus' phrasing recalls the winnowing fan of I.iii.26–30.*

43   Fair Play   *Hector's phrasing helps to explain what he meant earlier by "the Vain of Chivalry." Hector thinks of the battlefield as indistinguishable from the lists where chivalric bouts take place under conscientiously monitored rules of courtesy.*

45   the Hermit Pity   *Troilus compares Pity to a religious hermit, a man of peace.*

47   venom'd   *poisonous, deadly.*

48   ruthful   *sorrowful, breeding lamentation for the dead. Troilus' point is that by showing no "Ruth" (mercy), the Trojan swords will bring another kind of "ruth" (grief) to the Greeks.*

53   Retire   *retreat or retirement from battle.*

55   recourse of Tears   *both (a) their resort to tears, and (b) the repeated coursings of those tears through continual weeping.*

58   But by my Ruin   *only by my destruction.*

Let grow thy Sinews till their Knots be strong,
And tempt not yet the Brushes of the War.
Unarm thee, go; and doubt thou not, brave Boy,   35
I'll stand today for thee and me and Troy.

TROILUS   Brother, you have a Vice of Mercy in you,
Which better fits a Lion than a Man.

HECTOR   What Vice is that? Good Troilus, chide me
    for it.

TROILUS   When many times the captive Grecian falls,   40
Ev'n in the Fan and Wind of your fair Sword,
You bid them rise and live.

HECTOR   O 'tis Fair Play.

TROILUS   Fool's Play, by Heaven, Hector!

HECTOR   How now? How now?

TROILUS   For th' love of all the Gods,
Let's leave the Hermit Pity with our Mother,   45
And when we have our Armors buckl'd on,
The venom'd Vengeance ride upon our Swords;
Spur them to ruthful Work, rein them from Ruth.

HECTOR   Fie, savage, fie!

TROILUS   Hector, then 'tis Wars.

HECTOR   Troilus, I would not have you fight today.   50

TROILUS   Who should withhold me?
Not Fate, Obedience, nor the Hand of Mars,
Beck'ning with fiery Truncheon my Retire,
Not Priamus and Hecuba on Knees,
Their Eyes o'er-galled with recourse of Tears,   55
Not you, my Brother, with your true Sword
    drawn
Oppos'd to hinder me, should stop my Way.
But by my Ruin—

60 Stay *support.*

65 enrapt *seized by an ecstasy of inspired vision.*

68 engag'd *pledged, vowed [to fight].*

69 the Faith of Valor *fidelity to the demands of honor.*

73 shame Respect *bring shame to one who merits the highest respect.*

74 Voice *vow of support.*

75 forbid me *withhold from me.*

79 dreaming *subject to dreams that she takes to be omens.*

80 Bodements *warnings of doom.*

Enter Priam and Cassandra.

CASSANDRA   Lay hold upon him, Priam, hold him fast!
   He is thy Crutch: now if thou lose thy Stay,   60
   Thou, on him leaning, and all Troy on thee,
   Fall all togeth'r.
PRIAM   Come, Hector, come, go back!
   Thy Wife hath dreamt, thy Mother hath had
     Visions,
   Cassandra doth foresee, and I my self
   Am like a Prophet suddenly enrapt,   65
   To tell thee that this Day is ominous:
   Therefore come back.
HECTOR   Aeneas is a-field,
   And I do stand engag'd to many Greeks,
   Ev'n in the Faith of Valor, to appear
   This Morning to them.
PRIAM   Ay but thou shalt not go.   70
HECTOR   I must not break my Faith.
   You know me Dutiful: therefore, dear Sir,
   Let me not shame Respect, but give me Leave
   To take that Course by your Consent and Voice
   Which you do here forbid me, royal Priam.   75
CASSANDRA   O Priam, yield not to 'im.
ANDROMACHE   Do not, dear Father.
HECTOR   Andromache, I am offended with you:
   Upon the Love you bear me, get you in!
                  Exit Andromache.
TROILUS   This foolish, dreaming, superstitious
     Girl,
   Makes all these Bodements.

81–87   Look how . . . Hector!   *In these lines Cassandra speaks to Hector as if she were pointing out details in a picture of impending disaster that she carries in her prophetic mind.*

82   Vents   *openings, gashes.*

84   Andromach'   *Andromache; here elided for metrical purposes.* shrills her Dolors forth   *shrieks out her griefs.*

85   Destruction   *Most editors follow the Folio and print* distraction *(synonymous with* Frenzy*). Either word would fit the context: "destruction" would breed the frenzy here described, and "distraction" before Hector's death would simply be a foretaste of the even greater frenzy to follow on his destruction. All three of the nouns in this line personify the conditions described. Compare V.ii.31 for a similar choice between* destruction *and* distraction.
Amazement   *bewilderment, as of those lost in a maze.*

86   Antics   *idiots.*

89   soft   *wait a moment.*

90   deceive   *mislead, betray.*

91   amaz'd   *stupefied, paralyzed.*
Exclaim   *exclamation, outburst.*

S.D.   severally   *separately; in different directions.*

96   to lose my Arm or win my Sleeve   *What Troilus means is that he plans to use his arm to win back the sleeve that once adorned it.*

CASSANDRA   O farewell, dear Hector.   80
   Look how thou di'st, look how thy Eye turns
     pale;
   Look how thy Wounds do bleed at many Vents;
   Hark how Troy roars, how Hecuba cries out,
   How poor Andromach' shrills her Dolors forth.
   Behold Destruction, Frenzy, and Amazement,   85
   Like witless Antics one another meet,
   And all cry "Hector, Hector's dead, O Hector!"
TROILUS   Away, away!
CASSANDRA   Farewell. Yet soft: Hect'r, I take my
   Leave.
   Thou dost thy self and all our Troy deceive.   90
HECTOR   You are amaz'd, my Liege, at her Exclaim.
   Go in and cheer the Town. We'll forth and fight,
   Do Deeds worth Praise, and tell you them at
    night.
PRIAM   Farewell, the Gods with Safety stand about
   thee.   *Exeunt Priam and Hector severally.*
                                    Alarum.

TROILUS   They're at it, hark! —Proud Diomed,
   believe: 95
   I come to lose my Arm or win my Sleeve.

Enter Pandar.

PANDARUS   Do you hear, my Lord? Do you hear?
TROILUS   What now?
PANDARUS   Here's a Letter come from yond poor
   Girl.
TROILUS   Let me read.   100

607

101   **Tisick**   *phthisic, an asthmatic cough.*

104   **a' th's**   *of these.*

105   **Rheum**   *runny discharge of mucus.*

106   **Ache in my Bones**   *a symptom of syphilis. Evidently Thersites' curses are beginning to take effect.*
     curs'd   *bewitched.*

110   **Th' Effect . . . way.**   *The words have an effect that is the opposite of what they say.*

111   **Go, Wind, to Wind**   *The first* Wind *refers to the empty words; the second* Wind *refers to the breeze that will blow the paper away as Troilus tears the letter to pieces.*

112   **still**   *now as before.*

113   **edifies**   *nourishes, builds up.*

V.iv   *This scene takes place on the battlefield outside the walls of Troy.*

S.D.   **Excursions**   *sallies and skirmishes.*

1   **clapper-clawing**   *buffeting, pounding.*

3   **abhominable**   *abominable, vile, inhuman. This spelling probably preserves the Renaissance pronunciation of the word. It also preserves the usual Renaissance meaning, based on the belief that the word derived from a combination of* ab *(away from) and* homine *(man).*

4   **scurvy**   *contemptible.*

PANDARUS   A whoreson Tisick, a whoreson rascally
    Tisick, so troubles me, and the foolish Fortune
    of this Girl, and what one thing, what another,
    that I shall leave you one a' th's days; and I
    have a Rheum in mine Eyes too, and such an   105
    Ache in my Bones, that unless a man were curs'd
    I cannot tell what to think on't. What says
    she there?
TROILUS   Words, Words, mere Words, no Matter
    from the Heart:
    Th' Effect doth operate another way.   110
    —Go, Wind, to Wind: there turn and change
    together.
    My Love with Words and Errors still she feeds,
    But edifies another with her Deeds.   *Exeunt.*

Scene 4

Alarum. Enter Thersites. Excursions.

THERSITES   Now they are clapper-clawing one
    another. I'll go look on. That dissembling,
    abhominable Varlet Diomede has got that same
    scurvy, doting, foolish young Knave's Sleeve
    of Troy there in his Helm. I would fain see   5
    them meet, that the same young Troian Ass that
    loves the Whore there might send that Greekish

9   dissembling   *deceitful.*
         luxurious   *lecherous.*

10   Arrant   *knave, here one who is more "errant" than "arrant" (arrogant).*
         Policy   *craftiness; rational planning and strategy in general.*

13   Dog-fox   *male fox. Ulysses was proverbial for his fox-like wiliness.*

14   me   *for me. Thersites employs an archaic construction referred to by grammarians as the "ethic dative."*
         in Policy   *as a deceitful device.*

16   prouder   *more haughty and aloof.*

18–19 proclaim Barbarism   *proclaim a state of primordial anarchy. Thersites' image of the Greeks implies a parallel between them and the barbarian tribes that eventually overwhelmed the Roman Empire.*

19–20 Policy . . . Opinion   *Political cunning (indeed orderly government itself) begins to acquire a bad reputation.*

21   Sleeve   *Thersites refers to Diomed, who is parading Troilus' sleeve.*

22   take the River Styx   *begin crossing the river that leads into Hades.*

23   Thou doost miscall "Retire"   *You have incorrectly referred to a well-calculated withdrawal as if it were a cowardly retreat.*

25   Odds of Multitude   *overwhelming odds.*

whore-masterly Villain with the Sleeve back to
the dissembling, luxurious Drab of a Sleeve-
less Arrant. A' th' t'other side, the Policy   10
of those crafty, swearing Rascals, that stale
old Mouse-eaten dry Cheese Nestor, and that
same Dog-fox Ulysses, is not prov'd worth a
Blackberry. They set me up in Policy that
mongrel Cur Aiax against that Dog of as bad a   15
kind Achilles. And now is the Cur Aiax prouder
than the Cur Achilles and will not arm today.
Whereupon the Grecians began to proclaim
Barbarism, and Policy grows into an ill
Opinion.   20

Enter Diomed and Troilus.

Soft, here comes Sleeve and t'other.
TROILUS   Fly not, for shouldst thou take the River
  Styx,
I would swim after.
DIOMEDES   Thou doost miscall "Retire":
I do not fly, but advantageous Care
Withdrew me from the Odds of Multitude.   25
Have at thee!   *They fight.*
THERSITES   Hold thy Whore, Grecian! —Now for thy
  Whore, Troian! —Now the Sleeve, now the Sleeve!
     Exeunt Troilus and Diomedes fighting.

Enter Hector.

29	for Hector's Match *a suitable opponent for Hector (that is, a man of sufficient nobility to be Hector's equal).*
36	the wenching Rogues *the two rogues who are fighting over a whore.*
38	sort *sense.*
V.v	*The scene continues elsewhere on the battlefield.*
1	take *steal.*
4	chastis'd *punished. Thus far the only "chastisement" we have witnessed is the base command that Diomedes has just issued to his servant.*
5	her Knight by Proof *her knight by virtue of my valorous deeds in her honor.*

HECTOR   What, art Greek? Art thou for Hector's
    Match?
    Art thou of Blood and Honor?   30
THERSITES   No, no, I am a Rascal, a scurvy, railing
    Knave, a very filthy Rogue.
HECTOR   I do believe thee: live.
THERSITES   God 'a mercy, that thou wilt believe me!
    But a Plague break thy Neck for frighting me.   35
    What's become of the wenching Rogues? I think
    they have swallowed one another. I would laugh
    at that Miracle—yet in a sort Lechery eats it
    self. I'll seek them.   *Exit.*

Scene 5

Enter Diomed and Servant.

DIOMEDES   Go, go, my Servant, take thou Troilus'
    Horse;
    Present the fair Steed to my Lady Cressid.
    Fellow, commend my Service to her Beauty;
    Tell her I have chastis'd the am'rous Troian
    And am her Knight by Proof.
MAN   I go, my Lord.   *Exit.*   5

Enter Agamemnon.

6   **Renew**   *resume fighting.*

9   **Beam**   *lance.*

10   **pashed Corses**   *bashed corpses.*

13   **Patroclus ta'en or slain**   *In Homer's* Iliad *the death of Achilles' companion is a major turning point in the war. Here its first mention is buried in a catalogue of other casualties. Only later do we learn that Patroclus died at the hands of Hector.*

14   **dreadful Sagittary**   *a monstrous Centaur (half man and half horse) who was virtually invincible as an archer.*

19   **a thousand Hectors**   *Fighting in a field that includes neither Achilles nor Aiax, Hector appears both omnipresent and omnipotent.*

22   **scaling Sculls**   *scattering sculls (schools) of scaly fish.*

24   **strawy**   *straw-like in their vulnerability.*
        his Edge   *his sword, here compared to a scythe (a traditional emblem of Death).*

25   **Swath**   *the path of "straws" mowed down with each sweep of the blade.*

26   **leaves and takes**   *either spares or slays as he wishes.*

27   **Dexter'ty . . . Appetite**   *his skill so obedient to his will. Here* dexterity *involves a play on* dexter *(right), and thus refers to Hector's right arm as it wields his voracious scythe.*

29   **Proof . . . Impossibility**   *what he does seems impossible.*

AGAMEMNON   Renew, renew: the fierce Polidamas
      Hath beat down Menon; Bastard Margarelon
      Hath Doreus Prisoner
      And stands Colossus-wise, waving his Beam,
      Upon the pashed Corses of the Kings,   10
      Epistropus and Cedus; Polixenes is slain,
      Amphimacus and Thoas deadly hurt,
      Patroclus ta'en or slain, and Palamedes
      Sore hurt and bruis'd. The dreadful Sagittary
      Appals our Numbers. Haste we, Diomed,   15
      To reinforcement or we perish all.

Enter Nestor.

NESTOR   Go bear Patroclus' Body to Achilles,
      And bid the Snail-pac'd Aiax arm for Shame.
      There is a thousand Hectors in the Field:
      Now here he fights on Galathe his Horse,   20
      And there lacks Work; anon he's there a-foot,
      And there they fly or die, like scaling Sculls
      Before the belching Whale; then is he yonder,
      And there the strawy Greeks, ripe for his Edge,
      Fall down before him like a Mower's Swath.   25
      Here, there, and ev'ry where he leaves and
         takes,
      Dexter'ty so obeying Appetite
      That what he will he does, and does so much
      That Proof is call'd Impossibility.

Enter Ulysses.

615

30   O Courage   *be heartened.*

33   his mangl'd Myrmidons   *Achilles' fighting forces, who had gone into battle with Patroclus after Achilles' refusal to join the fray even though the Greeks were suffering terrible losses.*

35   Crying on Hector   *Ulysses' verb implicitly compares the Myrmidons to hunting dogs baying after a bear that has clawed them.*
        Aiax hath lost a Friend   *Doreus and Amphimacus (mentioned in lines 8 and 12) were both Grecian princes attending on Aiax.*

40   careless Force   *reckless might.*
        forceless Care   *an unforced motivation to fight for his cause.*

41   Lust   *sheer will power. Many editors follow the Folio here and print* Luck. *Either noun would fit the context.*
        in very spight of Cunning   *disdaining any concern for strategy and tactics.*

43   Ay there, there!   *Apparently Diomed is telling Aiax that he will join him in pursuit of Troilus.*
        draw together   *both (a) come together to work in cooperation, and (b) draw our swords in unison. Nestor is relieved that at last the Greeks are overcoming their internal divisions and directing all their energies against the adversary.*

45   Boy-queller   *boy-killer. Patroclus was an ardent protege of Achilles, and Achilles is clearly moved to avenge the death of a youth dear to him. But the primary point of this epithet would seem to be that Hector is too weak or cowardly to do to a real man what he did so effortlessly to a mere boy.*

ULYSSES   O Courage, Courage, Princes! Great
    Achilles   30
    Is arming, weeping, cursing, vowing Vengeance.
    Patroclus' Wounds have rous'd his drowsy Blood
    Together with his mangl'd Myrmidons,
    That noseless, handless, hack'd, and chipp'd,
      come to him
    Crying on Hector. Aiax hath lost a Friend   35
    And foams at Mouth, and he is arm'd and at it,
    Roaring for Troilus, who hath done today
    Mad and fantastic Execution,
    Engaging and redeeming of himself
    With such a careless Force and forceless Care   40
    As if that Lust, in very spight of Cunning,
    Bade him win all.

Enter Aiax.

AIAX   Troilus, thou Coward Troilus! *Exit.*
DIOMED   Ay there, there!
NESTOR   So, so, we draw together. *Exit.*

Enter Achilles.

ACHILLES   Where is this Hector?
    —Come, come, thou Boy-queller, show thy Face: 45
    Know what it is to meet Achilles angry.
    Hector, where's Hector? I will none but Hector.
                                   Exit.

V.vi   *The action continues at another point on the battlefield.*

3   correct   *discipline, punish.*

4–5   Were I . . . Correction!   *Even if I were the commanding general himself, I would surrender my position to you before I would yield to you the privilege of administering that chastisement.*

6   Traitor   *This noun was often used, as here, to refer to a person who was deceitful and treacherous. In chivalric tradition, to call a knight a traitor was to accuse him of being false to all the oaths (to God, King, and country) that gave him the right to bear arms; a soldier who failed to defend his name against such a charge was dishonored forever.*

7   my Horse   *Troilus cites only the cowardly act that Diomed has committed during the battle itself. But Troilus may also be associating the loss of his horse with the loss of his "Mare" (as women are sometimes contemptuously called in Shakespeare's plays).*

10   look upon   *stand back and watch.*

11   cogging   *conniving, cheating.*

Scene 6

Enter Aiax.

AIAX   Troilus, thou Coward, Troilus, show thy Head!

Enter Diomed.

DIOMED   Troilus! I say, where's Troilus?
AIAX   What wouldst thou?
DIOMED   I would correct him.
AIAX   Were I the Gen'ral, thou shouldst have my
      Office
   Ere that Correction! —Troilus, I say! What,
   Troilus!   5

Enter Troilus.

TROILUS   O Traitor Diomed, turn thy false Face, thou
      Traitor,
   And pay thy Life thou ow'st me for my Horse.
DIOMED   Ha, art thou there?
AIAX   I'll fight with him alone. Stand, Diomed.
DIOMED   He is my Prize, I will not look upon.   10
TROILUS   Come both you cogging Greeks, have at
      you both!   *Exeunt fighting.*

14   Pause if thou wilt.   *Hector is sparing Achilles rather than taking advantage of his vulnerability and killing him. Evidently in the hand-to-hand combat they have just had, Achilles has either become too fatigued to continue or has been deprived of his weapon by Hector's superior fighting.*

15   disdain thy Courtesy   *pour contempt on the magnanimity (gracious mercy) you have shown me. Achilles' reproach echoes what others, including Hector's brother Troilus (V.iii.37–48), have been saying about the Trojan champion all along.*

16   my Arms are out of Use   *I am out of practice.*

17   My Rest and Negligence   *Achilles refers to his long period of inactivity. What he is saying is that he is temporarily out of shape.*

24   carry him   *take him away from the battlefield as a prisoner of war.*

25   bring him off   *rescue him.*

26   wreak   *reck, care. Another meaning of* wreak, *avenge, seems inapplicable here.*

Enter Hector.

HECTOR   Yea Troilus, O well fought, my youngest
        Brother!

Enter Achilles.

ACHILLES   Now do I see thee, ha! Have at thee,
        Hector!   *They fight.*
HECTOR   Pause if thou wilt.
ACHILLES   I do disdain thy Courtesy, proud Troian: 15
        Be happy that my Arms are out of Use.
        My Rest and Negligence befriends thee now,
        But thou anon shalt hear of me again;
        Till when go seek thy Fortune.
HECTOR   Fare thee well.
        I would have been much more a Fresher Man   20
        Had I expected thee.   *Exit Achilles.*

Re-enter Troilus.

                —How now, my Brother!
TROILUS   Aiax hath ta'en Aeneas. Shall it be?
        No, by the Flame of yonder glorious Heaven,
        He shall not carry him. I'll be ta'en too,
        Or bring him off. —Fate, hear me what I say: 25
        I wreak not though I end my Life today.   *Exit.*

Enter one in Armor.

27   goodly Mark   *proper target.*

29   frush   *pound, batter.*

30   But I'll be Maister of it   *if I must in order to obtain it.*
      abide   *stay to fight.*

31   Hide   *Hector refers to the armor he covets. His image suggests
      that he will chase this warrior like a hunter pursuing a prized
      game animal. The implication of this episode is that, after
      fighting so valiantly in what has turned out to be a glorious
      day for the Trojans, Hector is now lowering himself to the level
      of a soldier whose only interest is in the spoils he can carry
      home from the field as trophies of triumph.*

V.vii   *The action continues in another part of the battlefield.*

2   Attend me where I wheel   *assist me wherever my movements
     take me.*

5   Empale   *fence in (as with the pales, or stakes, of a fortress).
     "Impale" (pierce with a spear) appears to have been a later
     sense, though it is tempting to read line 6 as an anticipation of
     it.*

6   execute your Arms   *put your weapons to proper use.
     Whether Achilles is merely reiterating the order he stated in
     line 5 or suggesting a second, thrusting action is not clear.*

7   Proceedings   *movements and actions.*

HECTOR   Stand, stand, thou Greek, thou art a
      goodly Mark.
   No, wilt thou not? I like thy Armor well;
   I'll frush it and unlock the Rivets all
   But I'll be Maister of it.   *Exit armed Soldier.*
                  Wilt thou not, Beast, abide?   30
   Why then fly on: I'll hunt thee for thy Hide.
                                          Exit.

Scene 7

Enter Achilles with Myrmidons.

ACHILLES   Come here about me, you my Myrmidons:
   Mark what I say. Attend me where I wheel;
   Strike not a Stroke, but keep your selves in
      Breath,
   And when I have the bloody Hector found,
   Empale him with your Weapons round about;   5
   In fellest manner execute your Arms.
   Follow me, Sirs, and my Proceedings eye:
   It is decreed Hector the Great must die.
                                       Exeunt.

Enter Thersites, watching Menelaus and Paris fighting.

THERSITES   The Cuckold and the Cuckold-maker are

623

10   **Bull**   *Menelaus (an allusion to the horns of the "Cuckold,"*
        line 9).
        Dog   *Paris ("the Cuckold-maker"). Thersites' name for Paris*
        derives from the sport of bull-baiting, where dogs were set upon
        a bull in an open-air arena similar to the Globe and the bear-
        baiting amphitheatres in the London suburbs.
        Low   *'loo (from* halloo*), a shout to urge dogs to attack their*
        prey.

11   **double-hen'd Spartan**   *Menelaus, King of Sparta. The*
        phrase **double-hen'd** *is usually emended to* **double-**
        horned *(on the assumption that Menelaus is both a bull and*
        a cuckold). But hen *can refer either (a) to a wife (in this case*
        one whose doubleness, duplicity, has given Menelaus a pair of
        horns), or (b) to a hen-hearted (weak, cowardly) man. It may
        be that Thersites is combining these senses.

12   **has the Game**   *either (a) has figured out his opponent's strat-*
        egy and developed a suitable defense, or (b) has the advantage.
        Ware   *beware, be on guard.*

18   **begot**   *conceived, born.*

21   **wherefore**   *therefore why.*

22   **most ominous to us**   *carries the most fearful omens for us.*

24   **tempts Judgment**   *risks retribution (presumably for hubris,*
        overstepping the bounds of permitted behavior, by piling one
        evil on top of another).

V.viii *The scene shifts to another part of the battlefield, where Hector*
        has just slain the soldier he began pursuing at the end of V.vi.

1   **Core**   *the corpse now left to rot without its "hide."*

at it. —Now Bull! —Now Dog! —Low, Paris,   10
low! —Now, my double-hen'd Spartan! —Low,
Paris, low! —The Bull has the Game! —Ware,
Horns, ho!   *Exeunt Paris and Menelaus.*

Enter Bastard (Margarelon).

BASTARD   Turn, Slave, and fight!
THERSITES   What art thou?   15
BASTARD   A Bastard Son of Priam's.
THERSITES   I am a Bastard too: I love Bastards.
    I am Bastard begot, Bastard instructed,
    Bastard in Mind, Bastard in Valor, in every
    thing Illegitimate. One Bear will not bite   20
    another, and wherefore should one Bastard?
    Take heed, the Quarrel's most ominous to us:
    if the Son of a Whore fight for a Whore, he
    tempts Judgment. Farewell, Bastard.   *Exit.*
BASTARD   The Divel take thee, Coward.   *Exit.*   25

Scene 8

Enter Hector.

HECTOR   Most putrefied Core, so Fair without,
    Thy goodly Armor thus hath cost thy Life.

6   ugly Night   *Achilles refers the fact that after a long day's battle, the sun is setting. But the phrase* ugly Night *can also apply to Achilles and his Myrmidons as emblems of (a) barbarity, (b) evil, and (c) death.*

7   vail   *both (a) descending, and (b) veiling (dropping a veil).*

9   forgo   *give over.*
     Vantage   *superior position, advantage.*

13   amain   *mightily (with main strength).*

14   Achilles . . . slain!   *The ignobility of this boast is comparable to Falstaff's claim to have killed Hotspur at the end of* 1 Henry IV.

15   Retire   *withdrawal from battle positions, retreat.*

17   The Dragon-wing . . . Earth   *Again, Achilles refers only to the descent of darkness. But his imagery foreshadows the fall of a civilized culture to what the play depicts as a horde of brutal predators, without honor, decency, law, or restraint—in the final analysis, without humanity.*

18   Stickler   *umpire or judge (a stickler for the rules).*

19   frankly   *freely.*

20   dainty Bait   *delicate morsel. Achilles' metaphor is apt. It was only because of Hector's "daintiness" (gentleness) in their earlier encounter that Achilles lived to see Hector's own negligence make him as defenseless as a piece of bait.*

Now is my Day's Work done: I'll take my
    Breath.
—Rest, Sword: thou hast thy fill of Blood
    and Death.   *He removes his Armor.*

Enter Achilles and his Myrmidons.

ACHILLES   Look, Hector, how the Sun begins to set,   5
    How ugly Night comes breathing at his Heels:
    Ev'n with the vail and dark'ning of the Sun
    To close the Day up, Hector's Life is done.
HECTOR   I am unarm'd: forgo this Vantage, Greek.
ACHILLES   Strike, Fellows, strike. This is the
    Man I seek.   *The Myrmidons slay Hector.*   10
    —So Ilion, fall thou next. Come, Troy, sink
    down.
    Here lies thy Heart, thy Sinews, and thy Bone.
    —On Myrmidons, and cry you all amain,
    "Achilles hath the mighty Hector slain!"   *Retreat.*
    Hark, a Retire upon our Grecian part.   15
ONE   The Troians' Trumpet sound the like, my Lord.
ACHILLES   The Dragon-wing of Night o'erspreads
    the Earth,
    And Stickler-like the Armies separates.
    My half-supp'd Sword, that frankly would have
    fed,
    Pleas'd with this dainty Bait, thus goes to Bed.   20
    Come tie his Body to my Horse's Tail:
    Along the Field I will the Troian trail.   *Exeunt.*

V.ix   *This scene shifts us to another part of the battlefield where the Greek forces are executing the retreat sounded in the previous scene.*

3   The Bruit is   *the report is that.*

4   Bragless   *not a subject for boasting. Aiax is envious, of course. But for reasons of which he is not aware, he nevertheless says something that has the ring of truth.*

7   pray   *request.*

Scene 9

Sound Retreat. Shout.
Enter Agamemnon, Aiax, Menelaus, Nestor,
Diomed, and the rest marching.

AGAMEMNON   Hark, hark, what Shout is that?
NESTOR   —Peace, Drums!
Soldier within   Achilles, Achilles! Hector's slain
      Achilles!
DIOMED   The Bruit is Hector's slain, and by Achilles.
AIAX   If it be so, yet Bragless let it be:
   Great Hector was as good a Man as he.   5
AGAMEMNON   March patiently along: let one be sent
   To pray Achilles see us at our Tent.
   If in his Death the Gods have us befriended,
   Great Troy is ours, and our sharp Wars are
      ended.   *Exeunt.*

629

V.x   *We now move to the Trojan side of the battlefield.*

1   Stand ho!   *Remain in your battle positions.*

5   In beastly sort   *both (a) by a victor who is acting in a bestial manner, and (b) as if Hector himself were no better than a beast that has been slaughtered in a hunt.*

7   smile at Troy   *show favor to Troy (by giving it a death that is mercifully swift).*

8   brief Plagues   *plagues that kill quickly.*

9   sure   *certain. Both sides view the death of Hector as the signal that Troy's fall is inevitable.*

10   discomfort   *discourage.*

13   Imminence   *both (a) threat of impending disaster, and (b) immanence, the quality of being in-dwelling.*

Scene 10

Enter Aeneas, Paris, Antenor, Deiphobus.

AENEAS   Stand ho! Yet are we Masters of the Field.

Enter Troilus.

TROILUS   Never go home, here starve we out the
    Night:
    Hector is slain.
ALL   Hector! The Gods forbid!
TROILUS   He's dead, and at the Murth'rer's Horse's
    Tail
    In beastly sort dragg'd through the shameful
    Field.   5
    —Frown on, you Heav'ns, effect your Rage with
    speed;
    Sit, Gods, upon your Thrones, and smile at
    Troy.
    I say at once let your brief Plagues be Mercy,
    And linger not our sure Destructions on!
AENEAS   My Lord, you do discomfort all the Host.   10
TROILUS   You understand me not that tell me so.
    I do not speak of Flight, of Fear, of Death,
    But dare all Imminence that Gods and Men

631

16   Scritch-owl   *screech-owl, proverbially associated with doom and lamentation.*
        aye   *forever.*

19   Niobes   *Niobe was a Phrygian Queen whose pride and impiety offended the Gods. In retribution, they killed all her children, induced her husband to commit suicide, and turned Niobe herself into a weeping rock atop Mount Sisyphus. In this passage* Niobes *is to be treated as a two-syllable word more or less synonymous with* Wells *(fountains of tears). The Prince alludes to her in the first soliloquy of* Hamlet, *I.ii.149.*

20   Cold   *frozen, lifeless.*

21   Scare . . . it self   *stun Troy into a paralysis of fear.*

25   Titan   *the Sun, here designated by the race of Gods (the Titans) of whom the Sun God (Helios) was a member.*

26   great-siz'd Coward   *This is usually taken as a reference to Achilles, who has killed Troy's champion in unfair fight and then degraded his corpse. Troilus may still be thinking of Diomed too, but it appears that the primary focus of his wrath has shifted from the personal to the general.*

28   still   *always.*

29   mouldeth Goblins   *creates frightful spirits of malice and retribution.*

33   Broker, Lackey   *base (slave-like) go-between.*

34   live aye with thy Name   *live forever with the name you have bequeathed to posterity (a recollection of II.ii.212–14).*

Address their Daungers in. Hector is gone:
Who shall tell Priam so, or Hecuba? 15
Let him that will a Scritch-owl aye be call'd
Go into Troy and say their Hector's dead.
There is a Word will Priam turn to Stone,
Make Wells and Niobes of the Maids and Wives,
Cold Statues of the Youth, and in a Word, 20
Scare Troy out of it self. But march away:
Hector is dead; there is no more to say.
—Stay yet, you vile abhominable Tents,
Thus proudly pitch'd upon our Phrygian Plains;
Let Titan rise as early as he dare, 25
I'll through and through you. —And thou
    great-siz'd Coward,
No space of Earth shall sunder our two Hates.
I'll haunt thee like a wicked Conscience still
That mouldeth Goblins swift as Frenzy's
    Thoughts.
—Strike a free March; to Troy with Comfort go. 30
Hope of Revenge shall hide our inward Woe.

Enter Pandarus.

PANDARUS   But hear you, hear you!
TROILUS   Hence, Broker, Lackey! Ignominy, Shame
    Pursue thy Life and live aye with thy Name.
                        Exeunt all but Pandarus.
PANDARUS   A goodly Med'cine for my aching Bones! 35
    —O World, World, World: thus is the poor
    Agent despis'd. —O Traitors and Bawds: how
    earnestly are you set a-work, and how ill

633

39   requited   *rewarded.*

41   Instance   *prior example.*

43   his Honey   *here, a combination of (a) his flower (sweetheart), or source of honey, (b) the fulfillment (honey) deriving from his access to that source, and (c) the sweet disposition reflecting his contentment.*
        his Sting   *the use of that power (his "armed tail") which defines him.*

44   subdu'd in armed Tail   *his "stinger" put down.*

45   Sweet Honey . . . fail   *as the bee ceases to collect honey, he also ceases to sing "sweet Notes" (to his broker, among others).*

47   painted Clothes   *either (a) ostentatious apparel, or (b) cloths with pictures painted on them for hanging in rooms for which tapestries would either be too costly or too elaborate.*

48   of Pandar's Hall   *members of Pandar's fraternity.*

49   half out   *half blinded already because of venereal diseases.*

52   Hold-door Trade   *bawds, who provide access to prostitutes.*

53   my Will . . . made   *I will be at Death's door myself.*

55   galled . . . Winchester   *diseased and bitter prostitute from Southwark (the suburb south of the Thames where brothels as well as theatres such as the Globe were to be found). Southwark was under the jurisdiction of the Bishop of Winchester.*

56   sweat   *Sweating treatments were standard for venereal disease.*

requited. Why should our Endeavor be so lov'd
and the Performance so loathed? What Verse for   40
it? What Instance for it? Let me see.
  Full merrily the humble Bee doth sing,
  Till he hath lost his Honey and his Sting.
  And being once subdu'd in armed Tail,
  Sweet Honey and sweet Notes together fail.   45
—Good Traders in the Flesh, set this in your
painted Clothes:
  As many as be here of Pandar's Hall,
  Your Eyes half out weep out at Pandar's Fall.
  Or if you cannot weep, yet give some Groans,   50
  Though not for me, yet for my aching Bones.
  Brethren and Sisters of the Hold-door Trade,
  Some two months hence my Will shall here be
    made.
  It should be now, but that my Fear is this:
  Some galled Goose of Winchester would hiss.   55
  Till then I'll sweat and seek about for Eases,
  And at that time bequeath you my Diseases.   *Exit.*

FINIS

Quality Printing and Binding by:
Horowitz/Rae Book Manufacturers, Inc.
300 Fairfield Road
Fairfield, NJ 07006 U.S.A.